S0-AHD-816

HISTORY OF THE LONDON STAGE

FANNY KEMBLE.

HISTORY
OF THE
LONDON STAGE
AND ITS FAMOUS PLAYERS
(1576–1903)

BY

H. BARTON BAKER

BENJAMIN BLOM  New York/London

THE AUTHOR

HAS MUCH PLEASURE IN

Inscribing this Volume

(BY PERMISSION) TO

SIR CHARLES WYNDHAM

AS THE DOYEN MANAGER

OF THE LONDON STAGE

First Published 1904
Reissued 1969 by
Benjamin Blom, Inc., Bronx, New York 10452
and 56 Doughty Street, London, W.C. 1

Library of Congress Catalog Card Number 72-81971

Printed in U.S.A. by
NOBLE OFFSET PRINTERS, INC.
NEW YORK 3, N. Y.

PREFACE

A FULL and complete history of the London stage would fill some scores of volumes—Geneste required ten for the history of the patent theatres and the Haymarket—he touches upon little else—from 1660 to 1830. With the space at my disposal I could do no more than generalise; but I have endeavoured to give a continuous and consecutive history of the rise, progress, changes, vicissitudes of the London stage from its foundation in 1576 to the present day—from the Blackfriars of Shakespeare and the Drury Lane of Garrick to "the Vic." and the Bower Saloon. My difficulty has been to select out of the plethora of materials such as would most vividly tell my story, as well as prove most acceptable to my readers. To condense within one volume the principal dramatic events, with some account of the authors who created them and the actors who embodied them, through a period of about three hundred and thirty years, distributed among the many scores of theatres that have risen, fallen, and still exist, from the time when James Burbage built The Theatre to the opening of the New Gaiety, has been a task to which much thought and labour have had to be given. In treating of the actors I have been compelled, except in rare cases, to confine myself entirely to their stage careers. That important omissions will be detected, that actors, concerning whom fuller details might be expected, are only glanced at, goes without saying; for all such shortcomings my plea must be lack of space.

Having been a constant playgoer from early boyhood, and associated with the stage both before and behind the curtain during the greater part of my life, I have been enabled to give personal impressions and reminiscences of some of the famous actors of the past—in their later days—as well as of those of the present.

In my very brief remarks upon the drama of the day I could scarcely refer to the enormous influence which Ibsen has exercised upon the work of Messrs. Pinero, H. A. Jones, Esmond, Haddon Chambers, and others of our leading dramatists, an influence which, whether for good or ill, is paramount over the dramatic literature of Europe.

The edition of 1889 has been thoroughly revised, the original text pruned, a great deal of new matter introduced, and the chronicles of the stage brought up to the autumn of 1903.

H. BARTON BAKER

CHRONOLOGICAL LIST

OF

THE LONDON THEATRES FROM THE EARLIEST PERIOD TO THE PRESENT TIME

I

THE ELIZABETHAN AND STUART THEATRES

II

THE RESTORATION THEATRES

[1] When a note of interrogation follows the date, it is doubtful. When the note stands alone, the date is unknown. A blank left in the second column of figures, denotes that the theatre is still standing. When two or more names are bracketed, it indicates that the theatre has been known by each of those titles.

III

BYGONE WEST END THEATRES

(Built during the Eighteenth and Nineteenth Centuries)

IV

THE WEST END THEATRES OF TO-DAY

THE WEST SUBURBAN THEATRES

THE NORTHERN THEATRES

(Past and Present)

[1] The old Richmond Theatre, built in 1765, was not pulled down until 1884.

THE SOUTHERN THEATRES

(PAST AND PRESENT)

THE EAST END THEATRES

(PAST AND PRESENT)

	BUILT	DESTROYED	PAGE
The Oriental / The Albion, Poplar	1867	?	409
The Theatre Royal, Stratford	*	—	409
The Borough, Stratford	1896	—	409

This, as far as I have been able to discover, is a complete list of the metropolitan theatres from 1576 to 1903, though doubtless others may have existed which have sunk into irretrievable oblivion.

I have omitted all mention of houses which have been used only for amateur performances. The most famous of these were, one in Catherine Street, afterwards the *Echo* office, and others situated in Gough Street and Rawstorne Street, upon the boards of which many an afterwards great actor first tried his wings. A more recent one, built about thirty or forty years ago, is the Bijou at Bayswater. Important performances are sometimes given. It was there *Nonna Vanna*, prohibited, no one knows why, by the Lord Chamberlain, was produced during 1903.

* The managers of the theatres marked with a star have neglected to furnish me with dates.

LIST OF ILLUSTRATIONS

PART I

THE STAGE UNDER ELIZABETH AND THE STUART KINGS

RICHARD BURBAGE.

THE LONDON STAGE

CHAPTER I

The Theatre—The Curtain—The Paris Garden—The Hope—The Rose—The Globe—The Swan—The Newington—The Blackfriars—The Fortune—The Red Bull—The Cockpit—The Whitefriars—The Salisbury Court—Audiences—Actors—Plays—Music—The Question of Scenery—A Play-day at the Blackfriars.

IN mediæval times the Miracle plays, Mysteries, and Moralities, the earliest forms of the Western drama, were represented in churches or on wooden movable platforms raised in the market places; but from Henry the Seventh's reign, when a passion for dramatic amusements began to develop among all classes, to the earlier years of "the Virgin Queen," the trained companies of actors, which many noblemen attached to their households, when not required by their lords, would roam from town to town giving public performances, usually in inn yards; and it was the ancient inn yard, with its open area, its two or three tiers of galleries with rooms at the back, that was taken as a model for the first English theatre, a model that has never since been departed from.

Upon the site of what is now Holywell Lane, Shoreditch, during the Middle Ages, stood the Priory of St. John the Baptist; at the Reformation it shared the common fate of religious houses, and after lying in ruins for some time, one Giles Allen purchased the ground and leased it out for building. One of these plots was taken by James Burbage, Burbadge, or Burbidge—the name is indifferently spelt—an actor in the Earl of Leicester's company, but a joiner by trade, in partnership with his father-in-law, John Braynes, and thereon they erected a circular wooden building, open to the sky, at a cost of £600 or £700, for theatrical and other amusements, which they named the Theatre,[1] and which was opened to the public in the autumn of 1576.

Not for long, however, did this novel venture enjoy a monopoly; during the following year a rival house sprang up in its immediate neighbourhood, and was called the Curtain; the name still survives in Curtain Road. Writing at this time, Stow says: "Many houses have been there builded [on the site of the Priory] for the lodgings of noblemen, of strangers born, and otherwise. And near unto are builded two publique houses for the acting and shew of Comedies, Tragedies, and Histories for recreation. Whereof the one is called the Courtein and the other the Theatre, both standing on the south side towards the field."

The Elizabethan drama, as we understand the term, was not yet born; Marlowe, the first of the great dramatists, did not produce his *Tamburlaine* until about eleven years afterwards, and the earliest known plays of John Lyly and George Peele do not date farther back than 1584. *Ralph Roister Doister*, *Gammer Gurton's Needle*, and *Gordubuc*, the first dramatic works in the English language that have any claim to be styled comedy and tragedy, were written at a much earlier

[1] Mr. Ordish, a weighty authority, in his *Early London Theatres*, opines that this was the first building erected in Europe for the performance of secular plays. In 1600, Paris had but two theatres, London nine or ten.

date, but only for private performance.[1] On the public stage were represented "Moralities," "Jigs," "Interludes,"[2] and such a barbarous medley of bombast and buffoonery as we have in the old plays of *Damon and Pithias*, *Appius and Virginia*, and *Cambyses*—which Shakespeare has immortalised by his reference to "the King Cambyses vein," in *Henry IV*. From these and similar specimens of the pre-Marlowe drama that have descended to us, we can form a tolerably accurate idea of the dramatic portion of the entertainment given at the earliest theatres. At the Theatre there was a movable stage for dramatic performances,[3] but the entertainment consisted mostly of tumbling, vaulting, rope dancing, and fencing. A passage in Lambard's *Perambulations of Kent* (1576) affords a curious hint as to the prices charged for admission. "Those who go to Paris Gardens, the Bell Savage,[4] or the Theatre to behold bear-baiting, interludes, or fence play, must not account of any pleasant spectacle unless first they pay one penny at the gate, another at the

[1] The first-named piece was written by Nicholas Udall, Master of Eton College, previous to 1553, and was probably acted by his scholars; the second was by John Still, also a clergyman, and played at Christ's College, Cambridge; while Lord Sackville's *Gordubuc*, or *Perrex and Porrex*, was performed before Queen Elizabeth at Whitehall by the gentlemen of the Inner Temple, in 1561.

[2] In the "Moralities," the vices and virtues were personified. The recently revived *Everyman* is a fair specimen of that species of composition. The "Jig" was made up of satirical verses, recited or sung by the clown to the accompaniment of pipe and tabor, to which he danced. "Interludes" were satirical dialogues on the follies and vices of the time; they were first introduced by John Heywood in the reign of Henry VII.

[3] Mr. Ordish conjectures that the word playhouse was derived from the Anglo-Saxon *plega-hus*, plega signifying a game or sport, while stage-play was so called from the circumstance that dramatic performances always took place on scaffolds or stages.

[4] The inn yards continued to be used for dramatic exhibitions for some years after this time, and the Bell Sauvage on Ludgate Hill was one of the most famous of these extemporised playhouses.

entry to the scaffold, and a third for a quiet sitting." The last must, indeed, have been a desideratum in these early theatres, since the unruliness of the audience, who frequently indulged in riots and tumults, was continually getting the managers into hot water with the civic authorities, most of whom were leavened with Puritanism. In 1580 the Lord Mayor appealed against Braynes and Burbage to the Lords of the Council, who at that very time had under consideration certain disturbances which had occurred on a certain Sunday[1] in the April of that year, and in this memorial his lordship disdainfully alludes to "the players of playes and tumblers" as being "a very superfluous sort of men," and opines that "the exercise of those playes is a great hindrance of the service of God." Here we have the germ of that fanaticism which grew year by year, until it was strong enough, under the gloomy reign of the saints, to sweep every pleasure out of existence. There was a constant struggle between the Court, as represented by the Privy Council, and the civic authorities about the players; the former repeatedly solicited the City to show indulgence to the players, as Her Majesty sometimes took delight in such pastimes, and these performances were necessary to enable them to attain more dexterity and perfection, the better to content Her Majesty.

The Theatre enjoyed but a brief career. In 1597, Giles Allen, the ground landlord, perhaps under pressure of the Puritan citizens, intimated to Messrs. Braynes and Burbage that he required the land for other

[1] The playhouses were open in London on Sundays, even in Charles the First's time; though it would appear that such amusements were never lawful on the Sabbath, and were forbidden by enactments at different periods. In 1595 there were performances on Christmas Day.

purposes. Now, according to the stipulations of the lease, Burbage had the power to remove the building at the end of his term; but Allen denied this right, and evidently thought he had the power of evading it. One morning, however, the actors and some assistants set about pulling down the house, and, in spite of the armed resistance of the ground landlord, amidst a great tumult, succeeded in carrying off the materials to Bankside, Southwark, and the timber thus saved helped to erect another theatre, which was afterwards called the Globe.

The Curtain was evidently a superior house to the Theatre; some of the most celebrated companies of the time appeared there, notably the Lord Chamberlain's, known in the next reign as the King's, of which Shakespeare was a member. Here it is probable that *Romeo and Juliet* and *Every Man in His Humour* were first presented. There is no known reference to the Curtain after 1623, though it may have existed until the final suppression of the theatres, between 1642 and 1647.

In the meantime theatrical amusements had been migrating southward, and at the close of the sixteenth and opening of the seventeenth century the Bankside, Southwark, was the great centre of theatrical London. In the petition of John Taylor, "the Water Poet," to James I. (1615) for the suppression of all theatres on the Middlesex side of the Thames, he states that 40,000 watermen plied for hire between Windsor and Gravesend, that half of these had been called into existence by the Southwark theatres and other places of amusement, which visitors always approached by the Thames, and he draws a direful picture of the ruin that will fall upon his craft if theatres are allowed to be erected within four miles of the city.

The most popular place of amusement, however, on

Bankside, was Paris Garden, afterwards better known as the Bear Garden.[1] About 1585, in order to vary the brutal amusements of bull-baiting and cock-fighting, a theatre was opened here; it was little more than a wooden frame set on trestles and wheels, so that it could be pushed aside to make room for the sports.

In 1613, after the destruction of the Globe, Philip Henslowe, Edward Alleyn's father-in-law and the author of the famous *Diary*, which throws such a wonderful light upon the theatrical arrangements of his time, rebuilt and greatly enlarged this house, which was thereafter known as the Hope. It is conjectured that the White Bear public-house—the name is, undoubtedly, a reminiscence of Paris Garden—occupies the site of it. Henslowe had built a theatre called the Rose within the precincts of the Bear Garden as early as 1592, in which it is probable that Shakespeare's *Titus Andronicus* and the first part of *Henry VI.*, Marlowe's *Jew of Malta*, and some of Greene's and Peele's plays were first performed. The Rose was the summer house of the Fortune, as the Globe was of the Blackfriars.

Now between Edward Alleyn,[2] master of the Bear Garden, and James Burbage there seems to have been a strong rivalry, and it was to oppose Alleyn that the manager of the Theatre transported the materials of the building to Bankside, and there erected the Globe, which was opened in 1597, just in the lusty spring of the Elizabethan drama. Marlowe, Greene, and Peele had done their work and passed away; Shakespeare had written his earlier plays, and, ere the century closed, Ben

[1] The Bear Garden survived even the Puritan rule, and continued to flourish until the early decades of the eighteenth century, when it was superseded in popular favour by the notorious Hockley-in-the-Hole, in Smithfield.

[2] Edward Alleyn was one of the finest actors of his day, the proprietor of the Fortune Theatre, and the founder of Dulwich College.

Jonson, Chapman, Thomas Heywood, and several minor lights had begun to wield their pens. A German traveller[1] who visited England in 1598 gives us the following curious description of the theatres of that period, and of Paris Garden: "Within the city are some theatres where English actors represent almost every day tragedies and comedies to very numerous audiences; these are combined with excellent music and variety of dances. There is still another place built in the form of a theatre, which serves for the baiting of bulls and bears that are fastened behind, and then worried by great English bull-dogs, but not without great risk to the dogs, from the horns of the one and the teeth of the other; and it sometimes happens they are killed upon the spot; fresh ones are immediately supplied in the place of those that are wounded or tired. To this entertainment, there often follows that of whipping a blinded bear, which is performed by five or six men, standing circularly with whips, which they exercise upon him without any mercy, as he cannot escape from them on account of his chain; he defends himself with all his force and skill, throwing down all who come within his reach, and are not active enough to get out of it, and tearing the whips out of their hands and breaking them. At these spectacles, and everywhere else, the English are constantly smoking tobacco, and in this manner they have pipes on purpose made of clay, into the further end of which they put the herb, so dry that it may be rubbed into powder, and putting fire to it, they draw the smoke into their mouths, which they puff out through their nostrils, like funnels, along with it plenty of phlegm and defluxion from the head. In

[1] Paul Hentznerus's *Journey into England in 1598*, translated by Horace Walpole.

these theatres fruits, such as apples, pears, and nuts, according to the season, are carried about to be sold, as well as ale and wine." John De Witt, the learned canon of St. Mary's Church, Utrecht, visited London in 1596, and wrote his impressions of the various sights he saw. Among other places he mentions are "four large and splendid playhouses"; the Theatre and the Curtain towards the north, and the Rose and the Swan in the south. He describes each as being oval in form, a beautiful structure, not of wood, but built or faced with flint and marble, and of considerable size, the boxes and galleries containing three thousand seats. There is a sketch of the Swan, showing the audience, the actors on the stage, the lord's room, the doors and the tiring-room at the back. There does not seem to be the slightest reason to doubt the authenticity of these documents, and their contents certainly give us a far more exalted idea of the resources and architectural pretensions of these early English theatres than has ever before been entertained.[1]

The Globe was a hexagonal building, and had for its sign[2] Atlas supporting the world, and underneath was written, *Totus mundus agit histrionem*, which motto, as *As You Like It* was first produced at this house, probably suggested the famous speech commencing "All the world's a stage."

Just after Shakespeare had retired, in 1613, during the performance of a play on the subject of Henry VIII., entitled, *All is True*,[3] the wadding of one of the cannons used for firing salutes, lodged in the thatch of the roof,

[1] The papers relating to this visit were found by Dr. Gädertz in the Royal Library, Berlin, in 1888.

[2] Not only did every trade and profession in those days mount a sign at its door, but even the theatres adopted the same fashion.

[3] Supposed to have been Shakespeare's *Henry VIII.*

and in two hours the house was a mass of smouldering ruins. But it was immediately rebuilt at a cost of £1,400. In a contemporary letter we read: "I hear much speech about this new playhouse, which is said to be the fairest that ever was in England."

The Globe, after the suppression of all places of amusement by the Puritans, was pulled down on the 15th of April, 1644; thirty-two years afterwards Richard Baxter was preaching in the wooden meeting-house raised upon the site, which is now covered by Barclay and Perkins' brewery.

The Swan, erected in Paris Garden by Mr. Langley about 1598, was used more for sports in the ring than stage plays. Of its history nothing is known beyond the circumstance that Middleton's *A Chaste Maid in Cheapside* was first acted there. The last mention of the Swan is by Shakerly Marmion, in 1632.

A house that perhaps stood nearly upon the site of the present Elephant and Castle Theatre—though that is uncertain—called "the Newington," of which little is known except that this also was the property of Edward Alleyn and Philip Henslowe, completes the list of the Southwark playhouses.

Shakespeare's close association with the Blackfriars and the Globe, as actor, author, and manager, renders everything connected with them of supreme interest. Less than twenty years ago, some documents were brought to light that afford new and very important information regarding the history of the former house, the site of which is now covered by the office of the *Times* and Playhouse Yard, facts that completely refute Mr. Payne Collier's dates. Within the precincts of the Blackfriars, at the time of the Reformation, stood a church dedicated to St. Ann, which, at the dissolution of the monasteries under Henry VIII., was seized upon by Sir Thomas Cawardine and converted into a storehouse for the properties used in the Court entertainments, as well as a place where the children employed in these spectacles were rehearsed. In the next reign two tennis courts were opened here, but were soon afterwards suppressed on account of the disorderly conduct of the frequenters. When Elizabeth came to the throne, the building seems again to have reverted to theatrical purposes. It was some time in 1596 that James Burbage obtained a lease of the premises from Sir Thomas's executor, Sir William More, and set about converting them into a theatre. The first tenants of the new playhouse were the Children of the Chapel, afterwards styled the Children of His Majesty's Revels.[1]

Papers relating to a Chancery suit discovered in the Record Office, and alluded to in the *Athenæum* for March 3rd, 1888, throw much new light upon the early history of the Blackfriars Theatre. The suit was brought against Richard Burbage, John Hemings, and others, in respect of the lease of this house, which the said Burbage, by deed dated 2nd September, 42 of

[1] These celebrated juvenile performers, as well as others called the Children of the Queen's Chapel, the Children of St. Paul's, were then attached to cathedrals and collegiate churches, and by an edict of Elizabeth (1585) were compulsorily trained for masques and other dramatic representations. Many of the plays of our greatest dramatists were originally represented by these youngsters, notably Ben Jonson's *Cynthia's Revels*, *The Poetaster*, most of John Lyly's, several of Chapman's, Dekker's, Marston's, Middleton's, etc. Their great popularity excited the jealousy of the adult actors; references to them abound in the Elizabethan drama, and everyone will recall the passage in *Hamlet:* "There is, sir, an aiery of children, little eyasses who cry out on the top of the question, and are most tyrannically clapped for 't: these are now the fashion, and so berattle the common stages (so they call them), that many, wearing rapiers, are afraid of goose quills and dare scarce come hither."

These juvenile companies, however, were excellent training schools, and gave many fine actors to the stage.

Elizabeth (1600), demised to Henry Evans, "who intended then presently to erect and sett upp a companye of boys . . . or others, to playe playes and interludes in the saide playhouse in such sort before tyme had been there vsed." By reason of the plague in anno 1, James I., Evans "grewe wearye" of the playhouse and desired to give up his interest in it. He surrendered the lease in August, anno 6, following. The complainant, in his replication, states that "during such time as the saide defendantes Heminges and Burbage and their companye contynewed playes and interludes in the said great hall in ffryers . . . they gott, and as yet dothe, more in one winter in the said greate Hall by a thousand powndes than they were vsed to gett in the Banckside." The use of the word "hall" is very suggestive as to the original form of the building. And very curious is another passage which goes on to state that Evans, in the 43 of Elizabeth, "was censured by the Right Honrable Courte of Starr Chamber for his vnorderlie carriage and behauior in takinge vp of gentlemens childeren against their wills and to ymploy them for playes." We likewise learn that the building was leased to this Henry Evans for forty pounds a year. The documents are given in full in the *Athenæum* for April 7th and 21st, 1888, and besides the interesting side-lights they throw upon the history of the theatre, seem to fully establish the fact that it was in 1600 that Shakespeare and his colleagues, including Richard Burbage, Lowin, Condell, Armin, Heming, succeeded the Children of the Queen's Revels as actors at the Blackfriars. When Burbage's company first appeared at the Globe it was known as the Lord Chamberlain's, but in the year 1603,[1] James allowed them to take the

[1] In the earlier days of the drama each company of actors was attached to some nobleman's household, and was known as his "servants." After

title of the King's Servants. They were enrolled in the Royal household, and each man was allowed four yards of "bastard scarlet," and a quarter of a yard of velvet for a cape. In an ancient letter, dated 1591, a portion of a volume of correspondence that passed between the English and Scotch Courts during the negotiations for the marriage of James with Anne of Denmark, it is stated that the King had expressed a great desire for the Queen's Company — Burbage's troupe—to visit Edinburgh, it being at that time in Lancashire; and we afterwards read that they had arrived as far as Carlisle. Although we are vouchsafed no further information upon the subject, there is little doubt that the royal request was complied with, and might account for King James's favour being afterwards so particularly extended to this company, and for Shakespeare's knowledge of Scotland.[1]

The theatre next in importance to the Blackfriars and Globe was the Fortune, so called from the image of the goddess which surmounted the principal entrance; this house was built by Alleyn in 1599, in Golden Lane, St. Luke's. Although as an aristocratic resort it could not compare with the Blackfriars, the greatest dramatists of

the building of regular theatres, however, these distinctions became only nominal, and were simply the titles under which the companies were licensed, and under which they performed at different theatres.

[1] Dr. Stefanson, of Copenhagen, in a paper read some few years ago before the Elizabethan Society, informed us that there is an entry in the accounts of the town of Elsinore which shows that a company of English actors performed there in 1585, and among the names are Will Kempe and Thomas Pope, both associates of Shakespeare. Now the years between 1585 and 1592 are the most obscure in the poet's career. Dr. Stefanson pointed out that Shakespeare's knowledge of Elsinore, its ancient customs and palace, which contains the portraits of the kings as indicated in the closet scene of *Hamlet*, is minutely correct. Might not Shakespeare have been in that company? Or, on the other hand, he might have obtained these particulars from Will Kempe.

the day, always excepting Shakespeare, wrote for its stage, and Alleyn was an actor who stood shoulder to shoulder with the great Burbage himself. The Fortune was destroyed by fire in 1621, but immediately rebuilt. In 1656, as it had fallen into decay under the Puritan régime, it was pulled down; and some idea may be formed of the area it occupied when it is stated that a street was cut through it, and twenty-three tenements, with gardens, raised upon the ground. Within the last twenty years a wall of the old theatre was enclosed within a box manufactory.

The remainder of the theatres erected before the Great Rebellion may be very briefly touched upon; conspicuous among these was the Red Bull, the site of which is now covered by Woodbridge Street, that faced one side of the Clerkenwell House of Detention. Of its date and origin nothing is known, though from the name we may conjecture that it was originally an inn yard. The earliest reference to the Red Bull that I can find is 1599, in which year a portion of the auditorium fell, possibly one of the inn galleries, during the performance of a puppet play; but later on, frequent allusions to this house, mostly disparaging, are to be found in the contemporary dramatists, who refer to it much in the same strain as did the burlesque writers of thirty years ago to the old Victoria; from which we may gather that its plays were of the blood-and-thunder school, and that its players were the "perriwig-pated fellows, who tore a passion to rags, to very tatters," referred to by Shakespeare.

Another notable theatre of the period was the Cockpit, in Drury Lane; the spot on which it stood was, until late years, marked by a squalid court, called Pitt Place; it is now covered by model lodging-houses. When the

Cockpit was first used for theatrical purposes is not known; the name sufficiently explains its origin, and probably after the actors had taken possession of the place, mains might have been fought as a relief to Melpomene or Thalia. Although the Cockpit was a private and therefore an aristocratic theatre, it seems to have been closely connected with the Red Bull, the company of which frequently performed there. On Shrove Tuesday, 1616–17, while "Queen Anne's Servants" (the Queen of James I.) were performing, the London apprentices sacked and set fire to the house. The Cockpit seems to have been in ill odour, and it is a significant fact that Shrovetide was the season when "the flat caps" considered it a privilege of their order to attack brothels and bagnios; but it has also been suggested that jealousy of the privileges of a private theatre may have had something to do with the riot. The Cockpit was speedily rebuilt, and appropriately renamed the Phœnix. Towards the close of the Protectorate, the rigorous edicts against theatrical amusements were relaxed; and in 1658, Davenant obtained permission to bring out an "opera," called *The Cruelty of the Spaniards*, at this house. The Phœnix continued to be used for dramatic representation after the Restoration, until the opening of the new theatre in Drury Lane.[1]

In theatrical annals, frequent allusion is made to a playhouse called the Whitefriars; recent researches, however, lead to the conclusion that this place was no more than the refectory or hall of the old Carmelite monastery, which had once almost adjoined the Temple, and that it was occasionally fitted up for dramatic exhibitions. Plays

[1] The Cockpit referred to in Pepys' *Diary*, after Aug. 18 and Oct. 11, was not this but the royal private theatre in Whitehall Palace.

were represented here as early as 1580, and after being dispossessed of the Blackfriars, the Children of the Revels would seem to have made it their headquarters. Apprentices and mechanics occasionally played here, and might have furnished Shakespeare with types of Bottom and his associates, whom they probably much resembled; but if it were ever a regular theatre, it was far inferior to its contemporaries.

Pepys writes that he saw Massinger's *Bondman* at "the White-fryars," but he might have meant Salisbury Court.

Salisbury Court, built in 1629, was the last theatre erected previous to the Restoration. This occupied a portion of the site of Dorset House, now covered by Salisbury Square, Fleet Street. It was suppressed in 1644; fell into decay, and was rebuilt in 1660; its second lease of life was a brief one, as it was destroyed in the great fire of 1666.

And now, having thus briefly sketched the history of the pre-Restoration theatres, let me endeavour to possess the reader with some conception of their arrangements, their audiences, and the manner in which plays were represented in them.

The circular or hexagonal form seems to have been the favourite amongst the builders of the Elizabethan theatres. The Globe was hexagonal, and the first Fortune Theatre was modelled exactly upon the lines of the Bankside house; when it was rebuilt after the fire, however, according to a picture extant, it had a flat façade. The dimensions of the first of the Golden Lane houses have been handed down to us, and they were identical with those of the Globe. The stage was 43 feet wide and, including the tiring-room at the back, 39½ deep; although it was only 32 feet from floor to ceiling, it had three tiers of galleries. The cost of the erection was £550, while that of the Globe was £600; but the latter was painted, and the Fortune was not. Both houses when rebuilt were probably greatly enlarged; the word "great" is frequently used by contemporaries when referring to the Globe.

There was a marked distinction between the public and private theatres; the latter were only three in number, the Blackfriars, the Cockpit, and Salisbury Court, and the performances given in them seem to have been in lieu of those which formerly took place in the great mansions. They were chiefly patronised by the nobility, who rented private boxes or rooms, of which they kept the keys, and who enjoyed the privilege of sitting upon the stage during the play.

At the private houses the performances were given by candle or torch light; whereas in the public ones, which were open only in summer, they commenced at three o'clock in the afternoon, at which hour a flag was hoisted on the roof, and trumpets blown to announce the opening-time. The Blackfriars was completely roofed in, and the pit was furnished with seats; while the Globe was only partly covered, and "the groundlings" or "undertakers," as the pittites were called, had to stand. The difference between the two audiences is set forth in Shirley's prologue to *The Doubtful Heir* (1640), which, written for the Blackfriars, was, for some reason, produced at the Globe:—

> "No shew, no dance, and what you most delight in,
> Grave undertakers, here's no target fighting . . .
> No clown, no squibs, no devil in't . . .
> But you that can content yourselves and sit,
> As you were now in the Blackfriar's pit,
> But will not deafen us with loud noise and tongues,
> Because we have no heart to break our lungs,
> Will pardon our vast stage, and not disgrace
> The play meant for your persons, not your place."

The private theatres, according to the *Historia Histrionica* of Wright, were very small, and "all these were built almost exactly alike for form and bigness." The public theatres were the resort of the commonality, who formed a noisy and unruly audience, romping, smoking, nut-cracking, drinking, playing at cards.

The prices of admission to the two classes of theatres ranged from twopence to half-a-crown; but a shilling seems to have been ordinarily the highest price in Shakespeare's time. Ben Jonson, in the induction to *Cynthia's Revels*, calls the stools upon the stage twelve-penny seats.

A further testimony to those already quoted regarding the superiority of the English theatres is to be found in that curious book of travels, of the year 1608, called *Coryat's Crudities*. During his stay in Venice the author writes: "I was at one of their playhouses, where I saw a comedy acted. The house is very beggarly and bare in comparison with our stately playhouses in England, neither can their acting compare with ours for apparell, shews, and musick. Here I observed certain things that I never saw before, for I saw women act, a thing I never saw before, *though I have heard that it hath been sometimes used in London*,[1] and they performed it with as good grace, action, gesture, and whatsoever convenient for a play as ever I saw a masculine actor."

Each company had its own dramatists, who wrote plays for its exclusive use; the Blackfriars and the Globe had incomparably the finest repertory; Shakespeare wrote only for those, and most of the masterpieces of Jonson, Beaumont and Fletcher, Webster,

[1] The italics are my own; as it is generally believed that the first English actress did not appear until after the Restoration, the suggestion in the text is curious, but no confirmation of it has been discovered.

Ford, Massinger, Middleton, Chapman, Cyril Tourneur, Shirley, etc., were there produced. After the two houses just named, the best plays were given at the Fortune.

And what of the actors who interpreted these marvellous dramas? To judge from contemporary opinion, they were worthy of the verses set down for them. The Elizabethan dramatists wrote for the day, without a thought of posterity; for the stage, not for the closet; and therefore it is highly improbable that Shakespeare and his associates would have given to the stage such gigantic conceptions as Macbeth, Lear, Hamlet, Volpone, Arbaces, Vittoria Corombona, Deflores, Vindice, and scores of others, unless the actors were capable of embodying them. And how thoroughly the art of acting was understood by these writers is testified to in Hamlet's speech to the players, which has been, and will be to all time, the text-book of the profession. Therefore, as a natural corollary to these arguments, we must believe that the greatest of all dramatic ages was the greatest of all histrionic. Upon the acting of Richard Burbage and Edward Alleyn, the first interpreters of some of the greatest of the poets' creations, the most glowing eulogies were pronounced; indeed, all the principal actors of the time are highly praised in contemporary literature. And it would be strange indeed if those glorious dramas, hot from the imagination of the writers, had not inspired a kindred genius in the souls of the players, so many of whom were dramatists themselves, imparting to their interpretations a power, a freshness, and an originality of which even the greatest of their successors could have felt only the afterglow.

Concerning their private life, Wright, in the *Historia Histrionica,* tells us that "all the actors lived in reputation, especially those of the Blackfriars, who were men of grave and sober behaviour." And it is worthy of remark that in all legal documents in which they are mentioned, the leading actors are invariably styled "gentlemen," which is a complete refutation of the common error that a certain statute of Elizabeth dubbed the entire profession rogues and vagabonds, whereas such terms applied only to wandering and unlicensed players. Indeed, such men as Burbage, Shakespeare, Alleyn, and many others, held a high social position, and were the friends and companions of the first nobility in the days when the aristocracy were not in the habit of consorting with their inferiors. From their proximity to the City, the Blackfriars actors were particularly exposed to the attacks of the Puritans, who generally affected that neighbourhood; these were continually petitioning the King, as their predecessors had in the days of the Theatre, to suppress the Blackfriars, on account of the great injury done to their business by the vast concourse of vehicles, and the crowds of people that flocked to the house.[1]

The average daily takings at the Blackfriars ranged from £20 to £30. The current expenses for rent, lighting, and the salaries of the inferior actors amounted to 45*s*., and the residue was divided among the principals, so that, considering the value of money in those days, it is not surprising that most of the shareholders died wealthy.

What little we know of the arrangements of the Elizabethan stage is chiefly derived from the plays, and, unfortunately, these leave us in great doubt as to the adjuncts and what we should now call the "mounting." Certain entries in Henslowe's *Diary* prove that the pieces were

[1] See Note at the end of the book.

dressed with a magnificence that would compare even with the productions of the present day. We read in that curious account-book that £21 was paid for two two-pile velvet cloaks at 20*s.* 5*d.* a yard, and for satin and taffeta at 12*s.* and 12*s.* 6*d.* a yard; in another place it is stated that £19 was given for a cloak; £6 13*s.* for Mrs. Frankford's gown[1] in *A Woman Killed with Kindness.* Now as money was then worth at least five times its present value, these sums must be multiplied by that number. And these splendid costumes were for the Fortune, a public and an inferior theatre.

The Blackfriars was celebrated for its fine orchestra; yet so far from this being an expense to the managers, the musicians appear to have paid them an annual stipend for the privilege of playing there: probably because it brought them before the notice of the aristocratic patrons.

We now come to the vexed and oft-discussed question, whether scenery of any kind was used to illustrate the Elizabethan drama. In the *Historia Histrionica,* which was published in 1699, it is distinctly stated that scenes were first introduced upon the public stage by Sir William Davenant at the Duke's old theatre in Lincoln's Inn Fields, in 1661, and the play, or rather opera, referred to was *The Siege of Rhodes.* Downes, the prompter, confirms this in his *History of the Stage.* Writing of this play, he says, "having new scenes and decorations, being the first that were ever introduced into England"—Downes, however, is not a trustworthy authority. Davenant's own words in the preface to the play are curious and somewhat ambiguous. "It has been often wished that our scenes (we having obliged ourselves to the variety of five changes, according to the

[1] More than poor Thomas Heywood received for writing the play.

ancient dramatic distinction made for time) had not been confined to about eleven feet the height and fifteen in depth, including the place of passage reserved for the music." We may gather from this that the scenes used in *The Siege of Rhodes* were little more than screens.[1] It should be noted that in the passage quoted from *Historia Histrionica*, the word public theatre is used; and as just previously the author has been discussing the difference between the public and private theatres, the word is at least suggestive. When Downes tells us that the scenes used in the *Siege of Rhodes* were the first ever introduced into England, he puts himself out of court, since we know that Ben Jonson's and Shirley's *Masques* were illustrated by scenic effects, devised by Inigo Jones, that would tax the powers even of a modern artist.[2]

Pages might be filled with quotations from the works of these dramatists in proof of the above assertion, but I must content myself with an extract from the stage directions in Shirley's *Masque of Peace*, performed before King Charles at Whitehall, in 1633, at the extraordinary cost of £20,000. The first scene represented a street with sumptuous palaces, lodges, porticoes, trees, and grounds; beyond, in a spacious plain, was the forum of Peace; "and over all was a clear sky with transparent clouds, which enlightened all the scene." This changed to a wooded landscape with bushes and byways. Then "there appeared in the foremost part of the heavens little by little to break forth a whitish cloud, bearing a

[1] Pepys notes going to see this play, July 2nd, but it is rather curious that he makes no mention of such a startling innovation as the introduction of movable scenes.

[2] It is said, but I cannot give the authority, that scenes were used in Sir John Suckling's *Aglaura*, produced at the Blackfriars in 1629, at a cost of three or four hundred pounds.

golden chariot, in which sat Peace; in another cloud, in a silver chariot, sat Law; and from a third descended Justice. Passing over several other transformations, we come to the last scene. The stage represented a plain, above which was a dark sky with dusky clouds, through these the new moon appeared, but with the faint light of approaching morning; from a certain part of the ground arose little by little a great vapour, which, when it came to the middle of the scene, began to fall downwards to the earth; and out of this rose another cloud, of a strange shape and colour, in which sat a young maid, with a dim torch in her hand, costumed in dark blue, sprinkled with silver spangles, and with white buskins trimmed with gold upon her legs, to represent the dawn," etc. Here we have scenic effects that Sir Henry Irving or Mr. Beerbohm Tree might be proud of.

That the stage arrangements of the *public* theatres were of a very plain description we may very well believe, but that no attempt was made to introduce scenic effects into the private houses, and above all into the Blackfriars, seems incredible; more especially when we find that such accessories were freely used in the old Mysteries and Moralities, at least as far back as Henry the Seventh's time. Among the entries in some manuscript accounts of the City and Corporation of Canterbury is the following: for a play called *The Three Kings of Colyn*, produced on Twelfth Night, 1501–2, at the Guildhall: "A castle made of painted canvas was erected in the room by way of scenery." The Elizabethan drama abounds in stage directions, which, if every kind of scenic effect was unknown, are perfectly meaningless. Even in so early a play as Lodge's and Greene's *A Looking Glass for London*, we read, "the magi beat the ground with their rods, and from under the same rises a brave arbour." There are several similar directions in this play. In a series of dramas upon the four ages of the world, written by Thomas Heywood for the Red Bull, numerous scenic effects are mentioned. In *The Brazen Age*, Jupiter strikes Hercules with a thunderbolt; his body sinks, and from the heavens descends a hand in a cloud, that, from the place where Hercules was burnt, brings up a star and fixes it in the firmament. In Shakespeare's *Cymbeline* (first folio) we read that Jupiter descends in thunder and lightning sitting upon an eagle, throwing a thunderbolt; Romeo, when forcing the tomb of all the Capulets, could not have used his crowbar against a curtain; and some kind of scenery must have been employed in *Macbeth*, *King Lear*, and the historical plays, in which numerous stage directions occur. Even realism was not unknown among the Elizabethans, for when *Macbeth* was played at the Globe, the Thane of Cawdor and Banquo made their first entrance upon horseback. The stage directions to the second act of Jonson's *Bartholemew Fair* are "a number of booths, stalls, etc., are set out"; and in Middleton's *Roaring Girl* there is a scene in which three different shops are represented with people sewing therein, and carrying on a cross dialogue, quite in the modern style. There is a passage in the induction to Ben Jonson's *Cynthia's Revels* that is very suggestive. "Slid, the boy, takes me for a piece of perspective, I hold my life, or some silk curtain[1] come to hang the stage here. I am none of your fresh pictures, that use to beautify the decayed dead arras of a public theatre."

[1] As a proof of the handsome manner in which the theatres were appointed, it may be stated that even the company of the Red Bull boasted that their curtain was of Naples silk.

The word perspective here evidently means a painting of some kind. There is scarcely a play among the many hundreds written at this period from which similar circumstantial evidence could not be drawn. Many of the stage situations, however, such as the balcony scene in *Romeo and Juliet*, the fall of Arthur from the battlements in *King John*, could have been carried out by means of a platform about ten feet high, that, supported by pillars, was raised at the back of the stage; curtains were hung in front of this erection, and only drawn when it was required. Sir Philip Sidney's description of the stage of his day[1] has been frequently quoted to prove that scenery was not used in the Elizabethan theatres; but the author of *Arcadia* died in the very infancy of the drama, 1586—years before the Blackfriars was founded, and before Shakespeare began to write. Thus his testimony goes for nothing.

The exact resources which the Elizabethan dramatists had at their command, however, is a point that is never likely to be satisfactorily cleared up. And now, setting aside theory and conjecture, let me endeavour to conjure up a vision of a play-day at the Blackfriars. But as no picture of this theatre has ever been discovered, the presentment, gathered from hints and passages scattered throughout many plays, must necessarily be a very imperfect one.

To eyes accustomed to the glare of our modern artificial illuminants, the interior lit up by candles would

[1] "Now you shall see these ladies walk to gather flowers, and then we must believe the stage to be a garden. By-and-by we hear news of a shipwreck in the same place, and then we are to blame if we accept it not for a rock. Upon the back of that comes out a hideous monster, with fire and smoke, and then the miserable beholders are bound to take it for a cave; while in the meantime two armies fly in, represented by four swords and bucklers," etc.

appear plunged in semi-darkness ; a silken curtain which runs upon an iron rod and opens in the middle at present conceals the stage, so we will begin by looking round at the auditorium. On three sides are tiers of galleries, well filled with splendidly dressed ladies and gentlemen, and beneath these are small rooms or boxes. The prices to the former have varied at different times from sixpence to a shilling ; and the latter from a shilling to two, or two-and-sixpence. In a small balcony on one side the stage is ranged the orchestra, and the musicians play before the piece and between the acts as in a modern theatre. Were we in the Globe, the noise from the groundlings would be deafening. There the audience indulge in nut-cracking, apple-eating, ale-drinking, card-playing, romping, flirting, and rioting indescribable ;[1] but here all is quiet and decorous. And now, at a triple flourish of trumpets, the curtains open and disclose the stage. As a tragedy is to be represented it is hung with black,[2] and, like the halls of the nobles, the boards are strewn with rushes ; the curtain at the back is still closed, and the walls at the sides are hidden by faded arras. Although the actors have not yet appeared, the stage is half-filled with ladies and gallants, seated upon three-legged stools, some of the gentlemen lying at their ladies' feet with their heads in their laps, and fanning themselves, as we see Hamlet in the play scene. And here we have the *jeunesse dorée* of Elizabeth's or James's Court, the Mercutios, the Tybalts, the Benedicts, the Don Pedros, and the Romeos ; the Beatrices, the Katherines, the Olivias, but

[1] Some very amusing satire upon the audiences of this time is to be found in Beaumont's *Knight of the Burning Pestle*.

[2] "Hung be the heavens with black."—*First Part of Henry VI.*, Act 1, Sc. 2.

not, I fear, the Desdemonas and Ophelias—their gorgeous costumes making a splendid contrast to the sombre background with the sheen of satin and velvet and the glitter of precious stones. It is a picture gallery; the close-cropped hair, the enormous ruffs, the huge trunk hose, the feet half concealed by the splendid roses in the shoes, the ladies in their pearled stomachers, and swelling farthingales stiff with gold and silver and pearl embroidery; we have seen it all in old portraits. At the back of each cavalier stands a page, a veritable Moth, whose duty it is to keep his master's pipe supplied with tobacco from "the fine lily pots," that, upon being opened, smell like conserve of roses, while between a pair of silver tongs he holds a glowing coal of juniper wood to ignite the Virginian weed, which is "drunk," as the phrase goes, from bowls of silver or clay of many curious shapes, so that the atmosphere resembles that of a modern music-hall. The actors are dressed in the costume of the period, many of the nobility being in the habit of sending them their cast-off suits. Comments are passed freely upon the play and the players; those of least judgment being, as usual, loudest in condemnation. Would I could picture Burbage in Hamlet and Shakespeare as the Ghost; but that is beyond the power of imagination—mine, at least—and so let this poor dim attempt at a presentment of the Elizabethan stage fade away.

No other English theatre has ever held so exalted a position, both from a dramatic and a histrionic point of view, as that occupied by the Blackfriars from 1609 until its suppression under the Commonwealth. Independent of the vulgar, it had never to descend to those wretched expedients to attract the crowd which for more than two hundred years have at different times shamed every London stage, while it gave to the world a dramatic literature incomparable in its grandeur and abundance. The Comédie Française is the only other theatre in the world of which so much can be said.

Note to page 10.—A distinguished Shakespearian student opines that *All Is True was* Shakespeare's play upon Henry VIII., and that it perished in the flames. It is well known that some of the highest authorities hold that the *Henry VIII.* included in Shakespeare's works was written by Fletcher. It would be impossible in this place to set forth the arguments upon which this contention is based, beyond a reference to the use of a redundant syllable at the end of the lines, which is a very rare occurrence in the greater poet, but quite a trick of Fletcher's, and a certain weak prettiness in the speeches of Wolsey and Catherine.

CHAPTER II

The Stage under the Commonwealth—The Red Bull—Cockpit—Vere Street Theatre—The First English Actress—Lincoln's Inn Fields—Dorset Gardens—Audiences—Actors—The Drama of the Time.

VERY curious and interesting are the records which have come down to us of the period which intervened between the final suppression of the theatres in 1647, and their reopening at the Restoration. The first edict was issued on September 6th, 1642; this seems, however, to have been generally evaded. But in the second edict all actors were threatened with imprisonment, and soon afterwards followed a third, which declared all players to be rogues and vagabonds, and authorised the justices to demolish all galleries and seats; it also enacted that any player discovered in the exercise of his vocation should be whipped for the first offence, and for the second declared an incorrigible rogue and vagabond, and every person found witnessing the performance of a stage play should be fined five shillings.[1]

What followed will best be told in the words of original authorities. My first quotation is from that very notable little book or pamphlet entitled *Historia Histrionica: an historical account of the English Stage*, etc., supposed to have been written by James Wright, of New Inn, and published 1699, to which I have referred

[1] This was the only edict by which the legitimate actor was ever branded as a rogue and a vagabond. See Note at the end of the book.

several times in the last chapter. The text is in the form of a dialogue between Lovewit and Trueman, which, after dwelling upon the actors and theatres of Elizabeth, James, and Charles the First's time, thus proceeds :—

"*Lovewit.*—But prythee, Trueman, what became of those players when the stage was put down, and the rebellion raised?

"*Trueman.*—Most of them, except Lowin, Taylor, and Pollard (who were superannuated), went into the King's army, and, like good men and true, served their old master, though in a different yet more honourable capacity. Robinson[1] was killed at the taking of a place (I think Basing House) by Harrison, he that was after hanged at Charing Cross, who refused him quarter, and shot him in the head when he had lain down his arms, abusing scripture at the same time by saying: *Cursed is he that doth the work of the Lord negligently.* Mohun was a captain, and (after the wars were ended here) served in Flanders, where he received pay as a major. Hart was a lieutenant of horse under Sir Thomas Dallison, in Prince Rupert's regiments; Burt was cornet in the same troop, and Shatterel quartermaster; Allen of the Cockpit was a major, and quartermaster-general at Oxford. I have not heard of one of these players of any note that sided with the other party, but only Swanston; and he professed himself a Presbyterian, took up the trade of a jeweller, and lived in Aldermanbury, within the territory of Father Calamy. The rest either lost or exposed their lives for their King. When

[1] Lowin was a famous Falstaff, and the original Volpone, Bosola, Sir Epicure Mammon; Taylor was Burbage's successor in tragedy; Robinson is mentioned in the first folio as one of the original actors in Shakespeare's plays.

the wars were over, and the Royalists totally subdued, most of 'em who were left alive gathered to London, and for a subsistence endeavoured to revive their old trade privately. They made up one company out of all the scattered members of several, and in the winter before the King's murder, 1648, they ventured to act some plays, with as much caution and privacy as could be, at the Cockpit. They continued undisturbed for three or four days; but, at last, as they were presenting the tragedy of the *Bloody Brother* (in which Lowin acted Aubrey; Taylor, Rollo; Pollard, the Cook; Burt, Latorch; and, I think, Hart, Otto), a party of foot soldiers beset the house, surprised them about the middle of the play, and carried 'em away in their habits, not admitting them to shift, to Hatton House, then a prison, where, having detained them some time, they plundered them of their clothes, and let 'em loose again. Afterwards, in Oliver's time, they used to act privately, three or four miles or more out of town, now here, now there; sometimes in noblemen's houses, in particular Holland House at Kensington, where the nobility and gentry who met (but in no great numbers) used to make a sum for them, each giving a broad piece, or the like. And Alexander Goffe, the woman actor at Blackfriars (who had made himself known to persons of quality), used to be the Jackal, and give notice of time and place. At Christmas and Bartholomew fair, they used to bribe the officer who commanded the guard at Whitehall, and were thereupon connived at to act for a few days at the Red Bull, but were sometimes, notwithstanding, disturbed by soldiers."

According to Kirkman, the dramatist, in his preface to *The Wits; or, Sport upon Sport* (1673), puppet plays upon scriptural, classical, and rustic subjects were given at the Red Bull during this interregnum by Mr. Robert Cox, and attracted crowded houses, that being the only kind of theatrical entertainment allowed by the Government.

In 1643 was published a pamphlet with the following lengthy title: "The Actor's Remonstrance or Complaint for the Silencing of their Profession, and Banishment from their several Playhouses, in which is fully set down their grievances from their Restraint, especially since Stage Players only are prohibited: the exercise of the Bear's College (Bear Garden), and the motions of Puppets being still in force and vigour."

This is one of the most curious theatrical brochures extant, abounding as it does in allusions to the manners and customs of the theatres of the preceding generation. The appeal is addressed to Phœbus and the Muses.

"Oppressed [the petitioners begin] with many calamities, and languishing to death under the burthen of a long and (for ought we know) everlasting restraint, wee, the *comedians*, *tragedians*, and *actors*, of all sorts and sizes, belonging to the famous private and publike houses within the City of London, and the suburbs thereof, in all humility present this our lamentable complaint.

"First, it is not unknowne to all the audiences that have frequented the private houses of Blackfriars, the Cockpit, and Salisbury Court, that wee have purged our stages from all obscene and scurrilous jests, such as might either be guilty of corrupting the manners, or defaming the persons of any men of note in the city or kingdom; that wee have endeavoured, as much as in us lies, to instruct one another in the true and genuine art of acting, to repress bawling and ranting, formerly in great request, and for to suit our language and action to the more gentle and natural garb of the times. Yet are wee, by authority, restrained from the practice of our profession, and left to live upon our shifts, or the expense of our former gettings, to the great impoverishment and utter undoïngs of ourselves, wives, children, and dependants. Besides, which is, of all others, our greatest grievance, that playes being put down, under the name of publike recreation, other recreations of farre more harmfull consequence are permitted still to stand, viz., that nurse of barbarism and beastlinesse, the Bear Garden, where, upon their usuall dayes, those demi-monsters are baited by ban dogs . . . pickpockets, which in an age are not heard of in any of our houses, repairing there, with other disturbers of the publike peace, which dare not be seen in our civill and well-goverened theatres, where none used to come but the best nobility and gentry."

It is complained that: "*Puppet Plays*, which are not so valuable as the *very musique between each act* at ours, are still kept up with uncontrolled allowance; witness the famous motion of *Bel and the Dragon*, so frequently visited at Holborne Bridge theese passed Christmasse holidays, whither citizens of all parts repaire, with farre more detriment to themselves than ever did the playes, comedies, and tradgedies being the lively representation of men's actions, in which vice is always sharply glanced at and punished, vertue rewarded and encouraged, and the most exact and naturall eloquence of our English language expressed and duly amplified, and yet for all this do we suffer in various ways. . . .

"Our *fooles*, who had wont to excite laughter with their countenances at their first appearance on the stage (hard shifts are better than none), are enforced, some of them at least, to maintain themselves by virtue of their baubles. Our *boyes*, ere we shall have libertie to act againe, will be grown out of use like crackt organ pipes, and have faces as old as our flags. Nay, our verie *doore keepers*, men and women, most grievously complain that by this cessation they are robbed of the privilege of stealing from us with licence; they cannot now seem to scratch their heads where they itch not, and drop shillings and half-crown pieces in at their collars. Our *musique*, that was held so delectable and precious, that they scorned to go to a tavern under twentie shillings salary for two hours, now wander with their instruments under their cloaks, I meane such as have any, into all houses of good fellowship, saluting every roome where there is company, with, *Will you have any musique, gentlemen?* For our *tire-men* and others that belonged formerly to our wardrobe, with the rest they are out of service, our stock of *cloathes* such as are not in tribulation for the generall use, being a sacrifice to moths. . . .

"The *tobacco-men* that used to walk up and down selling for a penny a pipe that which was not worth twelvepence a horseload, are now found tapsters in inns and tipling houses. Nay, such a terrible distresse and dissolution hath befallen us, that it hath quite unmade our hopes of future recoverie. For some of our ablest ordinarie *poets*, instead *of their annuall stipends and beneficiall second daies*, being, for meere necessitie, compelled to get a living by writing contemptible penny pamphlets, and feigning miraculous stories and unheard of battels. Nay, it is to be feared that shortly some of them will be incited to write ballads."

The petitioners conclude: "In consequence of theese evils by invoking the powerfull intercession of Phœbus, that they may be reinstated in their former homes and calling, and promise, in return, to admit none but reputable females into their sixpenny rooms, or boxes, to permit nothing but the best tobacco to be sold in the theatre, to avoid ribaldry, and, generally, so to demean themselves, that they shall no longer be deemed ungodly."

Mention has already been made of the first dawn of the revival—the performance of Sir William Davenant's *Cruelty of the Spaniards* at the Cockpit in 1656, which indicates that the rigours of fanaticism were beginning to relax. Though it has been alleged that the reason of this relaxation was Cromwell's hatred of the Spaniards, and that to place that nation in an odious light he would even condone a stage play.

As soon as Monk at the head of his army declared for the King, the actors who had survived the hard times crept out of their hiding-places, and were collected together by Rhodes, formerly prompter at the Black-friars, under whom they performed at the Red Bull. Rhodes afterwards played at the Cockpit and at Salisbury Court; but ere this the best of his actors had gone over to Killigrew, and it was probably the remnant of the old "book-keeper's" troupe that Pepys alludes to in the following passage, which is the last notice to be found of the St. John's Street Theatre.

"March 23rd, 1661.—To the Red Bull (where I had not been since plays came up again), up to the tiring rooms, where strange the confusion and disorder that is among them in fitting themselves, especially here where the clothes are very poor, and actors but common fellows. At last, into the pit where I think there was not above ten more than myself, and not one hundred in the whole house. And the play, which is called *All's Lost by Lust*, poorly done, and with so much disorder; among others, in the music room, the boy who was to sing a song not singing it right, his master fell about his ears, and beat him so that the whole house was in an uproar."

The great theatrical novelty of the Restoration was the introduction of women upon the stage. A company of French actors, in which women were included, had appeared at the Blackfriars, and afterwards at the Red Bull and the Fortune, in 1629; but very great hostility was manifested against them. In an article upon this subject in *The Drama, or Theatrical Magazine*, 1823, it is stated that "in 1656, Mrs. Coleman, the wife of Mr. Edward Coleman, represented Ianthe in the first part of Davenant's *Siege of Rhodes*, but the little she had to say was spoken in recitative." I have not been able, however, to find a verification of this statement. In *The Court Beggar*, played at the Cockpit in 1632, one of the characters says, "Women actors now grow in great repute." The passage may have referred to the French company just mentioned.

During the next thirty years, however, a marvellous change took place in public opinion, for in Davenant's patent it is stated: "Whereas the women's parts in plays have hitherto been acted by men, at which some have taken offence, we do give leave that for the time to come all women's parts be acted by women." Yet for several years after this was written boys and young men continued to share the heroines of tragedy and comedy with the actresses. In 1672, while the Drury Lane company, after the fire, were performing at Lincoln's Inn Fields, several plays—*Philaster*, *The Parson's Wedding*, *The Maiden Queen*—were acted entirely by women, and two of Dryden's coarsest prologues were written for the occasion.

On the 3rd of January, 1661, Pepys notes going to

see *Beggar's Bush* a second time, "it being very well done, and here the first time that I ever saw women come upon the stage." On the 7th of the same month, however, he saw Jonson's *Silent Woman*, with "Kinaston the boy" as Epicœne; and records his impression that, in female attire, he was the prettiest woman in the whole house, and as a man "likewise did appear the handsomest man in the house."

As the two most famous theatres of the Restoration, Drury Lane and Lincoln's Inn, are treated of in the next part, I will pass on to Dorset Gardens, "the splendid new house" that Davenant began to erect, just before his death, a little to the south of old Salisbury Court and close to the river, to which the company removed on November 9th, 1671.

Dorset Gardens was larger than either Lincoln's Inn Fields or Drury Lane; it was built by subscription, and the subscribers were called "Adventurers." I shall have more to say of these anon. The great feature of Dorset Gardens was the magnificence of its scenery and appointments, or in modern parlance, "its get up," which is referred to and satirised by Dryden in several of his prologues, where he writes of "the gaudy house with scenes,"[1] "the gay shows with gaudy scenes." The following passage from a prologue to *Tunbridge Wells*, a comedy written in 1678, animadverting upon the theatrical taste of that day, is so full of suggestion that with little alteration it might be well applied to our own:—

> "There's not a player but is turn'd a scout;
> And every scribbler sends his envoys out
> To fetch from Paris, Venice, or from Rome,
> Fantastic fopperies to please at home;

[1] "The gaudy house with scenes will serve for cits," would seem to point to the conclusion that Dorset Gardens was chiefly patronised by the *bourgeois*.

And that each act may rise to your desire,
Devils and witches must each scene inspire.
Wit rolls in waves, and showers down in fire;
With what strange care a play may now be writ,
When the best half's compos'd by painting it,
And in the air or dance lies all the wit."

Dorset Gardens continued to flourish until the amalgamation of the two companies,[1] after which it was only occasionally opened for the representation of plays that required elaborate scenery and machinery. In 1689 we find it styled the Queen's Theatre, Dorset Gardens, in honour, of course, of Queen Mary. But gradually, under the management of Christopher Rich, it fell into great degradation, being chiefly used as an arena for acrobats and wild beasts. In the prologue to Farquhar's *Constant Couple* (1700), allusion is made to a "strong man" who then had possession of it—

"Ah, friends! Poor Dorset garden-house is gone,
Quite lost to us; and, for some strange misdeed,
That strong man, Samson, 's pull'd it o'er our heads."

In April, 1703, it was announced that as soon as the damage it had sustained "by the late storms" could be repaired, the theatre would be opened for opera; but it does not appear that the promise was fulfilled. The last mention of Dorset Gardens is in Geneste, under the date of October 28th, 1706.

Besides these theatres there was one in Barbican, also established by letters patent, 1662, called the Nursery, for training boys and girls for the stage, somewhat after the style of the Children of the Revels in the time of Elizabeth and James; all obscene, scandalous, or offensive passages were to be omitted from the plays presented there. The Nursery is referred to by Oldham, and in

[1] See p. 51.

The Rehearsal; Pepys also mentions paying two visits to it. February 24th, 1667–8:—"To the Nursery, where none of us ever were before, where the house is better and the musique better than we looked for, and the acting not much worse, because I expected as bad as could be; and I was not much mistaken, for it was so." The most pointed reference, however, to the Nursery, is to be found in Dryden's *MacFlecknoe* (1682):—

"Near these a Nursery erects its head,
Where queens are formed, and future heroes bred,
Where unfledged actors learn to laugh and cry,
Where infant punks their tender voices try,
And little Maximins the gods defy;
Great Fletcher never treads in buskins here,
Nor greater Jonson dares in socks appear;
But gentle Simkin just reception finds
Amidst this monument of vanished minds."

Although many of the plays of Shakespeare and his contemporaries were revived, though with so many alterations and additions that the originals were almost lost sight of, the drama of the Restoration was modelled rather upon the French than the English school; the comedies were marked by a gross indecency of dialogue—though *that* was not borrowed from our neighbours—while the rhymed tragedies were stilted and unnatural. Chief among the writers for the Duke's Company was Mrs. Aphra Behn, whose comedies probably surpass in licentiousness all but a very few of those of her male contemporaries; yet it cannot be denied that, as dramatic compositions, they possess great merit; the plots are most ingenious, and situation succeeds situation with the rapidity and "go" of a Palais Royal farce, and if her characters have little variety—nearly all being drawn upon the same lines, the silly senile citizen, with a young and amorous wife, the daring gallant, the intriguing chambermaid, all modelled upon the Spanish comedy—she has verve and vigour in the incidents and dialogue that must have rendered her plays very attractive to the free and easy audiences of the time. The *répertoire* of the Duke's Company seems to have been even worse in point of morals than that of its rival; most of the notorious Edward Ravenscroft's pieces were written for Davenant, and the most abominable of all, *The London Cuckolds*. Etheredge's three comedies were produced here,[1] and most of Thomas Shadwell's works, though the latter, who was an inferior Ben Jonson, was rather coarse than licentious. The greater part of Dryden's plays were brought out at Drury Lane, but the vilest of them, *The Kind Keeper*, was given by the Duke's Company, as was also one of his finest, *The Spanish Friar*. Crowne, one of the best of the Restoration dramatists, wrote several plays for Lincoln's Inn Fields, and many of Tom D'Urfey's licentious productions found the same interpreters. Elkanah Settle, in whose writings the so-called heroic drama reached its highest absurdity, wrote eight of his seventeen extravagances for Lincoln's Inn Fields or Dorset Gardens. But in *The Orphan*, and *Venice Preserved* of Otway, the Duke's Company secured the two noblest tragedies written from the time of Charles I. to the present day.

The audiences were as licentious as the entertainment, and came but to see themselves and their manners reflected as in a looking-glass. Little of the play could

[1] Of these *The Man of Mode* was the most remarkable, as being the first of what Lamb styles the artificial school of comedy—a school which attained its greatest brilliancy in Congreve, and closed for ever with Sheridan.

have been heard amidst the uproar and clamour of the spectators, the gallants combing their long perriwigs and criticising the play aloud, or carrying on a flirtation with some masked female, or toying with the orange wenches, who were usually very important factors in the playhouses, and drove a profitable trade, since they charged sixpence each for their oranges. Nor were the humbler parts of the house behind the aristocratic in vice.

> "Our galleries were finely us'd of late,
> Where roosting masks sat cackling for a mate;
> They came not to see plays, but act their own,
> And had throng'd audiences when we had none.
> Our plays it was impossible to hear,
> The honest country men were forc'd to swear."
>
> *Epilogue to Sir Courtly Nice*, 1685.

A similar picture is given in Dryden's prologue for *The Women*, 1672—

> "Here's good accommodation in the pit;
> The grave demurely in the midst may sit,
> And so the hot Burgundian on the side
> Ply vizard masks, and o'er the benches stride.
> Here are convenient upper boxes too,
> For those that make the most triumphant show;
> All that keep coaches must not sit below.
> These gallants yon betwixt the acts retire,
> And at dull plays have something to admire," etc.

The young gallants frequently forced their way into the theatres without paying, or after staying in a little while demanded that their money should be returned; these abuses evoked an edict from the King in 1673, by which all such practices were suppressed.

PART II

THE HISTORY OF THE PATENT THEATRES, OF THE GREAT AND LITTLE THEATRE IN THE HAYMARKET, AND OF THE OPERA AND BALLET IN ENGLAND

ANN OLDFIELD.

CHAPTER I

The Four Theatres Royal, Drury Lane, 1663–1903—Their History, Actors, Traditions, and Literature—Also some account of the Theatres in Goodman's Fields.

COLLEY CIBBER, in his famous *Apology*, tells us that Charles II. at the Restoration granted two theatrical patents, one to Thomas Killigrew, Groom of the Chamber, and the other to Sir William Davenant, who had greatly distinguished himself in the Civil War; he thus conferred upon these two courtiers the monopoly of the London stage. The company of the first was called "The King's Servants," of the second, "The Duke of York's Servants." Davenant erected a theatre near Lincoln's Inn Fields, while Killigrew selected the site of a riding-yard in Drury Lane, that stood almost exactly upon the spot occupied by the present building. We must not, however, judge the Drury Lane of that day by its present aspect; it was still an aristocratic quarter of the town, wherein were to be found the residences of the Earls of Craven and Clare, the Marquis of Argyll, the Earl of Anglesey, and other nobles, imposing structures standing in grounds and gardens. Nell Gwynne lived here when she was attached to the theatre. It was not until the close of the century that these mansions, deserted by their noble owners, fell into disreputable hands, when streets and courts and alleys began to cover their pleasaunces; and in the time of

Queen Anne, as we may gather from Swift and Gay, the neighbourhood had become utterly disreputable.

The ground rent of the riding-yard was only £50 a year, and the cost of erecting the theatre £1,500; the dimensions of the building were 112 feet from east to west, and 59 feet from north to south. Although the patent was granted in August, 1660, the house was not ready until April 8th, 1663. But in the meantime Killigrew's company had been performing in a tennis court fitted up as a theatre in Vere Street, Clare Market, where, it is said, that on the 8th of December, 1660, the first English actress appeared in the character of Desdemona. A prologue spoken by the lady is to be found in Malone's *History of the Stage*. Her name is unknown. The first play acted at the new theatre was Beaumont and Fletcher's *The Humourous Lieutenant*. The performance was announced to commence at three, and the prices were: boxes 4*s*., pit 2*s*. 6*d*., middle gallery 1*s*. 6*d*., upper gallery 1*s*.[1]

In the travels of Balthasar de Monconys, published at Lyons in 1665, the following very interesting glimpse of the Theatre Royal, taken within two months of its opening, that is to say, on May 22nd, 1663, is given.

"L'après dinée nous fumes chez le Milord St. Alban et de là à la comedie dans la loge du Roy. Le théâtre est la plus propre et le plus bien que j'ai jamais vu, tout tapissé par le bas de bayette verte; aussi bien que toutes les loges qui en sont tapissés avec des bandes de cuir doré. Tous les bancs du parterre, où toutes les personnes de condition se mettent aussi, sont ranger en amphitheatre les uns plus hauts que les autres. Les changemens de théâtre, et les machines sont fort ingenieusement inventées et executées."

[1] It was not called the Theatre Royal, Drury Lane, until the next century, being usually spoken of as "The Theatre Royal."

M. Monconys, who was governor to the Duc de Chevreux, also visited the Duke's Theatre.

"L'après diné je fus à la comedie du Duc d'York où les changemens de scène me plurent beaucoup, mais non pas la froideur des actions et du parler tant des hommes que des femmes dans les pressans mouvements de colère et de crainte."

When the Theatre Royal opened, some of the best of Davenant's actors, probably by royal command, came from Lincoln's Inn to join Killigrew. His leading tragedians, Hart and Mohun, were men of high reputation; Hart was Shakespeare's grand-nephew, being the grandson of the poet's sister; contemporaries praised him enthusiastically, and it was said that in all the comedies and tragedies he was concerned in, he performed with that exactness and perfection that not any of his successors equalled him. Mohun, who had earned his title of Major in the civil wars, fighting on the side of the Cavaliers, was esteemed by the King, as a tragic actor, even above Hart; Lacey, a famous Falstaff, the original Bayes in *The Rehearsal*, mentioned in glowing terms by Pepys, was Charles's favourite actor; a picture representing him in three characters may be seen at Hampton Court. It was at Drury Lane, in 1665, that Nell Gwynne, who was a pupil of Hart's, made her first appearance as an actress in Dryden's *Indian Emperor*, and it was there, while speaking the epilogue to Dryden's *Tyrannic Love* (1669), that she first captivated the King. That very night, so the story goes, as soon as the curtain fell, he went behind the scenes and carried her off.

The company also included the two beautiful Marshall sisters, Anne and "Becky"; Mrs. Davenport, the romantic story of whose mock marriage with the Earl of Oxford is told by De Grammont; Pepys' inamorata, Mrs.[1] Knipp, and many others famous in their day, but now forgotten. Colley Cibber, in his "Apology," bears witness to the social importance enjoyed by the two companies. "Ten of the King's company," he writes, "were in the royal household establishment, having each ten yards of scarlet cloth, with a proper quantity of lace, allowed them for liveries, and in their warrants from the Lord Chamberlain were styled 'Gentlemen of the Great Chamber.' Whether the like appointments were extended to the Duke's company, I am not certain; but they were both in high estimation with the public, and so much the delight and concern of the Court, that they were not only supported by royalty being frequently present at their public presentations, but by its taking cognisance of their private government, insomuch, that their particular differences, pretensions, or complaints, were generally ended by the King's or Duke's personal command or decision. Besides their being thorough masters of their art, these actors set forward with two critical advantages, which perhaps may never happen again in as many ages. The one was their immediate opening after so long an interdiction of plays during the civil war and the anarchy that had followed it.[2] What eager appetites from so long a fast must those guests have had to that high and fresh variety of entertainments which Shakespeare had prepared for them. . . . The other advantage I was speaking of is that before the Restoration no actresses were seen upon the English

[1] Actresses were styled "Mrs." in the playbills until late in the eighteenth century, "Miss" being a term of reproach in those days for any but very young girls.

[2] Wright (*Historia Histrionica*) informs us that for several years after the Restoration whole sharers in the King's company got £1,000 per annum.

stage. The characters of women, in former theatres, were performed by boys or young men of the most effeminate aspect."

Very brief was the existence of the first Drury Lane Theatre, as it was burned down in January, 1672. During the rebuilding, the company performed at the house in Lincoln's Inn Fields,[1] which had been abandoned by the Duke's company in the preceding year upon their removal to Dorset Gardens.

The new Drury Lane was designed by Sir Christopher Wren; it cost £4,000, and was opened on March 26th, 1674. That no attempt, however, was made to rival the magnificence of the Duke's House may be gathered from a prologue written by Dryden for the occasion, which opens thus:—

> "A plain built house after so long a stay,
> Will send you half unsatisfied away;
> When, fallen from your expected pomp, you find
> A bare convenience only is designed.
> You, who each day can theatres behold,
> Like Nero's palace shining all with gold,
> Our mean ungilded stage will scorn, we fear,
> And for the homely room disdain the cheer."

Cibber gives a very good idea of the arrangement of the stage, which, he tells us, projected in a semi-oval figure right forward to the front bench of the pit, with side wings for the entrances in place of stage boxes, so that the whole action of the play was conducted beyond the pillars of the proscenium. Playgoers who remember the stage of the old Haymarket Opera House, burned down in 1867, will be better able to realise this form than those accustomed only to the modern theatres, in which the proscenium, on account of our elaborate scenic effects,

[1] See the following chapter.

has been virtually abolished, thus confining the dramatic action strictly within the stage frame. The form, however, was considerably altered, even during Cibber's time, by the enlargement of the auditorium and the introduction of stage boxes; but he contends for the superiority of the old fashion, as the most subtle shades of facial expression could be seen, and the softest whispers and most delicate intonations of the voice could be heard and better appreciated by the spectators.

"These two excellent companies, the King's and the Duke's," again to quote Cibber, "were both prosperous for some years, till their variety of plays began to be exhausted.[1] Then, of course, the better actors (which the King's seems to have been allowed) could not fail of drawing the greater audiences. Sir William Davenant, therefore, master of the Duke's company, to make head against their success, was forced to add spectacle and music to action; and to introduce a new species of plays, since called dramatic operas, of which kind were *The Tempest*, *Psyche*, *Circe*,[2] and others, all set off with the expensive decorations of scenes and habits, with the best voices and dancers. This sensual supply of sight and sound coming in to the assistance of the weaker party, it was no wonder they should grow too hard for sense and simple nature, when it is considered how many more people there are that can see and hear, than think and judge. So wanton a change of the public taste, there-

[1] We are informed in the *Apology* that they had a private rule or argument, that both houses were so happily tied down to, which was that no play acted at one house should ever be attempted at the other. All the capital plays of Shakespeare, Fletcher, Ben Jonson, were divided between them by the approbation of the Court and their own alternate choice; so that while Hart was famous for Othello, Betterton had no less reputation for Hamlet. Geneste, however, doubts that any such absolute rule existed.

[2] The first was Davenant's alteration of Shakespeare's play; the second was by Shadwell; the third by Charles Davenant.

fore, began to fall as heavy upon the King's company as their greater excellence in action had before fallen upon their competitors. . . . Not to dwell too long upon this part of my history, which I have only collected from oral tradition, I shall content myself with telling you that Mohun and Hart, now grown old, and the younger actors, as Goodman, Clark, and others, being impatient to get into their parts, and growing intractable, the audiences, too, of both houses, then falling off, the patentees of each, by the King's advice, which perhaps amounted to a command, united their interests and both companies into one, exclusive of all others, in the year 1684.[1] This union being so much in favour of the Duke's company, was the cause of Hart leaving the stage, and Mohun survived not long after."

The Duke's comedians, it would appear, endeavoured to mimic Mohun's manner, when reduced by age and infirmity, a baseness which Lord Rochester reproved in the following fine verses:—

> "And these are they who durst expose the age
> Of the great wonder of the English stage,
> Whom nature seem'd to form for your delight,
> And bade him speak as she bade Shakespeare write:
> These blades, indeed, are cripples in their art,
> Mimic the foot, but not the speaking part;
> Let them the Traitor, or Volpone try,
> Could they rage like *Cethegus*, or like *Cassius* die?"

[1] This date is incorrect. The union took place in 1682 (November 16th). Thomas Killigrew died in the March of the same year, but it seems that long previous to his death he had mortgaged the patent to Lacey, Mohun, and Hart, who were the veritable directors of the company. The names signed to the agreement for the amalgamation are Charles Davenant, William Smith, and Betterton on one side, and Charles Hart and Edward Kynaston on the other; Charles, Thomas Killigrew's son, who succeeded his father as Master of the Revels, was to receive £3 for every performance: Hart and Kynaston five shillings per diem, and ten shillings if they acted. Harris, Hart, Mohun, and Nell Gwynne left the stage after the union.

The union of the two companies, however, did not much mend matters. Whether it was that the great religious and political issues which then, and for years afterwards, so engrossed the public mind that they left little room there for such diversions, or whether it proceeded from apathy about things theatrical, a reaction from the eagerness with which they had been enjoyed at the Restoration, it would be useless to discuss, but for some years previously there had been a great falling off in public patronage. Something of this seems to have been attributable to the attractions of French and Italian companies. In the epilogue written for the King's company on their visit to Oxford in 1673, Dryden says:—

> "A French troop first swept all things in its way,
> But those Monsieurs were too quick to stay,
> Yet, to our cost, in that short time, we find
> They left their itch for novelty behind.
> The Italian merry-andrews took their place,
> And quite debauched the stage with lewd grimace:
> Instead of wit and humour, your delight
> Was there to see two hobby-horses fight," etc.

To such a low ebb had theatrical business fallen in 1690, that Charles Davenant, who had succeeded to the patent rights on the death of his mother and the retirement of his brother Alexander, sold his interest to a roguish lawyer, named Christopher Rich, for £80. It has been previously stated in the account of Dorset Gardens, that that house had been built by a subscription of gentlemen, who were called "Adventurers"; these, receiving no interest for their investment, however, had ceased to trouble themselves about the affairs of the theatre. Thus did this lawyer obtain absolute power,[1] which he used in the most unworthy manner,

[1] This account differs from that given by Cibber; I have followed Geneste.

imposing his own terms upon the actors, who were most miserably paid.[1] Verbruggen and Powel, both performers in the first rank, received but £2 a week each; Goodman, an excellent actor, and another named Griffin, were reduced to such straits that they had to sleep in one bed, and possessed but one shirt between them. Cibber tells a laughable story, how one, having an assignation with some fair Lindabrides, insisted upon wearing the garment out of his turn, and how the dispute was decided in their garret at the point of the sword. On more than one occasion Goodman took to the highway to eke out his miserable stipend.[2]

When "the Adventurers" applied for dividends, Rich evaded their claims, and, when pressed, so wearied out the suitors by every species of legal chicanery that at length he was left in undisturbed possession of the theatre. In 1695, however, the long-enduring actors revolted and laid their grievances before the Court; after obtaining a personal interview with King William, who, doubtless at the intercession of his beloved Mary, a great lover of the theatre, treated them with marked kindness, they were granted a licence to open the old theatre in Lincoln's Inn Fields, which, since the temporary tenancy of the King's company, it would seem, had been reconverted into a tennis court.

[1] For a very detailed and interesting account of the disputes and lawsuits between Rich and his actors, see some articles, "Actors and Managers under Queen Anne," which appeared in the *Athenæum* during August, 1888.

[2] Goodman's was an adventurous career. He had begun life by being expelled from Cambridge for defacing a picture of the Duke of Monmouth, at that time Chancellor of the University; he then took to the stage, and afterwards to the highway; was concerned in Sir John Fenwick's plot, turned King's evidence; and ended as the lover of Charles the Second's old mistress, the Duchess of Cleveland. He was a famous representative of Lee's Alexander, but of late years would never play it unless "my duchess" was present.

All the principal members of the Theatre Royal company—Betterton, Mrs. Barry, Mrs. Bracegirdle, etc.—seceded, leaving behind only the young and inferior actors. "The great Mr. Congreve," who then stood at the head of the dramatic authors of the time, went with them, took an active share in the management, and gave to this house his immortal comedy, *Love for Love*, which had been written for Drury Lane. The play, with Betterton, who, like another Delaunay, could play the gay young lover at sixty, Dogget, Underhill, Sandford, Mrs. Bracegirdle, Mrs. Barry, and Mrs. Bowman in the cast, proved a great success. The publication, however, of Jeremy Collier's famous *Short View of the Profaneness and Immorality of the English Stage*, in 1697, dealt a terrible blow at what little prosperity the theatres still enjoyed, and aroused the old spirit of Puritanism, which had been scotched, not killed. Yet the castigation was well deserved, for the licentiousness of the stage both before and behind the curtain had become a monstrous evil.

The sensation created by the book was enormous, scores of pamphlets refuting or defending its views were written, and the falling off in the audiences plainly showed that its remonstrances had struck home.

At the beginning of 1699 the King's Chamberlain sent an order to both playhouses calling the attention of the actors to the profane and indecent expressions often used in plays, and warning them, at their peril, not again so to offend; while in 1704 the wearing of vizard masks by the women was forbidden by an edict of Queen Anne.

During ten years Betterton and his associates performed at Lincoln's Inn Fields, Congreve, who received a share of the profits, continuing to take an active part in the management. But the famous actors of the Restoration, both male and female, were long past their maturity, and a new generation, destined to be scarcely less celebrated—Wilks, Cibber, Barton Booth, Mrs. Porter, Mrs. Oldfield—was rising to take their places.

In 1705, Lincoln's Inn Fields was again deserted, and the company went over to Sir John Vanbrugh's new theatre in the Haymarket, of which an account will be found in a future chapter.

In the meantime Rich still continued to wield the sceptre of Drury Lane, and to cajole and cheat as before, until another eruption in his company took place, and the best actors among those who had remained with him after the first revolt also seceded to the new house. The rivalry between the two companies was bitter and unscrupulous; and in 1699 the Grand Jury of Middlesex, which, no doubt, was strongly leavened with Puritanism, coupled the two theatres with the Bear Garden as public nuisances. And even the friendly testimony of Wright, who wrote his *Historia Histrionica* in this year, goes far to confirm this judgment. "Whereas of late," he writes, "the play-houses are so extremely pestered with vizard masks and their trade (occasioning continual quarrels and abuses), that many of the more civilized part of the town are uneasy in their company, and shun the theatre as they would a house of scandal." He adds that an audience can hardly be drawn without "the additional invitation of a Signor Fedeli, a Monsieur l'Abbé, or some such foreign regale expressed at the bottom of the bill."

It would be tedious to enter into the various complications and disputes in which Rich involved himself with his actors and "the Adventurers," so, "brief let me be." In 1709, Sir Thomas Skipworth, who, Cibber tells us, owned one-fourth of the united patent, was so disgusted with his unremunerative investment that he made Colonel Brett a present of it. The new possessor, determined to put the gift to some use, and having influence at Court, backed up the complaints and remonstrances of the actors against the injustice with which they were treated so effectually, that in the year last named, the Chamberlain silenced the patent by his authority, and closed the theatre.

Soon after Rich had been deprived of his patent rights, Mr. William Collier, a member of Parliament, with considerable interest at Court, obtained a licence to open Drury Lane during the Queen's pleasure, and as the old patentee refused to give up possession, Collier employed people to force an entrance, but only to find that Rich had previously removed everything portable in the shape of dresses and properties.[1] Collier's speculation turning out anything but successful, he transferred his interest in this theatre to Cibber, Dogget, and Wilks.

Before entering upon the history of the famous Triumvirate, let me take a retrospective glance, necessarily very brief, at the actors and literature of the house during the first thirty-six years of its existence.

Upon Mohun, Hart, and others of the Restoration period I have already touched; but there remain those whom Cibber has styled "the best set of English actors yet known"; actors whose portraits he has drawn in colours so vivid that they can never fade. At the head of the list stands Betterton, the friend of Tillotson, the mentor of Pope, and the critic of Dryden, of whom Steele wrote in *The Tatler*, on the occasion of his funeral, "a man whom I always very much admired,

[1] See *Tatler*, No. 99, for a most amusing description of the *fracas*.

and from whose actions I had received more strong impressions of what is great and noble in human nature than from the arguments of the most solemn philosophers, or the descriptions of the most charming poets I have ever read."

In another place this fine critic has said: "I have hardly a notion that any performer of antiquity could surpass Mr. Betterton in any of the occasions in which he has appeared upon the stage"; and again he tells us that when Betterton played Hamlet, at seventy, in manner, gesture, and voice he appeared "a young man of great expectation, vivacity, and enterprise." The great actor's last appearance upon the stage was as Melantius, in *The Maid's Tragedy*, on April 10th, 1710. Three days afterwards, on account of the violent means to which he had resorted to suppress an attack of gout, he was dead.

Kynaston, when he left off playing heroines, became a fine actor of heroic tragedy. Another admirable performer was Mountfort, who was murdered by the notorious duellist, Lord Mohun. The "great" Mrs. Barry was one of the grandest tragedy queens that ever trod the stage; while of the celebrated Mrs. Bracegirdle, Cibber says that all the extravagance and frantic passion of Lee's Alexander the Great was excusable when she played Statira; that scarcely an audience saw her that were not half her lovers, without a suspected favourite among them. In an age of general dissoluteness she bore an immaculate reputation, and, in spite of the sneers and scandal of certain profligate writers of the time, seems to have merited it. Mrs. Mountfort was called "a miracle of fine acting," and there were many others, such as Sandford, Nokes, Leigh, Underhill, whose names will be familiar to every reader of *The*

Tatler, and whose full-length portraits will be found in the *Apology*.

Equally brilliant during this period were the literary annals of Drury Lane. With very few exceptions, all the dramatic works of "Glorious John" were first produced upon this stage. And with all their faults, the stilted rant of the heroic rhymed tragedies, and the licentiousness of the comedies, they contain much of Dryden's finest work; those who are unacquainted with his plays can have but a limited appreciation of his poetical powers. "Mad Nat Lee," really a man of genius, though tainted by insanity, wrote almost entirely for the King's Company—*The Rival Queens* (*Alexander the Great*), the only one of his plays now remembered, kept the stage until within living memory; Southerne also, whose *Oronooko* and *Isabella, or The Fatal Marriage*, were favourite tragedies up to our grandfathers' days; Crowne, the author of *Sir Courtly Nice*, famous among the comedies of the eighteenth century, favoured Drury Lane; Sir Charles Sedley's two best comedies, *Bellamira* and *The Mulberry Garden*, were brought out here in 1667 and 1668. It was to this theatre that Congreve gave *The Old Bachelor* and *The Double Dealer;* Wycherly, his *Love in a Wood*, *The Country Wife*, and *The Plain Dealer;* Farquhar, all his best pieces except *The Beaux Stratagem;* Vanbrugh, *The Relapse* and one or two minor works; Mrs. Centliver, *The Busy Body* and that admirable comedy of intrigue *The Wonder;* Steele, his four plays; and with the exception of a wretched tragedy called *Xerxes*, all Colley Cibber's works were first brought out at the Theatre Royal; of these, *She Wou'd and She Wou'd Not*, *The Careless Husband*, and *The Provoked Husband*—in which he was part author with Vanbrugh—are not only works of a very high order of merit, but are comparatively free from the grossness of their predecessors.

Between the two houses there was a splendid array of dramatic genius which could only be overshadowed by the Titans of the Shakespearian age. The prevailing faults of the writers are licentiousness and the brutal cynicism that denies all virtue both to man and woman, and not infrequently lapses into the vilest obscenity. Jeremy Collier's book did much to modify this evil, and Steele and Cibber were the first to bring into vogue a purer school of comedy, though the lachrymose sentimentalism of the former, in such comedies as *The Lying Lover*, *The Conscious Lovers*, *The Tender Husband*, did much to defeat his good intentions.

Notwithstanding the brilliancy of its histrionic and literary record, the retrospect of the stage from the Restoration to the end of Queen Anne's reign is anything but satisfactory; the national passion for theatrical amusements, which had been one of the most marked features of the reigns of Elizabeth and the two first Stuart kings, burst forth with something of its old enthusiasm during the early years of the reign of the second Charles, and then sank again into indifference.

The management known as *The Triumvirate* was one of the most prosperous in the annals of the London stage. From a histrionic point of view, these three actors were a host in themselves; Cibber, who was never happy out of the society of a lord, who was a member of White's Club, the only actor that ever obtained that privilege until just recently,[1] was an incomparable fop and fine gentleman. Wilks, although he had few natural gifts for the stage, yet by study and

[1] I understand that Mr. Bourchier has the privilege of standing at the famous bow window.

application became the finest light comedian of his day; certain contemporaries also highly praise his tragic powers; but these, probably, did not extend beyond sound yet conventional acting. Few actors have had the privilege to create so many famous characters. It was for him Mrs. Centliver wrote Don Felix in *The Wonder*, and Farquhar, Sir Harry Wildair in *The Constant Couple*, Mirabel in *The Inconstant*, Captain Plume in *The Recruiting Officer*, and in these, perhaps, he never had an equal; while his Prince Hal was pronounced to be a performance of the highest excellence. Dogget was equally admirable in his own peculiar line, and was a consummate artist in dressing and make up; he chiefly shone in old men and characters of low life; he was the original Fondlewife in Congreve's *Old Bachelor*, and Ben in the same author's *Love for Love*. He had a passion for speculating on the Stock Exchange, and was so enthusiastic a Whig that in his will he left a sum of money for a coat and badge to be annually rowed for by Thames watermen on the 1st of August, to celebrate the accession of the House of Hanover. Three individuals of more opposite tastes were never linked together; Dogget, the miserly money-grubber; Cibber, the fashionable rake, who squandered his money at the gaming-table and in other modish follies, while Wilks was entirely absorbed in his profession, and was lavish in expenditure only upon stage dresses.[1] Nevertheless, the union prospered to an extraordinary degree, for when the common interests of the partners were in question they always agreed.

[1] This does not seem to have extended to the *ensemble*, however. In a newspaper of 1723, while criticising the performance, the writer says: "King Duncan has not had a new habit for the last century; Julius Cæsar was as ragged as a colt, and his guards were a ragged regiment. Only the parts played by the managers were well dressed."

"In the twenty years we were our own directors," writes Cibber, "we never had a creditor that had occasion to come twice for his bill; every Monday morning discharged us of all demands before we took a shilling for our own use. And from this time we neither asked any actor, nor were desired by them to sign any agreement whatsoever. The rate of their respective salaries were only entered in our daily pay roll, which plain record everyone looked upon as good as city security."

Dogget's Whig fanaticism, however, by-and-by brought about a change in the government. The rising tragedian of the day, the man who by a consensus of opinion was hailed as the successor of Betterton, was Barton Booth, and when Addison's *Cato* was produced in 1713, he created such an impression in the part of the Roman Censor that Lord Bolingbroke suggested he should be admitted to a share of the patent, and as Booth was a pet with the aristocracy, a carriage and six almost nightly waiting at the stage door to convey him to some noble house, the suggestion was little short of a command.

Dogget was so indignant at being controlled by a Tory lord that he withdrew in high dudgeon, and ultimately received £600 for his interest in the patent, the exact sum which Booth paid for his admission. Booth was a gentleman by birth, and a scholar, and these advantages were apparent in his acting; but he had not the versatility of either of his great predecessors, Hart or Betterton. He was successful only in heavy tragedy; he was a fine Othello, and a grand Lear. Foremost among the ladies under the triumvirate management was famous Ann Oldfield, who was advanced from behind the bar of the Mitre Tavern, in

St. James's Market, kept by her aunt, to be the associate of duchesses; she was the original and inimitable Lady Betty Modish of Cibber's *Careless Husband*, and the old actor writes: "I have often seen her in private societies, where women of the best rank might have borrowed some part of her behaviour without the least diminution of their sense or dignity." She was equally great in tragedy. Chetwood says, in his *History of the Stage*, "her piercing, flaming eye, with manner and action suiting, used to make me shrink with awe." She was the original Jane Shore in Rowe's tragedy of that name (1714). The mantle of Mrs. Barry, however, was said to have fallen upon the shoulders of Mrs. Porter; Dr. Johnson told Mrs. Siddons that in the vehemence of tragic rage he had never seen her equalled; she was the original Alicia in *Jane Shore*, and Leonora in Young's *Revenge;* but her greatest parts were Queen Katherine in *Henry VIII.*, and Queen Elizabeth in Bankes's *Unhappy Favourite.*

At the death of Queen Anne in 1714, the licence of Drury Lane, through the influence of Sir Richard Steele, had been changed into a patent for his lifetime and that of two of his heirs. When, however, in 1719, Sir Richard quarrelled with his patron, the Duke of Newcastle, then Lord Chamberlain, over the Sunderland Peerage Bill, His Grace, to avenge himself, suspended the patent and closed the theatre. Much was said about "the insolence of the actors," and Colley Cibber was included in Steele's disgrace. This was probably on account of a dispute the future Poet Laureate had had with the Master of the Revels,[1] Charles Killigrew, the latter claiming a forty-shilling fee for each

[1] This ancient office was finally abolished on the passing of the Licensing Act, 1737.

new play acted, while Cibber argued that the patent gave the managers of Drury Lane absolute power in such matters. It was only by submission, however, to this ancient functionary that the Triumvirate were able to obtain a temporary licence to renew their performances, and it was not until Sir Robert Walpole returned to office in 1721 that the patent rights were restored. Though his office was little more than a sinecure, and the managers were constantly complaining that he did little or nothing to earn the money, Steele was paid £700 a year as director, as well as in consideration of the patent, which was made out in his name.

During twenty years Drury Lane enjoyed an almost uninterrupted prosperity, though the share netted by each manager, £1,500, would not be thought much in these days. Wilks died first, then Booth, after which Cibber retired.

After the death and retirement of the Triumvirate, dark days again fell upon Drury Lane. In 1732 a gentleman named Highmore purchased Cibber's share for £3,000, and shortly afterwards acquired that of Mrs. Wilks; but a revolt of the company, stirred up by Colley's worthless son,[1] obliged him to close the house a ruined man, and sell his interest at a great sacrifice to Charles Fleetwood, a young fellow of good family, who, together with Giffard, the manager of Goodman's Fields, the purchaser of Mrs. Booth's moiety, now became proprietor of the patent rights. Fleetwood was a spendthrift, a gambler, a man utterly devoid of honesty and honour, always deeply in debt

[1] Theophilus Cibber, who was drowned in October, 1758, crossing over from Ireland, the husband of the great Mrs. Cibber, famous for his impersonation of Ancient Pistol, by which name he is frequently referred to by his contemporaries; he was a very disreputable personage.

and difficulties, and under his direction dramatic art sank to a very low level.

The first gleam of light that illumined this gloomy prospect was the appearance of Charles Macklin as Shylock. As early as 1725 the young Irish actor had essayed a more natural style of acting at Lincoln's Inn Fields, and had been discharged for flying in the face of tradition. Some years afterwards he was engaged by Fleetwood for Drury Lane. Shakespeare's *Merchant of Venice* had not been performed for forty years, a spurious version by Lord Lansdowne, called *The Jew of Venice*, in which the actors rendered Shylock as a low comedy part, having taken its place. Macklin now proposed to revive the original text, and to play Shylock as a tragic character. Manager and actors were aghast at such a daring proposal, and it was only when business was hopelessly bad that, in the season of 1741, Fleetwood consented to the experiment being made. Yet even after the play was announced his courage gave way, and he begged Macklin to forego his intention. But the Irishman was firm. The play was produced on January 11th, and his impassioned fervour and natural acting took the jaded town by storm. A German critic, named Lichtenberg, who saw him in after life play the part, gives a good idea of the leading features of the impersonation. "Picture to yourself," he writes, "a somewhat portly man, with a yellowish, coarse face, a nose by no means deficient in length, breadth, or thickness, and a mouth, in the cutting of which Nature's knife seems to have slipped as far as the ear, on one side at least, as it appeared to me. His dress is black and long, his trousers likewise long and wide; his three-cornered hat is red. The words he speaks on coming on the stage are slow and full of import. 'Three thousand ducats.' The two *th's* and the two *s's*, especially the last after the *t*, Macklin mouths with such unction that one would think he were at once tasting the ducats, and all that could be purchased with them. Three such words spoken in that situation marks the whole character. In the scene, when for the first time he misses his daughter, he appears without his hat, with his hair standing on end, and in some places a finger's length above the crown, as if the wind from the gallows had blown it up. Both hands are firmly clenched, and all his movements are abrupt and convulsive." So terribly malignant was his action and expression in the court scene that a shudder went through an audience that had been accustomed to roar with laughter at this situation. Even George II., who so despised "blays and boetry," was appalled by the performance, and could not sleep after witnessing it; while Pope immortalised the actor in the couplet:—

> "This is the Jew
> That Shakespeare drew."

Macklin had given the first blow to the old school of acting; he had aroused a desire for something new, fresh, and unconventional; but he lacked the stability of character, the tact, and the genius to carry out the revolution he had initiated; it was reserved for a far greater actor, David Garrick, to develop his ideas, and give them practical effect.

Before touching on the career of David Garrick, it will be necessary to the proper understanding of his connection with Drury Lane to give some account of the theatre at which he made his first appearance upon the stage.

In 1729 a Mr. Thomas Odell, who after the passing

of the Licensing Act was made Deputy Licenser of Plays in the Lord Chamberlain's office, converted a silk-throwster's shop in Leman Street, Whitechapel, into a theatre,[1] and engaged as his stage manager an actor from Dublin, named Henry Giffard.[2] Odell, not understanding anything about theatres, very soon transferred his rights in the building to Giffard, who, finding the speculation a promising one, to quote Chetwood's words (*History of the Stage*), "in the year 1733 caused to be built (in Ayliffe Street, close by) an entire new, beautiful, convenient theatre, by the same architect with that of Covent Garden: where dramatic pieces were performed with the utmost elegance and propriety." Strange to relate, this remote Temple of Thespis was destined not only to be the scene of the début of David Garrick, but indirectly to bring about a most important piece of legislation that shaped the destinies of the stage, and all connected with it, for over a century.

Henry Fielding's *Pasquin*, and *The Historical Register*, in which Sir Robert Walpole is so severely satirised and ridiculed, is commonly held responsible for having pro-

[1] There was a yet earlier theatre in Goodman's Fields, however, according to the following passage extracted from an old periodical called *The Observator*, which was published about the beginning of the eighteenth century. In 1703, it informs its readers, in the character of Tutchin, that "the great playhouse has calved a young one in Goodman's Fields, in the passage by the Ship Tavern, betwixt Prescot and Chambers Street." To this information *Observator* replies: "It is a very good place in Rosemary Lane precinct, and I know no reason why the quality at both ends of the town should not have the same diversions. This will be a great ease to the ladies of Rag Fair, who are now forced to trudge as far as Lincoln's Inn Fields to mix themselves with quality. The mumpers of Knockvargis will now have the playhouse come to them who were not able to stump it to the other end of the town on their wooden legs; the Does in Tower Hill Park and Rosemary Lane purlieu will be foddered nearer home this winter, and the sailors will have better entertainment for their loose coin."

[2] It was here, in 1730, Fielding's second piece, *The Temple Beau*, was first produced.

voked that Minister in 1737 to introduce the famous Licensing Act; but it was really the immediate result of a play never acted, called *The Golden Rump*. The MS. of this piece, by a hand unknown, was sent to Giffard, who, frightened at its audacious abuse of the King and his ministers, carried it to Walpole. It was the last straw, and, after reading it, Sir Robert at once brought in a Bill which not only strictly limited the metropolitan theatres to two, but established a censorship over the drama as well. Giffard received £1,000 for his loyalty, but it destroyed the legal status of his theatre.

Giffard seems to have had a good company, and several of his actors afterwards rose to distinction; notably Walker, the original Captain Macheath in *The Beggar's Opera*, and the finest Faulconbridge of which there is any tradition; Yates, afterwards a famous member of Garrick's *corps dramatique* at Drury Lane, and the original Sir Oliver Surface; Bullock, a low comedian highly praised; Harry Woodward, then a boy; Mrs. Giffard, who subsequently held a leading position in the patent houses, and Giffard himself, a man of no inconsiderable talent. After the passing of the Act, Giffard took his company to Lincoln's Inn Fields, which breach of the law, as he rented the house from Rich, the manager of Covent Garden, the patentees seem to have winked at. But the speculation did not prove a success, and in the following year he returned to Goodman's Fields.

There never was an Act of Parliament so stringently worded that its enactments could not in some way be evaded; so Giffard hit upon the expedient of issuing tickets at one, two, and three shillings for a concert "at the late theatre in Ayliffe Street," and performing a play *gratis* between the two parts. The plays selected were those of the regular dramatic repertory,[1] yet no one seems to have interfered with him, Whitechapel probably being considered at that time a part of the metropolis far too remote to come into rivalry with Covent Garden.

At the close of the "thirties," David Garrick, then in the wine business with his brother Peter in Durham Yard, Adelphi, was haunting the theatres and coffee-houses and every place where the actors resorted, chafing at the restraint which his friends put upon his inclination. One night, when he was behind the scenes at Goodman's Fields, Yates, who was playing Harlequin, was taken suddenly ill, and young Garrick, who just before had made a hit in an amateur performance[2] got up by Cave, the printer, in the old room over St. John's Gate, Clerkenwell, was easily prevailed upon to take his place. Harlequin, except in Rich's pantomimes, was not a mere acrobat in those days; he was a speaking part, an impromptu wit, and Garrick seems to have acquitted himself well on the occasion, for soon afterwards he accompanied Giffard's company to Ipswich, where he played under the name of Lydgate. Determined now to be an actor, Garrick, on his return to London, tried both the patent houses, and, finding they would none of him, made his début at the unlicensed theatre in Goodman's Fields, October 9th, 1741, as Richard III.

As usual, the entertainment was called "a concert of

[1] It is worth noting that Giffard here revived *The Winter's Tale,* for the first time for one hundred years.

[2] As a boy of eleven, Garrick had organised a company of juvenile players for a performance of *The Recruiting Officer,* in which he took the part of Kite, and as he grew up his love of amateur acting was frequently indulged in at his native city, Lichfield.

vocal and instrumental music" in two parts, admission to which was by tickets at one, two, and three shillings, to be obtained at the Fleece Tavern, near the theatre. And between the two parts of the concert was presented gratis, "an historical play called *The Life and Death of King Richard III.*," etc., etc. "The part of King Richard by a young gentleman who never appeared on any stage." This, as we know, was a playbill fib.

Having made himself well known as a young man about town with very original ideas upon acting, many of Garrick's friends journeyed from the west to witness his performance. From the first his success was assured; accustomed to the cold and stilted declamation, without heart, soul, or impulse, of the time, the effect of his fire and passion upon the audience was electrical; the marvellous tent scene, the tiger-like ferocity of the last act, and the awful agony of the death scene were such as had never been witnessed in living memory. The press declared his reception to have been the greatest and most extraordinary ever known on such an occasion. After a few nights all fashionable London was rushing east to see the new actor. Pope, who had sat at Betterton's feet, said magnificently, "That young man never had a rival and never will have a rival"; and William Pitt pronounced him to be the only actor in England.

Nevertheless, "Garrick's easy and familiar yet forcible style of delivery at first threw the critics into some hesitation concerning the propriety as well as novelty of his manner," says Davies (*Life of Garrick*). "They had been long accustomed to an elevation of the voice, with a sudden mechanical depression of its tones, calculated to excite admiration and to entrap applause; to the just modulation of the words, and concurring expression of the features from the genuine workings of nature they had been strangers, at least for some time. Quin, after he had seen Garrick in some important character, declared peremptorily that if the young fellow was right, he and the rest of the players had been wrong."

Aaron Hill, in his dedication to *The Fatal Vision*, 1716, animadverts upon the affected, vicious, and unnatural tone of voice so common among actors of the time. Antony Aston, in writing of Mrs. Barry, says: "Neither she, nor any of the actresses of those times, had any tone in their speech, so much lately in use." This sing-song delivery was undoubtedly borrowed from the Parisian stage, where it was the mode during the time of Louis XV. Against these vices of style Garrick used the most potent of all weapons, ridicule. When playing Bayes in *The Rehearsal*, he would check the actors who spoke naturally and proceed to teach them how to deliver the speeches in true theatrical manner. For this purpose he selected some of the most eminent performers, and assumed the manner and deportment of each in his turn. He would begin with Delane, who, next to Quin, was the leading tragedian of the time. Retiring to the back of the stage, drawing his left arm across his heart, resting his right elbow upon it, and raising a finger to his nose, he would come forward with a stately gait, nodding his head as he advanced, and deliver a speech in the exact tones of this declamatory tragedian. After that he would proceed to imitate other prominent performers of the day. He never, however, mimicked Quin, whom he considered an excellent actor in parts that suited him—and Quin was a duellist who had killed his man.

At Goodman's Fields, Garrick ran the whole gamut of

stage characters; he played burlesque as Bayes, he appeared as *jeune premier* in the parts of Chamont and Lothario, as a comedy old man, Fondlewife, in *The Old Bachelor*, as the tragedian in Hamlet, and as a low comedian in *The Lying Valet*.

The theatre closed on May 27th, 1742, in the midst of a most brilliant success, not to open again. The patentees of Drury Lane and Covent Garden, thoroughly roused by the alarming diminution in their receipts, determined to enforce the recently passed Act of Parliament; so with the co-operation of Sir John Bernard, a London magistrate, and the original mover of the Act, they so far intimidated Garrick and Giffard, that the one seems to have been reduced to the necessity of making an engagement with Fleetwood, and the other of shutting up his theatre.

Odell's old theatre in Leman Street, which after Giffard's resignation had been used only for rope-dancing and such-like exhibitions, was now reopened as a playhouse, but with an unknown company. The last time I can find any mention of Goodman's Fields is under date 1751. But whether it is Odell's or Giffard's theatre I cannot determine. The latter seems to have been converted into a warehouse, which was burned down in 1802.

Garrick was engaged by Fleetwood at a salary of six hundred guineas per annum, the largest sum that had ever yet been paid to an actor, Quin receiving only five hundred pounds. On the 11th of May, 1742, he made his first appearance at Drury Lane as Chamont in *The Orphan*. He then performed for six nights at Goodman's Fields, returned to Drury Lane on the 28th, played Lear, and on the 31st appeared as Richard. This was the last time he acted in London that season, being engaged for Dublin, where his success was as great as in London. He reappeared at Drury Lane for the season on October 5th, in the same year, as Bayes.

Notwithstanding Fleetwood's unthrifty habits, Drury Lane, thanks to Macklin, who was the manager, seems to have been tolerably prosperous for a time, but towards the close of the year 1743, the patentee's reckless extravagance had thrown its affairs into the utmost confusion; bailiffs were in possession, actors' salaries were unpaid, and they themselves treated with insolence, while the stage was disgraced by the most contemptible exhibitions from Sadler's Wells. It was a repetition of the old story of Christopher Rich. The company determined to secede, and waited upon the Lord Chamberlain in the hope of obtaining a licence to open the Haymarket. This was peremptorily refused, and consequently they had no alternative but to return to Fleetwood. He consented to take back all the recalcitrants except Macklin, whom he regarded as the ringleader. Garrick offered to pay Macklin £6 a week out of his own pocket until matters could be smoothed over, but the hot-headed Irishman would not listen to any compromise, and on the first night of the season, December 5th, 1743, with the aid of some friends, organised a riot in the theatre. Garrick was hissed and not allowed to speak; pamphlets were issued on both sides; and Fleetwood engaged some thirty bruisers, headed by the notorious Jack Broughton, the first of the champion prize-fighters, to deal with the rioters, who, as usual, chiefly congregated in the pit. The most disgraceful scenes were almost nightly enacted within the theatre, until Macklin was again engaged; though he did not gain this victory without having to make submission in a prologue written for the occasion, in which he protested—

> "No revolution plots are mine, again
> You see, thank Heaven, the quietest of men."

But Fleetwood's reign was nearly over; impaired in health and fortune, and hopelessly embarrassed, he had mortgaged the patent for £3,000, and had borrowed £7,000 on the dresses, scenery, and properties of the house, and now the lender was in possession as receiver. Fleetwood advertised that the patent was to be sold before a Master in Chancery. Two City men determined to be the purchasers, provided that James Lacy, who was at that time assistant manager to Rich at Covent Garden, would undertake the management. Lacy had formerly been a manufacturer at Norwich, but through misfortunes in business, and a taste for theatricals, he took to the stage, played under Rich at Lincoln's Inn Fields, and under Fielding at the Haymarket; he was also the builder of Ranelagh Music House, which he sold for £4,000. Lacy was to be a joint partner, but the purchasers were to lay down the whole of the money required, and to hold Lacy's third in the mortgage until his share of the profits enabled him to discharge his obligation.

After some complications, into which I need not enter, the matter was settled, and requiring a partner, Lacy proposed to David Garrick, who, having money, reputation, and ability, was a most desirable one, to join him; by the advice of his friends, Garrick accepted. The new patent was granted, and it was stipulated that the two partners were to be equal sharers in the profits, except that Garrick was to be paid a salary for acting.

Drury Lane opened under this new management on

September 15th, 1746. The business of the theatre was divided between the partners, Garrick entirely superintending the stage. Order, decency, and decorum were now strictly enforced; punctuality was insisted upon at rehearsals, at which as much attention was paid to the business of the scene as though the audience was already present; he also insisted upon the actors being perfect in their parts, and those who did not conform to his rules were suspended. Nor were his reforms less notable before the curtain; at the bottom of a bill for October, 1747, was printed the following notice: "As the admittance of persons behind the scenes has occasioned a general complaint on account of the frequent interruption in the performance, it is hoped that gentlemen won't be offended that no money will be taken there for the future." This struck a death-blow at the intolerable abuse of allowing spectators to be seated on the stage during the performance—a subject upon which I shall have more to say in a future chapter—but the rule does not seem to have been rigidly enforced, at least after a time. (See next chapter.)

Garrick gathered about him a noble company, including Macklin; Spranger Barry, who at Covent Garden had achieved a success scarcely inferior to his own; Mrs. Pritchard, a grand *tragédienne;* Mrs. Cibber, most tender and exquisite of Juliets and Ophelias; delightful Peg Woffington, most inimitable of high-comedy actresses, a Sir Harry Wildair second only to Wilks, and a tragic actress as well; Kitty Clive, unapproachable in the broader comedy, etc.

On March 19th, 1748, *Macbeth*, freed from most of Davenant's alterations, though still a long way from the text, was revived. The music, supposed to be by Locke, which had been foisted into Davenant's version, was

DAVID GARRICK.

EDMUND KEAN.

retained; the singing witches were dressed in the most charming costumes, some of white satin and lace, and were rouged and powdered, and made to look as attractive as possible. Garrick wore a scarlet coat, silk stockings, and a powdered wig; and Mrs. Pritchard, as Lady Macbeth, was attired as a fashionable lady of the period. But their acting was marvellous, especially in the murder scene. Garrick's dagger soliloquy filled the audience with terror. "When," says Murphy (*Life of Garrick*), "he re-entered with the bloody dagger in his hand, he was absolutely scared out of his senses; his distraction of mind and agonising horrors were finely contrasted by Mrs. Pritchard's seeming apathy, tranquillity, and confidence. Their looks and actions supplied the place of words, and their terrifying whispers made the scene awful and tremendous." Yet he failed as Othello, a circumstance, perhaps, greatly owing to the smallness of his stature.

In 1750, both Barry and Mrs. Cibber went over to Covent Garden, which possessed by far the stronger company. This was the season of the famous *Romeo and Juliet* rivalry, which will be referred to in the chapter on Covent Garden. Garrick had to fight against the opposition house by producing pantomime, though he had promised never to resort to it. In a prologue, on the opening night, he told the audience that if they would not come to see Lear and Hamlet, he must give them Harlequin. And he did it so well that Rich trembled upon his throne.[1] Garrick never disgraced Drury Lane by any unworthy production; some of the tragedies and comedies were terribly dull, but they never compromised the dignity of the stage. In a piece called *The Chinese Festival*, brought out in 1755, however, the pit and

[1] See the next chapter.

gallery took such offence at the introduction of foreign dancers, that although the performance was by the King's command, and His Majesty was present, a riot ensued, great damage was done to the theatre, and Garrick's house in Southampton Street narrowly escaped being sacked. During this season Mrs. Cibber returned.

The range of characters that Garrick sustained during a single season is surprising: Ranger, Hamlet, Archer, Romeo, Benedick, Lear, Sir John Brute, Don Felix, Bayes, Lothario, Kitely, Lord Chalkstone (a gouty old man), Abel Drugger, in the mutilated version of Ben Jonson's *Alchemist*, Leon (*Rule a Wife and Have a Wife*), Leontes, Lord Townley, etc.

Drury Lane experienced a great loss in 1758, when Harry Woodward, most delightful of light comedians, of Prince Hals, of Copper Captains, of Petruchios, seceded to go into partnership with Barry at Dublin.

Although Garrick had set his face against allowing the audience upon the stage, the nuisance still continued on benefit nights; and as it brought a large sum of money to the *bénéficiaires*, it was difficult to abolish. It was this consideration that in 1762 induced him to enlarge Drury Lane so as to increase the capacity of the auditorium, which would then hold £335.

A year later, however, the musical pieces at Covent Garden, such as *The Beggar's Opera* and *Love in a Village*, proved so attractive that the nightly takings at Drury Lane fell to £30, £15, and even £5 a night. It was at this time that Garrick took his Continental trip, and created as great a sensation in France and Italy as he had among his own countrymen. A clever young actor named Powell, who made a very decided hit, took the place of Roscius until his return.[1]

[1] His career was a brief one; he became manager of the Bristol theatre, and died in that city. There is a tablet to his memory in the cathedral.

A magnificent reception was accorded the great actor when he reappeared on Drury Lane stage on September 14th, 1765, as Benedick. The King honoured the performance by his presence, the house was filled to overflowing, and his entrance was hailed by a succession of ringing cheers. It was said that a finer polish and elegance marked his acting on his return, and all the enthusiasm of nearly a quarter of a century back was reawakened among the public; night after night the theatre was crammed, and from that time until his retirement, Garrick never played to a bad house.

In the January of the following year, Mrs. Cibber died. Barry returned to Drury Lane, after an absence of ten years, in 1767, and with him Mrs. Dancer, afterwards his wife, who, it was said, rivalled even Sarah Siddons as Lady Randolph. Mrs. Abington, finest of fine ladies, and most incomparable of *comédiennes*, Parsons, Baddeley, Dodd, King, and Ross, were now members of the company. Mrs. Pritchard retired in 1768, and Kitty Clive, after forty years' service, during the following season.

Garrick made a curious experiment at the end of 1772, when he altered *Hamlet* (Hamlet was one of his finest parts); he cut out the plot, in which Laertes seconds the King, for the destruction of the Prince, and excised Osric and the grave-diggers. Sad to relate, this barbarous version of the play kept the stage for several years.

Writing to *Notes and Queries* a few years back, Lieut.-Colonel Alexander Fergusson says:—

"Recently I have had occasion to inspect some old family correspondence which had successively passed through the hands of Mr. Upcott and Mr. Dawson Turner, and came upon what purports to be a weekly pay list of Drury Lane Theatre of the year 1773. The paper, which is unsigned, is a very large sheet of what in the present day would be called 'toned,' but in the last generation 'whitey-brown,' paper of a very coarse description, and is voluminous, seeing there are on it some 180 names, representing an expenditure of £522 7*s.* 6*d.* a week.

DRURY LANE THEATRE PAY LIST, 13th February, 1773, at £87 1*s.* 3*d.* diem, or £522 7*s.* 6*d.* per week.

	£	*s.*	*d.*
Men.			
James Lacy, Esq.	16	13	0
David Garrick, Esq.	16	13	0
	17	10	0
Mr. S. Barry and Wife	50	0	0
Mr. King	8	0	0
Mr. Reddish	8	0	0
Mr. Jefferson[1]	8	0	0
Mr. Dame and W. (wife)	8	0	0
Mr. Dibdin	6	0	0
Mr. Bannister and W.	6	0	0
Mr. Clinch	2	10	0
Women.			
Mrs. Abington	8	0	0
Miss Pope	8	0	0
Miss Young	7	0	0
Singers.			
Mr. Vernon	8	0	0
Mrs. Smith	6	6	0
Miss Venables	6	6	0
Dancers.			
Mr. Daigville and W.	6	0	0
Signora Vidini	5	0	0
Mrs. Sutton	5	0	0
Mr. Grimaldi and W.	5	0	0

[1] This was an ancestor — great-grandfather, I believe — of Joseph Jefferson. Grimaldi was the father of the famous "Joe."

Besides to many performers of less account, there are also payments to men dressers, women dressers, properties, music, band, £49; soldiers, £4 4*s.*; numberers, 30*s.*; house barber, £1 4*s.*; candlewoman, 12*s.*; pensioner, Mr. Waldgrave, 10*s.* 6*d.*; and last, but not least, the item 'sinking fund,' £21."[1]

On the 29th of December, 1775, *The Merchant of Venice* was performed at Drury Lane; King was the Shylock, and Portia was played "by a young lady, being her first appearance." The young lady was a country actress named Siddons, whom Garrick had brought up from Cheltenham on the report of King and "fighting" Parson Bates, the editor of *The Morning Post.* It was not her first appearance, however, as she had sustained the silent part of Venus in the revival of the Shakespearian Jubilee Procession, which had been transferred to the Drury Lane stage after its exhibition at Stratford-on-Avon in 1763, and was afterwards frequently revived. Mrs. Siddons as Portia proved a terrible fiasco; her voice was weak, her movements were awkward, her dress was old, faded, and in bad taste. After appearing in one or two other characters, with a similar result, she played Lady Anne to Garrick's Richard. Nervousness seems to have utterly overpowered her, and the critics pronounced the young actress "lamentable." After that, full of bitterness and disappointment, she went back to the country to gain confidence and mature her latent genius.

[1] In 1765, the expenses of Drury Lane were under £70 a night, and the company consisted of 160 performers, among whom were names of high celebrity. At the head of the company was Garrick at a salary of per night, £2 15*s.* 6*d.*; Mr. Yates (the famous Othello) and his wife, £3 6*s.* 8*d.*; Palmer and his wife, £2; King, the celebrated Sir Peter Teazle and Lord Ogleby, £1 6*s.* 8*d.*; Parsons, 6*s.* 8*d.*; Mrs. Cibber, £2 10*s.*; Mrs. Pritchard, £2 6*s.* 8*d.*; Mrs. Clive, £1 15*s.*; Miss Pope, the best of chambermaids 13*s.* 4*d.*; Signor Guestinelli, the chief singer, £1 3*s.* 4*d.*; Signor Grimaldi and his wife, chief dancer, £1.

Early in 1776, warned by failing powers, Garrick announced his retirement from the stage, and a series of farewell performances of his great characters brought people from the remotest parts of the kingdom, and even from the Continent, to Drury Lane. It was on the 10th of June, 1776, that, in the character of Don Felix in *The Wonder*, the curtain fell for the last time upon the greatest actor—to judge by the universal pæan of praise that rose from the greatest men of every variety of taste and prejudice—that England, or perhaps the world, has ever known. There was not a dry eye within the walls of the theatre that night; and, as slowly and reluctantly he passed behind the curtain, a mournful cry of "Farewell" broke from hundreds of quivering lips like a mighty sob.

On September 21st, 1776, Richard Brinsley Sheridan succeeded to the vacant throne in partnership with his father-in-law, Thomas Linley, the composer, and Dr. Ford. £35,000 was Garrick's price for his share of the patent; of this Sheridan took two-fourteenths, Linley the same, and Dr. Ford three-fourteenths. Two years later Sheridan bought Lacy's share for £45,000. Moore wonders how this impecunious young man, who, at the time, had hardly sufficient for his household expenses, became possessed of all these thousands, and succeeding biographers have agreed with the poet in regarding it as an unsolved mystery. But there is a passage in Lockhart's *Life of Scott* that throws light upon the puzzle. It occurs in Sir Walter's diary (January 13th, 1826), just after Moore's biography of the great wit was published; Scott is referring to a visit of Charles Mathews (the elder), and the various subjects they conversed about. "Mathews says it is very simple in Tom Moore to admire how Sheridan came by the means of paying the price of Drury Lane Theatre, when all the world knows he never paid it at all; and that Lacy, who sold it, was reduced to want by his breach of faith." As Sheridan never paid anyone, it is not likely he would have made exception in the case of Garrick and Lacy; the former received the money for Linley's and Ford's share, but probably never a farthing from Brinsley.

The production of the *School for Scandal*, at the commencement of 1777, rendered Sheridan's first season a remarkably fortunate one. The famous comedy was a prodigious success from the first night, thanks to the screen scene, the most superlatively effective situation in the whole round of comedy. Mrs. Abington was Lady Teazle; Smith, the prince of fine gentlemen, Charles; Jack Palmer, the plausible, Joseph; King, a distinguished actor of old men, Sir Peter; Yates, equally good in tragedy and comedy, Sir Oliver; Dodd and Parsons, two of Lamb's favourites, Sir Benjamin and Crabtree; Baddeley,[1] of Twelfth-Night cake memory, Moses; Miss Pope, an admirable actress, Mrs. Candour. It was a wonderful cast.

The attraction of 1773 and the two following seasons was Henderson, upon whom it was considered that the mantle of Roscius had fallen.

On October 10th, 1782, Mrs. Siddons made her *rentrée* as the heroine of Southerne's *Isabella, or The Fatal Marriage*. And with what a difference since her last appearance! Her beautiful face and form, the exquisite tones of her voice, her deep tenderness, seized upon every heart, and her overwhelming agony

[1] Baddeley left a sum of money to provide a cake to be cut in the green-room of Drury Lane on every Twelfth Night in memory of him. For several years Sir Augustus Harris turned the celebration into a huge reception after the performance, but long since it has gone back to a more select gathering.

thrilled every soul as it had never been thrilled before. Men wept, women fell into hysterics, transports of applause shook the house; the excitement and enthusiasm were almost terrible in their intensity, and the curtain fell amidst such acclamations as perhaps even Garrick had never roused. The salary she was engaged at was £5 a week. This very inadequate stipend was, of course, quickly increased; but notwithstanding the rush and houses nightly crowded to the ceiling, at the end of the season she was in receipt of only £20. Her benefit, however, realised a large sum.

It was not until the second season, February 2nd, 1784, that she played the part she is now best remembered by, Lady Macbeth; in this she had memories of Mrs. Pritchard to struggle against, and old playgoers considered her inferior to Garrick's great actress in the part. So nervous was Sheridan regarding such comparisons that he begged her, on the first night, even at the last moment, to cut out, in the sleep-walking scene, the business of washing her hands in pantomime, which had never been done before, Mrs. Pritchard holding the lamp throughout the scene. But she was firm against his entreaties, and was justified by the result.

On September 30th, 1783, John Philip Kemble made his first appearance at Drury Lane in the character of Hamlet; he created considerable attention, but no enthusiasm. Two years later, inimitable Dora Jordan came up from Yorkshire and opened here as Peggy in *The Country Girl*, to add a new joy to London life. How she could act in serious parts, in Viola, Charles Lamb has described in one of the most exquisite passages of *The Essays of Elia.*

In the meantime, Sir Christopher Wren's theatre had fallen into such decay that in 1791 it was found necessary to pull it down. And on June the 4th the grand old house that had stood in six reigns, which had witnessed the triumphs of Hart, Mohun, Betterton, Booth, Garrick, of Mrs. Barry, Mrs. Porter, Mrs. Pritchard, Mrs. Siddons, Mrs. Bracegirdle, Mrs. Oldfield, Mrs. Woffington, Mrs. Abington, and many other peerless actors and actresses, closed its doors for ever, and next day was handed over to pickaxe and shovel.

The new Drury Lane was opened on March 12th, 1794, with, it being the first day of Lent, a selection from Handel's oratorios and the Coronation March; the stage was set to resemble a Gothic cathedral. The old theatre had held 2,000 people, the new accommodated 3,611, or nearly 600 more than the present building. The numbers were as follows: the pit, 800; the boxes, 1,828; the two-shilling gallery, 675; the one-shilling, 308; money, £1,771. The dimensions of the house were: the opening of the curtain, 43 feet; height, 38 feet; height from pit to ceiling, 56 feet.

The season for dramatic performances did not commence until April 21st, when a grand revival of *Macbeth* was presented, with Kemble and Mrs. Siddons in the leading rôles; Charles Kemble making his first appearance in London as Malcolm. Some modern effects were anticipated by arranging that the ghost of Banquo should be invisible, while the gorgeous setting of the banquet scene was the talk of the town, and for the first time since the days of Dorset Garden we hear rather more of the scenery than of the acting. An epilogue, written by George Colman, was spoken by Miss Farren, in which defiance was hurled at the Fire Fiend:—

> "The very ravages of fire we scout,
> For we have wherewithal to put it out;
> In ample reservoirs our firm reliance
> When streams set conflagration at defiance."

The curtain was then raised to show the stage turned into a vast lake, upon which a man was rowing a boat, while a cascade tumbled down at the back; upon this an iron curtain was lowered, and tapped with a hammer to show that there was no deception; it was declared to be an impossibility that fire could ever obtain a mastery over such elaborate precautions, indeed, it was sarcastically remarked that a little fire would do good both to actors and dramatists, though it could not singe a feather among the audience. And yet within fifteen years this boasted flame-proof building was burned to the ground.

Sheridan, unfortunately for the success of the theatre, was again the manager. Neither the reign of Christopher Rich nor Charles Fleetwood was more disgraceful to the stage than that of the brilliant wit upon whose self-entailed ruin so much false sentiment has been shed by partial biographers. Neither actors, tradespeople, nor workpeople were paid; even Kemble and his sister were more than once driven by their necessities to the sordid resource of refusing to go on the stage until arrears of salary were settled. Such strikes were of every night occurrence among other members of the company, and, their just demands sometimes being refused, incompetent persons were put into their parts. Even the poorest employés were not paid their wages; Fanny Kemble, in her "Records," tells us how, on Saturday morning, the workpeople would assail him with, "For God's sake, Mr. Sheridan, pay us our salaries. For Heaven's sake let us have something this week"; how he would faithfully promise that their wants should be attended to, and then, after emptying the treasury of the week's receipts, would slip out of the theatre by another door, and leave them penniless. Neither did he expend any money upon the theatrical stock; the wardrobe for the ordinary dramatic *répertoire* was little better than a collection of rags, and the scenery was dingy and dilapidated. "He never paid the slightest attention to the economy of the establishment," says one of his biographers, Dr. Watkins, "nor took any pains to uphold its credit; his talents were excited only to exhaust the resources of the theatre for his private purposes." Failure was the natural consequence of such a state of affairs.

King had been Sheridan's first manager, but from 1788 to 1796 John Kemble filled that most unthankful post. Besides being out of pocket a large sum for arrears of salary, Kemble was the scapegoat who had to bear the brunt of infuriated creditors, and was once arrested for a debt of the unprincipled lessee for which he had made himself responsible. Worn out and disgusted at last, he resigned his office to Wroughton, though he continued to be a member of the company. In the year 1800, however, Sheridan, who had enormous influence over the great tragedian, as indeed he had over everyone upon whom he cared to exercise his irresistible fascination, again prevailed upon Kemble to be his lieutenant, promising him a share of the profits. But finding that he had no intention of fulfilling the bargain, John Philip, in 1802, finally severed his connection with Drury Lane, and purchased a sixth of the Covent Garden patent.

The records of Kemble's management are little more than a list of Shakespearian and other revivals of the legitimate drama, interspersed with ponderous new plays such as *The Iron Chest*, 1796, in which he made such a deadly fiasco. The most notable of these latter productions was Sheridan's translation of Kotzebue's *Pizarro*, 1799. Stuffed with patriotic speeches, at a time when

England was at fever heat, with the two Kembles in picturesque parts, and Mrs. Siddons and Mrs. Jordan as the two heroines, it drew crowded houses.

With the new century came a new species of play, borrowed from the German, a corollary to Mrs. Radcliffe's and Monk Lewis's romances. *The Castle Spectre* of the latter writer had been the success of 1798. Holcroft's *A Tale of Mystery*, brought out at Covent Garden in 1802, is credited with being the first of the melodramas. These plays were carried on partly in dialogue, partly in dumbshow, the whole action to the accompaniment of music. Sheridan, finding that these compositions drew more money than the legitimate, deluged the stage with them. Now began the reign of grand processions, costly dresses, real elephants, performing dogs, and real water. Covent Garden, in self-defence, was obliged to follow suit, and such pieces as *The Miller and his Men*, *The Dog of Montargis*, *The Dumb Maid of Genoa*, with a sword combat, in which every blow had to keep time to music, *The Bleeding Nun of Lindenberg*, *Timour the Tartar*, *The Forty Thieves*, *Aladdin*—the Arabian Nights stories were played seriously in those days—and scores of others, entirely overshadowed the legitimate.

On the 24th of February, 1809, Drury Lane was burned down for the second time in its history, and into such low esteem had the National Theatre fallen that, but for Samuel Whitbread, the principal shareholder, it would not have been rebuilt. Through his indefatigable exertions, however, £400,000 was raised by subscription,[1] and after a long delay the new house was commenced.

[1] £60,000 of this enormous sum went in securing patent rights. The second Drury Lane patent, which, as I have previously explained, dated

Sheridan's application for the management was refused by the directors, chiefly through the firmness of Whitbread, and the fourth and present Theatre Royal, Drury Lane, built by Holland after the model, it is said, of the great theatre at Bordeaux, was opened on October 10th, 1812, under the direction of Samuel James Arnold, a dramatic author, and first manager of the Lyceum, assisted by a committee of lords and gentlemen, among whom were the Earls of Dudley and Essex, Lord Byron, Samuel Whitbread, Douglas Kinnaird, etc.

The new house was inaugurated with a great flourish of trumpets and beating of drums. In the previous August the committee had advertised a free and open competition for an address to be spoken on the opening night; an invitation to which, however doubtful it might have been for the interests of the theatre, posterity is indebted for those inimitable *jeux d'esprit*, "the Rejected Addresses" of James and Horace Smith. As not one of the hundred and twelve sent in was considered worthy

only from 1719, was granted for a term of years, and was afterwards renewed from time to time. The rights of both the original patents granted to Killigrew and Davenant had been acquired by Christopher Rich, and by him transmitted to his son John, who, while manager of Covent Garden, according to the tolerably well-authenticated story, bought the actual document from a Mr. Clarke, to whom, most probably, thriftless, impecunious Charles Killigrew had pawned it, for £100 and a hogshead of claret. When the new theatre was being erected, inquiries began to be made about this patent, of which nothing had been heard for about a century, and it was then discovered to be in the possession of the Covent Garden patentees, to whom £20,000 was paid for its redemption; Sheridan received a second £20,000, while an equal sum was paid to the Linley and other interests in the Drury Lane patent created in 1776. On the opening of the theatre a new term of twenty-five years was granted; this expired during Bunn's management in 1837, and, as he made no application for a renewal, he was questioned by the Lord Chamberlain as to the authority upon which he was keeping the house open; he then produced the veritable patent of Killigrew, together with a receipt for £9,561 19*s.* 5*d.* from the proprietor of Covent Garden, dated December 17th, 1813, which was the last instalment of the purchase money.

of the occasion, Lord Byron was prevailed upon to write the address, which was delivered by Elliston. The decision, however, did not pass without a protest upon the part of the rejected, for on the second or third night a Dr. Busby and his son addressed the audience from the boxes upon the supposed injustice with which their effusions had been treated, both having sent in a poem; the Doctor offered to recite his, and to appeal to the judgment of the audience whether it was not better than Lord Byron's.

Although the new Drury Lane company included Elliston, Dowton, Robert Palmer, Wewitzer, the last of the Garrick Company,[1] Raymond, Rae, Wroughton, Jack Bannister, Wrench, Mrs. Glover, Mrs. Edwin, Miss Duncan, Miss Kelly, Miss Mellon, it was inferior as a whole to that of Covent Garden, which could boast of John and Charles Kemble, Young, Emery, Liston, Sally Booth. Neither was the amateur management particularly successful; the first season closed with a heavy loss, and the second commenced under very depressing circumstances.

Several new actors appeared, but all failed, until, on the 26th of January, 1814, an obscure country tragedian, named Edmund Kean, who had been engaged in sheer desperation, and brought up from Exeter, a very model of a strolling player, shabby, almost shoeless, whom the mediocrities treated at rehearsal with unconcealed contempt, made his appearance here as Shylock to an indifferent and half-filled house. But when the curtain fell upon the fourth act it was upon such a burst of enthusiasm as had not been heard since the night on

[1] Wewitzer, the last surviving man of the Garrick Company, lived until 1831. But Mrs. John Kemble, Brereton's widow, *née* Priscilla Hopkins, survived until 1845, dying at the age of ninety.

which Mrs. Siddons first played Isabella. The next day all London was ringing with the fame of the new actor. Richard was his next impersonation. "Just returned from seeing Kean in Richard," wrote Byron in his diary. "By Jove, he is a soul! Life, nature, truth, without exaggeration or diminution." Coleridge said it was reading Shakespeare by flashes of lightning. The receipts rose from £100 to £600 nightly. After his third appearance, Whitbread raised his salary from £8 to £20. One week the committee presented him with £100, the next with £500, while splendid presents flowed in upon him from all sides; society fawned upon him, flattered him, courted him, and made him the idol of the hour. Hamlet, Othello, a stupendous performance, Iago, Luke in *Riches*, followed in quick succession.

For the sixty-eight nights during which Kean performed, the receipts were £38,942, while the total for the season was £68,329, yet the theatre closed with a loss to the directors of £20,000. It is said that disappointment at the failure of the speculation which he had done so much to promote so preyed upon Whitbread's mind, that it was the immediate cause of his terrible suicide in 1815.

During the second season, Kean appeared as Macbeth, but his great hits were Zanga, in *The Revenge*, and Sir Giles Overreach. "He looks like Michael Angelo's 'Rebellious Angel'!" exclaimed Southey, appalled by the awful expression of his features in the great scene of Zanga. "Like the Arch-fiend himself!" exclaimed another. A writer in *Blackwood's* wrote that his last scene of Sir Giles was "the most terrific exhibition of human passions that had been witnessed on the modern stage." Maturin's *Bertram*, and Sir Edward Mortimer in *The Iron Chest*, in which Kemble had failed, were among his greatest triumphs.

Rivals sprang up to contest the bays with him, among them Junius Brutus Booth, the father of Edwin, who had played Richard at Covent Garden in imitation of Kean, and was thought by some to be his equal. So the Drury Lane management engaged Booth to play Iago to their Othello. It was one of the most memorable contests that even that stage ever witnessed. Never did Kean act as he acted on that night, "He glared anon upon the now diminutive Iago," wrote Barry Cornwall, "he seized and tossed him aside with irresistible vehemence. The fury and whirlwind of the passions seemed to have endowed him with supernatural strength. His eyes were glittering and bloodshot, his veins were swollen, and his whole figure restless and violent." He played Abel Drugger, Garrick's old part, and Tom Tug in *The Waterman*, and sang the songs—he had a very sweet voice. One of his greatest parts was Lear, which he acted from the text. People thought that his wonderful effects were spontaneous. On the contrary, "he studied and slaved beyond any actor I ever knew," said a contemporary. He would shut himself up in his room all day to rehearse the production of a single line.

During six years Kean was the Atlas that supported the burden of the huge theatre. Rivals rose, but all paled before the splendour of his overwhelming genius.

Within a few years "the committee of noblemen and gentlemen," having lost £80,000 since the opening of the new theatre, grew tired of so unprofitable a burden, and in 1819 Drury Lane passed into the hands of that eccentric genius whom Lamb has so magnificently apostrophised in one of his essays, Robert

William Elliston. Elliston had been before the London public since 1796; In 1804 he had made a marked success at Old Drury as the Duke Aranza in Tobin's *Honeymoon*, and he had already been a manager at the Olympic. Elliston was one of the finest representatives of high comedy the stage has ever known, and in his best days would probably have carried the palm away even from Charles Kemble. The terms under which he undertook the tremendous responsibilities of "the National Theatre" were simply ruinous. The rental was to be £10,200 per annum, exclusive of all rates; yet there were 635 perpetual free admissions, or renter's tickets, another creation of Sheridan's; and, as if this were not enough, the new lessee engaged, before the end of the second season, to spend £6,000 in beautifying the building. He opened with a grand company, Kean, Pope, Holland, Harley, Oxberry, Dowton, Munden, Mrs. W. West, Mrs. Egerton, Mrs. Glover, Miss Kelly, Mrs. Orger, etc., and his success was considerable. One of Elliston's earliest and greatest hits, however, was a wretched melodrama, called *The Cataract of the Ganges*, in which a real waterfall drew more money than all the histrionic talent.

Elliston magnificently redeemed his bond by spending, in 1822, £22,000 upon the building; the interior was entirely remodelled by Beazley, the ceiling was lowered fourteen feet, and the boxes were brought forward five feet, thus somewhat diminishing the capacity of the auditorium, and leaving it much as it was until the recent alterations.[1] When Kean came back from his American

[1] The portico in Catherine Street, and colonnade in Little Russell Street, were not added until 1831. Drury Lane underwent extensive renovation in 1866. The present dimensions of the building are 131 feet from north to south, and 237 feet from east to west; beyond this is a space of 93 feet devoted to scene rooms, making the entire length 330 feet.

tour, in 1822, he returned to Drury Lane. Elliston celebrated his arrival by a street procession, and the great actor was escorted to the stage door by a troop of horsemen—bruisers, jockeys, prize-fighters, publicans—followed up by a rabble rout that gathered through the streets; Elliston in a carriage and four and six outriders, and Kean's coach drawn by four negroes. Fancy Sir Henry Irving going to the theatre in that style!

The great event of the engagement was another contest, this time between Kean and Charles Young, in which they acted Othello and Iago, Jaffier and Pierre, and other parts in now forgotten plays. The excitement and enthusiasm of the audiences were boundless. A critic in *The Examiner* wrote that it was impossible to convey an idea of those performances to persons who had not witnessed them. "For it is not in human nature to reach the pitch of excellence attained by Mr. Kean on the two occasions, without some extraordinary stimulus."

Though the public support was generous, it could not keep pace with the gigantic expenditure, nor, it must be added, with the thriftless personal extravagance of the manager, and, after struggling with debt and difficulties for some time, Elliston, in 1826, was a bankrupt.

The shareholders treated him with heartless and impolitic severity; during his seven years' lesseeship he had spent £30,000 in improving their property, and had paid them £66,000 in rent; to them £5,500 was the total of his liabilities, and for this debt he offered ample security; but they would have nothing but their bond, and closed the doors against him.

A notable first appearance in the last year of Elliston's management was that of Ellen Tree, who commenced her first London engagement here in September, 1826, as Donna Violante in *The Wonder* with pronounced success.[1] With the exception of one bright interval under Macready, the sun of Drury Lane set with Elliston.

Elliston was succeeded by Stephen Price, who was satirically nicknamed the American "Chesterfield." It was under his management that Charles Kean made his début October 1st, 1827, as young Norval in *Douglas*. Charles was not seventeen at the time, and left Eton to take to the stage for his own and his mother's support, his father, through dissipation and extravagance, having fallen into embarrassments from which he never extricated himself. There was a crowded house, and the youth was warmly received, but he made no mark. He played several other parts, and the audience dwindled nightly. At Christmas in the following year he returned as Romeo, and met with only a cold reception. Mr. Price took the theatre at a rental of £10,600, which he did not pay, and at the end of his fourth season the shareholders had not only to lose their money, but to pay *him* to give up possession.

There was, however, at least one creditable act connected with Price's management; when, owing to the difficulties at Covent Garden, Charles Kemble could not give Joey Grimaldi a farewell benefit at the house with which his name had been so long associated, Price offered him the use of Drury Lane. In 1815, Grimaldi had a serious illness, and from that time he never knew a single day's health. At length his sufferings became so acute, that men were obliged to be kept waiting at

[1] Three years previously she had appeared as Olivia in *Twelfth Night*, for her sister Maria's benefit at Covent Garden, but that was only tentative. She remained at Drury Lane for three years, after which she transferred her services to the rival house, where she played Romeo to Fanny Kemble's Juliet. She was the original Ion (at the Haymarket) in Sergeant Talfourd's tragedy of that name, and was the original representative of several of Sheridan Knowles's heroines—Mariana in *The Wife*, the Queen in the *Rose of Arragon*, the Countess in *Love*.

the side scenes to catch him in their arms when he came staggering and exhausted off the stage; his sinews were gathered up into knots by the cramp that followed their every exertion; and during the waits, his limbs had to be chafed to enable him to go on with the performance. He had taken a farewell benefit at Sadler's Wells in March, 1828, and on June 27th, in the same year, he made his last public appearance at Drury Lane. The scene was very affecting; he was to act the clown in one scene of *Harlequin Hoax*, and speak a farewell address. But what a difference from the old days,[1] when he used to come bounding upon the stage full of life and vigour, amidst a roar of delight from the expectant audience! The roar of applause was more enthusiastic than ever; but instead of the sprightly Joey of old, a prematurely aged man, unable to stand, was carried before the footlights on a chair; yet the old humour sparkled as brilliantly as ever; his old jokes, his old songs never provoked louder shouts of laughter than on the last occasion he was ever to utter them.

"It is four years," he said in his farewell speech, "since I jumped my last jump, filched my last oyster, and boiled my last sausage. To-night has seen me assume the motley for a short time; it clung to my skin as I took it off, and the old cap and bells rang mournfully as I quitted them for ever." When the last word was spoken Harley led him, utterly overcome, off the stage amidst a tremendous sympathetic demonstration, and when he quitted the theatre, a huge crowd followed his vehicle, cheering him the whole way home to Pentonville. He realised close upon £600 by this benefit, and the Drury Lane fund allowed him £100 a year for the remainder of his life.

[1] See "Sadler's Wells."

Alexander Lee, musical composer and publisher, was the next tenant of the National Theatre. There is an entry in Macready's Diary to the effect that on July 31st, 1830, he entered into an engagement with Mr. A. Lee for three years at Drury Lane; £30 per week the first year and £40 the second and third, with a half clear benefit each year. Lee had no money, but presently found a backer in Captain Polhill, the member for Bedford. In consequence of constant quarrels between Mrs. Waylett, whom Lee had married, and an actress favoured by the Captain, Lee's reign came quickly to an end, and Polhill appointed Bunn, "the poet Bunn" of *Punch*, who had been Elliston's stage-manager in 1823, in his place. Captain Polhill retired from the management in 1834, with a loss of £50,000. And from that time until 1839, Bunn was sole lessee.

There was not a style of entertainment that Bunn did not essay; he began with the legitimate drama, and descended, in 1839, to tight-rope dancers and Van Amburg, the lion tamer. It must be added in extenuation, however, that he received more royal patronage through the "Lion King" than for any other form of entertainment he presented, Queen Victoria commanding two special performances. Opera, however, was the staple fare; he gave English versions of Weber's and Rossini's operas, mutilated, it is true, but competently rendered; he treated his patrons to German opera, and Jullien's Promenade Concerts, varied by *tableaux vivants*, and Macready, Phelps, and Mrs. Warner in tragedy. He boasts in his book, *The Stage*, that nearly every great actor of the day appeared under his management, as well as every great European singer and dancer. Yet Alfred Bunn was simply a showman, and he made Drury Lane only a big booth. But he could not make it pay, and at the end of five years had to retire thousands in debt.

An actor named Hammond, at that time manager of the Strand Theatre, where we shall meet him again, was rash enough to be tempted by a rental reduced to £5,000 a year. But although he engaged Macready, Elton, Phelps, and Mrs. Warner, he had to close early in March.

Jullien and Eliason filled out the remainder of the season with their concerts.

At Christmas, 1841, Macready, after failing at Covent Garden, was again tempted to try his fortune in management. He produced *The Two Gentlemen of Verona*, poor Gerald Griffin's *Gisippus*, Byron's *Marino Faliero*, Handel's *Acis and Galatea*, but the last only was a monetary success. Through an obstinate policy, or rather over-punctilious regard for his public pledges, he would not permit it to be sung more than three times a week, and thus frittered away its attraction. Yet we cannot but admire the fine artistic sense and proud probity of the man, who preferred losing his money to breaking faith with his supporters and countenancing those long runs which are death to art. In the company were James Anderson, Samuel Phelps, Keeley, Harley, Elton, Mrs. Nisbett, Mrs. Stirling, Mrs. Keeley, Miss Priscilla Horton.

Macready, in his opening bill, announced that the grand saloon attached to the boxes should be protected "from all improper intrusion." With a determined hand he swept away those shameful abuses which had hitherto disgraced the auditorium of our theatres, and introduced an order and decorum until then unknown.

The second season opened with a performance of *As You Like It*, and a cast which probably was never equalled. Mrs. Nisbett, Rosalind; Mrs. Stirling, Celia; Mrs. Keeley, Audrey; Macready, Jacques; Anderson, Orlando; Phelps, Adam; Graham, Oliver; Keeley, Touchstone; Compton, William; Ryder, the Banished Duke—his first appearance in London; George Bennett, Duke Frederick; Elton, the First Lord, etc. A splendid revival of *King John* followed with an equally fine cast, Helen Faucit as Constance; Westland Marston's *Patrician's Daughter* and Browning's *The Blot on the Scutcheon* were the novelties; and there was a revival of Dryden's *King Arthur*, with Purcell's famous music, all before Christmas.

In connection with *King Arthur*, James Anderson, in his memoirs, tells a remarkable story. During the rehearsals Tom Cooke, the musical director, was in despair of being able to find anyone who could do justice to the solos in *Come, if you dare!* Anderson, who had noticed the fine voice of a young chorus singer named Sims Reeves, suggested him as a solution of the difficulty, and was laughed at by Cooke for the proposal. Macready, however, impressed by Anderson's persistency, desired Cooke to try the young man alone.

"In less than twenty minutes Cooke returned in raptures of delight. Rushing up to me, he embraced me again and again, swearing, in his odd way, that we must change places—*I* must conduct the orchestra, and *he* take my place on the stage. The result was delightful; Mr. Reeves made a great hit, and was nightly encored in his magnificent solos. Shortly after this he went to Italy."

Finding the "legitimate" unprofitable, Macready, in April, 1843, engaged Clara Novello, and produced *Sappho*, a grand opera; Milton's *Comus* followed, and a new play by Knowles. But it was all in vain; the enormous rental, the cruel burden of renter's tickets, which half filled the best seats on the best nights, and indifferent public support, sent the unfortunate manager adrift, wrecked in health and fortune.

This was the last season in which the patent rights were enjoyed by the two great theatres; the new Licensing Act was passed in that year.[1] It was the end of the *ancien régime*, and from that time a new order of things dramatic obtained.

After Macready, Bunn again. In 1844 he engaged Charles Kean, who since his début seventeen years before had been gaining fame and fortune, for a series of performances, which almost rivalled the successes of the father; but operas, ballets, extravaganzas, and pantomimes were Bunn's principal productions; indeed, Drury Lane was for years an opera-house rather than a theatre. Here were produced Balfe's *Bohemian Girl*, for which Bunn wrote the idiotic libretto, *The Maid of Athens*, and many other of his works; Benedict's *Brides of Venice;* Wallace's *Maritana*, etc., sung by Miss Romer, Madame Anna Thillon, Miss Rainforth, Borrani, Stretton, Weiss, and Sims Reeves, who was engaged in 1847–8.

In the latter year the Cirque National, from the Champs Elysées, performed at Drury Lane, and on June 14th (1848), a French company appeared in a version of *Monte Cristo* which extended over two nights. A serious riot was the consequence of this new departure in stage art, and the circus returned, to be succeeded by more opera. After which Bunn had to retire to Boulogne, and depend upon a friend for mere subsistence.

[1] See the chapter on the Olympic for a detailed account of the effects of this revolutionary measure.

On December 26th, 1849, James Anderson undertook the management, with a respectable but by no means brilliant company. His most notable productions were *Ingomar*—no man ever played the part as Anderson did—and *Azael*, the latter splendidly mounted—the *Temple of Isis* was a wonderful set. But neither the legitimate nor the spectacular would draw, and Anderson retired, a ruined man, in the summer of the great Exhibition year. He was immediately followed by an American circus, that cleared thousands. Such was the taste of the day.

Old Drury was the scene of another notable "Farewell" on February 26th, 1851, when Macready made his last appearance upon the stage in the character of Macbeth. Macready had the bad taste to despise—or pretend to despise—the profession to which he owed fortune, position, reputation, and cast no "longing, lingering glance" behind, such as had marked the farewell of Garrick, of Kemble, of Siddons, who passionately loved their art. On that morning he wrote in his Diary: "My first thought when I awoke was that this day was to be the close of my professional life. I meditated on it, and not one feeling of regret intermingled with the placid satisfaction accompanying my performance of every act, needfully preparative to the coming event." This is not the utterance of an artist, but of a mere workman, and after reading it I can never believe that Macready was more than a very fine conventional actor, one who, had he been gifted with the divine afflatus, could not have been so destitute of enthusiasm, of sentiment, of soul. He was the product and the representative of a sordidly inartistic age. In writing of the night he says: "To attempt any description of the house, of the wild enthusiasm of applause, every little portion of the vast assembly in motion, the prolongation, the deafening cheers would be useless." The object of the ovation was the person least moved by it. A grand farewell dinner was given him at the London Tavern, at which some very great people, literary, artistic, aristocratic, were present. We shall meet Macready again at Covent Garden.

In the autumn season, Gye, of Covent Garden, ventured upon this forlorn hope with tragedy and opera; but although the theatre was called for a time "The Grand National Opera House," prices raised, and competent artists engaged, it would not pay. In the July of 1852 a Mr. Sheridan Smith was manager for one week, and for the same space of time a Mr. De Vere wielded Garrick's sceptre; in the October of the same year Mr. George Bolton was a six days' monarch: none of these gentlemen having the wherewithal to meet the first week's expenses.

At the close of the year last named, the directors let the theatre to Mr. E. T. Smith, publican and ex-policeman, at a rental of £3,500. What a falling off was there from the Elliston and Macready days! *Uncle Tom's Cabin*, then in the full flush of its popularity, inaugurated a seven years' reign on Boxing Night, 1852. It was a lucky hit, for the whole nation was in one of its periodical fits of sickly sentiment over Mrs. Stowe's highly coloured fiction. *Gold*, the earliest dramatic version of Charles Reade's *Never Too Late to Mend*, followed, and completed the prosperity of the season. During 1853 and 1854, Gustavus Brooke, whom we shall meet at the Olympic, drew crowded houses. But following in Bunn's footsteps, Smith made Drury Lane an opera-house rather than a theatre.

Italian opera was given at cheap prices in 1853 and in succeeding seasons: stalls, four shillings; dress-circle, half-a-crown ; second circles and pit, one shilling ; and the two galleries, sixpence ; while one guinea was the highest price charged for a private box. And at this tariff the public could hear Madame Gassier, Lucy Escott, Miss Huddart, Hamilton Braham, Bettini, Borrani, etc. But Smith, like Bunn, was a showman and of a lower grade; he, Smith, alternated Gustavus Brooke, Miss Glynn, and Charles Mathews with Chinese conjurers and a man-fly who crawled upon the ceiling, and the great Rachel with a circus. Yet he might have succeeded in making the speculation remunerative had he confined his energies within reasonable bounds ; but he was at the same time lessee of Drury Lane, the Alhambra, Her Majesty's, and a travelling circus ; landlord of the Radnor Tavern, at the top of Chancery Lane, wine merchant, auctioneer, picture dealer, land agent, bill discounter, newspaper proprietor, etc., etc. No wonder that, between so many stools, he ultimately came to the ground.

Dion Boucicault, after his quarrel with Webster, in the early autumn of 1862, opened Drury Lane for a season with *The Colleen Bawn*, Madame Celeste, himself, and his wife being the principal attractions. This was followed by the *Relief of Lucknow*. In the December of the same year, Edmund Falconer, having made £13,000 by *The Peep o' Day* at the Lyceum, was ambitious to try his fortunes at the National Theatre. His opening piece, *Bonnie Dundee*, upon which he spent a large sum, was a direful failure. In 1863 he entered into partnership with his acting manager, F. B. Chatterton, and produced finely mounted revivals of *King John*, *Henry IV.*, *Manfred*, *Faust*, and *Comus*, with Phelps, Walter Montgomery, Mrs. Hermann Vezin, and a fairly good company to interpret them. Phelps's delineation of

Byron's sombre hero was, with Werner, I think, the finest thing in tragedy the Sadler's Wells manager ever did. His address to Astarte had in it a ring of pathetic passion that he seldom rose to, and the declamatory speeches were given with a power of elocution that one never hears nowadays. The scenic effects were grand; no scene more stupendous than the Hall of Ahrimanes, with the Demon seated on his globe of fire surrounded by his satellites, could be imagined. The part had been performed at Drury Lane many years before by an actor named Denvil, who made a great hit in it. When Phelps was playing the part, Denvil was taking checks at the gallery door.

Within three years Falconer lost all his money, and Chatterton was then accepted by the committee as sole lessee at a rental of £6,000 per annum, and £10 a night for every additional performance over 200. When we compare this with the sum paid by E. T. Smith a few years previously, we gather how rapidly theatrical property was even then rising in the market.

Chatterton followed on with Shakespeare and Byron and the old comedies, interpreted by Phelps, Walter Montgomery, Barry Sullivan, John Ryder, Helen Faucit, Mrs. Hermann Vezin, Miss Neilson. But he afterwards told the world that Shakespeare spelt ruin, and Byron, bankruptcy. So in 1868 he brought out *The Great City*, the first of those panoramic dramas of modern life which have since attained to such extraordinary proportions on this very stage. The introduction of a real cab and a real horse was then considered a marvel of realism.

A series of adaptations of Scott's novels, with beautiful Adelaide Neilson as Rebecca and Amy Robsart, Phelps in the double rôle of King James and Trapbois in *The Fortunes of Nigel*, and other romantic dramas, together with the annual pantomime and William Beverley's transformation scene, kept the theatre going for a time. But by-and-by both actors and entertainments deteriorated in quality, falling from bad to worse. He made a final effort during his last season, engaged Mrs. Hermann Vezin, Ryder, and Charles Dillon as the star, produced *Macbeth*, *Othello*, *The Winter's Tale*, *Belphegor*, and other plays; but Dillon was only a wreck. Even the pantomime did not draw, and on February 4th, 1879, Chatterton retired with liabilities amounting to £36,000. Drury Lane, however, was not responsible for all the losses; he was at this time manager of the Adelphi and Princess's as well, and neither was paying.

November 6th, 1879, enter "Augustus Druriolanus," as his friends used to call the future knight. The story of how Augustus Harris became lessee of Drury Lane, as told by himself, reads like a bit of smart fiction. Passing the house one day, he saw a notice on the doors that it was closed. He had always cherished a belief that he could work Drury Lane and make it a success, by means of gorgeous pantomimes. Someone offered to find him the money to carry out his ideas. Relying upon this promise, he proposed himself as a tenant to the committee of proprietors, who, after some hesitation, touching his youth—he was only twenty-seven—agreed to let him the theatre, on condition that he would pay £1,000 down. At that time all his worldly wealth was £3 15*s*. He hurried off to his backer, but the gentleman backed out, and suggested a dinner at the Aquarium instead. To continue in his own words, "I was ready to go anywhere and catch at a straw. At the Aquarium he, the ex-backer, introduced me to Mr. Rendle" (afterwards his father-in-law) "in these words, 'Allow me to introduce my friend, Mr. Augustus Harris, the new lessee of Drury Lane. I believe you were one of the unsuccessful proposers for the theatre,' and then, turning to me, he said, 'Mr. Rendle wanted to give the Vokeses another chance at the Lane.'"

Harris proposed to join forces with Mr. Rendle, he to find the work, his partner the money, confessing candidly in the same breath his financial position. "I saw him several times, and told him that with £3,000 I would undertake to open the house and produce my pantomime. This was a bold venture, seeing that this year Covent Garden was going to do pantomime on the most lavish scale! A bold venture! I look back, and it seems madness! Well, sir, I think Rendle got tired of me, and to get rid of me at last said, 'Look here, Harris, I will find £2,000, on condition you find the first £1,000.' 'Agreed,' I cried, 'I'll do it.'" And perhaps at that moment he did not possess as many pence! Off he went to a refreshment contractor, and obtained from him a promise of £250 as soon as the lease was signed; then with great difficulty he induced a relative to do a little bill for another £250. That afternoon, while walking in the park, he met a couple of friends, who invited him home to dinner with them. Over the wine and cigars he asked for a loan of £250, and got it. "Next day I bounced into Rendle's office. 'Got £750, can't get any more.' My frankness, my earnestness, more than my plans, I think, won him, and he lent me the money; but the capital was £2,750, not £3,000."

Harris started the most prosperous reign that any monarch of Old Drury had enjoyed since David Garrick with George Rignold in *Henry V.;* then followed the pantomime, *Blue Beard;* both were successful. Next season he began the series of spectacular sensational dramas with *The World; Youth, Pluck, A Million of*

Money, A Sailor's Knot, etc., followed one another, all of the same pattern. During his management, however, he produced six of Shakespeare's plays and a few romantic dramas, such as *The Spanish Armada, The Royal Oak.* In the summer of 1881 he brought over the Saxe-Meiningen Company, a notable engagement, which exercised an important influence upon English stage art. In the following year Ristori appeared once more as Elizabeth, Lady Macbeth, and in other of her favourite rôles. The company of the Theâtre Français was here in 1893, and previous to this, in 1886, the manager started opera seasons with the finest artistes to be found—the De Reszkes, Mme. Melba, Lassalle, Emma Eames, Nordica, etc. Of his Covent Garden seasons I shall have something to say at the end of the next chapter.

Each Christmas brought forth a pantomime more gorgeous and elaborate than its predecessors. Truly they were not the pantomimes of old; they were all glitter, pageantry, costume, scenery, processions, and mechanical effects, and sometimes not even Dan Leno and Herbert Campbell could save them from being dreary—*but* they *paid*, the manager made money, the shareholders got good dividends—so *n'importe!*

Being Sheriff of the City of London in 1891, on the occasion of the German Emperor's visit, Harris received the honour of knighthood.

The number of his undertakings, which included six or seven theatres, innumerable travelling companies, a newspaper, besides ordinary business speculations, exhausted his physique, and he fell a victim to a wasting disease at the age of forty-five, June 22nd, 1896. During the next season, Drury Lane was carried on under the name of his widow, but since then it has been managed by a syndicate, with Arthur Collins, who was Sir Augustus's business man, as manager. He has followed faithfully in the steps of his predecessor, and produced an annual sensational drama, *The White Heather*, *The Price of Peace*, *The Millionaire*, *The Best of Friends*, exhausting earth, fire, and water, both above and beneath, for blood-curdling situations, until one anxiously asks, what has he left undone, what will be the next startler? And each Christmas he has given us the usual gorgeous pantomime with the usual people. In 1901, £15,000 was spent upon reconstructing and redecorating the house, great improvements being effected, not only in the auditorium, but in the mechanical arrangement of the stage. In the following year, Mr. Collins returned to a custom that had lately lapsed, and opened the great theatre for a summer season with a very elaborate production of *Ben Hur*. This year he has gone one better with Sir Henry Irving and *Dante*, which, though disappointing as a play, was probably the most stupendous "get up" that any stage has yet shown.

The Fortunatus cap that was bestowed upon Sir Augustus has been inherited by his successor, as the handsome dividends that the shareholders receive each year, and the splendid reserve fund which is constantly being added to, amply testify. I wonder if the ghosts of a century of ruined managers ever revisit the scene of their earthly misfortunes? If so, how mortifying the contrast must be!

CHAPTER II

The Lincoln's Inn Fields Theatres, 1660–1743, and the Three Theatres Royal, Covent Garden, 1732-1903—Their famous Actors and Actresses—The origin of English Pantomime—A retrospect of histrionic and dramatic Art and Literature from Betterton to Macready.

UNDER date November 20th, 1660, Pepys wrote in his *Diary:* "Mr. Shipley and I went to the new playhouse near Lincoln's Inn Fields (which was formerly Gibbon's tennis court), where the play of *Beggar's Bush* was newly begun, and so we went in and saw it well acted. It is the finest playhouse, I believe, that ever was in England."

This theatre had been opened a week or two previously under the patent[1] granted by Charles II. to Sir William Davenant, poet, dramatist, and soldier. Pepys' reference to it as "the finest playhouse" is curious, since within eight years after its erection, Sir William found it to be too small, and started building a new house in Dorset Gardens. He died in the same year (1668), leaving his interest in the patent to Lady Davenant, who was assisted in the management by Harris and Betterton. At the lady's death, Charles and Alexander Davenant succeeded to her rights. On the retirement of the latter in 1690, Charles sold his interest to Christopher Rich. The fortunes of the house during the few following years have been sketched in the chapter on Drury Lane, and how, when the Lord Chamberlain silenced

[1] See Chapter I.

his patent, rogue Rich, being possessed of the lease of Davenant's old theatre in Lincoln's Inn Fields, at once set about rebuilding it. It was not, however, until after the accession of George I. that he could obtain leave again to exercise the rights of his patent. But ere the curtain rose upon the new stage the crafty lawyer had gone to render up his last account, and it was his son John who opened the house, December 8th, 1714. It is described by contemporaries as a handsome building, the interior superbly adorned with mirrors on each side, the stage furnished with new scenery, and "more extended" than Drury Lane.

John Rich had a taste for acting, and at first essayed tragedy; but, being a man entirely devoid of education, he made a dismal failure. Yet there was a strong dramatic genius in this coarse, illiterate man, and it burst forth when, in 1717, he appeared as Harlequin, in a pantomime called *Harlequin Executed*. Borrowed from the Italian Arlecchino, Harlequin had hitherto been a speaking part; it was Rich, or Lun, as he chose to call himself in the bills, who, simply from his inability to speak upon the stage, originated the silent Harlequin,[1] yet by mere dumb action he could rival the power and pathos of the most accomplished tragedian.

"On his last revival of *The Sorcerer*," writes Jackson, in his *History of the Scottish Stage*, "I saw him practise the hatching of Harlequin by the heat of the sun, in order to point out the business to Miles, who, though excellent in the line of dumb significance, found it no easy matter to retain the lesson Rich had taught him—this certainly was a masterpiece in dumbshow—from the

[1] The speaking Harlequin was common, however, for many years afterwards; we find Garrick performing it at Goodman's Fields (see p. 68), and long afterwards Harry Woodward was famous in the character.

first chipping of the egg, his receiving of motion, his feeling of the ground, his standing upright, to his quick Harlequin trip round the empty shell, through the whole progression, every limb had its tongue and every motion a voice, which spoke with most miraculous organ to the understanding and sensation of the observers."

Early in 1723 the managers of Drury Lane, in rivalry to Rich, produced a pantomime by Dr. Thurmond, a dancing-master, entitled *Harlequin Doctor Faustus*, which, constructed on a much more elaborate scale than those hitherto given at Lincoln's Inn Fields, may be considered as the first English pantomime. Not to be outdone, in the December of the same year, Rich brought out his famous *Necromancer; or Harlequin Executed*, which far surpassed in splendour all that had yet been seen. The prologue to this piece is very suggestive as to the relative positions of the two houses.

> "Yon rival theatre by success made great,
> Plotting destruction to our sinking State,
> Turn'd our own arms upon us—and woe be to us—
> They needs must raise the Devil to undo us;
> Straight our enchanter gave his spirit wing,
> And conjur'd all the town within this ring."

A continuous rivalry was now carried on between the two theatres, and pantomime became the great attraction at both; for while at Drury Lane Booth, Wilks, Cibber, and Mrs. Oldfield could draw but £500 a week to the Treasury, the Genius of Nonsense would swell the receipts to £1,000. The price to the boxes was raised from four to five shillings at pantomime time; but the following curious notice was put upon the bill of the play: "The advance money to be returned to those who choose to go out before the overture of the entertainment." As late as 1747 we find a similar notice in Garrick's bills. Yet when Garrick became one of the managers of Drury Lane he promised the audience that he would not attempt to gain their patronage by such spurious attractions as pantomimes; but in spite of the appeal he made to the public to support him in his laudable resolve,[1] he was very soon compelled to rescind his promise, and follow in the footsteps of his predecessors.

The opening of the old English pantomime was really modelled with certain modifications upon the masque of the Elizabethan and the Stuart days, that by its gorgeous scenery and mechanical effects anticipated the spectacular display of a later date.[2] The story was usually founded upon a classical subject, and was illustrated with music and grand scenic effects; on to this was tacked a comic transformation after the Italian style. Harlequin was turned into a magician, who, by a touch of his bat, could transform a palace into a hut, men and women into wheelbarrows and chairs, and colonnades into beds of tulips or serpents, and all these mechanical tricks were worked as deftly nearly two centuries ago as they are now. Harlequin was the hero, for the clown was simply a rustic servant of Pantaloon's, and played a very unimportant part in the piece until the genius of Grimaldi developed him into a new dramatic creation. It may be mentioned that the tight spangled dress was not worn by Harlequin until the nineteenth century. From the days of *The Necromancer* pantomimes never ceased

[1] "'Tis yours this night to bid the reign commence
Of rescu'd nature and reviving sense;
To chase the charms of sound, the pomp of show,
For useful mirth and salutary woe;
Bid scenic virtue form the rising age,
And truth diffuse her radiance from the stage."

[2] See p. 23.

to be the best trump card a manager could play at either of the patent houses.

The opening of the new Lincoln's Inn Fields theatre drew away several members of the Drury Lane company. In 1717 James Quin, who had just before made his début at the latter house, passed over to Lincoln's Inn Fields, with which, and Covent Garden, his future career was mostly associated. It was not until 1720, however, that he made his great hit in the character of Falstaff; he was acknowledged to be the best representative of the fat knight since Betterton. As a tragedian he was the most stilted of declaimers—

> "Heavy and phlegmatic, he trod the stage,
> Too proud for tenderness, too dull for rage,"

wrote Churchill in *The Rosciad*, yet until Garrick rose he was indisputably the first actor of his day.

A most serious riot occurred at the Portugal Street Theatre in 1721 through the practice of allowing certain privileged persons to sit upon the stage during the performance. As an illustration of the theatrical manners of the age this incident is worth pages of description. One night, in a principal scene of *Macbeth*, a nobleman crossed from one side of the stage to the other, in front of the actors, to speak to a friend; when Rich remonstrated with him upon the impropriety of such behaviour my lord struck him in the face. Rich and Quin drew their swords, the rest of the company supported them, and the beaux took the offender's side. But the players proving too strong, their foes were driven out of the theatre. Reinforced, the rioters soon returned, smashed the handsome mirrors that lined the proscenium, threw torches among the scenery, tore up the seats, and it was not until the military were called out that the disturbance was quelled. From that time a fashion, which had been introduced by Charles II., of posting a guard on each side the stage, was revived, and partly survives to the present day in the soldiers that attend the performances at Drury Lane and Covent Garden.

Perhaps the greatest event of Rich's management was the production of Gay's *Beggar's Opera* (1727–8). This "Newgate Pastoral" took the town by storm, and drew crowded houses for sixty-two nights. Ladies had their fans painted with subjects from the piece; Sir Robert Walpole and Townshend went to see themselves satirised as the two thieves and receivers, Peachum and Lockit; Walker, the original Macheath, and Lavinia Fenton, the Polly Peachum, became the darlings of the town. At the end of the season the Duke of Bolton carried Polly away, and afterwards made her his duchess—a position which she well became by her wit, her taste, her understanding, and her manners.

Towards the end of 1731 John Rich, on account of Lincoln's Inn Fields having fallen into decay,[1] set on foot a subscription for erecting a new theatre in Bow Street, Covent Garden. A year afterwards he vacated the old house. And here the story of the Portugal Street theatre may be said to end. In 1733–4 it was opened by the celebrated Porpora with an Italian opera company, in opposition to Handel at the King's Theatre, and became the more fashionable house of the two. After that it was let for balls, concerts, and was occasionally taken by actors whom the patent theatres left out in the cold. The latest date, as far as I can discover, at which it was used as a theatre was 1742–3, when it was opened by Giffard for a short time after the final

[1] As the house had been opened only seventeen years, this would lead us to suppose that the "rebuilding" must have been very superficial.

closing of Goodman's Fields. The building afterwards served at different times as a barrack, an auction-room, a china warehouse, and it was not until 1848, when it was pulled down for the enlargement of the museum of the College of Surgeons, that the last remains of the theatre finally disappeared.

Most of the great actors and actresses who flourished between 1662 and 1730 had appeared within those walls. And here were produced Congreve's two greatest comedies, and two of the greatest in the world's literature, *Love for Love*, 1695, *The Way of the World*, 1700, and his one tragedy, *The Mourning Bride*, which, if it does not contain "the true Promethean fire," is a work of great merit, especially in its versification, and was the model for Rowe, Young, and the best writers in the tragic vein who immediately followed him.

Six thousand pounds being quickly subscribed for the new theatre, the building was at once commenced. Its progress seems to have excited considerable interest among "the quality," and the precincts became quite a fashionable resort, a number of people assembling every day to watch the masons at work. Rich paid the Duke of Bedford £100 a year as ground rent; this, at the old manager's death, was raised to £300, and in 1792 to £940. The house was decorated in gorgeous style by the Italian artist, Amiconi, who painted a magnificent ceiling, representing the gods banqueting in the clouds; the scenery, said to have been very fine, was by the same artist, assisted by George Lambert, the founder of the Beefsteak Club. It was but a small theatre; from the stage to the back of the boxes the length was only fifty-one feet, and it would hold when full not more than £200, although space was economised to such an extent that only twenty-one inches were allowed to each person. The prices of admission were—boxes, 5*s.*; pit, 3*s.* 6*d.*; galleries, 2*s.* and 1*s.*; and seats on the stage, 10*s.* 6*d.*; there were two entrances, one under the Piazza, and the other in Bow Street.

On the first night, December 7th, 1732, so great was the demand for places that pit and boxes were amalgamated at 5*s.* The opening piece was Congreve's *Way of the World.* This was followed by a revival of the *Beggar's Opera,* with the original cast, which ran twenty nights, while the rest of the company played at Lincoln's Inn Fields.

During the first few years of its existence there is little that is interesting in the history of Covent Garden; season after season old tragedies and old comedies, occasionally varied by a new play, succeeded each other in regular succession. The company also remained pretty much the same, except when death removed the veterans. A dead level of conventional dulness and mediocrity reigned throughout the theatrical world, and no first appearance of any interest took place at Covent Garden until Peg Woffington, whose saucy face still looks down upon us from the walls of the Garrick Club, already the idol of Dublin, having, after many rebuffs, forced her way into the presence of John Rich and his seven-and-twenty cats, prevailed upon the eccentric manager to engage her. She opened on November 8th, 1740, as Sylvia, in the *Recruiting Officer.* On the 20th of the same month she played Sir Harry Wildair in the *Constant Couple,* and electrified the town by a performance such as had not been seen since Wilks played the part. She repeated the character twenty times during the season to crowded houses. No woman before, or since, ever made so delightful a stage rake, so elegant, so fascinating, so debonair, that even ladies fell in love

PEG WOFFINGTON.

SARAH SIDDONS.

with her. In the following season she went over to Drury Lane. But it was at Covent Garden, in 1757, while playing Rosalind, that she was death-stricken.

She had complained of feeling unwell all through the performance, but when, in the epilogue, she came to the line, "If I were among you I would kiss as many as had beards that pleased me," her voice broke, she faltered, then screaming "O God! O God!" tottered to the stage door, and was caught by someone standing there. She lingered on for three years, but never again was the brilliant actress seen upon the stage. She was only forty-four years of age.

In 1744 the noted George Anne Bellamy made her first appearance upon these boards as Monimia in *The Orphan.* She was such a mere child at the time that Quin objected to play with her, but so admirably did she acquit herself, that at the end of the performance he caught her in his arms and exclaimed, "Thou art a divine creature, and the true spirit is in thee." In after years, though far inferior in genius to those great actresses, she rivalled both Mrs. Cibber and Woffington. For this, however, she was more indebted to her beauty and brilliant conversational gifts, in which she almost equalled "the lovely Peggy," between her and whom there was deadly rivalry, than to her histrionic powers. She was Garrick's Juliet during the famous run of Shakespeare's tragedy at Drury Lane.[1]

[1] In 1785, worn down by poverty, degradation, and sickness, the once charming George Anne Bellamy, who had intoxicated the town by her charms of manner and person, now so decrepit that she could not rise from the armchair in which she was seated upon the stage, took leave of the public at Drury Lane, where a benefit had been organised to save from utter starvation the woman who once, in her magnificent generosity, gave £1,000 towards the better clothing of our soldiers abroad, and never passed a sentinel on guard afterwards without a blessing. Some time before her death she published her very amusing memoirs.

Pantomime still reigned supreme at Covent Garden as it had at Lincoln's Inn Fields; John Rich had little more consideration for the dignity of the drama than had his father, and when acting would not draw he did not scruple to supplement it with wild beasts, tumblers, contortionists, and rope-dancers. And yet he divided with Drury Lane all the histrionic ability of the time. But he always believed himself to be a crushed tragedian; took pupils and gave *levées* at which he delighted to spout scenes from *Richard the Third*, in his ludicrous fashion. He was jealous of every successful actor. When poor George Anne Bellamy made her great hit as Juliet, he declared it was not owing to her acting, but to his arrangement of the funeral procession; and when Barry was drawing crowded houses, he would peep through the curtain of a night and mutter to himself, "What, you are come again, are you? Much good may it do you!—I don't envy your taste." Tate Wilkinson in his *Memoirs*, and Jackson in his *History of the Scottish Stage*, tell many amusing stories of Rich's eccentricities, and of his extraordinary habit of calling everyone out of his or her name.

When the new theatre first opened Quin was in the height of his popularity; haughty, absolute, overbearing, every actor, and even John Rich himself, trembled before him. In 1746 Garrick accepted an engagement to play at Covent Garden with Quin, against Quin, and in Quin's stronghold. It was in Rowe's *Fair Penitent* the battle of the schools was fought: the elder actor was Horatio, Garrick "the gallant, gay Lothario." It was a marvellous contrast, the monotonous cadences, the dreary pauses, the sawing of the air, the dignified indifference to the sentiments he was uttering, which marked Quin's style; and the passion, the impulse, the deep intensity of his rival; and although the old school had still many adherents, the public verdict was not long in doubt.

In 1750 a far more formidable rival, "silver-tongued" Spranger Barry, divided the suffrages of the town with Garrick in Romeo; playgoers were astonished at the play running twelve nights at Drury Lane and thirteen at the Covent Garden, and wits composed epigrams upon the extraordinary event. Barry's fine person, handsome face, and musical voice gave him a great advantage over "little David," and, in addition, he had Mrs. Cibber, the most passionately pathetic of actresses, for his Juliet. A lady after seeing the play at both houses remarked that if she had been the Juliet to Garrick she should have expected he would have come up to her, and if she had been the Juliet to Barry she would certainly have jumped down to him.

But when the two played Lear against one another, Garrick's supremacy asserted itself. Wonderful stories, however, are told of Barry's Othello, of ladies shrieking with terror at his delivery of the line, "I'll tear her all to pieces"; of actors who were so vividly impressed that they could not sleep after witnessing it.[1] At fifty this Apollo had become old and infirm, and Reynolds, the dramatist,

[1] Churchill, however, (*The Rosciad*), who, though severe and sarcastic upon most of the actors of the time, could yet praise highly where praise was merited, in his picture of Barry gives one the idea of a conventional and somewhat affected actor:—

> "Who else can speak so very, very fine,
> That sense may kindly end with every line."

Again:

> "When he appears most perfect, still we find
> Something which jars upon and hurts the mind:
> Whatever lights upon a part are thrown,
> We see too plainly they are not his own.
> No flame from nature ever yet he caught,
> Nor knew a feeling which he was not taught;
> He raised his trophies on the base apart,
> And conn'd his passions as he conn'd his part."

gives a sadly contrasted picture of him as the noble Moor in a full suit of gold-laced scarlet, a little cocked hat, knee-breeches, and silk stockings, that conspicuously displayed a pair of gouty legs.

Rich died in 1761, leaving the theatre to his son-in-law, John Beard,[1] the vocalist, for himself and wife, with the proviso that the property should be sold whenever he could obtain £60,000 for it; and it was for this sum that George Colman the elder, Harris, Rutherford, and Powell, in 1767, purchased the patent.

The event was celebrated in an "occasional prologue" to *The Rehearsal*, written by Whitehead, and spoken by Powell, on the opening night of the season, four lines of which ran :—

> "For Brentford's State two kings could once suffice,
> In ours behold *four kings of Brentford* rise,
> All smelling to one nosegay's od'rous savour
> The balmy nosegay of the public favour."

The company at this time included Powell, a very fine tragedian, of whom mention has been made in the previous chapter, "Gentlemen" Smith, Bensley, Shuter, Macklin, Woodward, Yates, Hull, Mrs. Yates, Mrs. Bellamy, Mrs. Mattocks, Mrs. Ward, Miss Macklin, Mrs. Buckley, etc.

Rich had depended principally upon pantomimes, and Beard upon light musical pieces, but the new management resorted to a more legitimate entertainment to draw the public. Before the end of the first season, however, the partners were divided into two factions, with Harris

[1] Miss Rich was Beard's second wife, his first was Lady Hamilton Herbert, the daughter of the Earl of Waldegrave. Beard was a very worthy fellow, and until the appearance of Incledon, was unequalled as an English ballad singer. The elder Dibdin considered him the finest of all our native tenors.

and Rutherford on one side and Colman and Powell on the other. It seems to have been, as usual, a case of *cherchez la femme;* a Mrs. Lessingham, a favourite of Harris's, not having the parts assigned her which she fancied, succeeded in irritating her *cher ami* against Colman, who was the stage director, and to such a height did hostilities rise at last, that after the close of the season, in June 1768, Colman took possession of the keys and refused Harris admission to the theatre. The latter, together with Rutherford and a posse of roughs, broke into the house through a window in Hart Street and carried off a considerable part of the wardrobe, books, and other property. This led to a lawsuit, which was not settled until 1770; a quarrel between Harris and the lady who had caused all this disturbance, in the interim, however, considerably tended to an amicable arrangement by which Colman was reinstated as manager.

March 15th, 1773, marked an important era in dramatic history, for on that night Oliver Goldsmith's *She Stoops to Conquer* was produced at Covent Garden. And it required all the influence of Dr. Johnson and his literary *coterie* to induce Colman to accept the piece. Several of the company refused to play in a comedy that was so *ungenteel.* But the audience soon caught the spirit of the author, and nature once more asserted her sway upon the stage over the inane artificialities of the school of Hugh Kelly.[1]

That same year Lewis, the most mercurial of comedians, made his first appearance in London; and Macklin, at the age of eighty-four, performed Macbeth for the first time on the metropolitan stage, and had the courage to substitute Highland tartans—a costume which survived until Charles Kean's famous revival of

[1] See p. 155.

the tragedy at the Princess's—for Garrick's gold-laced scarlet coat.

It was said at the time that he looked more like an old Scotch piper than a prince of the blood royal, and that his performance was very uneven; so while some applauded, others hissed. This opposition, he asserted, proceeded from his brother actors; law proceedings and affidavits followed, and the next time he appeared as Macbeth he was met with howls of disapprobation; more than that, the audience insisted upon his discharge upon the spot, and would not listen to a word until an actor brought a board upon the stage, upon which was written: "At the command of the public, Mr. Macklin is discharged." The next season, however, found him re-established in favour.

Colman sold his share of the patent in 1774, and as Powell was dead and Rutherford was a mere cypher, Harris took that absolute position in the direction of the theatre which he retained until his death.

Spranger Barry made his last appearance upon the stage here as Jaffier, in October, 1776, and died in the following January. Harry Woodward passed away in the same year. In 1780 we find the irrepressible nonagenarian, Macklin, playing Sir Pertinax Macsycophant in his own comedy, *The Man of the World*, for the *first time* in London.

From 1779 to his premature death in 1785, Henderson, who, as I have said before, was generally considered to be Garrick's successor, was the leading attraction at Covent Gorden. We shall meet him at the Haymarket in an earlier part of his career.

Covent Garden underwent so many alterations in 1787 that it was virtually rebuilt, and five years later was again greatly enlarged.

A very remarkable farewell was witnessed at Covent Garden on May 7th, 1789, when Macklin, at the age of ninety-nine, took leave of the stage in his great part of Shylock, which he had recreated fifty-seven years previously at Drury Lane, before Bolingbroke, Swift, Steele, and Pope. Memory had long been failing the wonderful old man, and his dazed look when he entered the green-room, and his strange questions, prepared everyone for a breakdown. He delivered the first two or three speeches correctly, but evidently without any understanding; then he stopped, tried to go on again, but all was blank, and coming forward to the footlights, he begged the audience, in a broken voice, to pardon him, and allow his substitute, who had been kept ready dressed at the wings, to finish the performance. He lived to his hundred and eighth year, but never again set foot upon the stage.

Full justice has scarcely been done to Macklin's remarkable powers; it was he who, in 1741, initiated that sweeping reform in the histrionic art which Garrick perfected,[1] and it was he who, as we have just seen, in 1773, made the first attempt at appropriate costume upon the English stage. Churchill, however, describes his acting as "hard, affected, and constrained," and he had a harsh and unprepossessing countenance. Macklin was a dramatic author of some ability; *The Man of the World* kept the stage until Phelps's retirement; he was

[1] As Garrick and Macklin were fast friends long before the former appeared upon the stage, and used to spend hours together walking up and down beneath the Covent Garden Piazza, discussing the state of the drama, it is very probable that these conversations gave Garrick his first idea of a new style of acting, which his natural powers so admirably adapted him to carry out. In regard to Macklin's age there is a doubt, but he always asserted that he was born in the year of the Battle of the Boyne, 1690, and there is considerable evidence to prove the correctness of his assertion.

also the author of another very good comedy, *Love à la Mode.*

Charles Incledon, perhaps the greatest tenor this country has ever produced, made his first appearance at Covent Garden as Dermot in *The Poor Soldier* in 1790. He had been a man-of-war's-man, though previous to his entering the navy he had received some musical education as a chorister at Exeter Cathedral from the famous organist, Jackson. Incledon must have been a marvellous ballad-singer; when Rauzzini heard him at Bath, rolling his voice grandly up like a surge of the sea till, touching the top note, it died away in sweetness, he exclaimed in rapture, "*Corpo di Dio!* it was very lucky there was some roof above, or you would be heard by the angels in heaven and make them jealous." He himself used to tell a story of the effect he produced upon Mrs. Siddons: "She paid me one of the finest compliments I ever received. I sang 'The Storm' after dinner; she cried and sobbed like a child. Taking both my hands she said, 'All that I and my brother ever did is nothing to the effect you produce.'" "I remember," says William Robson, in *The Old Playgoer*, "when the *élite* of taste and science and literature were assembled to pay the well-deserved compliment of a dinner to John Kemble, and to present him with a handsome piece of plate on his retirement, Incledon sang, when requested, his best song, 'The Storm.' The effect was sublime, the silence holy, the feeling intense; and while Talma was recovering from his astonishment, Kemble placed his hand on the arm of the great French actor and said, in an agitated, emphatic, and proud tone, '*That* is an English singer.'" Munden adds that Talma jumped up from his seat and embraced him. Yet Incledon never received more than £16 a week. His last appearance in London was under Elliston at Drury Lane in 1820.

Mrs. Glover, afterwards the most incomparable of "old women," made her London début here in 1797. In the first year of the nineteenth century, George Frederick Cooke, who, like Kean, had been for years a country stroller, at the age of forty-five created a veritable sensation upon these boards as Richard. The story of his life is a sad record of wasted genius—wasted by the vilest dissipation. Never did actor more sorely try the patience of an indulgent public. Sometimes he would disappoint a crowded house by not appearing at all; at others he would present himself in a state of speechless intoxication. Illness was the culprit's excuse for his shortcomings, and in spite of their indignation the audience could not repress a roar of laughter when one night, after several ineffectual efforts to proceed, he laid his hand upon his heart, and hiccoughed, "My old complaint, ladies and gentlemen, my old complaint." His last appearance at Covent Garden, and in London, was June 5th, 1810, when he played Falstaff. Two years afterwards he died in Boston, U.S., being the first of the great English actors who starred in America.

Cooke left behind an enormous reputation; some considered him superior to Kean in the character of Richard. A few years ago a criticism upon Cooke, written by Charles Lamb for the columns of the *Morning Post* (January 2nd, 1802), was reproduced in the *Athenæum*. It is a fine piece of analysis, which brings the actor and his style vividly before us. I have only space, however, to quote one or two of the salient points. "He has a tongue that can wheedle the devil. It has been the policy of that ancient and grey simulator, in all ages, to hide his horns and claws. The Richard of Mr. Cooke perpetually obtrudes his. We see the effect of his deceit uniformly successful; but we do not comprehend *how* it succeeds. . . . The hypocrisy is too glaring and visible. . . . We are inclined to admit that in the delivery of *single sentences*, in a *new* and often *felicitous* light thrown on *old* and hitherto misconstrued passages, no actor that we have seen has gone beyond Mr. Cooke. He is always *alive* to the scene before him, and by the *fire* and *novelty* of his manner he seems likely to infuse some *warm blood* into the *frozen declamatory style* into which our theatres have for some time past been degenerating."

There is a vivid description of Cooke's Sir Giles Overreach in Lockhart's *Life of Scott*, contained in a letter of Sir Walter to Joanna Baillie (March 13th, 1813), "I saw him [John Kemble] play Sir Giles Overreach, the Richard III. of middling life, last night; but he came not within a hundred miles of Cooke, whose terrible visage, and short, abrupt, and savage utterance gave a reality almost to that extraordinary scene in which he boasts of his own successful villainy to a nobleman of worth and honour, of whose alliance he is ambitious. Cooke, somehow, contrived to impress upon the audience the idea of such a monster of enormity as had learned to pique himself even upon his own atrocious character." Washington Irving describes his acting as Iago in the third act of *Othello*. "He grasped Kemble's left hand with his own, and then fixed his right, like a claw, on his shoulder. In this position, drawing himself up to him with his short arm, he breathed his poisonous whispers into his ears. Kemble coiled and twisted his hand, writhing to get away, his right hand clasping his brows, and darting his eye back on Iago."

These several criticisms convey one impression, that

of an actor of superlative power, who, by his terrific intensity, took an audience captive, and rendered them utterly oblivious, at the time, of his exaggerations and contempt of nature. His Sir Pertinax Macsycophant and Archy Macsarcasm (*Love à la Mode*) were, according to contemporary opinion, excellent performances. With all his shortcomings, which would be fatal to him according to present ideas of stage art, George Frederick Cooke must have been a very extraordinary actor.

It was in 1803 that John Kemble, after his final break with Sheridan, purchased a sixth part of the Covent Garden patent for £23,000, though thirty-six years previously the whole had fetched only £60,000. He succeeded Lewis, whose share it was he had bought, as stage-manager and general director. Mrs. Siddons shortly afterwards quitted Drury Lane and joined her brother in his new venture.

At the end of the next year, Covent Garden witnessed one of those extraordinary furores which occasionally seize upon the British public for some rather ordinary personage or exhibition, while superior talent goes to the wall. A boy actor, named Master Betty, and called "the tenth wonder of the world," was at that time turning the brains of provincial audiences, and although the Covent Garden company included Kemble, Siddons, Cooke, Munden, the management considered it worth while to offer this juvenile prodigy £50 a night. By one o'clock on December 1st, 1804, the date of his first appearance, a prodigious concourse filled Bow Street. Towards evening the crowd assumed such alarming proportions that it was considered necessary to send for a guard of soldiers to clear the entrance and to form passages and approaches, that a probable catastrophe might be averted. Within a few minutes after the doors were opened the theatre was crammed, seats, lobbies, passages even that did not command a glimpse of the stage; gentlemen wedged into suffocating corners were only kept from fainting by ladies' fans, while swooning persons of both sexes had to be dragged out of the human mass every few minutes. Drury Lane took £300 from the overflow. The roar of applause that burst forth as this infant phenomenon, who appeared in a version of Voltaire's *Mérope* called *Barbarossa*, dressed as the slave Achmet, stepped from the wings, was overwhelming, and as the audience had come determined to adore this new fetish, his success was proportionate to his reception. London enthusiasm surpassed even the extravagances of the provinces; duchesses contended for the honour of driving the young Roscius, as he was called, about in their carriages; if he were indisposed, bulletins were regularly issued; William Pitt adjourned the House of Commons in order to see him play some particular part, and the University of Cambridge made him the subject for a prize medal. Yet he was only a clever boy who had been well parrotted: the books from which he studied were marked for every inflection of the voice, and for every movement of the arms and legs. The craze, however, was of short duration; when he returned in the next season he drew but indifferent houses.

On September 30th, 1808, Covent Garden was burned to the ground, twenty-three firemen perishing in the ruins. The loss of property was estimated at £150,000, of which only £50,000 was covered by insurance.

Before passing on to the new theatre, let me endeavour to give some idea of the aspect of the old house. A drawing of the interior of Covent Garden, made about 1763, shows us the stage lit at the back by six chandeliers, each with twelve candles in brass sockets. Garrick abolished these at Drury Lane when he returned from the Continent, substituting concealed lamps in their place and introducing footlights. Tate Wilkinson, in his delightful *Wandering Patentee*, gives a vivid picture of the appearance of the theatre at this period. "On crowded nights an amphitheatre of seats was raised upon the stage, where there would be groups of ill-dressed lads and persons sitting on the stage in front three or four feet deep; so that, in fact, a performer on a popular night could not step with safety, lest he should thereby hurt or affend, or be thrown down amidst scores of idle or tipsy apprentices. But it was the beaux who usually affected that part of the house. There was only one entrance on each side the stage, which was always particularly crowded. First they sported their own figures to gratify self-consequence and impede and interfere with the performers who had to come on and go off the stage. They loved to affront the audience, particularly the gallery part, who would answer by showering down oranges and half-eaten apples, to the great terror of the ladies in the pit, who were so closely wedged they could not move." Fancy the absurdity of Macbeth fresh from the murder of Duncan having to push his way through a throng of beaux. Riots so often arose from these causes that royal proclamations were issued, even as far back as 1673, forbidding spectators to be admitted to the stage, but the evil continued until Garrick suppressed it at Drury Lane in 1762.[1]

[1] In his very first playbill, as noted in the previous chapter, Garrick prohibited the admission of strangers to the stage. Long before that the Triumvirate made a successful stand against this custom, Cibber assuming the right of refusing admission by the stage door, without distinction; but it was at the risk of his life, so furious were the beaux at being denied their privilege. Under Fleetwood and John Rich the abuse was again permitted.

With a stage half proscenium, and lit by candles, there was not much scope for scenic effects, nevertheless Garrick engaged the famous Dutch artist Louthenberg; but it was only to paint for his pantomimes and spectacles, while the legitimate drama went dingy enough.

From the days of Dorset Garden, stage upholstery, as it is now called, with the exceptions just mentioned, was utterly neglected; no appeal was made to the eye; good plays and bad plays were finely acted, the actor was all-sufficient, and no gorgeous setting was considered necessary for the dramatic pictures.

Eight months after the disastrous fire, a new and more splendid Covent Garden rose from the ashes of the old. Both Kemble and Mrs. Siddons had lost their stage wardrobes, which were consumed in the flames. But generous friends came forward to their assistance. The Duke of Northumberland sent Kemble the munificent sum of £10,000, and returned him the bond on the day the first stone of the new house was laid, requesting that it might be thrown in to heighten the flames. The Prince of Wales presented him with £1,000, and laid the foundation stone on December 31st, 1803. New Covent Garden cost £150,000, £100,000 of which was raised in shares of £500 each. Smirke was the architect, his model being the Temple of Minerva in the Acropolis at Athens; and the statues of Tragedy and Comedy, niched under the Doric portico in Bow Street, were by Flaxman.

On account of the great expense of the undertaking, Kemble raised the prices of admission; the boxes were advanced from six to seven shillings, and pit from three-and-sixpence to four shillings, and a third tier of boxes was erected and let for £12,000 a year. This, and a patriotic opposition to the engagement of Madame

Catalani, led to the famous, or infamous, Old Price riots. The opening night was September 18th, 1804; the plays were *Macbeth* and *The Quaker*. As Kemble, after *God Save the King*, stepped forward to speak the opening address, he was saluted with groans, hisses, cat-calls, and shouts of "Old Prices!" Not one word of the play was heard. The Riot Act was read from the stage; constables and even soldiers were called in, but the rioters held their ground. This went on night after night with ever-increasing violence. Men stuck the letters O. P. on their hats and waistcoats; ladies wore O. P. medals. Dustmen's bells, coachmen's horns, watchmen's rattles, and a kind of carmagnole called the O. P. dance, nightly drowned every word the actors spoke. After a struggle of sixty-one nights, Kemble was obliged to give in, lower the pit to the old price, and do away with the private boxes.

The ordinary expenses of Covent Garden at this period were £300 a night; there was a quadruple company for tragedy, comedy, opera, and ballet. Between the years 1809 and 1821, tragedy was represented by Kemble, Cooke, Macready, Young, Charles Kemble, Conway, Terry, Abbot, Mrs. Siddons, Miss O'Neill, Mrs. Bunn, etc., etc.; comedy by Munden, Johnstone, Liston, Jones, C. Kemble, Farren, Fawcett, Blanchard, Mathews, Emery, Farley, Yates; Mesdames Jordan, Davison, Brunton, Gibbs, C. Kemble, Foote, Davenport, etc.; in opera by Braham, Incledon, Sinclair, Philips; Mesdames Catalani, Stephens, Maria Tree, Love, Fearon; in pantomime by Byrne, Farley, Grimaldi, Bologna, Ellar. Between the two dates named above the receipts were £1,000,000, averaging £80,000 a season.

During those years some notable first appearances

and two famous farewells had taken place on the boards of Covent Garden. In 1813, that most delicious of English vocalists, "enchanting Kitty Stephens," as James Smith lovingly called her, made her début at the age of nineteen as Mandane in Dr. Arne's *Artaxerxes*, and was hailed as the rival of Catalani. Competent critics opined that no English cantatrice, either before or after her, has ever built so pure and perfect an English style upon an elaborate Italian basis. Leigh Hunt said that her bird-like triumphs in the part of Polly (Peachum) were like nothing else heard on the stage, and left all competition behind. A lady of unimpeachable character, in 1838 she became Countess of Essex. It is not many years ago since she passed away at the great age of eighty-eight.

Although she appeared on two occasions afterwards, namely, in 1817 and 1819, Mrs. Siddons took her leave of the stage on June 29th, 1812, as Lady Macbeth; with true artistic feeling, the audience insisted that the play should terminate with the sleep-walking scene, so that the last grand impression might not be disturbed. The consensus of eulogy by all who saw her act in her great days, as in the case of Garrick, renders the greatness of her genius indisputable. "The enthusiasm she excited," to quote Hazlitt, "had something idolatrous about it; she was regarded less with admiration than with wonder, as if a being of a superior order had dropped from another sphere to awe the world with the majesty of her appearance. We can conceive nothing grander. . . . She embodied to our imagination the fables of mythology, of the heroic and deified mortals of older time. . . . She was tragedy personified." During the latter years of her professional life, however, she became unwieldy in person, and stagey, heavy, and monotonous in style; when she appeared for the last time in 1817, as Lady Randolph, no spark of that superlative genius, over which Hazlitt rhapsodised, lit up the performance.[1]

Wonderful stories are told of her power over the spectators. Macready relates that when she played Aspasia in *Tamburlaine*, after seeing her lover strangled before her eyes, so terrible was her agony as she fell lifeless upon the stage, that the audience believed she was really dead, and only the assurances of the manager could pacify them. One night Charles Young was playing Beverley to her Mrs. Beverley in *The Gamester*, and in the great scene was so overwhelmed by her pathos that he could not speak. Unto the last she received the homage of the great; even the Duke of Wellington attended her receptions, and carriages were drawn up before her door nearly all day long.

At Covent Garden, on October 6th, 1814, her successor to the robe of Melpomene, Miss O'Neill, from Dublin, made her first appearance in London as Juliet, and at once achieved an enormous success. Macready, in his *Reminiscences*, tells us of her artless unconsciousness, her freedom from affectation, her fervid *Italian* passion in the balcony scene, and adds, "Throughout my whole experience, hers was the only representation of Juliet I have ever seen." Hazlitt writes: "Her highest effort, perhaps, was in portraying tremulous joy, a rapture bordering on frenzy, an inspiration of delight, portentous of sudden and fearful disaster. We never remember to have been more delighted by her acting than when we had seen her in Isabella, at the return of Biron, clasp him in wild rapture, forgetting her dreadful

[1] See Macready's *Reminiscences*.

condition,[1] gaze on him with eyes lit up with strange fire, and reply to his question by laughter in which horror and transport mingled." In tenderness and pathos she is said to have equalled Mrs. Siddons in her early days; but she had never the ideality, never rose to the sublimity of that marvellous actress in pure tragedy. Her stage career was very short; in 1819 she married Sir William Wrixon Beecher, and retired from the stage.

In that same year the beautiful Maria Foote, then only sixteen, was introduced to the London public on these boards, as Amanthis in *The Child of Nature*, but did not create any particular impression. It was not until she brought her breach of promise case against "Pea Green" Hayne that she became the rage. Miss Foote seems to have been rather a very excellent amateur than an actress; it was said of her that she danced and sang more like a highly accomplished lady than a professional. Mrs. Bancroft has given us some very interesting glimpses of the once popular favourite in her last days, in *On and Off the Stage*. "I was never a great actress," she used to say, "though people thought me fascinating, and I suppose I was." And no doubt it was that innate fascination in which lay the secret of her charm. She was the original Virginia in *Virginius*, and Macready highly commends her performance of the character. As everyone knows, she married the eccentric Lord Petersham, afterwards Earl of Harrington.

On September 16th, 1816, William Charles Macready made his first bow to a London audience upon these boards as Orestes in Ambrose Philips's *Distressed Mother*. Though well received, he created no sensa-

[1] Biron is Isabella's husband, but, believing him dead, she has married Villeroy.

tion, and his progress in public favour was not rapid, for he had two formidable rivals in the theatre, Charles Young and Charles Kemble, who divided the principal tragic parts between them, and Macready was for some years relegated to a series of melodramatic heroes, such as Gambia in *The Slave*, and Rob Roy, varied by repulsive villains, such as Pescara in Shiel's *Apostate*, and Wallenberg in Maturin's *Manuel*.

In less than a year after Macready's début, on June 29th, 1817, John Philip Kemble bade farewell to the footlights in his greatest character, Coriolanus. And never did he play the part more grandly. "As he approached the last act," writes Mr. Fitzgerald, in his book on the Kembles, "a gloom seemed to settle down on the audience; and when at the end he came slowly forward to make his address, he was greeted with a shout like thunder of 'No farewell!' It was long before he could obtain silence, or could control his feelings sufficiently to speak. At last he faltered out, 'I have now appeared before you for the last time: this night closes my professional life.' At this a tremendous tumult broke out, with cries of 'No, no!' . . . At the end he withdrew with a long and lingering gaze, just as Garrick had done." Unlike Mrs. Siddons, he retained all his grandeur to the last, and seems to have retired in the ripe autumn of his powers. A grand dinner was given in his honour, at which Lord Holland took the chair, and the Duke of Bedford, the Marquis of Lansdowne, and others of the highest nobility, together with the most eminent men connected with literature and art, were present. Indeed, not even Garrick left the stage with such *éclat* as attended the retirement of "the noblest Roman of them all."[1]

[1] For a full appreciation of Kemble's acting, see pp. 148–9.

Yet, notwithstanding the magnificent companies he gathered about him, the Kemble management was far from satisfactory in its relations to art. The hugeness of the theatre in time rendered the acting, even of Mrs. Siddons, coarse and stilted; all the resources of the house were chiefly lavished upon spectacles, such as *Blue Beard*, with its gorgeous show and real elephants. But for this, Sheridan's reckless management at Drury Lane was chiefly responsible; where, as I have previously said, the author of the *School for Scandal* engaged performing dogs, or anything that would draw a tasteless, ignorant public, indifferent to everything save sensation and raree-show, and Covent Garden in self-defence was compelled to follow his lead or play to empty benches.

John Kemble, on his retirement, made over his share of the Covent Garden patent to his brother Charles, most inimitable of Mercutios, Mirabels, Petruchios, Doricourts, most perfect of light comedians. Differences soon arose between Charles Kemble and Henry Harris, the son of Colman's old partner, who was the principal shareholder; this quarrel at length led to litigation and a Chancery suit.

The disagreement between the partners was ultimately settled by a compromise, and Harris retired, upon Kemble and the other shareholders undertaking to pay for the theatre the monstrous rental of £12,500 per annum. A committee of management was formed, and, as is usual under such circumstances, made a terrible fiasco; Young, Miss Stephens, and Liston seceded and went over to the other house, which, under Elliston, was already plethoric with talent. So Drury Lane became the fashion, and Covent Garden was literally a desert. In 1823, Macready followed his old associates. And these defections were brought about to save, all told, about £20 a week. Failure was the inevitable result of such mistakes; the committee was bankrupt, and Charles Kemble undertook the sole direction of the theatre.

King John, with appropriate scenery and dresses, revived in 1823, was the earliest of the archæological Shakespearian revivals, and initiated a new departure in theatrical art. When Dance endeavoured to persuade John Kemble to dress his Roman characters a little more in accordance with antiquity, he replied that he did not wish to be taken for an antiquary. Planché, who arranged the revival of *King John*, had similar prejudices to contend against. Farley wanted to know, if all the money was spent upon Shakespeare, what was he to do for his Easter piece? And when the actors were shown the peculiar pot-shaped helmets they had to wear, they declared the audience would roar at them. "And so they did," writes Planché, "but it was with approbation."

The curious caprices of the public's moral judgment in this country were well exemplified in 1825 by the different receptions accorded to Kean, at Drury Lane, after his *crim. con.* trial over Alderman Cox's wife, and that given to Miss Foote after her action for breach of promise against "Pea Green" Hayne. While the former was hooted off the stage, the latter attracted the largest audience ever assembled within the walls of that theatre; seats were taken weeks in advance, guineas were paid for places in the orchestra, and the total receipts amounted to £900 16*s.* The actress's appearance as Letitia Hardy was greeted with waving of hats and handkerchiefs and hysterical sobs from the ladies, while every point that could in any way be twisted into an allusion to her recent experiences was greeted with bursts of acclamation. Undoubtedly Maria Foote was more sinned against than sinning,[1] but so was Kean, though in a less degree.

Charles Kemble was neither a judicious nor a fortunate manager,[2] and by the year 1829 the affairs of the theatre were in such a disastrous condition that the bailiffs were in possession for taxes. Inevitable ruin seemed to stare the hapless lessee in the face, when his daughter Fanny, then only in her seventeenth year, stepped into the breach, appeared as Juliet, and redeemed the fortunes of the house.

It had got abroad that, as the young lady was not intended for the stage, it was an act of heroic self-sacrifice; and as she was likewise very beautiful, the public flocked in their thousands, and the critics went into raptures over her Juliet, Euphrasia, Belvidera, Mrs. Beverley. But Miss Kemble, notwithstanding the over-flowing houses she drew, which enabled her father in the one season to pay off £13,000 of his debts, was not a genius; she had no true sympathy with her art, and was chiefly conspicuous, like Macready, after her short-lived triumph, for casting scorn and contempt upon everything and everybody connected with it.

[1] When scarcely seventeen, she had been seduced by Colonel Berkeley, afterwards Earl Fitzhardinge, under a promise of marriage, and lived under his protection for five years. Joseph Hayne, of Burdrop Park, a sporting cad, a great patron of prize-fighters, ignorant of this circumstance, made her an offer of marriage. Berkeley was despicable enough to betray to him the secret of his liaison with the lady, and even hinted that it still continued, which was a falsehood. Thereupon Hayne broke off the marriage. Soon afterwards, however, he renewed the engagement. The bridal day was fixed; the morning came, but no bridegroom. His friends had spirited him away into the country, and kept him there by force. When he got away from them, he fixed the day for the second time, and Miss Foote gave up her profession, sold her wardrobe, and for the second time her *fiancé* failed to put in an appearance. The jury awarded £3,000.

[2] Some idea of the state of affairs may be gathered from the fact that between May 17th and July 22nd 11,000 orders were issued.

In May, 1832, Laporte, who is better known by his connection with the opera-house, became manager of Covent Garden, and on the 30th of that month, Charles Young, the most successful actor of the Kemble school, took his farewell of the stage. Although almost exclusively a tragedian of the heavy order, Fanny Kemble tells us, in her *Records of a Girlhood*, that he had no tragic mental power, but a perception and a passion for humour, and that he constantly indulged in private in ludicrous stories, personal mimicry, admirable imitations of national accent, a power of grimace that equalled Grimaldi's, and the most irresistible comical way of resuming in the midst of the broadest buffoonery the stately dignity of his own natural countenance, voice, and manner.

I think, however, Mrs. Butler has scarcely done Young justice. After he played Iago to Kean's Othello at Drury Lane in 1822, even the great Edmund shrank from comparison. "I have never seen Young act," he said. "Everyone has said he could not hold a farthing rushlight to me, but he can. He *is* an actor, and though I flatter myself he could not act Othello as I do, yet what chance should I have in Iago after his d——d musical voice. Tell him he has made as great a hit in Iago as ever I did in Othello." From 1822 until his retirement, Young never played for less than £50 a night, as high a sum as Kean ever received. When, in 1808, *Julius Cæsar* was played at Covent Garden with John Kemble as Brutus, Charles Kemble as Marc Antony, and Young as Cassius, the success of the last was second to neither of his great rivals.

The year after Young bade adieu to the footlights, Covent Garden was the scene of one of the most notable, and at the same time saddest, of theatrical farewells.

On March 23rd, 1833, Edmund Kean and his son Charles stood together for the first time upon the London stage, as Othello and Iago.[1]

The house was crammed to suffocation. Brandy had long since shattered the reputation, the genius, and the health of the great actor. He had been very ill throughout the winter, and was utterly unfit to sustain the fatigue and excitement of such a night; but he went through the part, dying as he went, until he came to the "farewell," in which in the old days he used to stir the very souls of the spectators; he broke down on the words "Othello's occupation's gone!" Then, gasping for breath, he began, "Be sure thou prove——" but, unable to proceed, he fell upon his son's shoulder, moaning, "I am dying—speak to them for me." And so the curtain descended upon him for ever.

In that same year, 1833, Covent Garden passed under the management of Bunn, who was already lessee of Drury Lane. After two years he resigned in favour of Osbaldiston, of transpontine fame, who, although he engaged Charles Kemble and Macready and an excellent company, endeavoured to attract the public by reduced prices, always a fatal step in London theatres, and the usual disastrous result followed the experiment.

The stages of the patent houses had been sinking lower and lower in public estimation since the retirement of John Kemble, and the downfall of Elliston at Drury Lane; an utter indifference to theatrical amusements,

[1] Edmund Kean was very bitter against Charles for having taken to the stage against his strict prohibition, but a reconciliation had taken place between father and son several years previously, when the elder Kean acted for Charles's benefit at Glasgow in October, 1828, the former playing Brutus, the latter, Titus, in Howard Payne's tragedy *Brutus; or, the Fall of Tarquin.*

similar to that which marked the closing years of the seventeenth century,[1] infected the public.

The situation is graphically described in one of Wilson's *Noctes Ambrosianæ*. Says Christopher North to Tickler, "The drama, I fear, is in a bad way in London, Tim, and if so, it cannot be very flourishing in the provinces. Mr. Mathews acknowledges[2] that fashion is fatal to it. 'I meet young gentlemen now,' says he, 'who formerly used to think it almost a crime not to go to the theatre; but they now ask, "Whereabouts is Covent Garden Theatre?" although the same people would faint away if it were thought they had not been to the Italian Opera. If they are asked whether they have seen Kean or not lately, they will say, "Kean—Kean? No; where does he act? I have not been there these three years." Formerly it was the fashion to go to the theatre; but now a lady cannot show her face at table next day, and say she has been to the theatre. If they are asked whether they have been at Covent Garden or Drury Lane, they say, "Oh dear no; I never go there, it is too low!" . . . I remember the time when it was no shame to go to see the legitimate drama. It was the fashion to go and see Miss O'Neill *for a season*, and Mr. Kean *for a season;* if they were real and sincere admirers of those actors they would have followed them; but we found the theatres at which they acted dropped down from £600 to £200.'" Some of Mathews' utterances may have been tinged by sarcasm, but they were perfectly correct in the main.

Years before this was written, Scott, when it was

[1] See p. 52.

[2] Mathews, among other leading members of the profession, appeared before the Committee on Sir James Graham's Bill to give evidence as to the state of the drama.

mooted that he should write for the stage, says in one of his letters (1819):—

"I do not think the character of the audience in London is such that one could have the least pleasure in pleasing them. One half come to prosecute their debaucheries, so openly that it would degrade a bagnio; another set to snooze off their beef-steaks and port wine; a third are critics of the fourth column of the newspaper; fashion, wit, or literature there is not, and, on the whole, I would far rather write verses for mine honest friend *Punch* and his audience. The only thing that could tempt me to be so silly, would be to assist a friend in such a degrading task, who was to have the whole profit and shame of it."

How much of this state of things was due to the public and how much to the managers, it would be difficult to say; but I think it will be evident to every one who has read these pages that personal extravagance, blundering, and a lack of business capacity was at the bottom of many of the failures I have recorded.

It was Osbaldiston who introduced the last of the English classical *tragédiennes*, Miss Helen Faucit, to the London public. Her first appearance upon the stage was at Richmond in 1833, when she was only thirteen. In that charming series of articles which appeared in *Blackwood* several years ago, and has since been republished, on "Some of Shakespeare's Female Characters," she has thus prettily described how she came to be an actress.

"One hot afternoon my sister and myself, finding it yet too sunny to walk down to the river—we had to pass the theatre (in Richmond by the Thames) on the way—took refuge in a cool place to rest awhile. On the stage was a flight of steps and a balcony, left standing, no doubt, after rehearsal, or prepared for that of the next day. After sitting on the steps for a while, my sister exclaimed, 'Why, this might do for Romeo and Juliet's balcony. Go up, birdie, and I will be your Romeo.' Upon this, amid much laughter and with no little stumbling over the words, we went through the balcony scene, I being prompter. . . . My sister and I went away to the river, leaving the shadowy gloom of the stage as we found it. To our surprise and consternation, we learned some time after that there had been a listener. When our friends arrived some days later, the lessee told them that having occasion to go from the dwelling-house to his private box, he heard voices, listened, and remained during the time of our merry rehearsal. He spoke in such warm terms of the Juliet's voice, its adaptability to the character, her figure—I was tall for my age—and so forth, that in the end he prevailed on my friends to let me make a trial on his stage. To this, at my then very tender age, they were loth to consent. But I was to be announced simply as a young lady—her first appearance. At the worst a failure would not matter; and, at any rate, the experiment would show whether I had gifts or not in that direction. Thus did a little frolic prove to be the turning-point of my life."

Three years after her appearance at Richmond, she appeared at Covent Garden as Julia in *The Hunchback*, with such success that the manager offered her a three years' engagement. Miss Faucit was thereafter the original Pauline in *The Lady of Lyons*, in which she made her first great impression. Her range of characters was very wide. She was a famous Juliet, a fine Lady Macbeth, and a celebrated Rosalind. The writer of these pages saw her play the last-named part only when the freshness and spontaneity of youth had long departed, at one of her last appearances, at the Haymarket, but its noble, subtle intellectuality rendered it a living commentary upon the text of Shakespeare; in its perfect refinement, its minute touches, its delicate elaboration, its supreme *finish*, it formed a remarkable contrast between the old school and the new.

What a splendid eulogy is that of De Quincey upon her Antigone, which she played here in 1845, and through the provinces, and at Dublin as well. But in London, Sophocles' immortal tragedy, though illustrated by Mendelssohn's music, was only *un succès d'estime*. "Then, suddenly—oh heavens, what a revelation of beauty!—forth stepped, walking in brightness, the most faultless of Grecian marbles, Miss Helen Faucit, as Antigone. What perfection of Athenian sculpture—the noble figure, the lovely arms, the fluent drapery! What an unveiling of the statuesque! Is it Hebe? Is it Aurora? Is it a goddess that moves before us? Perfect she is in form, perfect in attitude. It flattered one's patriotic feelings to see this noble young countrywoman, realising so exquisitely and restoring to our imagination the noblest of Grecian girls." "It is hard to say," wrote Alison, "whether her Rosalind is the more charming, or her Lady Teazle the most fascinating, her Belvidera the more moving, or her Juliet the more heart-rending."

One of the last great efforts to bring back to Covent Garden something of its ancient glory was the Macready management, which commenced on September 30th, 1837, with a splendid revival of *The Winter's Tale*, and a fine company, including Phelps, Harley, Elton, James Anderson (his first appearance in London), Miss Faucit, Miss Huddart, Miss Taylor, a delightful comedy actress, etc. Between the opening night and Christmas, in addition to *The Winter's Tale*, *Hamlet*, *Othello*, *The Bridal* (an alteration of *The Maid's Tragedy*), *Werner*,

Macbeth, and several legitimate comedies were produced, and entailed a loss of £3,000 in two months.

After Christmas, the pantomime was preceded by a revival of *King Lear*, from the text; then came Bulwer's *Lady of Lyons*, which proved a trump card, though only after it had been played some little time. *Coriolanus* followed; but though mounted in the most perfect manner, failed to attract, and was played on one occasion to £55.

The next season opened with a company forty-six in number, the very pick of the profession. *Coriolanus* was performed on the first night, with Vandenhoff in the title rôle. A wonderful revival of *The Tempest* followed, with Macready as Prospero; George Bennett, Caliban; Helen Faucit, Miranda; Phelps, Antonio; Anderson, Ferdinand. This was a decided success, and for fifty-five nights the receipts averaged £230 a night.

There is a very significant passage in James Anderson's memoirs. "Had the manager only followed the advice of his officers, it might have gone one hundred nights more to like receipts. But no, he would never give the public what it wanted, but only what he liked; this he considered consistent with his pledges to give novelty and variety. . . . He had a temper and will peculiar to himself; he would manage the theatre in his own way, and that was how he came to lose his money. Instead of running *The Tempest* nightly to fine houses, he chose to revive a dull old piece called *The Royal Oak*, which we played to empty benches."

Henry V., grandly cast, was the last of Macready's Shakespearian revivals at Covent Garden, and in the July of 1839 he retired, a heavy loser.

Madame Vestris was the next candidate for this crown of thorns, and gathered about her an admirable company—Harley, the Keeleys, Mrs. Nisbett, Charles

Mathews, Anderson, etc. *Love's Labour's Lost* was her opening piece, September 30th, 1839. A blunder marred the inauguration. Madame closed the shilling gallery; the offended deities of the high Olympus filled the lower gallery and pit to overflowing on the first night, and hooted and yelled and damned the play, which would otherwise have proved successful. Light pieces from the Olympic and opera were then tried; but the success of the season was Sheridan Knowles's *Love,* with Anderson as Huon, and Ellen Tree as the Countess. It ran fifty nights to large audiences, and then unfortunately had to be withdrawn in consequence of Miss Tree having made other engagements. Leigh Hunt's *Legend of Florence,* in which "the fair Ellen" is said to have played divinely as Ginevra, fell flat.

An event worth noting in the early part of 1840 was the production of *Romeo and Juliet,* according to the text of Shakespeare, doubtless for the first time since the Commonwealth period, for Miss Jane Mordaunt, Mrs. Nisbett's sister, to appear as the heroine; but she made no impression.

It was in this season that Charles Kemble returned to the stage for a few nights "at Her Majesty's command," and played to greater houses than he had been ever able to draw in his younger days. "In Don Felix, Charles Surface, and Benedick, he was incomparably fine," says Mr. Anderson, "but more especially so in Mercutio. In this part I had a better chance of watching his acting, as I played Romeo to him, and I will say truthfully that I never saw, and shall never see again, anything in comedy acting so superlatively fine as his Mercutio. He was at this time considerably over seventy years of age, but acted like a man of forty." [1]

[1] George Vandenhoff, in his *Leaves from an Actor's Note-Book*, tells a good story illustrative of Charles Kemble's powers; Vandenhoff played

The season came to a close on May 29th with *The Merry Wives of Windsor.* "I much fear," to again quote Mr. Anderson's personal experiences, "that, notwithstanding all the wonderful endeavours to deserve success, there was a heavy loss at the treasury. . . . Under Madame's management, nothing was in any way slighted or neglected. Even the most trifling piece produced was given with earnest care and expense."

The next season opened with *The Merry Wives of Windsor;* followed by a revival of Beaumont and Fletcher's comedy, *The Spanish Curate*, and a new play of Knowles's; but nothing drew until Boucicault's *London Assurance* was produced in March, 1841. It ran sixty-nine nights, and ended the season, when, Madame being about £600 short of a rental of as many thousands, the proprietors, who by their greed had done much to ruin their own property, closed the doors against her.

The dramatic annals of Covent Garden virtually ended with the Vestris management. Charles Kemble again opened the theatre in 1842 to bring out his daughter, Adelaide, the singer, a great artiste, as Norma. Then Bunn once more ventured upon the speculation. But both seasons were very brief.

In the following year the Anti-Corn Law League opened the house as a bazaar. In 1844–6, Jullien's famous concerts and *bals masqués* were given there, and in 1847, after undergoing considerable alterations, the

Mercutio at Covent Garden, when the last of the Kembles had retired. Next day, in the green-room, after complimenting the young man upon his performance, Mr. Kemble offered to give him a few hints; he was then nearly seventy years of age, and was dressed at the time in his ordinary street attire, but he gave the Queen Mab speech with a grace and beauty such as the young actor had never conceived, reducing him to despair at his own crude efforts.

Theatre Royal, Covent Garden, was converted into the Royal "Italian Opera." Delafield, the *entrepreneur,* spent £40,000 in adapting the theatre to the new style of entertainment, and in two years lost £60,000 besides. In 1850, Mr. Gye became lessee, and held that position with varying fortunes until 1856. On the 4th of March in that year, at the close of a *bal masqué* given by Wizard Anderson, the old home of the Kembles was again destroyed by fire.

Some account of the present theatre and its annals as an opera house will be found at the end of the next chapter.

Having thus brought this imperfect sketch of the great patent theatres to a conclusion, it may be useful to take a retrospective glance at the various phases through which the actor's art passed during the eighteenth and nineteenth centuries, or rather from Betterton to the retirement of Macready, and add a few notes upon the drama of the same period.

When we remember the very decided Gallic tastes of the King and his courtiers, among whom were numbered Killigrew and Davenant, the patentees of the two theatres of the time, it cannot be doubted that the Restoration actors modelled their style upon that of the French school. Betterton accompanied Davenant to Paris to study the arrangements of the theatres, and must have seen the great Baron act, and Champmeslé, and Dumesnil, and knowing the royal preference, would certainly have profited thereby. When he returned to London he gave hints to Elizabeth Barry, though she had probably already been trained in the French method by one who was well acquainted with it, her lover, Rochester. An ideal grandeur and a magnificent declamation were the distinguishing features of French classic tragedy, and in the great French artistes just mentioned these were combined with a power and intensity that rendered the artificial natural. I believe that the acting of Betterton and his associates was of this order.

But with this noble actor, the glories, the very soul of the school, departed; even Barton Booth seems to have fallen short of the splendid powers of his prototype and master, Betterton, though Aaron Hill finely said of him, "the blind might have seen him in his voice, and the deaf have heard him in his visage." After Booth, turgid declamation, rant without passion, a stilted utterance that disdained nature, the very dry bones and dust of tradition, were all that survived; mediocrity reigned supreme, and tragedy was represented by such conventional actors as Ryan, Boheme, Mills, Delane, and Quin, until the coming of David Garrick. Writing of the first time he saw this great genius act, Richard Cumberland says: "It seemed as if a whole century had been swept over in the transition of a single scene; old things were done away, and a new order at once brought forward, bright and luminous, and clearly destined to expel the barbarism and bigotry of a tasteless age, too long attached to prejudices of custom, and superstitiously devoted to the illusions of imposing declamation."

And Cumberland's was but the echo of universal opinion. Garrick was a phenomenal actor; without any previous apprenticeship, preparation or drudgery, at a remote end of the town which had hitherto been as unknown to fashion as the wilds of Africa, without preliminary puff of any kind, he took the whole play-going public by storm. There is no parallel to this in theatrical history. From Richard III. to Abel Drugger, from King Lear to Don Felix, from Macbeth to Bayes, his tragic force, his keen sense of humour, his marvellous *genius* carried all before it. Yet he did not quite obliterate the old artificial style. "Even Mrs. Cibber," Cumberland says, "in a high-pitched key sang or recitatived her speeches like a French actress."

Being inimitable, unapproachable, Garrick founded no school, left behind him no imitator—unless it were Henderson, whose early death gave John Kemble the lead in tragedy and brought back the artificial and declamatory style that reigned supreme until the advent of Edmund Kean. Both the actors last named formed schools; one half the mediocrities spouted and paused and strutted, John Kembles in miniature; the other half ranted in hoarse accents and rushed about the stage and fancied they were Keans. But the grandeur, the majesty with which the one invested certain characters, and those marvellous flashes of genius by which the other carried every spectator out of himself, in fine, the informing soul of each was absent in his imitators; even Charles Young, the finest representative of the Kemble cult, though he had something of the stately grace and dignity of the original, never knew those moments of inspiration, as when Kemble, in Coriolanus, dashed in among the flying soldiers as though he had indeed the strength and power to sweep a score of them before him like blades of grass.

Sir Walter Scott has exactly defined the limits of his genius in the following passage:—

"John Kemble certainly is a great artist. It is a pity he shows too much of his machinery. I wish he could be double-capped, as they say of watches; but the fault of too much study certainly does not belong to many of his tribe. He is, I think, very great in those parts especially where character is tinged by some acquired and systematic habits, like those of the Stoic philosophy in Cato and Brutus, or of misanthropy in Penruddock; but sudden turns and natural bursts of passion are not his *forte*. . . .

"He seems to me always to play best those characters in which there is a predominating tinge of some over-mastering passion, or acquired habit of acting and speaking, colouring the whole man. The patrician pride of Coriolanus, the stoicism of Brutus and Cato, the rapid and hurried vehemence of Hotspur, mark the class of characters I mean. But he fails where a ready and pliable yielding to the events and passions of life makes what may be termed a more natural personage. Accordingly, I think his Macbeth, Lear, and especially his Richard, inferior in spirit and truth. In Hamlet, the natural fixed melancholy of the prince places him within Kemble's range; yet many delicate and sudden turns of passion slip through his fingers. He is a lordly vessel, goodly and magnificent when going large before the wind, but wanting the facility to go 'ready about,' so that he is sometimes among the breakers before he can wear ship."

Edmund Kean approached nearest to Garrick; there was the same electrical passion, the same abandon in both; but Kean had many tricks and mannerisms, and he had had years of practice in the provinces before he astounded a Drury Lane audience, while, as it has been already said, all his apparently spontaneous effects were the result of deep study.

After Kean came Macready, a mannerist, lacking all enthusiasm for his art, nay, more, despising it; yet by dint of dogged application and a naturally fine intellectual grasp developing into a noble actor. But Edmund Kean, "the little man with a great soul," was really the last of the English tragedians, the last who could "pluck out the heart of the mystery" of Shakespeare's great creations, the last who could soar into the regions of ideal passion and carry his spectators with him.

Macready was the founder of the modern school, of which Irving is the present representative, though he had more of the ideal and was nearer to the demi-gods than any of his followers. Yet for all that he was only a supremely fine melodramatic actor, as his greatest successes were not in Shakespeare or in the poetic drama, but in such plays as *Virginius*, *William Tell*, *Richelieu*, *Werner*.

Tragic acting, indeed, began to decline with the tragic drama, and after Barton Booth, if not after Betterton, tragedians became phenomenal; even Garrick's company did not possess a tragic actor of the first rank. Macklin was hard and harsh; Thomas Sheridan was a stilted declaimer; Mossop, a mouther and ranter of the most pronounced type; Reddish and John Palmer were good actors in many parts, but not in the first rank; and Smith, in tragedy, was the most mediocre of heroes. The ladies, however, well sustained the traditions of Ann Marshall, Mrs. Betterton, Mrs. Barry, and Mrs. Porter. Mrs. Pritchard, Mrs. Spranger Barry, Mrs. Cibber,[1] Mrs. Yates, were tragic actresses of the highest order, and little inferior to these was that glorious *comédienne*, Peg Woffington, and, perhaps, Miss Younge.

The strength of Garrick's companies, especially the later ones, lay in their comic talent, and this supremacy of comedy lasted till the end of the eighteenth and during

[1] Churchill pronounced a fine eulogy upon this great actress in the lines—

> "To melt the heart with sympathetic woe,
> Awake the sigh and teach the tear to flow,
> To put on Henry's wild distracted glare,
> And freeze the soul with horror and despair."

the first years of the nineteenth century. Woodward, King, Smith, Parsons, Dodd, Weston, Edwin, Suett, Mathews, Liston, Bannister, Emery, Quick, Dowton, Elliston, Charles Kemble, Kitty Clive, Mrs. Abington, Dora Jordan, these were the perfection of comedians; each was a Garrick or a Siddons in comedy, and, indeed, Garrick himself was as great in comedy as in tragedy. How few names, not half a dozen, are inscribed upon the roll of Melpomene to balance this glowing record of the goddess of laughter. And many another name little inferior to those quoted might be added.

That the dramatic art, which is always in its highest vigour in the heroic ages of nations and wanes before the advance of the artifical conditions of life, had passed its meridian even in Garrick's days may be gathered from the fact that up to the time of the Triumvirate the public went to see the *play, well acted all round*, as when Cibber, Booth, Wilks, Dogget, Mrs. Oldfield, etc., performed together and stood shoulder to shoulder in respective merit, and would have thought it very bad art for one to overshadow all the rest. It was Garrick who inaugurated the star system, for he was the first of a line of great actors who were a head and shoulders above their contemporaries; and so for a hundred and fifty years the general public has been drawn, not by the excellence of a play or a company, but by the talent or popularity of one or two actors or actresses, tragic or comic.

Were it possible to recall out of Hades the Hamlet of Betterton, the Richard of Garrick, the Coriolanus of Kemble, the Othello of Kean, and the Virginius of Macready, the cultured playgoer would find it hard to determine which was the grandest performance; but the votes of the many would be given *en masse* to Garrick,

Kean, and Macready, to the first two for their universality, to the last because he would be most *en rapport* with the spirit of the age, which is nothing if not realistic. We are out of touch with the heroic, with enthusiasm, with passion, and the modern actor, to compromise with the Philistinism of his audience, endeavours to render tragedy natural, that is, commonplace, which is just about equal to a painter attempting to render Raphael or Michael Angelo in unison with Teniers.

What is there of realism in Shakespeare's *Macbeth?* The barbarous, half-savage Highlander of history has been transfigured by the poet into one of the great psychological studies of the world, his utterances are couched in the sublimest poetry; Macbeth might have *thought* all that Shakespeare has made him say, as any coarse and ignorant man might *feel* all the pangs of Othello, yet be without the power to give them utterance; and it is this marvellous gift of the mighty dramatist to interpret and give a voice to the dumb soul of ordinary humanity, through which he appeals to all humanity, cultured or ignorant. Nevertheless, like all tragic geniuses from Æschylus and Sophocles, he is an idealist and can never be adequately rendered by the familiar realism of recent actors.

Figuratively, the English stage has been developed by successive waves of idealism and realism, the latter ever the stronger, with a strength increasing with each successive ebb and flow. In comedy the artificial brilliancy, the perfect finish, the subtle minutiæ of the characters of Congreve, Farquhar, and Vanbrugh, with modification ever tending to the familiar, extended from Wilks to Charles Kemble and expired with the latter.

During the second half of the eighteenth century, in consequence of the failure of dramatic genius, the actor held the stage without a rival, supreme over the dramatist; and the reign of the scene-painter and the mechanist was still afar off. Tragedy died with Otway, and there is not a work of the eighteenth century that has the ring of true passion in it: Congreve's *Mourning Bride*, of which I have made previous mention; Rowe's *Jane Shore* (1713), stilted and artificial, though not without merit; Young's *Revenge* (1721), which, in the part of Zanga, has afforded splendid opportunities to most of our great tragedians; Moore's *Gamester* (1753), powerful in conception, but most bald and prosaic in execution, about which cling memories of some of the finest efforts of Mrs. Siddons and Miss O'Neill, are the only works worth mentioning. Any number of dull, stilted plays were produced under the name of tragedies, several written by men of great ability, such as Dr. Johnson's *Irene* and James Thomson's *Sophonisba*, but all have long since sunk into oblivion. Among them, however, was one that was hailed as an almost more than Shakespearian effort—Home's tragedy of *Douglas*, in which both Spranger Barry's wife and Mrs. Siddons acted so wonderfully as Lady Randolph. One need not be so very old to remember the day when every schoolboy learned to spout the famous speech, "My name is Norval," and in Scotland it shared with *Rob Roy* the distinction of being regarded as the national play, and woe to the actor who was not perfect in the text, for every little boy in the gallery knew it by heart. The story of the enthusiastic Scot who at one of the earlier representations of the piece at Covent Garden rose up in the pit, and, addressing the audience, exclaimed, "Where's your Wully Shakespeare the noo?" is well known. It is extremely difficult for modern taste to discover in what the greatness of *Douglas* consisted.

The great successes achieved by the Booths, the Garricks, and the Kembles were in the plays of Shakespeare, Jonson, Beaumont and Fletcher. But what garbled versions they were of those great writers, more especially of Shakespeare. Every dramatic manipulator, from Dryden and Davenant to Nahum Tate and Theophilus Cibber, thought he could improve upon "the sweet Swan of Avon"; the consequence was that not a single play of his was given without impertinent interpolations and monstrous alterations, amounting in some to an absolute change of plot and motive. Indeed, it is only within the memory of the present generation that Garrick's version of *Romeo and Juliet* and Cibber's *Richard III.* have given place to Shakespeare's; and Macready first restored the Fool to *King Lear.*

A comparison between the dramatic literature of the first three decades and the last seventy years of the eighteenth century is startling in its contrast. Wycherley, Vanbrugh, Congreve, Farquhar, Cibber, Steele were all plying their pens during the first period, and such a galaxy of comedy writers producing in the same era has no parallel in our own or in any other history. The great work of the second period is *The School for Scandal;* but fine as is the wit of Sheridan, Congreve's is finer, and were it not for the screen scene, which is probably the finest situation in the whole range of comedy, the work would be little more than a clever plagiary upon "Tom Jones," Wycherley's *Plain Dealer*, and Molière's *Le Misanthrope. The Rivals*, previously produced at Covent Garden, was damned on the first night, January 17th, 1775. Sheridan held it was through the incompetence of the actor who personated Sir Lucius. Yet it was finely cast, with Shuter, Woodward, Lewis, and Quick in the principal parts. Certain alterations, however, being made, the first night's judgment was speedily reversed by contemporaries, as it has been by posterity.

A few comedies that preceded Sheridan's great works must not go unmentioned. Colman the elder's *Jealous Wife* (1761), and *The Clandestine Marriage* (1766), an admirable work; Arthur Murphy's *The Way to keep Him* (1760), and *All in the Wrong* (1761), two spirited comedies; and above all, Goldsmith's delightful *She Stoops to Conquer*, given to Covent Garden in 1773. A reference to this work renders necessary some account of the school of comedy it was destined to displace.

A new species of comedy called the sentimental had become the fashion during the first half of the eighteenth century. Steele's three comedies, *The Tender Husband* (1703), *The Lying Lover* (1704), and *The Conscious Lovers* (1721), were the earliest specimens of this form of composition; but they found no imitators until Hugh Kelly produced his *False Delicacy* (1768), which, though far from being so contemptible a piece of work as many critics have represented it to be, is overcharged with superfine writing. Cumberland followed in Kelly's steps with melodramatic additions, while in the hands of Holcroft and Mrs. Inchbald the style degenerated into the domestic drama of the last century. So great was the success of *False Delicacy* that it ran eight successive nights, and would have gone longer, but Garrick had pledged himself to the public that no new piece should run beyond that limit. It was, however, performed twenty times afterwards during the season.

The comedies of Colman the younger were popular not only in their day, but certain of them, such as *John Bull*, *The Poor Gentleman*—both written for Covent

Garden—and *The Heir at Law* (for the Haymarket) were favourites within these five-and-twenty years. They were essentially of the sentimental school, stilted in the serious scenes, and though humorous, almost destitute of wit. Nevertheless these plays are remarkable, as, in conjunction with those of Holcroft, Cumberland, and Mrs. Inchbald, they mark a new era in stage literature; hitherto kings and nobles only had filled the tragic scene, and the beaux and belles the comic, but the authors just named, infected by the spirit of the French Revolution, chose most of their heroes and heroines from among the people, and their comic characters from a class that is almost entirely absent from the works of Congreve and even Sheridan. Colman was the creator of that terrible bore, the virtuous peasant, who always carried his entire wardrobe in a coloured pocket-handkerchief at the end of a stick, who was always fighting in defence of the hapless village maiden, eternally spouting platitudes, was as eager as the stage sailor to bestow his last shilling upon anyone in want, and always expressed joy by stamping about and singing "Ri fol, riddi iddi ido," a conventional figure that was driven from the stage by the burlesques of H. J. Byron. One of the most notable of Colman's pieces was the once famous *Mountaineers*, written for Covent Garden (1793); the mad lover, Octavian, was a favourite part with Kemble, Kean, Elliston, and many of their successors; indeed, the last words that Edmund Kean ever uttered were from the dying speech of Octavian, "Farewell, Flo—Floranthe."

Mrs. Inchbald was one of the dramatic luminaries of the Bow Street house during the last two decades of the eighteenth century, but no audience could now endure any one of her works. Yet *Such Things Are*, a most wretched agglomeration of twaddle, nightly crowded the theatre to the ceiling; hundreds were turned away from the doors, and the lucky authoress realised £900 by it. *Wives as they Were and Maids as they Are*, *Lovers' Vows*, *Everyone has his Fault*, kept the stage for many years; but the sentiment is mawkish and overstrained, the comic scenes, though occasionally sprightly, cannot boast of much wit, while the characters are of the most conventional type. Mrs. Cowley's bright comedy, *The Belle's Stratagem* (1780), which was given a new lease of life by Irving's and Ellen Terry's admirable acting, and most of Holcroft's works, including the only one of his that has kept the stage, *The Road to Ruin* (1792), were produced at Covent Garden. Several of Cumberland's plays first saw the footlights at that house, but his best-known works were given to Drury Lane; notably, *The Wheel of Fortune* (1795), which, in the misanthrope Penruddock, furnished John Kemble with one of his finest impersonations; a few will remember Samuel Phelps's admirable rendering of this part.

A dramatic novelty that originated in the second half of the eighteenth century was the musical farce and operatic drama, for although *The Beggar's Opera* was the progenitor of all, it did not find imitators for many years. Of these musical pieces, Charles Dibdin's *Quaker*, *The Padlock*, *The Waterman*, and Isaac Bickerstaff's delicious *Love in a Village*, with its charming comedy and delightful airs, and his *Lionel and Clarissa*, now quite forgotten, may be taken as types. These and others in the same style, *Inkle and Yarico*, *Rosina*, *No Song no Supper*, *The Miller and his Men*, etc., etc., with music by some of our best composers, were among the most popular of English dramatic entertainments.

During the nineteenth century, the great theatres added little to the literature of the country. Such as it is, Covent Garden had the lion's share. Here were produced some of Morton's best works: *Town and Country*, in which the character of Plastic may claim to be the first of that long series of gentlemanly villains, of which Captain Hawkesly in *Still Waters Run Deep* is the most pronounced development; *The School of Reform*, in which the elder Emery played so magnificently as Tyke; and *Speed the Plough*, performed not so many years ago, were among the number. For this house O'Keefe wrote his *Wild Oats*, George Colman the younger *The Poor Gentleman* (1800) and *John Bull* (1803), with Fawcett as Job Thornberry; Cooke, Peregrine; Blanchard, Sir Simon; Lewis, Tom Shuffleton; Johnstone, Dennis; Emery, Dan.

In tragedy, Shiel's *Evadne* and *The Apostate*, which, though containing passages of real poetry, owed their success almost entirely to the grand acting of Miss O'Neill, Charles Young, and Macready, are the only tragic productions that need be mentioned previous to the rise of Sheridan Knowles. *Virginius*, the first of Knowles's plays produced in London, was brought out at Covent Garden, on May 17th, 1820; the title rôle was probably Macready's grandest effort, and the tragedy was received with the greatest enthusiasm.

Knowles was hailed as a Shakespeare Redivivus, and it must be admitted that to an audience surfeited with the sham classicism of such plays as Ambrose Phillips's *Distressed Mother*, which even Macready had selected to make his London début in, there was a reality of flesh and blood about the new writer's treatment of the pathetic old Roman story, marvellously refreshing. *Virginius* is a powerful play with fine dramatic situations, and, well acted, must always command the tears and sympathies of the spectators; but we have only to compare it with John Webster's grand old tragedy, *Appius and Virginia*, to perceive how much the modern author falls short of the capabilities of the subject. With the exception of two or three isolated passages, the blank verse is little better than inverted and distorted prose. In those days, when even the educated were ignorant of Elizabethan dramatic literature, Knowles was accounted to be an imitator of that school; but his knowledge of the great masters of his art was probably confined to the acted plays of Shakespeare and Massinger, and his model was the latter.

The Hunchback, with Fanny Kemble, then in the height of her fame, as the heroine, was also contributed to Covent Garden; her acting as Julia is said to have drawn more tears than any stage representation since Kemble and Siddons appeared in *The Stranger*. Knowles himself played Master Walter; but, burly in form, below the middle height, and pedantic in utterance, he could have been but a poor representative of his hero; Charles Kemble, the original Sir Thomas Clifford, said afterwards that the only person who did not understand the author was the gentleman who played Master Walter. With an obscure plot that Knowles himself could never quite satisfactorily explain, no very strong situations, and almost invariably played to empty benches, it kept the stage only because Julia was a showy part—that every lady used to be ambitious to act. *The Love Chase* was rendered a passing success by Mrs. Nisbett's brilliant performance of Constance; but it is utterly artificial. Macready gave life to *William Tell* by his splendid acting, but the play virtually died with him. A showy but somewhat stilted heroine, a good stage part, and two excellent dramatic situations kept *The Wife* alive for many years. The rest of his plays passed away with the original representatives.

Bulwer Lytton's dramas were far more successful. His first dramatic essay, *The Lady of Lyons*, in spite of its stilted diction and improbable plot, has drawn more money into theatrical treasuries in town and country than any other play of the pre-sensational period. The cause is not far to seek; it lies in the vividness of the action, without which the literary merit of a play counts for nothing. Within a few days of its production it was entitled *The Adventurer*, and it was not until a run of nine nights had assured him of success that the author would permit his name to appear upon the bills. *Richelieu*, a much better work, less bombastic, and with really fine stage situations, quickly followed, and met with equal favour, though Macready was doubtful of it up to the last moment.

Money, produced at the Haymarket in 1840, was another of Bulwer's successes. It was got up regardless of cost; D'Orsay was called in to suggest the costumes, and the tailor of the "Last of the Dandies" made them. The cast was a record. Macready and Helen Faucit, Evelyn and Clara; Walter Lacy, Blount; Webster, Graves; Mrs. Glover, Lady Franklin; Wrench, Dudley Smooth; Miss Horton, Georgina; Strickland, Sir John Vesey. The comedy has been revived again and again for long runs up to within a very recent period, the last revival being, I think, at the Garrick. But its characters are out of date, and it has now probably been consigned to limbo.

Serjeant Talfourd's noble but coldly classical play *Ion* preceded Bulwer's in date. Byron's *Werner*, *Sardanapalus*, and *The Foscari* were brought out at Drury Lane, and afforded Macready some of his greatest triumphs, and *Marino Faliero* at Covent Garden. There were *The Patrician's Daughter* and other poetical plays by

Westland Marston—all dead and gone, but Boucicault's clever hotchpotch *London Assurance* was performed only a few years ago at the Criterion, with Wyndham as Dazzle.

After the early forties, dramatic literature was buried under an avalanche of melodrama; Lovel's *The Wife's Secret*, *Love's Sacrifice*, and a few others of the quasi-poetical school occasionally came to the front, but they have all passed into oblivion, and it is very improbable they will ever be drawn out of it. In the course of the following pages I shall have to make frequent references to the new school, originated by Pinero and Jones, which has once more raised the drama to the dignity of literature; but any general survey of the dramatic authors of our own time would only give rise to controversy.

CHAPTER III

The Great Haymarket Theatre—A sketch of the history of the Italian Opera and Opera Ballet in London, and some account of the famous Singers and Dancers who have appeared between 1705 and 1903

TAKING the West End theatres in chronological order, the great theatre in the Haymarket must precede the little one. It was the strained relations between Christopher Rich and the leading members of his company that first suggested to Sir John Vanbrugh the project of building a new theatre in the Haymarket, "for which," says Cibber, "he raised a subscription of thirty persons of quality, at one hundred pounds each, in consideration whereof every subscriber for his own life was to be admitted to whatever entertainments should be publicly performed there, without further payment for his entrance. Of this theatre I saw the first stone laid, on which was inscribed 'The Little Whig,' in honour to a lady of extraordinary beauty,[1] then the celebrated toast and pride of that party. In the year 1705, when this house was finished, Betterton and his co-partners dissolved their own agreement, and threw themselves under the direction of Sir John Vanbrugh and Mr. Congreve." And Colley goes on to tell us, in his diffuse manner, that the actors depended upon the genius of those two famous writers and the splendour of the new house to draw the public; "but," he adds, "almost every proper quality and convenience of a good

[1] Lady Sunderland.

theatre had been sacrificed or neglected to show the spectator a vast triumphal piece of architecture. For what could their vast columns, their gilded cornices, their immoderate high roofs avail, when scarcely one word in two could be distinctly heard in it? Nor had it then the form it now stands in, which necessity two or three years afterwards reduced it to. At the first opening, the flat ceiling, that is now over the orchestra, was then a semi-oval arch, that sprung fifteen feet higher from above the cornice. The ceiling over the pit, too, was still more raised, being one level line from the highest back part of the upper gallery to the front of the stage; the front boxes were a continual semicircle to the bare walls of the house on each side. This extraordinary and superfluous space occasioned such an undulation from the voice of every actor, that generally what they said sounded like the gabbling of so many people in the lofty aisles of a cathedral. The tone of a trumpet, or the swell of an eunuch's holding note, it is true, might be sweetened by it; but the articulate sounds of a speaking voice were drowned by the hollow reverberations of one word upon another. To this inconvenience why might we not add that of its situation? for at that time it had not the advantage of the large city, which has since been built in its neighbourhood; those costly spaces of Hanover, Grosvenor, and Cavendish Squares, with the many great and adjacent streets about them, were then but so many green fields of pasture, from whence they could draw little or no sustenance unless it were that of a milk diet. The City, the Inns of Court, and the middle part of the town, which were the most constant support of a theatre, and chiefly to be relied on, were now too far out of the reach of an easy walk, and coach hire is often too hard a tax upon the pit and gallery."

It was in 1705 that the first opera in the Italian style, with recitatives, was performed in this country at Drury Lane; it was called *Arsinoë, Queen of Cyprus*, written by Motteaux; it so hit the fashionable taste that the lessees decided to open the Queen's Theatre, as the new house was christened (April 9th, 1705), in honour of the reigning sovereign, with one of these exotics, a translation from the Italian, entitled *The Triumph of Love.* It proved an utter failure, being performed only three nights, after which the manager had to turn to the drama, and in October Vanbrugh produced his admirable comedy *The Confederacy.* But whether it was on account of the bad acoustic properties of the house, or from other causes, comedy was little more successful than opera, and neither *The Confederacy*, nor two or three other works from the same pen, drew the public to the Queen's. Congreve quickly retired from the unfortunate speculation, and Sir John Vanbrugh was glad to let the house to a Mr. Owen Swiney, Rich's factotum and man of business, who was to pay £5 for every acting day, and not more than £700 for the entire year. Swiney commenced operations in October, 1706; and business improved under the new manager, who brought some fresh blood into the *corps dramatique.*

The union of the two companies under Colonel Brett, however,[1] and the growing taste for Italian singers and Italian music, brought about an arrangement with Swiney, by which the Queen's Theatre was to be devoted entirely to opera, while the actors were ordered to return to Drury Lane, there to remain under the patentees, Her Majesty's only company of comedians. The reader of the previous chapters will already have learned how this happy arrangement came to an end,

[1] See p. 56.

how another revolt of the actors brought a number of them back to the Haymarket, where on certain nights they varied the operatic with the dramatic, considerable alterations having been made in the house to adapt it for the speaking voice.

There would be little interest in following all the complications between actors and managers that occurred at this period. By-and-by, Collier, the new patentee of Drury Lane, became also the lessee of the Queen's; after which the actors went back to their old quarters at Drury Lane, and the Haymarket was finally delivered over to the lyric drama. And with this arrangement really commences the history of Italian opera in England.

Every reader of the *Spectator* will remember how felicitously Addison[1] has ridiculed the absurdities and crudities of the opera, as it existed in his time. Some great star or stars were brought from Italy to sustain the principal parts, while the minor characters were sustained by English singers; so the lover pleaded to his mistress in a tongue unknown to her, and the lady replied with equal fervour in rhythmical cadences of which he understood not a syllable; heroes addressed their soldiers or their slaves in the liquid accents of Rome or Naples, and were answered in the dialect of Cockayne.[2] Mrs. Tofts, a very fine singer, was the first of our English *prime donne;* associated with her

[1] Much of Addison's virulence against Italian opera, however, resulted from the failure of his own effort at the lyric drama, *Rosamond*, with music by Thomas Clayton, described as "a jargon of sounds," brought out at the Queen's in 1707.

[2] According to Dr. Burney (*History of Music*), the music of these early operas was neither dramatic, passionate, pathetic, nor graceful. The first violin accompaniment was printed over the voice part, and if the words indicated sorrow it was marked *slow*, if they implied pleasure it was marked *quick*.

was Margarite L'Epine, and Valentini, the first of those male soprani who so long enchanted English ears. There were several native singers of note; Leveredge, a famous basso, and Hughes, a tenor. The absurdities of such a mongrel dialect were too transparent, and, to use Addison's words, "the audience grew tired of understanding half the opera, and therefore, to ease themselves entirely of the fatigue of thinking, have so ordered it at present that the whole opera is performed in an unknown tongue."

The last of those hybrid productions was *Pyrrhus and Demetrius*, 1708,[1] and in that same year arrived the famous Nicolini, a name familiar to every reader of the *Spectator*. Two years later, George Frederick Handel, George the First's Chapel Master at Hanover, was invited over to England; Aaron Hill, the author of several plays, who was then director of the Queen's Theatre under Collier, engaged the great German composer to write an opera upon a subject taken from Tasso, and on February 24th, 1711, Handel's first opera, *Rinaldo*, was produced at that house, and ran fifteen nights. *Rinaldo*, though the earliest, was one of the finest works that Handel gave to the stage; among the music are to be found the two beautiful and well-known airs "Cara Sposa" and "Lascia ch'io pianga." Elaborate scenic effects were introduced into these operas, much to the scorn of the *Spectator*. "How would the wits of King Charles's time have laughed to have seen Nicolini exposed to a tempest in robes of ermine, and sailing in an open boat upon a sea of pasteboard. What a field of raillery would they have been let into, had they been entertained with painted dragons spitting

[1] The first opera produced in this country wholly in Italian was Buononcini's *Almahide*, 1710.

wildfire, enchanted chariots drawn by Flanders mares, and real cascades in artificial landskips. . . . *Rinaldo* is filled with thunder and lightning, illuminations and fireworks."

Another opera, called *Hydaspes*, afforded excellent fun for Mr. *Spectator*. In this Nicolini was thrown into an amphitheatre to be devoured by a lion, to whom he appealed in the minor key, softly whispering in the feline ear the story of his love; then defying the beast in *bravura* passages, telling him he may tear his bosom but cannot touch his heart, and after cajoling the monarch of the forest into listening to these dulcet strains, Hydaspes took a mean advantage of his tenderness and throttled him.

To the powers of Nicolini the *Tatler* gives ungrudging praise. "Nicolini sets off the character he bears in every opera by his action as much as he does the words of it by his voice; every limb and finger contributes to the part he acts, insomuch that a deaf man might go along with him in the sense of it. There is scarcely a beautiful posture in an old statue which he does not plant himself in, as the different circumstances of the story give occasion for it; he performs the most ordinary action in a manner suitable to the greatness of his character, and shows the prince even in the giving of a letter or the despatch of a letter." Nicolini's salary, however, was only 800 guineas a year. Yet so early as 1711 we hear of Swiney, bankrupt through excess of expenses over receipts, having to fly the country.

About the same time as *Rinaldo*, an opera by Gasparini, founded upon Shakespeare's *Hamlet*, and entitled *Ambletto*, was brought out, the overture of which must have been very remarkable for such a subject, consisting, as it did, of four movements closing with a *jig!*

Handel's most formidable rival was Buononcini. He very equally divided the town with the German master, although he was infinitely inferior to him.

Swift has immortalised the Italian in his witty epigram :—

> "Some say that Signor Buononcini
> Compared to Handel's a mere ninny;
> While others say that to him Handel
> Is hardly fit to hold a candle.
> Strange, that such difference should be
> 'Twixt tweedle-dum and tweedle-dee!"

The Duchess of Marlborough, not Sarah, however, thought so much of Buononcini's talents, that she settled £500 a year upon him.

Handel composed no fewer than thirty-five Italian operas, some of the airs from which he afterwards introduced into his oratorios. "Whatever pleasure," says Mr. Hogarth, in his *Memoirs of the Opera*, "they must have given to the audiences of that age, they would fail to do so now; and, indeed, their performance would be impracticable. The music was written for a class of voices, the male soprano, which no longer exists, and for these no performers could now be found. A series of recitatives and airs, with only an occasional duet, and a concluding chorus of the slightest kind, would appear meagre and dull to ears accustomed to the brilliant concerted pieces and finales of the modern stage; and Handel's accompaniments would seem thin and poor amidst the richness and variety of the modern orchestra." In 1785, when the celebrated Madame Mara made her first appearance at the King's Theatre, Handel's operas were already regarded as old-fashioned and out of date.

It was not only between the composers that the taste

of the town was divided, for each singer had his or her partisans, who would scruple at nothing for the glorification of the favourite and the mortification of her rival. This spirit manifested itself very strongly at the time when Mrs. Tofts and Margarite L'Epine were the *dive* of the day, but it never rose to such a height as when the fashionable world was at war over the merits of the celebrated Cuzzoni and Faustina. No one was too great to join in this absurd partisanship, even Sir Robert Walpole was infected by it, being a supporter of Faustina. His lady, however, attempted to hold the balance between the two, and one day, when her husband was away, invited both Faustina and Cuzzoni to dinner. But no truce, however brief, could exist between these bitter enemies; at table they began by bickering, went on to quarrelling, and from wordy war proceeded to blows and scratches, playing havoc with the china. On another occasion, Lady Walpole engaged both the *dive* to sing at a concert at her house. Fearing another *émeute*, she dared not allow them to meet; so while one was performing she lured the other to a remote apartment, under the pretence of showing her something curious; and when it came to her turn to entertain the company, her ladyship had to resort to the same ruse with her rival.

The Cuzzoni party was headed by the Countess of Pembroke, whose followers used to hoot whenever Faustina appeared upon the stage. The *London Journal* for June 10th, 1727, says: "A great disturbance happened at the opera, occasioned by the partisans of the two celebrated rival ladies, Cuzzoni and Faustina. The contention was at first only carried on by hissing on one side and clapping on the other; but proceeded at length to the melodious use of catcalls and other accompaniments, which manifested the zeal and politeness of that illustrious assembly."

At length this continuous turmoil became so unendurable that the managers of the King's Theatre—the name had been changed at the accession of George I.—determined to rid themselves of one of these firebrands. Having discovered that Lady Pembroke had extracted an oath from Cuzzoni that she would never take one shilling less than Faustina, they, at the commencement of a new season, offered her one sovereign less than her rival, and by this means so disgusted the lady that she quitted the country.

In the year 1720 a Royal Academy of Music was established at the King's Theatre, for which Handel was engaged to write a series of operas. The affair was a terrible failure, £15,000 was lost by the end of the year, and subscribers were so backward in paying up, that legal proceedings were threatened against them in the public papers. This brought about a new mode of subscription, which, with certain modifications, has continued to the present day. Tickets were issued for a season of fifty nights on payment of ten guineas down, an engagement to pay five more on February 1st, and the remaining five on May 1st. Within seven years the whole of the capital, £50,000, was lost, and the Academy ceased to exist in 1728.

One of the great features of the Opera House now was the gorgeous masquerades arranged by Heidegger, who was bandmaster to George I., and prided himself on being the ugliest man in Europe; these, in splendour, it was said, far surpassed even those of Italy. In 1724, however, in consequence of a sermon preached by the Bishop of London, these balls were prohibited, and it was not until past the middle of the century that they were revived. It is worth noting that it was in the King's Theatre that Handel's *Esther*, the first oratorio ever heard in England, was given, and in the next year, 1732, his exquisite *Acis and Galatea* was produced at the same house.

All other operatic events, however, at this period were thrown into the shade by the appearance, in 1734, of the marvellous Farinelli. Dr. Burney says that without the assistance of gesture or graceful attitude, he astonished and enchanted his hearers by the force, extent, and mellifluous tones of his voice, even when he had nothing to execute or express. No intervals were too close, too wide, too rapid for his execution. Composers were unable to write passages difficult enough to display the full extent of his powers. On his arrival in England, at a private rehearsal given in the apartments of Cuzzoni, the manager of the opera observed that the band did not follow him, but were all gaping with wonder. He desired them to be attentive, but they confessed they were unable to keep pace with the singer, and were not only disabled, but overwhelmed by his talent. He could hold on and swell a note to such a surpassing length, that people could scarcely be persuaded but that it was continued by some hidden wind instrument while he took breath. He seems, however, to have been partly indebted for this power to the formation of his lungs, which were capable of holding an immense volume of air. His voice was said to have had the power of tranquillising the half-insane Ferdinand VI.; and an enthusiastic Englishwoman exclaimed blasphemously, after hearing him, "One God, one Farinelli."

Farinelli received a salary of £15,000 a year and a clear benefit, which was worth another £2,000. Yet, so capricious is fashion, that two years afterwards he sang to a £35 house.

Senesino was another famous male soprano, who sang in Handel's operas in 1726. After him came Caffarelli, of whom a curious story is told. He had been a pupil under the great Porpora; during five years the master made him sing only scales; at the end of that time the pupil asked when he was to be taught to sing. "You have nothing more to learn," answered Porpora, "you are now the greatest singer in the world." And so he proved himself to be.

As we have noted in a previous chapter, Porpora directed an Italian opera company at Lincoln's Inn Fields in 1733 and 1734, after which he went over to the King's Theatre for a time while Handel, in partnership with Heidegger, took opera to Covent Garden.

Among the singers who interpreted Handel's operas was Anastasia Robinson, the unacknowledged wife of that eccentric genius the Earl of Peterborough, a pure and noble woman whose whole life was one self-sacrifice, and whom George Meredith has taken as the heroine of one of his novels.

In 1741 the King's Theatre was under the management of the Earl of Middlesex. From the retirement of Handel from the operatic stage in 1740 until the advent of Glück with his *Orfeo*, in 1770, the art of musical composition made little progress, and the only event that claims notice in this brief *résumé* was the production, in 1762, of Dr. Arne's *Artaxerxes*, an opera which until far into the last century was regarded as our one classical work. It is now merely curious as a specimen of a dead and gone school of weak and florid music, which, even at the date of this production, was rapidly dying out in its birthplace, Italy.

Writing in 1747, Horace Walpole gives a curious and sarcastic account of an opera by Vaneschi, called *Fetonte*.

"It is in what they call the French manner; but about as like it as my lady Pomfret's hash of plural persons and singular verbs was to Italian. They sing to jigs and dance to church music. Phaeton is run away with by horses that go at a foot's pace, like the Electress's coach, with such long traces that the postilion was in one street and the coachman in another. Then comes Jupiter with a farthing candle to light a squib and a half; and that they call fireworks. Reginello, the first man, is so old and so tall that he seems to have been growing ever since the invention of opera," etc.

Sheridan, who without any tangible means seems to have been always able to enter into the most costly speculations, in partnership with Harris of Covent Garden, in 1778, gave £22,000 for the opera patent, and undertook it at a rental of £1,200 a year. Harris very soon retired and Brinsley sold his interest to Taylor, who continued to be *impresario* until 1804.

Sir John Vanbrugh's theatre on the 17th of June, 1789, was burned to the ground, at a loss of £73,000; set fire to, it is believed, by the leader of the orchestra, who had a grudge against Ravelli, the acting manager. The conflagration happened in the daytime, when the singers were at rehearsal, but no lives were lost. While the new house was in the course of erection, the company migrated to the Pantheon.[1]

[1] The Pantheon in Oxford Street was built, in 1770, by Wyatt at a cost of £60,000 for concerts, balls, and other amusements. It opened in 1772, being intended for a kind of winter Ranelagh. Horace Walpole highly eulogises in one of his letters the beauty of its decorations, the ceilings and panels of the ballroom being painted after the style of Raphael's loggias. Masquerades were given here, and in 1784, Lunardi's famous balloon was exhibited. It was fitted up as an opera house after the destruction of the King's Theatre. Curious to relate, in 1792, just after the company had vacated the Pantheon, it was burned to the ground. It was rebuilt on the old plan; but in 1811 was reconstructed after the model of the great theatre at Milan, for the

The exterior of the old King's Theatre, according to a print still extant, was unworthy of the architect of Blenheim: it was a dull, heavy building of red brick, roofed with black glazed tiles, and having a frontage only thirty-five feet in width; with its three circular-headed doors and windows it looked more like a meeting-house than a theatre. And now let us turn to the interesting *Musical Reminiscences of Lord Mount Edgcumbe* for a picture of the old and new house, and of the old and new régime. Writing of the former he says: "The boxes were then much larger and more commodious than they are now. . . . The front was then occupied by open public boxes, or an amphitheatre (as it is called in French theatres), communicating with the pit. Both of these were filled exclusively with the highest classes of society, all, without exception, in full dress, then universally worn. The audiences thus assembled were considered as indisputably presenting a finer spectacle than any other theatre in Europe, and absolutely astonished the foreign performers, to whom such a sight was entirely new. At the end of the performance the company of the pit and boxes repaired to the coffee-room, which was then the best assembly in London, private ones being rarely given on opera nights; and all the first society was regularly to be seen there. Over the front box was the five-shilling gallery, then resorted to by respectable persons not in full dress; and above that an upper gallery, to which the admission was three shillings. Subsequently the house was encircled with private boxes, yet still the prices remained

performance of Italian comic operas. The stage was ninety feet deep and fifty-six wide, and the pit held 1,200 people. It was opened on February 25th, 1812, with Tom Dibdin's opera, *The Cabinet*, at opera prices. But the speculation failed, and two years afterwards scenery, fittings, all were sold off, and the licence was never again renewed.

the same, and the pit preserved its respectability, and even grandeur, till the old house was burned down in 1789."

"Formerly," he continues, "every lady possessing an opera box considered it as much her home as her house, and was as sure to be found there, few missing any of the performances. If prevented from going, the *loan* of her box and the gratuitous use of the tickets was a favour always cheerfully offered and thankfully received, as a matter of course, without any idea of payment. Then, too, it was a favour to ask gentlemen to belong to a box, when subscribing to one was actually advantageous. Now no lady can propose to them to give her more than double the price of admission at the door, so that, having paid so exorbitantly, everyone is glad to be reimbursed at least a part of the great expense which she must often support alone. Boxes and tickets are therefore no longer given, they are let for what can be got; for which traffic the circulating libraries afford an easy accommodation. Many, too, which are not taken for the season, are disposed of in the same manner, and are almost put up to auction, their price varying from three to eight or even ten guineas, according to the performance of the evening or other accidental circumstances."

The foundation-stone of the second King's Theatre was laid by the Right Honourable John Hobart, Earl of Buckinghamshire, on April 3rd, 1790; the architect was Michael Novosielski, and the building was opened on the 26th of March, 1791, but only with a music and dancing licence, and no legal status could be obtained for the house until after the burning down of the Pantheon in the following year; that place of amusement having, while the company performed there, assumed the title of the King's Theatre, and appropriated the patent. Mr. O'Reilly, the manager of the Oxford Street house, had contracted debts to the amount of £30,000, and it was arranged by a committee, over which the Prince of Wales presided, that these liabilities should be taken over by the shareholders of the new theatre in order to get back the original licence. This was a crushing burden to begin with, and sank more than one enterprising manager.

During the three seasons that the new Drury Lane was building the company performed here,[1] after which the house was given up entirely to opera.

The great *prime donne* of the first twelve years of the new house were Mara, Banti, Grassini, and Mrs. Billington; while from 1804 to 1806 inclusive, Braham was a leading tenor. Lord Mount Edgcumbe, an unexceptionable judge, pronounced Banti to have been the most "delightful singer" he ever heard. She died at Bologna in 1806, and left her larynx, which was of extraordinary size, to be preserved in a bottle in the museum of that town. Mrs. Billington was a beautiful singer, but an indifferent actress. She had received a careful training in Italy, and her vocal powers were greatly appreciated there. Once, however, she nearly fell a victim to the superstition of the people. While singing at Naples an eruption of Vesuvius burst forth; the Neapolitans, thinking it a judgment upon them for countenancing an English heretic, were about to spring upon the stage and seize her, when fortunately the eruption ceased and their fury melted into enthusiastic applause.

Mara retired in 1794; Banti, as we have seen, died

[1] Dramatic performances had been frequently given in the old house. Spranger Barry opened it in 1766, etc.

in 1806; the same year witnessed the last appearance of Grassini in England and the retirement of Mrs. Billington. The last-named lady took Mozart's *Clemenza di Tito* for her benefit. It was the first time the great composer's music was heard in London. The principal parts were sung by the *bénéficiaire* and Braham. But the Italians of the company neither understood nor relished the music, one of the concerted pieces being more difficult to study than half a dozen whole operas of the Italian school. So after a few repetitions this fine opera was laid aside and neglected. It had been produced by the suggestion of the Prince of Wales, who seems to have been the only Englishman at that time capable of appreciating Mozart's genius, and the score was supplied from his own library. The same season Braham quitted the Italian stage and devoted himself entirely to English music. Thus five of the constellations of the Opera House disappeared almost simultaneously.

It was, however, in that same year, 1806, that Madame Catalani, who had already won golden opinions on the Continent, first appeared in London. Passing through Paris on her way to England, she sang before Napoleon, who was greatly delighted with her. "Where are you going," he demanded, "that you wish to leave Paris?" "To London, sire," she replied. "You must remain in Paris," was the peremptory rejoinder. "You will be well paid and your talents better appreciated here; 10,000 francs a year, two months' leave of absence. That is settled. Adieu." The lady, however, contrived to escape across the Channel and to fulfil her engagement. Her terms were 2,000 guineas for the season. But the next year she increased them to 5,000 guineas. The manager objected that it left him nothing for his other artists. "What do you want else when you have my wife's talent?" demanded her husband, Valabrèque. "She and four or five puppets (*poupées*) are enough." And that was all the public got, and for a time it sufficed to crowd the theatre. Finally, her terms became so enormous that managers, especially when the public began to grow tired of "the four or five puppets," even with Madame, feared to incur the responsibility of engaging her. How history repeats itself. Does not this read like a reminiscence of a celebrated songstress of our own day? Catalani left the King's Theatre in 1813, and after that was heard chiefly at concerts. She gained by these entertainments £10,000 in one season of four months in London, and doubled that sum in a tour through the English provinces, Scotland, and Ireland. Yet even these sums are moderate when compared with Patti's earnings.

Catalani herself seems to have been a simple-minded, good-natured creature, and more than one story is told of her charitable disposition. But her husband was a low-bred, avaricious fellow. He called her his *poule d'or*, which she certainly was to him. Captain Gronow relates in his *Reminiscences* that when she was at Stowe, Valabrèque sent in a bill to the Marquis of Buckingham for seventeen hundred pounds for seventeen songs his wife had sung in company, although she was on the footing of a guest. But he was usually left behind when she was invited to distinguished houses. She is described by contemporaries as being very beautiful, not a great actress, but making up for all deficiencies by the charm of her manner. Her voice, Captain Gronow says, "was transcendent." But she appears to have preferred to astonish her audience by extraordinary feats of execution, such as leaping two octaves at once, and by the most florid *fioturi*, rather than pleasing them by purity of style. These faults, as an inevitable consequence, increased with time. One of her favourite feats was to sing the "Non più andrai" of *Figaro*, and by mere force of lungs and volume of voice to rise above all the brass of the orchestra. Her last appearance in opera took place in 1824, in Mayer's *Il Fanatico per la Musica;* but she cut out everything that did not tend to the display of her *bravura* powers, and walked through the part without condescending to act. Each night the audience grew thinner, until she finally withdrew from the stage. Her last appearance in public was at Dublin in 1828.

Between 1804 and 1807 a Mr. Goold was the manager of the King's Theatre. At his death, in the year last named, it again came into the hands of Taylor, to whom I have previously referred. Taylor was always in debt and difficulties, and, during the greater part of the time that he was director, lived within the King's Bench or its "rules." "How can you conduct the King's Theatre, perpetually in durance as you are?" remarked a friend. "My dear fellow," replied the manager, "how could I possibly conduct it if I were at liberty? I should be eaten up, sir—devoured. Here comes a dancer—'Mr. Taylor, I want such a dress'; another—'I want such and such ornaments.' One singer demands to sing a part different from the one allotted to him, another to have an addition to his appointments. No; let me be shut up, and then they go to my secretary; he, they know, cannot go beyond his line, but if they get at *me*—pshaw! no man at large can manage that theatre; and, in faith, no man who undertakes it ought to be at large."

Taylor had a partner named Waters, who was Goold's executor; between the two, as affairs grew worse, there were continual disagreements. At length Taylor closed the theatre. Waters tried to get possession, but Taylor's people resisted. Free fights were of constant occurrence, until the former at length succeeded in forcing an entrance. This was in 1813. Waters carried on the management from 1814 to 1820, when, overwhelmed by debt, he was compelled to retire. The house was then taken by Mr. Ebers, a bookseller, who gave to the world his experiences of its management in a volume entitled, *Seven Years of the King's Theatre.* During that period he never lost a less sum than £3,000 in a season, frequently considerably more. Thus, from its establishment in this country, we find that Italian opera, spite of the fashionable patronage which had always been accorded it, was not only an unprofitable, but a ruinous speculation to all who undertook it.

The following passages, however, extracted from a theatrical magazine of the period are very suggestive as to the cause of Mr. Ebers's failure, and are extremely important as describing the style in which operas were put upon the stage of the King's Theatre in 1823:—

"It is with feelings of the liveliest indignation that we direct the attention of our readers to the continuance of disreputable abuses, which render this magnificent establishment a living monument of national dishonour. When a foreigner views the imposing exterior of the opera-house, its numerous columns, its splendid piazzas, and its colossal dimensions, he reasonably expects that the interior will exhibit corresponding attractions, and hurries to the theatre buoyant with the hope of anticipated delight. He pays his half-guinea, and is introduced into this fancied temple of elegance and grandeur. The filthy condition of the corridors, where the dirt of ages reposes in undisturbed tranquillity, secure from the lustrations of a scrubbing-brush, soon convinces our enthusiast that no lord of the vestibule protects the flowing train of a countess from plebeian pollution. He hurries on and fixes his gaze on that venerable specimen of the antique, the drop-curtain, whose faded hues and tarnished dinginess are only surpassed by the murky sails of a coal-lighter. The indulgent spectator overlooks these glaring violations of common decency, and recollecting that the musical department is under the direction of a committee of noblemen of acknowledged taste and ample fortune, he makes sure that this union of talent and wealth will procure him the highest treat that a *fanatico per musica* can possibly desire. But here again he is doomed to disappointment; his high-wrought expectations terminate in a mixed feeling of scorn, contempt, and indignation. This is no fanciful picture, but a feeble attempt at delineating the various emotions which a foreigner experiences at the wretched want of effective management in the King's Theatre." The writer then goes on to animadvert upon the badness of the singers, the lack of variety in the operas produced, broken promises, and general incompetence.

A month or two afterwards the same journal comments very strongly upon the curtain being rung down and the lights put out in the middle of the ballet. It might have been want of means to carry on the management properly that was at the bottom of these terrible shortcomings, but it was certainly hopeless to expect public patronage for such an ill-directed establishment.

In 1818 the auditorium of the King's Theatre was reconstructed and modelled in the form in which many of us remember it, by Nash and Repton, who, in 1820, added the colonnades, the entire alteration costing £50,000. The shape was horse-shoe; in dimensions it was within a few feet of La Scala. Its length from the curtain to the back of the boxes was 102 feet; the extreme width, 75 feet; the stage was 60 feet long and 80 feet wide. The subscription to the new theatre was increased to sixty representations, and the charges to thirty guineas a seat. But during Catalani's engagement the price of a box to hold six was advanced from 180 guineas to 300.

Although the first two decades of the last century were not very remarkable for great singers, they were peculiarly rich in great works. Catalani introduced Mozart's *Le Nozze di Figaro*, being herself the original Susanna in London.[1] In 1811 the immortal composer's *Cosi fan tutte* was heard for the first time, and received with unbounded delight. *Il Flauto Magico* followed, but the company was inadequate to the interpretation of this difficult work, and it failed. The year 1817 should be marked with a red letter in operatic annals, since it witnessed the production of the incomparable *Don Giovanni*, brought out in the teeth of a strong cabal and immense difficulties. Its success was triumphant. It was played twenty-three nights to overflowing houses, and restored the exhausted treasury to a flourishing condition. The original cast embraced Madame Camporese, Madame Fodor, Signors Crivelli, Ambrogetti,[2] Naldi, and Agrisani. In the same year Madame Pasta, then a mere girl, no older than the century, made her début, but

[1] Madame Vestris sang the part here in 1816, in the purest style of Italian vocalisation, it is said.

[2] Ambrogetti was a great artiste; being cast for the part of the Father in an operatic version of Mrs. Opie's *Father and Daughter*, called *Agnese*, he studied in Bedlam every form of madness. But his acting was so terrible that the public could not endure it, and the opera failed through the very greatness of the performance. The realism that in our time has drawn crowds to see *Drink* and *Resurrection* was not appreciated a hundred years ago.

seems to have given little indication of her future pre-eminent genius, and created no attention. With the appearance of Signor Garcia in 1818 began the reign of Rossini, he introducing the *Barbière*, the first opera of that composer heard in England. From 1821 to 1828, fourteen out of the thirty-four operas sung were by the great Italian *maestro;* Mozart came next. Rossini visited London in 1824 to conduct his opera of *Zelmira.* Madame Rossini, a singer of great eminence in Italy, sustained the principal part; but, although she was still beautiful in person and grand in style, she was *passée*, and was coldly received. It was her last appearance upon the stage.

In 1825, Velluti, the last of the male soprani, appeared. Thirty years had elapsed since this class of voice had been heard by the English public. So strong were the prejudices entertained against the new singer that it was only after much hesitation that the management decided to permit his appearance. Lord Mount Edgcumbe describes the event:—

"At the moment when he was expected to appear, the most profound silence reigned in one of the most crowded audiences I ever saw, broken on his entering by loud applauses of encouragement. The first note he uttered gave a shock of surprise, almost of disgust, to inexperienced ears; but his performance was listened to with attention and great applause throughout, with but few expressions of disapprobation, speedily suppressed. The opera he chose for his début was *Il Crociato in Egitto*, by a German composer named Meyerbeer, till then unknown in this country. The music was quite of the new school, but not copied from Rossini; it was original, odd, flighty, and might even be termed fantastic."

Might not this be the mild criticism of an old gentleman of a dozen years ago upon Wagner? His lordship's remarks upon Rossini's works, in which he complains of the sudden change of motives, the absence of airs, and the noisy instrumentation, so different from the thin melodious operas of his youth, are equally suggestive. Rossini and Meyerbeer were to him what Wagner was to his grandchildren.

Ebers's unfortunate seven years terminated in 1827, after which the house, at a rental of £800 per annum, passed into the hands of Laporte and Laurent, who continued the management through good and evil fortune until 1842. At the accession of Victoria, the King's Theatre was renamed Her Majesty's.

From 1824 to 1846 was the golden age of opera in this country, if not for the *impresarii*, at least for the public, as between those two dates the lyric drama was interpreted by artists such as, perhaps, those of no other period in its history can compare. Pasta reappeared in 1824, when she was at the height of those marvellous powers that rendered her the greatest lyric artist the world has ever heard. "Pasta," says Hogarth, "was what a musical performer ought to be, but is so very seldom—a complete impersonation of the character she assumed. We thought not of admiring the great vocalist; we even forgot that it was Pasta who stood before us while we were thrilled with horror by the frenzy of the desperate Medea, or wept for the sorrows of the lovelorn Nina" (Paiesello's *Nina*). After a long and, as it had been supposed, final retirement from the stage, she reappeared for one night in 1850 in selections from *Anna Bullena*. The melancholy scene is admirably pictured by Mr. Chorley. Her toilet was neglected, her hair absurdly dressed, as, indeed, was her whole figure. Among the audience was Rachel, who cruelly and openly ridiculed the whole performance, and Madame Viardot, then in the height of her fame, came to hear Pasta for the first time. "She attempted the final mad scene of the opera, the most complicated and brilliant among the mad scenes on the modern stage, an example of vocal display till then unparalleled. By that time, tired, unprepared, in ruin as she was, she had rallied a little. When, on Anne Boleyn's hearing the coronation music for her rival, the heroine searches for her own crown upon her brow, Madame Pasta wildly turned in the direction of the festive sounds, the old irresistible charm broke out; nay, even in the final song, with its roulades and its scales of shakes ascending by a semitone, the consummate vocalist and tragedian was able to combine form with meaning, the moment of the situation was indicated at least to the younger artist. 'You are right,' was Madame Viardot's quick and heartfelt response (her eyes full of tears) to a friend beside her. 'You are right. It is like the *Cenacolo* of Da Vinci at Milan—a wreck of a picture, but the picture is the greatest in the world.'"

Sontag came to London in 1828, but her Berlin (she was a Prussian by birth) and Paris idolaters had aroused such marvellous expectations in the English public that she was a disappointment. Gradually, however, a reaction took place, and ere the season was over she had become an established favourite. Upon her marriage with Count Rossi, a Piedmontese noble, she retired from the stage. The revolution of 1848 stripping him of his possessions, she again resumed her profession, reappearing at Her Majesty's during the seasons of 1849–50; and, most curious to relate, although now a middle-aged woman, appealing to a new generation of opera-goers, and immediately following Jenny Lind, her second success was as brilliant as her first. Her style, like Catalani's, was excessively florid; she excelled in light opera.

The year after Sontag's début, 1829, a yet greater artiste made her bow before an English public—Madame Malibran, the original Amina in this country. Someone—Chorley, I think—has felicitously called her the Garrick of the Italian stage, to mark her great diversity of style as compared with Pasta, whom he calls the Siddons of opera. A romantic pathos hovers around the memory of this glorious artiste. Her history was a sad one: a harsh father (Garcia) in her childhood, an unhappy marriage with a man double her age in her girlhood, and then her early death at twenty-eight, just after she was united to De Begnis, the man of her choice. In private life she was as warm-hearted and generous as she was great in public. "Boundless as were Malibran's resources, keen as was her intelligence, dazzling as was her genius, she never produced a single type in opera for other women to adopt. She passed over the stage like a meteor, as an apparition of wonder rather than as one who, on her departure, left her mantle behind for others to take up and wear."

Each season now brought forth a new prodigy. In 1830 appeared Lablache, whose first part was Geronimo in *Il Matrimonio Segreto*. "Musical history," says Chorley, "contains no account of a bass singer so gifted by nature, so accomplished by art, so popular without measure or drawbacks, as Louis Lablache. His shoe was as big as a child's boat, one could have clad a child in one of his gloves," and yet, he goes on to say, that so perfectly artistic was he in dress and bearing that the spectator was never shocked by his abnormal size.

Rubini created immense enthusiasm upon his appearance in 1831. The fascination of his voice was irresistible; even his brother artistes would linger at the wings while he was singing, loth to lose a single note. The compass of his voice was marvellous; he could begin on the high B flat without preparation, and hold on it for a considerable time. At Milan the people flocked in crowds to hear this wonderful effect, and never failed to encore it. One night, raising his eyes to heaven, extending his arms, inflating his chest, and opening his mouth, he endeavoured as usual to give forth the wonderful note. But B flat would not come. Greatly disconcerted, the tenor brought all the force of his splendid lungs into play and gave it forth with immense vigour. But he could feel that he had in some way injured himself. He went through the performance, however, as brilliantly as ever. When it was over he sent for a surgeon, who very soon discovered that he had broken his collar-bone—it had been unable to resist the tension of his lungs. "Can a man go on singing with a broken clavicle?" he inquired. "Certainly," replied the doctor; "and if you take care not to lift any weight, you will experience no disagreeable effects." And he did go on singing for years afterwards.

Tamburini appeared in 1832, Grisi in 1834, Persiani in 1838, and Mario in 1839. Out of this combination was formed the world-famous *Puritani* quartette, Rubini, Lablache, Tamburini, and Grisi; such a one had never before been approached upon the lyric stage, and probably never will be again. In 1842 a noble artiste burst upon the town, Miss Adelaide Kemble, "the greatest English singer (though not the best of this century)," says Chorley, "a poetical and thoughtful artiste, whose name will never be lost as long as the art of dramatic singing is spoken of." He says that in

Norma she could compare with Pasta, and could be preferred (apart from voice and person) to Grisi. "In comedy, her Susanna was good enough for any opera-house in Europe, no matter how high the standard."

Tamburini's name is inextricably associated with what may be regarded as the last of the theatrical riots. The favourite baritone had been superseded by an inferior artiste named Colletti, upon which his colleagues of the theatre organised a clique to compel his re-engagement, and enlisted upon their side the fashionable part of the audience. On Colletti's appearance he was saluted with a storm of hisses from the omnibus boxes, and shouts of "Tamburini!" Laporte appeared, but could not make himself heard. At length the noble occupants of one of the boxes, headed by a Prince of the Blood, still living, leaped upon the stage, the curtain fell, the invaders waving their hats, shouted "Victory!" and Laporte was obliged to give way. The affair is the subject of one of the Ingoldsby Legends, "The row in an omnibus box." At the death of Laporte, in 1842, Her Majesty's passed under the direction of Mr. Lumley, who had been concerned in the previous management. The event of his first season was the début of Ronconi, who, in the greatness of his acting, rivalled even Lablache, and that with a voice limited in compass, inferior in quality, and possessing little power of execution; added to these drawbacks were a low stature and commonplace features. He was the original Rigoletto in London. Verdi was heard for the first time in this country in *Ernani*, in 1845. People hardly knew what to make of the new style, and its reception was anything but cordial.

Early in 1846 there rose a rumour that a new opera speculation was to be initiated at Covent Garden. A disagreement between Lumley and his conductor Costa, ended in all except one of "la vieille garde"—Grisi, Mario, Tamburini, Costa and Lablache—seceding from Her Majesty's, and opening, under Persiani's husband, the great dramatic house for opera. The one who alone remained true to the old theatre was the great basso.

Never was such acrimony, such furious disputes, or such an unscrupulous paper war carried on between two rival establishments as marked the commencement of the operatic year of 1847. Both houses appear to have suffered severely by the competition; Madame Persiani was ill and unable to appear through the losses sustained by her husband. And Lumley seems to have been in little better plight, when the appearance of Jenny Lind suddenly raised his fortunes to the very pinnacle of success.

Bunn had engaged "the Swedish Nightingale" in 1845 to appear at Drury Lane. Lumley, however, protested that Her Majesty's was the only place in London at which she could make her début, and so induced her to sign another agreement. Bunn was offered £2,000 to cancel his arrangement, which he refused; but afterwards so terrified her by letters and paragraphs in the public papers, that she feared to set her foot on English ground. Late one night Lumley started for Vienna; as ruin was close upon him, he was ready to undertake any obligation to get her over, and after binding himself to pay all damages[1] that she might incur through her breach of faith with Bunn, at last succeeded in securing his prize. The contest between the three managements, for Covent Garden was backing up Drury Lane, raised the expectations of the public to fever heat.

[1] When the case was tried, Bunn, who put his damages at £10,000, was awarded by the jury £2,500.

A new complication arose when the Lord Chamberlain refused to license *Roberto Il Diavalo*, in which she had arranged to appear. This difficulty, however, was overcome, and the eventful night at length arrived.

"Rarely," says Lumley, in his *Reminiscences*, "was ever seen such excitement at Her Majesty's Theatre. The crowd at the doors might have led to a suspicion of an *émeute* in a capital less orderly than London; and the struggle for entrance was violent beyond precedent—so violent, indeed, that the phrase 'a Jenny Lind crush' became a proverbial expression. Nor was this crowd the result of a hasty gathering. From an early hour in the afternoon, the Haymarket became so thronged as to be impassable to pedestrians. As to the file of carriages, it seemed as interminable as it was dense." Describing the performance, Chorley says: "She appeared as Alice in *Robert* (it was the first representation of Meyerbeer's opera in Italian in this country), an appearance not to be risked by any singer the least nervous. The girl, dragged hastily down the stage in the midst of a crowd, has at once, and when out of breath, to begin on an accented note, without time to think or look around her. I have never seen anyone so composed as Mdlle. Lind on that night. Though the thunder of welcome was loud and long enough to stop the orchestra and to bewilder a veteran, and though it was acknowledged with due modesty, her hands did not tremble—one even arranged a ring on the finger of the other—and her voice spoke out as firmly as if neither fear nor failure was possible. . . . The scenes of Alice, thoroughly well given and perfectly suited to the powers of their giver, were waited for, listened to in breathless silence, and received with applause which was neither encouragement, nor appreciation, nor enthusiasm, so much as idolatry. Woe to those during that season who ventured to say or to write that any other great singer had ever sung in the Haymarket Opera House! To my cost, I know they were consigned to such ignominy as belongs to the idiotic slanderer. Old and seemingly solid friendships were broken, and for ever, in that year."

But Mdlle. Lind was only a shooting star. Prudery and certain religious scruples with which she had become imbued through sanctimonious friends and episcopal patrons determined her to quit the stage, and there were great wailings and weepings, and a tremendous demonstration when, on May 18th, 1849, the wonderful songstress, but doubtful artiste, made her last bow behind the footlights.

Sophie Cruvelli, who had fled overwhelmed by the Swedish vocalist's success, returned, and Madame Sontag, as before mentioned, stepped into the breach and kept Lumley's fortunes afloat a little longer.

In 1848, Mr. Sims Reeves made his first appearance at the Italian Opera as Carlo, in *Linda di Chamouni*, and was received with enthusiasm, but, in consequence of a disagreement with the management, he appeared but once. He reappeared in the next season with Miss Catherine Hayes in *Lucia di Lammermoor* as Edgardo.[1] In 1849 he sang Elvino in *La Somnambula*, and in the next year, Ernani. He was a superb artiste and a great singer, but though highly successful at the Italian Opera, it is in English opera and oratorio that he will be chiefly remembered.

The year 1851 was marked by the first production of Beethoven's *Fidelio* in this country; Cruvelli being the

[1] He had sung this part at Drury Lane in 1847, after making a great success in it that same year at La Scala. Berlioz, who was the conductor at Drury Lane, was very enthusiastic about the English tenor.

original Fidelio—a magnificent performance. In 1852 the struggle between the two houses ended in the discomfiture of Her Majesty's, and landed Lumley in the bankruptcy court.

The theatre now remained closed until the burning of Covent Garden in 1856, upon which Lumley once more became director of the old house; but he was terribly handicapped by Lord Ward, who, at the time of his bankruptcy, had bought in the theatrical properties, and now required him to make over the lease of the house as security. Fortune, however, returned to him with the advent of Giuglini, the last of the pure Italian tenors, and of that exquisite vocalist and actress Piccolomini, who, in *La Traviata*, created a furore second only to Jenny Lind. The début of Titiens in 1858, as Valentine in *Les Huguenots*, roused great excitement, both out of doors and behind the scenes. Even the rehearsals became exciting events. "As her powerful voice," says Lumley, "rang through the theatre and excited the plaudits of all present, so the latent fire of Giuglini (the Raoul) became kindled in its turn, and, one artiste vying with the other in power and passion of musical declamation, each rehearsal became a brilliant performance. Indeed, so strongly were both artistes and connoisseurs impressed with the merits of Mdlle. Titiens, that fears were expressed lest she should utterly 'swamp' the favourite tenor. 'He will never be able to come up to that powerful voice in the last act,' said one. I foresaw that their fears were groundless, and the result proved I was right, for in his personation of Raoul, Giuglini raised himself to the pinnacle of his profession." The success at night was magnificent; the Queen was present, and, upon leaving her box, told the *impresario* that it was beautiful. And those who can remember Teresa Titiens in this opera will more than endorse that verdict; physically she was anything but an ideal Valentine, but by the power of her genius, in the great duet, she literally transformed herself, and cast such a glamour over the spectator that one saw not a big and somewhat coarse-looking woman, but a heroic girl. As Norma, Lucrezia Borgia, Fidelio, as Anna, and in other parts, her acting was as magnificent as her vocalisation. I can personally remember a striking instance of her power over the audience. When *Lohengrin* was first produced at Her Majesty's, Titiens was the Ortruda. The Wagnerites strenuously put down every attempt at applause during the action of the first act. But early in the second, after the meeting between Elsa and Ortruda, and the latter burst forth into the invocation to the infernal gods, such was the extraordinary power of the great prima donna, of her attitude, as she threw up her arms, of her splendid organ as it rose like a trumpet blast above the crash of the instrumentation, that all else was forgotten, and the whole house burst forth into a roar of applause. Giuglini possessed a voice of entrancing beauty, its liquid sweetness was incomparable; but his career was very brief, he died the victim of his own popularity.

Lumley finally retired in 1858, and in 1860, E. T. Smith, giving the *impresario*, who had gone over to Boulogne out of the reach of his creditors, £16,000 for "the goodwill," added Her Majesty's Theatre to his numerous speculations—for one year. He opened, in April, with English opera, brought out Macfarren's *Robin Hood*, with Sims Reeves and a very competent cast, and signalised his brief management by producing on Boxing Night the first pantomime, *Tom Thumb*, ever seen upon this stage.[1] On the 26th of April, 1862, Mapleson, who had been E. T. Smith's acting manager, undertook the direction of the house. During the winter season of 1864, the Pyne and Harrison Company occupied the theatre, and followed up their predecessor's experiment by adding a Christmas pantomime to their other attractions.[2]

It was in the season of 1867, the year in which the house was burned to the ground, that that glorious artiste, Christine Nilsson, made her début here as Margherita, and achieved a triumph. Personally, at least, Gounod's heroine never had so ideal a representative; the slender, graceful figure, the fair hair, the beautiful, dreamy, northern face, with its deep-set, grey-blue eyes, the exquisite voice, that thrilled like a silver bell, the poetry and passion of her acting were all that could be conceived of the creation of Gounod's music. Her Violetta, her Mignon, her Alice, her Desdemona (in Rossini's *Otello*) were all wonderfully beautiful performances. Among her greatest successes was the double rôle of Margherita and Helen in Boito's *Mefistofele*. I never heard wilder enthusiasm than she roused in the prison scene, after her solo and the duet with

[1] Arditi told a good tale of his showman proclivities. One Oaks day, when he was the *impresario* of Her Majesty's, he invited Arditi, Titiens, Giuglini, and one or two others, to drive down to Epsom with him. A drag and a spanking turn-out were provided. It was noticed, as they drove along the road, that the conveyance excited a great deal of attention; everybody stared at it and made remarks as it passed. During a halt, Giuglini happened to pass round at the back of the drag, and there to his horror he saw a board on which were inscribed in glaring letters the words, "E. T. Smith's Operatic Company." There were ructions, and everyone refused to go a step further until the advertisement was removed.

[2] Falconer opened the house in November, 1866, with *Oonagh*, the longest play on record. At *two o'clock* on the *Sunday* morning, the stage carpenters pulled the carpet from underneath the feet of the actors; before they could scramble to their feet someone rang down the curtain, and the play was never finished.

Campanini, as Faust, who was that night in fine form; men sprang up on their seats, and cheered in a babel of tongues, and waved their hats, and ladies their pocket-handkerchiefs, in indescribable excitement.

But I have advanced far into the chronicles of the new house.

Before pursuing the story of the opera further, I must retrace my steps to give some account of the sister art, which for some years not only shared in importance with the lyric, but at one time threatened almost to supersede it.

The opera ballet dates in this country from 1734, when Mademoiselle Sallé appeared at Covent Garden and created a wonderful furore. On her benefit night men fought their way to the doors sword in hand, and when she took her leave, purses of gold and bonbons of guineas were showered upon the stage.[1] Contemporaries are enthusiastic in their praise of her acting as Galatea in the ballet of *Pygmalion and Galatea.* After her departure there was a long pause before her successor appeared. On the Continent the rage for this graceful form of entertainment compelled opera composers to introduce the *danseur* and *danseuse* into all their works, however inappropriate might be their presence.[2] "You must write me the music for a *chacone* to this," said Vestris the eldest (*le dieu de danse*, as he called himself) to Glück, when the latter was writing the *Iphigenia in Tauris.* "Do you think the Greeks knew anything

[1] Yet twenty years later, when Garrick brought a troupe of French dancers to Drury Lane, there was a riot among the pittites, and after the performance, they marched to Southampton Street and broke his windows. But the opera in those days was exclusively patronised by the aristocracy.

[2] The ballet was popular in Italy as early as the beginning of the sixteenth century; it was introduced into France by Catherine de Medicis, and was in vogue all over Europe in the seventeenth century.

about a *chacone?*" answered Glück indignantly. "Did they not?" exclaimed Vestris, with a look of astonishment; "how I pity them!"

Our continual wars with France rendered it very difficult to get good dancers, for in that country alone was there thorough training in this art. Sometimes the Parisians let us have a *danseuse* whose popularity was on the wane, such as Mademoiselle Guimard, who appeared at the King's Theatre in 1789. Lord Mount Edgcumbe says that, "although sixty years of age, she was full of grace, and danced most exquisitely." But the lady was not nearly so old as his lordship represents, having been born in 1743. Madeleine Guimard was a noble woman as well as a fine artiste, and during the terrible distress that preceded the revolution, spent a large portion of her earnings in relieving the starving people, and this without breathing a word to anyone of her charitable deeds. The wars with the Republic and the Empire entirely cut off our supplies of Parisian *danseuses* for the next twenty years and more; and even for some time after the peace the French were very loth to allow *perfide Albion* to have any but second-class artistes whom they did not care to keep, and as the opera-dancers were trained by an academy under the immediate control of a Minister, none could leave the country without permission.

Upon becoming lessee of the Opera House, in 1821, Mr. Ebers resolved to make a desperate effort to bring over some of the stars of the Parisian ballet. Of such importance were these negotiations, that they had to be conducted through the medium of the English ambassador at Paris, who put himself in communication with the Baron de la Ferté, the Intendant of the Theatres. The artistes especially desired were the then reigning favourites of the dance — Albert and Noblet. The Intendant received the application with all suavity, but threw every possible obstacle in the way of granting it. After, however, as much duplicity and diplomacy as might have been required to bring about a treaty between two hostile nations, it was arranged that the desired ones should be spared to Albion for two months. For their services, Albert was to receive £50 for each performance, and Noblet £550 for the entire engagement; in addition to which, £25 was to be allowed each for the expenses of the journey. Two other celebrated dancers, Coulon and Bias, were engaged upon the same terms, together with three others, two males at £430 and £240 each, and a lady at £270. The incense offered to Noblet might have turned any female brain. She was run after by the aristocracy, invited everywhere, literally worshipped; she was the universal theme of conversation; the fashionable world could think of nothing else. The Earl of Fife, then one of the principal patrons of the opera, placed a carriage at her disposal during her stay, and every Sunday gave dinner-parties in her honour.

No sooner were her rehearsals announced than all the men of fashion, and all who were, or would be thought, judges of the graceful, eagerly solicited for admission to them, paying for the privilege as at a regular representation. Nor was the curiosity confined to the gentlemen; ladies of the first rank and fashion found their way to the theatre, and participated in the interest excited by the new arrivals.

These children of Terpsichore, being so splendidly received, did not care to leave their comfortable quarters at the expiration of the given time. Upon which there was great excitement .in Paris; the perfidy of Albion had this time passed beyond the limits of endurance, since it treacherously desired to deprive France even of its dancers. Urgent remonstrances were made by the French Academy, and the Baron de la Ferté sent over a special envoy to negotiate the return of the recalcitrants. After a very heated correspondence, it was arranged that they should remain in London until the end of the season, and that henceforth two first and two second dancers should be allowed to come over every season from the schools of the Academy, and that in return a pledge must be given that no dancer should be brought from Paris contrary to the wishes of the Academy. A treaty to this effect was drawn up in full form, signed, sealed, and witnessed.

From this year, 1821, considerably more than a hundred and fifty years after the Continent, however, the ballet rose to the dignity of an institution. In the accounts of the season, Mr. Ebers stated that while the opera cost £8,636, the expenses of the ballet were £10,678. The prima donna, Madame Camporese, an immense favourite and a fine singer, received only £1,650 for the season, while the principal male dancer, Albert, was paid £1,785, and the *première danseuse*, Noblet, £1,537. There was the same discrepancy throughout. De Begnis and his wife Ronzi de Begnis, Madame Vestris, and Ambrogetti, all fine artistes, received but £600 each; while two second dancers, Bias and Deshayes, were paid respectively £650 and £930. It had been stipulated in the first treaty that, at the end of Albert and Noblet's engagement, two other dancers of equal fame, Paul and Anatole, should take their places; consequently, when the former arranged to remain until the end of the season, the manager found himself saddled with double expenses, which, to gratify his aristocratic patrons, he had to endure. In addition to the salaries before stated, Paul took £1,200 for half the season, Anatole £1,300, and the Vestrises, the dancers, father and son, £1,200. The most curious feature in these accounts is the enormous sums paid to a class of artistes who have wholly disappeared—the male dancers, who actually received larger salaries than the *danseuse.* No ballet was possible without their assistance, and many of them were not only consummate pantomimists, but very beautiful executants. Albert is said to have been the most graceful dancer that was ever seen at the London opera, while Paul "seemed literally to fly as he bounded from the stage, so light and zephyry were his motions."

Yet the ballets were as wretchedly mounted as the operas. Ebers himself writes: "The same scenes, the same dresses, and the same decorations figured in every performance, till the eye was wearied and the imagination disgusted by seeing different countries and ages all exhibiting the same scenes and costumes. Nor was the scarcity of dresses confined to the *coryphées* and *figurantes* of the ballet and the inferior characters of the opera; the *premiers sujets* were as sparingly appointed. Every other theatre gave correct scenery and costume, with every possible degree of magnificence; it was only at the opera scenes and dresses were mean and inappropriate." He mentions it as worthy of particular note that he introduced repeated changes of dress in the same performance, and that in the ballet of *Aline* the dresses were three times varied.

But it was not until the advent of the world-famous Taglioni and Fanny Elssler that the ballet attained its highest development and popularity. A critic happily defined Taglioni as the poetry, Elssler as the wit of motion. Their style was entirely different. Nothing like the chaste and exquisite movements of the former in *La Sylphide*, *La Fille de Danube*, *Giselle*, *L'Ombre* have ever been seen before or since. But Elssler was more than a *danseuse*—"she was the only artist of the century, perhaps, who combined in so striking a degree the two talents of actress and dancer."

"Nothing in execution was too daring for her, nothing too pointed," says Chorley in his *Musical Recollections*. "If Mdlle. Taglioni flew, she flashed. The one floated on to the stage like a nymph, the other showered every sparkling fascination round her like a sorceress. Her versatility, too, was complete; she had every style, every national humour under her feet—she could be Spanish for the Spaniards, or Russian for the Northerns, or Neapolitan for those who love the delicious Tarantula. But beyond these, Mdlle. Elssler, as an actress, commanded powers of high and subtle rarity."

One of her greatest triumphs was in the ballet of the *Tarantula*, which is the story of a girl who pretends to be tarantula-mad that she may dance an elderly suitor into declining her hand. "The manner in which she wrought its whimsical scenes up to a climax; the grace, the daring, the incessant brilliancy, the feverish buoyancy, and the sly humour with which she managed to let the public into the secret that her madness was only feigned, raised this ridiculous farce to the level of a work of art." In private life, it is said that the most prudish man or woman might have passed days in her society without being recalled to any recollection of the scanty stage dress, and the attitudes more fitted for sculpture than for social life; in short, by any look, gesture, or allusion belonging to the dancer's craft. In America, divines offered her their pews at meeting-houses, students serenaded her, rich men showered gold and diamonds upon her instead of bouquets.

Besides these empresses of the dance, there were queens that were scarcely inferior to them: the charming Cerito, Adèle Dumilâtre, the very incarnation of grace, and fascinating Carlotta Grisi. In 1843, Dumilâtre, in *Les Houris*, nightly crowded Fop's Alley; and in *Un Bal sous Louis XIV.*, the *minuet de la cour*, in which Elssler was her cavalier, became the rage. *Ondine* with Cerito made an equal sensation, while the divine Fanny eclipsed them all in *Le Delire d'un Peintre* and the world-famous *Cachuca*, which was ground on every organ, whistled by every boy, and attempted on the boards of every provincial theatre. And with this wonderful combination of dancers were musical stars of equal splendour—Grisi, Persiani, Mario, Lablache, etc.

On June 10th, 1843, there appeared in the theatrical news of the *Examiner* the following paragraph: "A Spanish *danseuse*, Donna Lola Montez, made her appearance between the acts of the opera on Saturday, and executed a characteristic step called 'El Olano.' The Donna was destitute of those graces which impart such a charm to the French and Italian dancers; but there was a certain intensity of expression, and, as it seemed, a certain nationality, which gave her a peculiar interest. In spite of the encouraging reception she met, she has not danced since Saturday, which remains a mystery." Such was the announcement of the first public appearance of this thereafter notorious person. Mr. Lumley accounts for "the mystery." He says the lady was introduced to him by a certain nobleman as the daughter of a celebrated Spanish patriot and martyr, and represented as a dancer of consummate ability; he very soon discovered that in both particulars he had been deceived—that she was not a Spaniard, but an Englishwoman, and, although singularly beautiful, and with a certain novelty of style, had no pretensions to the name of artiste or *danseuse.* Yet the public received her with every sign of enthusiasm. Nevertheless, he would not allow her to appear after the first two or three nights. The story told of her exit is that the *impresario* having made some disparaging remarks upon her dancing, she broke her umbrella over his head.

The novelty of 1845 was the "Viennoise" children. A dancing-mistress of Vienna had trained thirty-six little girls into a *corps de ballet.* Their marvellous success in the Austrian capital induced the English manager to offer to engage them. The Austrian authorities interposed; they feared to trust these young lambs within the wolf-fold of the heretics—at least, so it was whispered. But all difficulties were ultimately overcome, and the little ladies were allowed to appear before a London public. Their success was very great. They were splendidly trained, and executed their dances with a precision little short of marvellous. Their greatest performance was the *Pas de Miroir*, in which one division performed a very elaborate dance before a gauze intended to represent a mirror, while another set on the opposite side went through the reverse movements so accurately that the illusion of a reflected dance was perfect.

Lucille Grahn, who, the critics said, combined the ideal forms of Taglioni with the realism of Elssler and the sprightliness of Carlotta Grisi, appeared in the same season. Nor among the *danseuses* must we forget the *danseurs*, the celebrated Perrot, St. Léon, and M. Charles. The ballet of *Eoline*, with Lucille Grahn, rivalled the past popularity of the *Sylphide* and *Ondine;* and the

Mazurka d'Extase, with Perrot, excited almost as much enthusiasm as Elssler's *Pas de Fascination.* Taglioni reappeared, after an absence, that same year.

But the great event of all was the famous *Pas de Quatre.* How it was brought about must be told in the words of its projector, Mr. Lumley. "With such materials in my grasp as the four celebrated *danseuses*—Taglioni, Carlotta Grisi, Cerito, and Lucille Grahn—it was my ambition to unite them all in one striking *divertissement.* But ambition, even seconded by managerial will, scarcely sufficed to put so audacious a project into execution. The government of a great state was but a trifle compared to the government of such subjects as those whom I was *supposed* to be able to command; for these were subjects who considered themselves far above mortal control, or, more properly speaking, each was a queen in her own right—alone, absolute, supreme. . . . But there existed difficulties even beyond a manager's calculations. Material obstacles were easily overcome. When it was feared that Carlotta Grisi would not be able to leave Paris in time to rehearse and appear for the occasion, a vessel was chartered from the Steam Navigation Company to waft the sylph at a moment's notice across the Channel; a special train was engaged and ready at Dover; relays of horses were in waiting to aid the flight of the *danseuse* all the way from Paris to Calais. In the execution of the project the difficulty was again manifold. Every twinkle of each foot in every *pas* had to be nicely weighed in the balance, so as to give no preponderance. Each *danseuse* was to shine in her peculiar style and grace to the last stretch of perfection, but no one was to outshine the others unless in her own individual belief. Lastly, the famous *Pas de Quatre* was composed with all the art of which the distinguished dancing-master, Perrot, was capable. All was at length adjusted. Satisfaction was in every mind; the *Pas de Quatre* was rehearsed—was announced; the very morning of the event had arrived, no further hindrances were expected. Suddenly, while I was engaged with the lawyers in my room, poor Perrot rushed unannounced into my presence in a state of intense despair. He uttered frantic exclamations, tore his hair, and at last found breath to say all was over, that the *Pas de Quatre* had fallen to the ground, and could never be given. With difficulty the unfortunate ballet-master was calmed down to a sufficient state of reason to be able to explain the cause of his anguish. When all was ready, I had desired Perrot to regulate the order in which the separate *pas* of each *danseuse* should come. The place of honour, the *last* in such cases, as in regal processions, had been ceded without over-much hesitation to Mdlle. Taglioni. Of the remaining ladies, who claimed equal rights, founded on talent and popularity, neither would appear before the others. '*Mon Dieu!*' exclaimed the ballet-master, 'Cerito will not begin before Carlotta, nor Carlotta before Cerito; there is no way to make them stir—all is finished!' 'The solution is easy,' said I; 'let the *oldest* take her unquestionable right to the envied position.' The ballet-master smote his forehead, smiled assent, and bounded from the room upon the stage. The judgment of the manager was announced. The ladies tittered, laughed, drew back, and were now as much disinclined to accept the right of position as they had been before eager to claim it. The order of the ladies being settled, the *Grand Pas de Quatre* was finally performed on the same night before a delighted audience, who little knew how nearly they had been deprived of their promised treat."

The excitement out of doors was as great as it was within; the house was crowded to suffocation every night; from the palace to the shop-counter it was the one absorbing topic of conversation. The excitement crossed the Channel, foreign newspapers teemed with histories of its wonders. Foreign courts received accounts of its captivations with official despatches. "It was literally a European event." The wonderful *Pas* was revived in 1847 with Rosati, a new luminary, in place of Lucille Grahn, the other three being as before. *Les Quatre Saisons*, another very remarkable ballet, produced in 1848, with Carlotta Grisi, Cerito, Marie Taglioni, Rosati, Perrot, and St. Léon, was received with almost equal enthusiasm.

But already the tide was turning. The first decline of the ballet may be traced to the appearance of Jenny Lind, to the development of that craze which admitted of no rivalry. Languid swells began to be bored with trying to understand the story of those poetic and elaborate entertainments, and cared only for the detached dances. One of, if not *the* last of the great opera ballets was *Le Corsair*, 1856. Rosati, last of the line of opera *danseuses*, was the Medora, Ronzani the Conrad. But in spite of the splendour of the production, upon which an immense sum was expended, it was a failure. Gradually the ballet sank in importance, until it became only an adjunct to the opera, as in *Guglielmo Tell*, *Roberto Il Diavolo*. In 1857 a troupe of Spanish dancers appeared at the Haymarket, of which the famous Perea Nena was the principal, and revolutionised the art. The marvellous rapidity and variety of her steps, which were worked up to a delirium of motion, created a great sensation; the sylph-like beauty, the poetic vivacity of Taglioni and Elssler were seen no more; many dancers imitated Perea Nena, but they could neither approach the facility of her steps nor the exquisite voluptuous Spanish grace of the original; they simply vulgarised the terpsichorean art. Only twice since the fifties has London been afforded a glimpse of the poetry of motion—when Madame Dor appeared in *Babil and Bijou* in 1872, and Adelina Rossi in the magnificent ballet *Excelsior* at Her Majesty's in 1885. Both, but especially the latter, were fine examples of the classic school.

Ballet, except in Drury Lane pantomime, is now a monopoly of the variety theatre; the Empire and the Alhambra mount these productions with a splendour never dreamed of in the days of Taglioni and Elssler, but the *prima ballerina* is extinct. Dancing must now be reckoned among the lost arts.

To return to the story of the opera. Earl Dudley held Lumley's lease, which did not expire until 1891, so he determined to rebuild the theatre, after the fire. It was completed in 1872, at a cost of £50,000. But no tenant could be found. As the greater number of the stalls and boxes were let upon lease, the expenses would exceed the receipts, though the house were to be crammed every night. It was sold by auction in 1874 for £31,000.

The religious Christy minstrels, Moody and Sankey, were the first tenants, and proved "a draw." But on April 30th, 1877, Mapleson ventured again to become lessee, and opened the new house as Her Majesty's Opera, with *Norma*. It was almost the last appearance of Titiens. A few short weeks afterwards her glorious voice was hushed in death.

The most remarkable début at the new house was that of Etelka Gerster, a supremely fine singer, who made a great impression as Gilda, Amina, Lucia, Margherita,

Linda. The reappearance of Tamberlik after a long absence was another remarkable event. Rossini's Otello was the part chosen. In the old days he, like Rubini, was celebrated for giving the high B flat from the chest, and everyone in the audience was on the tiptoe of expectation for this wonderful note. He acted and sang magnificently, though the middle register of his voice was a little worn. At last, in the scene with Iago (Faure) in the third act, the eagerly anticipated note rang through the house. It was like an electric shock, and evoked a frantic shout of applause, renewed again and again.

Nilsson sang during several seasons, Trebelli remained faithful to her old home, Minnie Hauk made a success as Carmen, the company was usually fairly good, sometimes excellent; but the house never paid, it never could pay.

Carl Rosa had seasons here in 1879, 1880, and 1882. Mayer brought Sarah Bernhardt and a French opera company in 1886; there were promenade concerts in the next year under Van Biene. Mapleson started the opera season of 1889; then it was taken over by a company, with a capital of £40,000, which in less than a year came to grief. French plays by the Gymnase Company, and Sarah Bernhardt, 1890, as *Jeanne d'Arc*. But in the year before the grand old house fell into the most utter degradation. In 1889 it was the scene of a boxing tournament, and the stage which had been trodden by some of the grandest lyric artistes of the day was given up to bruisers. A "gorgeous" pantomime was, however, produced at the close of the year. But the end was at hand. In 1892, all the effects were sold off, and soon afterwards the building was demolished.[1]

[1] Attached to the old Opera House, that was burned down in 1867, was a small theatre called the Bijou, which was used occasionally for concerts

To complete this brief sketch of the opera in England, I must go back to Covent Garden, after the fire. The ruins were scarcely cold ere the rebuilding was decided upon. The Duke of Bedford granted a ground lease for ninety years at a rental of £850, more than an acre of additional land being acquired by the demolition of the Piazza Hotel and other houses. The huge theatre cost £70,000. The area of the stage, exclusive of the bow in front of the proscenium, is 90 feet by 88 feet; the length of the entire building on the Bow Street side is 127 feet, on the Hart Street side, 210 feet. It was opened on May 15th, 1858, by Gye with *Les Huguenots*, in which Mario and Grisi sustained the chief parts; followed by *La Traviata* with Bosio. Some of the most famous débuts which have taken place at the present house are those of Adelina Patti, 1861, Pauline Lucca, Albani, Santley, Trebelli, Faure, Tamberlik, Gayarré.

In 1869 the management of the two opera houses was amalgamated, the first result of which was the withdrawal of Costa, and this was followed by the secession of Mdlles. Christine Nilsson and Ilma Di Murska, Foli, Santley, and others. Before 1871 the impossible fusion was dissolved, and Messrs. Gye and Mapleson were once more in active opposition, the latter at Drury Lane, where he gave operatic performances until he returned to his old quarters in the Haymarket.

Mr. Gye's management was chiefly remarkable for the superior manner in which the operas were mounted, a detail that had never received much attention at the other house, but it was, at the same time, responsible for an evil which finally threatened to crush Italian opera

and light entertainments. Mathews and his wife gave their entertainment "Charles Mathews at Home," here in 1862.

out of existence—the star prima donna, who was paid such enormous sums that a satisfactory *ensemble* was rendered impossible. A Philistine public, whose artistic sympathies were *nil*, whose musical tastes simply depended upon the fashion of the moment, were brought to the belief that there was nothing worth hearing except Madame Patti, and it was only on the nights that lady and one or two others sang that the house was filled.

It was reserved for the energy of Augustus Harris—who, after successfully experimenting with Italian Opera at Drury Lane in 1886, undertook the management of Covent Garden for the following season—to pluck up courage to refuse the terms of and dispense with the services of the star prima donna. Opera was grown musty with worn-out traditions; everything was hackneyed, conventional, lifeless; the operatic stage was a generation behind the dramatic; a realistic age was disgusted at its dreary artificiality. The new *impresario* reformed this altogether. The introduction of the De Reszkes, Lassalle, and other fine male artistes, rendered the men rather than the women the chief draw; Madame Melba, however, has of late sung the public back to their old love. To enumerate all the great singers that Sir Augustus Harris introduced to the London public would be to name most of the greatest of the day, notably Madame Calvé. It was under his management that the *Meistersinger* was first heard in England, notwithstanding that up to the last a certain royal personage was opposed to the experiment, though after hearing that great masterpiece the Prince handsomely acknowledged his mistake. *Tristan und Isolde*, the *Valkyrie* were also added to the repertory by this dauntless *entrepreneur*, who had the audacity even to eliminate the word "Italian" from the bills, which, as the libretto was quite as frequently sung in French and German, as in the tongue of Rossini, had long become an absurd anomaly, and substitute for it "The Royal Opera." The worn-out, oleaginous, wooden-faced choristers, in their dingy or tawdry costumes, whose action and expression were invariable, whether they were witnessing a wedding or a murder, gave place to fresh voices, youth, sympathy, and bright, appropriate dresses.

Since the death of Harris, Covent Garden has been managed by a syndicate of "noblemen and gentlemen," who have expended large sums upon remodelling and refurnishing the stage, and in bringing the house up to present-day requirements, though no improvements can ever render it, inferior as it is to almost every opera house on the Continent, worthy to be the lyric theatre of the greatest city of the world.[1]

For several seasons the trend has been entirely in the direction of Wagner. The magnificent productions of the "Ring," and the success which has attended them, and the preponderance of the great German *maestro's* works over those of all other composers, have unmistakably indicated the musical proclivities of the day. But of late there have been signs, if not of reaction, at least of a reawakened taste for lighter and more tuneful operas, thanks chiefly to the splendid singing of Madame Melba, and the no less splendid powers, both vocal and histrionic, of that grand artiste, Madame Calvé.

There is another remarkable circumstance connected with the revivification of opera by Sir Augustus Harris: he solved the problem that had baffled all his predecessors—how to make opera pay, and he has bequeathed the secret to his heirs.

[1] See note 2, at the end.

CHAPTER IV

The Little Theatre in the Haymarket—Its Rise, Progress, Fortunes, and those who have shared in them, 1720–1903

AFTER Drury Lane, there is not a theatre in London so rich in memories of the great actors who have strutted and fretted their hours upon the stage as "the little theatre in the Haymarket." In the old days of the patent monopoly it was a kind of a chapel-at-ease to Drury Lane and Covent Garden, doing duty for them during the summer months, and here candidates for admission to those mighty universities of the histrionic art most frequently first sought the suffrages of a metropolitan audience. In 1720, one John Potter, a carpenter, purchased the site of an old inn called "The King's Head," and erected thereupon a small theatre. As the building, decorations, scenery, and dresses cost in all only fifteen hundred pounds, it could not have been a very splendid affair.

Colley Cibber complained that Sir John Vanbrugh's great house, on the opposite side, was built in the country; but during the fourteen years that followed its erection, Hanover and Grosvenor Squares were built, and new streets were being laid out on all sides of them; yet still to the north and the west green fields, and farmhouses, and milkmaids, and hayricks were within a few minutes' walk. Having no patent or licence, Mr. Potter opened with a company of young amateurs, who had been acting at a tavern in St. Alban's Street.

On December 15th, 1720, a newspaper of the day published the following advertisement: "At the New Theatre in the Haymarket, between Little Suffolk Street and James Street, which is now completely furnished, will be presented a French Comedy, as soon as the rest of the actors arrive from Paris, who are duly expected. Boxes and pit, five shillings; gallery, two-and-sixpence." On the 29th of the same month, the rest of the actors having, I presume, arrived, the house was opened with *La Fille à la Mode, ou le Badaud de Paris,* "under the patronage of a distinguished nobleman," the company, according to the fashion of the day, styling themselves "the French Comedians of his Grace the Duke of Montague." Performances at first were given four times a week, then two were found to be sufficient, and the prices of admission were lowered, boxes to four shillings, pit to half a crown, and gallery to eighteen-pence. As the aristocracy alone would support foreign entertainments, the French speculation languished, and on the 4th of the following May came to an end. In 1726 we find the Haymarket in the possession of acrobats, tumblers, and the famous rope-dancer, Signora Violante, who, in Dublin, first trained Peg Woffington for the stage.

Of the history of "the little theatre in the Haymarket"—so called to distinguish it from its big brother opposite—during the early years of its existence, we can obtain only stray glimpses through the medium of advertisements in old newspapers, for its doings were considered quite beneath the notice of the dramatic historians of the time. Colley Cibber does not deign to mention it in his *Apology*. It lived only upon sufferance. Occasionally a temporary licence was obtained, through the influence of some nobleman, for regular dramatic performances; at others it was opened by amateurs, or by authors who could not obtain a home for their bantlings at Lincoln's Inn or Drury Lane. An extraordinary production of this kind was brought out here in 1729 by one Johnson, a dancing-master of Chester. It was called *Hurlothrumbo, or the Supernatural.* A contemporary describes the author as playing a part called Lord Flame, and "speaking sometimes in one key, sometimes in another; sometimes dancing, sometimes fiddling, sometimes walking upon stilts." This curious medley had a run of thirty nights.

Fielding is the first great name connected with this house. It was here, in 1730, that he produced his once-famous burlesque *The Tragedy of Tragedies, or the Life and Death of Tom Thumb the Great.* Like the yet more famous *Rehearsal,* it was a satire upon the heavy tragedies of the day, and, though greatly altered to fall in with the humour of succeeding generations, it kept the stage until within living memory. Lord Grizzle was one of Liston's favourite parts. Swift is accredited with saying that he never laughed but twice, and one of these occasions was at a performance of *Tom Thumb.* About eight out of the twenty-seven dramatic pieces which flowed from the facile pen of the author of *Tom Jones* were first produced upon the Haymarket stage. Most of them are in the burlesque style—indeed, Fielding was undoubtedly the father of modern burlesque, and one or two of his efforts in that line, founded on classic subjects, with songs and duets that might almost have been written by Byron or Brough, could with very little alteration have been revived at the old Strand Theatre. His comedy was intensely personal; no public abuse and no public character, from the Prime Minister to the actors at the neighbouring theatre, escaped flagellation by that keen and daring wit.

The first English company of any note that performed at the Haymarket were the Drury Lane rebels, under Theophilus Cibber.[1] The patentees appealed to the law, and one of the actors, Harper, was arrested to make a trial case, under the old Act of Elizabeth, which accounted all players wandering from place to place or *playing in unlicensed* buildings as rogues and vagabonds.[2] Popular feeling, however, was all on the side of Harper, who was a householder and a man of means, so he was acquitted of the charge, and the house remained open until the following May.

Fielding, having found some "adventurers" to risk their money, undertook the management of the Haymarket in 1734; but he opened either on sufferance or in defiance of the law, as the following advertisement will show: "March 5th, 1735, The Great Mogul's Company of English Comedians, newly imported at the New Theatre in the Haymarket. Sealed tickets for Monday, March 8th, being the third day of the entertainment, may be had at the Two Blue Posts, Bow Street, Covent Garden, and at the Bedford Coffee House, in the Great Piazza." We find but few familiar names among this company; Macklin's is the only one of any repute, he not having returned to Drury Lane with the rest of the revolted company. Fielding's management lasted until the passing of the Licensing Act (1737), which his bitter satire upon Sir Robert Walpole, under the name of Quidam in *The Historical Register*, played here in the year just named, did much to bring about.[3]

The Act was extremely unpopular, and audiences loved to damn new plays simply because they were licensed. A fine opportunity of displaying their animus

[1] See p. 63. [2] See note "Rogues and Vagabonds," at the end. [3] See p. 67.

was afforded by the announcement (1738) that a French company was about to give a series of representations "under distinguished patronage" at "the little theatre." As it was publicly threatened that the performance would be violently interfered with, a detachment of soldiers was ordered to the Haymarket, and one of the Westminster magistrates, Justice Deveil, took a seat in the pit as the representative of law and order.

Nothing so exasperated John Bull in those days as to flourish the French flag before his eyes, for he was nothing if not national. As soon as possible after the doors were opened the house was crammed from floor to ceiling, and the audience sounded the note of preparation by singing in chorus "The Roast Beef of Old England." When the curtain rose, the actors were discovered standing between two files of Grenadier Guards, the soldiers with fixed bayonets and resting upon their firelocks. A roar of indignation greeted this sight; the whole pit rose and, turning to the Justice, demanded that the military should be withdrawn. He dared not resist the appeal, and gave the men the signal to retire. But when the actors opened their mouths, their words were drowned by howls, hisses, catcalls, and every kind of diabolical noise, while patriotic individuals demanded to know why English actors should be prohibited from appearing upon that stage and foreigners obtain permission and protection. Deveil promised that if the performance was permitted to go on he would lay the grievance before the King, but shouts of "No treaties!" was the unanimous answer. As they could not make their voices heard, the unfortunate French people ranged themselves for a dance; then from all parts of the house rained a hailstorm of peas, covering the stage and rendering dancing impossible. The Justice called for a candle to read the Riot Act, and threatened to summon the military to disperse the audience, but the attitude of the rioters was so menacing that it remained a threat and nothing more. The French and Spanish ambassadors and their wives, and other aristocratic patrons, now hurried from their boxes; while the management, finding it useless to oppose the storm, ordered the curtain to be dropped. "And," says a contemporary writer, "no battle gained by Marlborough ever elicited more frantic enthusiasm than did this victory over foreign actors."

For several years after the passing of the obnoxious Act "the little theatre" led but a vagabond existence; it was only occasionally taken by some adventurer, who, having nothing to lose, could evade or defy the law.

In the February of 1744 another rebellious subject of the lords of the patent opened this refuge for destitute and quarrelsome players. This was Charles Macklin, who was already one of the foremost actors of the day. Macklin was a teacher of his art, and, with a slight sprinkling of professionals, his company was made up of amateurs and pupils. Among the latter was a young fellow about town, well known at the Bedford Coffee House for his wit, named Samuel Foote, who here made his first appearance upon any stage as Othello to his tutor's Iago.[1] The future droll was short and stout, with a round, full, flat face, and his appearance as the Moor must have been extremely funny.

In September, 1744, Theophilus Cibber again revolted against his manager, and, with some other malcontents, on September 11th in that year, once more opened "the little theatre" with Shakespeare's *Romeo*

[1] This could scarcely have been funnier than when, more than a century later, Sothern played Othello to Buckstone's Iago on these same boards.

SAMUEL FOOTE.

and Juliet, which was played for the first time "for one hundred years."[1]

Since 1680 a garbled version of the tragedy, by Otway, entitled *Caius Marius*, in which the Veronese lovers were converted into ancient Romans, had possessed the stage.[2] The success of the revival was announced the next morning in the *General Advertiser*, wherein it was stated that "many persons of distinction were last night in the pit and gallery, who could not find room in the boxes." On the 14th it was "bespoke by several ladies of quality." Theophilus's daughter Jane was the Juliet. How he contrived to drive the proverbial coach and four through the Act of Parliament is explained by the following advertisement which appeared in the *Advertiser*. "At Mr. Cibber's academy, in the Haymarket, will be a concert; after which will be exhibited *gratis* a rehearsal in the form of a play, called *Romeo and Juliet*." But in the course of a few weeks, on October 22nd, the house was closed by order of the Lord Chamberlain.

During this brief season it would seem that Theophilus also revived *Cymbeline* for the first time since the Restoration. When he left the theatre, Mrs. Charke, Colley Cibber's notorious daughter, who always played male parts and wore male attire in private life, tried to keep the company together, but was very soon expelled.

[1] That is, according to Mr. Cibber; but Pepys records seeing *Romeo and Juliet* at the Opera House (Lincoln's Inn Fields Theatre) in March, 1662. This could hardly be James Howard's version, as that was produced at Drury Lane. It must not be supposed that Cibber gave the play from the text; it was announced as revised and altered by himself, but the alterations were chiefly borrowed from *Caius Marius*.

[2] In Fielding's *Tom Thumb*, Huncamunca exclaims: "Oh Tom Thumb, Tom Thumb, wherefore art thou Tom Thumb?" In the notes to the play the author quotes the lines, not from Shakespeare, but from Otway, where it stands: "Oh Marius, Marius, wherefore art thou Marius?"—a proof of how little Shakespeare was known at the time.

The result of Foote's appearance in tragedy was an engagement at Drury Lane for comedy parts. There he made so great a success as a mimic in the character of Bayes in *The Rehearsal*, that, finding himself overshadowed by the genius of Garrick, he determined to turn manager on his own account. Failing to procure a licence, he took a leaf out of Mr. Cibber's book, and on April 22nd, 1747, announced that a concert of music would on that day be performed at the theatre in the Haymarket, after which would be presented *gratis* a new entertainment, called *The Diversions of the Morning*, and a farce taken from *The Old Bachelor*, entitled *The Credulous Husband*—Fondlewife, Mr. Foote—and an epilogue by the B—d—d (Bedford) Coffee House. The Diversions and the Epilogue consisted of a mimicry of the best-known men of the day—actors, doctors, lawyers, statesmen. The managers of the patent houses could not tolerate such an infringement of their rights as a performance by one of the most popular comedians of the time. They appealed to the Westminster magistrates, and on the second night the constables entered the theatre and dispersed the audience.

But Foote was not so easily to be put down. The very next morning he published the following announcement in the *General Advertiser:* "On Saturday afternoon, exactly at twelve o'clock, at the new theatre in the Haymarket, Mr. Foote begs the favour of his friends to come and drink a dish of chocolate with him, and 'tis hoped there will be a great deal of company and some joyous spirits. He will endeavour to make the morning as diverting as possible. Tickets to be had for this entertainment at George's Coffee House, Temple Bar, without which no one will be admitted. N.B.—Sir Dilbury Diddle will be there, and Lady Betty Frisk has absolutely promised." No one knew what this advertisement meant, and a crowded house was the natural result. When the curtain rose, Foote came forward and informed the audience that, "as he was training some young performers for the stage, he would, with their permission, whilst chocolate was getting ready, proceed with his instructions before them." Then some young people, engaged for the purpose, were brought upon the stage, and, under the pretence of instructing them in the art of acting, he introduced his imitations.

The authorities did not again interfere with him, so he altered the time of his entertainment from morning to evening, and the title to "Tea"; and to drink a dish of tea with Mr. Foote, as going to his theatre came to be styled, was the rage of the season. Next year he called his performance "An Auction of Pictures." Here is one of his advertisements: "At the forty-ninth day's sale at his auction-room in the Haymarket, Mr. Foote will exhibit a choice collection of pictures—some entirely new lots, consisting of a poet, a beau, a Frenchman, a miser, a tailor, a sot, two young gentlemen, and a ghost; two of which are originals, the rest copies from the best masters." In this he mimicked the peculiarities of Justice Deveil, Cock, the auctioneer, and the notorious orator, Henley. To the attractions of his "Auction" he presently added a "Cat Concert," in ridicule of the Italian opera, and engaged a man so celebrated for his imitations of those tuneful animals that he was known as Cat Harris. And fashion, as usual, flocked to the Haymarket to hear and see its tastes turned into ridicule.

In 1749 the little theatre nearly came to an untimely end through a hoax perpetrated for a wager by the Duke of Montagu. One morning the town was thrown into a wonderful state of excitement by the announcement that, on a certain evening, the "Great Bottle Conjurer" would appear at the Haymarket; that, among other extraordinary feats, he would put himself into a quart bottle and sing a song therein; that he would summon up the spirits of dead relations for anyone desirous of seeing them, and enable the living to converse with the dead. There was, and is, no limit to English gullibility, and the house was crammed, not with the ignorant and vulgar, but with the fashionable world. After a long delay, during which the dupes grew very impatient, a person came forward and informed the audience that the bottle conjurer was unable to appear that evening, but if they would come again the next, he would undertake to squeeze himself into a pint bottle instead of a quart. The spectators, being deficient in a sense of humour, resented the joke; the Duke of Cumberland, who was among the gulls, drew his sword, and leaping upon the stage, called upon everybody to follow him. The people, ripe for mischief, were too loyal to decline a prince's invitation. The seats were smashed, the scenery was torn down, the wreckage carried into the street, where a bonfire was made of it; and but for the timely appearance of the authorities, the building itself would have been added to the fuel.

During the winter months, Foote was engaged at one or the other of the winter theatres, where many of his best pieces were produced, and afterwards transferred in the summer months to the Haymarket. His satire was not keener or more impartial than Fielding's, but the great novelist's characters were performed by only ordinary actors, while Foote, who was one of the most extraordinary mimics that ever lived, embodied his own caricatures, and thereby increased their poignancy tenfold. The audacity of his personalities was astounding. In

The Orators (1762), he personated, under the name of Peter Paragraph, a noted printer, publisher, and alderman of Dublin, known as one-legged George Faulkener. The Irishman brought an action of libel against him: a trial ensued. Next season at the Haymarket, the incorrigible wit introduced a new scene into the piece, representing the trial, in which he caricatured judge, counsel, and jury. In *The Mayor of Garrat*, one of his wittiest pieces, under the name of Matthew Mug, he held up to public derision the silly old Duke of Newcastle, of whom he used to say that he always appeared as if he had lost an hour in the morning, and was looking for it all the rest of the day.

One of his most notorious caricatures was Mr. Cadwallader in *The Author*. The original of this character was an intimate friend of his, a Welsh gentleman named Ap-Rice, an enormously corpulent person, with a broad, staring face, an incoherent way of speaking, a loud voice, an awkward gait, a trick of rolling his head about from side to side, and of sucking his wrists. Here was a splendid subject for our mimic, and he produced him to the life, to the huge delight of the audience, among which more than once was to be found Ap-Rice himself, who, in happy ignorance that he was gazing upon his own reflection, laughed as loudly and applauded as vigorously as anybody. But it was impossible that he could long remain in this blissful ignorance, for so unmistakable was the imitation to everybody but the victim, that he could not enter a coffee-room, or be seen in any public place, without people whispering, "There's Cadwallader!" or someone calling after him, "This is my Becky, my dear Becky"—one of the phrases in the play. When the Welshman at length realised the fact, he was furious, and obtained an injunction from the Lord Chamberlain to restrain the performance.

In *A Trip to Calais*, under the name of Lady Kitty Crocodile, Foote threatened to hold up to public censure the bigamous Duchess of Kingston. The piece was never played; but in another version, called *The Capuchin*, he gibbeted an infamous scoundrel, Jackson, a hedge parson, one of the duchess's creatures. In revenge this fellow bribed a discharged coachman of Foote's to bring a hideous accusation against his master. The charge broke down, but it broke Foote's heart; he was never the same man again.

Ten years before this, in 1766, Foote had obtained a patent for his theatre at the cost of a limb. While on a visit at Lord Mexborough's during the hunting season, the Duke of York, for a frolic, mounted him upon a blood horse. The animal threw him, and his leg, being fractured in two places, had to be amputated. Considering that he ought to make the victim of his ill-timed jest some amends, the Duke interceded with the King, and obtained a patent, by which Foote was legally permitted to keep open the Haymarket between May 14th and September 14th. And thus, after a vagabond existence of forty-six years, "the little theatre" was at last raised to the dignity of a lawful dramatic temple. Thereupon the manager made some extensive alterations and improvements in the house, which had hitherto been little better than a barn. Immediately after the Jackson affair, in 1777, he sold his interest to George Colman, recently one of the patentees of Covent Garden, for an annuity of £1,600 per annum. He lived only a few months afterwards.

Before commencing his second season, Colman new-roofed the house, furbished up the decorations, converted the side-slips of the gallery into a third tier of boxes, and added an approach of a few feet wide, which was dignified by the name of a lobby. "In Foote's time," says Colman the younger, "there was scarcely any space between the boxes and the pit; so that the attention of the audience in this part of the theatre was frequently disturbed by post-horns and the out-of-door cries of 'extraordinary news from France.' But, after all, the passages to the side-boxes were so narrow that two stout gentlemen could scarcely pass one another; and I often thought it would be better to furnish my side-box customers with a bell to tie round their necks at the pay-door, to give warning of their approach and prevent jostling." Scenery and decorations were of the barest description, while the costumes, being always of the fashion of the day, were regulated by the means of the performers.

Although Harry Woodward, Baddeley, the elder Bannister, and other actors of note occasionally appeared upon the Haymarket stage, the members of Foote's regular company, whatever might have been their merits, can scarcely be counted among the noted actors of the eighteenth century. Exceptions, however, must be made in favour of three comedians—first, Ned Shuter, whom Garrick pronounced to be the greatest comic genius he had ever known. Shuter was the original old Hardcastle and Sir Anthony Absolute. Strange to say, he was a follower of that most bitter enemy of the players, George Whitefield; he would sometimes attend five different meeting-houses on Sundays, and when very drunk could scarcely be restrained from preaching in the streets. This maudlin religion and his liberal donations so impressed the famous preacher, that on the occasion of one of Shuter's benefits he actually recommended the congregation to attend—*just that once.* The second, Weston, Foote took out of a booth at Bartholomew

Fair. It was for him he wrote the part of Jerry Sneak, in *The Mayor of Garrat.* To judge by contemporary criticism, Weston must have been a wonderful actor in such parts as Scrub in *The Beaux' Stratagem*, and Abel Drugger, in which he was thought to excel even Garrick. But a long probation of miserable strolling had utterly demoralised him, and in 1776 he died the victim of habitual intemperance. Quick, George the Third's favourite actor, made his first appearance here as one of the pupils in Foote's *Orators*, in 1767. His impersonations of Dogberry and Tony Lumpkin were among the finest the stage has seen.

Foote's patent died with him, and it was under an annual licence, which in 1811 was extended from four to five months, that his successor opened the house. With the accession of the elder Colman to the managerial throne began the golden era of "the little theatre," which for the next forty years and more continued in full meridian splendour. Three notable first appearances inaugurated Colman's first season: charming Miss Farren, afterwards Countess of Derby, a finished actress of the fine ladies of comedy, but little above mediocrity in serious parts. Edwin, Weston's successor, and his equal in humour though not in art, for he was terribly addicted to "gagging." Like Weston, his sottishness was a disease. A contemporary says: "I have seen him brought to the stage-door in the bottom of a chaise, senseless and motionless; if the clothes could be put upon him, and he was pushed on to the lamps, he rubbed his stupid eyes for a minute; consciousness and brilliant humour awakened together; and his acting seemed only the richer for the bestial indulgence that had overwhelmed him." Henderson, whom we have met both at Drury Lane and Covent Garden, was the most important of the three; his Shylock, Hamlet, and Falstaff

—in the last some thought him superior to Quin—drew to Colman's treasury between four and five thousand pounds within a month. It was Henderson who, by his fine recitation, first brought Cowper's "Johnny Gilpin" into popularity. He afterwards went to Drury Lane, but death in 1785 cut short his career, which promised great things. It now became the routine for the best performers of the two great winter theatres to appear at the Haymarket during the summer months, and actors and actresses who had successfully passed through a provincial probation here made their first trial for the highest honours of their profession.

In 1789, failing health of body and mind obliged the elder Colman to relinquish the management to his son. All his best work had been done for the great houses, and his pen added nothing of permanent value to the repertory of the Haymarket. He died in 1794. The reign of George the younger commenced with a terrible calamity. On February 3rd, 1794,[1] their Majesties commanded a play at this theatre. An enormous crowd awaited the opening of the doors, and the rush was so terrible that fifteen persons were trampled to death, and many others greatly injured. The house was closed in consequence; but people soon forget such catastrophes, and when the summer came the theatre was as crowded as ever. George the younger almost monopolised the Haymarket stage, as far as new plays went, with his own productions. In the year 1800 the company included John Emery, Charles Kemble, Fawcett, Jack Bannister, Dicky Suett,[2] Farley, Barrymore, Irish John-

[1] During the rebuilding of Drury Lane, which took place this year, the patentees allowed the theatre to be opened under their authority for the winter months.

[2] Those who would know something about these actors, I refer to the *Essays of Elia*, wherein Charles Lamb has immortalised more than one of them.

stone, Mrs. Mountain, Mrs. Davenport, Mrs. Gibbs, etc. Elliston, whom we have met at Drury Lane, and shall meet again at the Olympic and the Surrey, made his début here in 1796; and Charles Mathews the elder, in 1802. Liston's first appearance was in 1805.

In that year there occurred at the Haymarket one of the most curious riots in theatrical annals. In 1767, Foote produced a burlesque, the author of which was never discovered, entitled, *The Tailors: a Tragedy for Warm Weather*. Dowton announced the revival of this piece for his benefit. As the title implies, it was a satire upon the sartorial craft, and upon the bills being issued, an indignation meeting was convened among the knights of the needle, who vowed to oppose the performance by might and main. Menacing letters were sent to Dowton telling him that seventeen thousand tailors would attend to hiss the piece, and one, who signed himself DEATH, added that ten thousand more could be found if necessary. These threats were laughed at by the actors; but when night came it was discovered that the craft were in earnest, and that, with few exceptions, they had contrived to secure every seat in the house, while a mob without still squeezed for admission. The moment Dowton appeared upon the stage there rose a hideous uproar, and someone threw a pair of shears at him. Not a word would the rioters listen to, nor would they accept any compromise in the way of changing the piece. Within howled and hissed *sans* intermission hundreds of exasperated tailors; outside howled and bellowed thousands of raging tailors, who attempted to storm the house. So formidable did the riot wax, that a magistrate had to be sent for and special constables called out; but these were helpless against overwhelming odds, so a troop of Life Guards was ultimately summoned, who, after making sixteen prisoners, put the rest to flight.

In the season of 1807, Charles Young, a tragedian of the Kemble school, who came to be acknowledged as John Philip's legitimate successor in classic tragedy, made his début as Hamlet, and created a marked impression.

A curious exhibition was presented here in 1810, when a middle-aged West Indian, named Robert Coates, who had already rendered himself the sensation of the town by his extraordinary costume and equipage, appeared as Romeo, dressed in a sky-blue spangled cloak, red pantaloons, muslin vest, a full-bottomed wig, and an opera-hat. His acting was on a par with his make-up, and convulsed the house with laughter, while as a climax, his small-clothes, being over tight, gave way in the seams.

Never was burlesque so comical as his dying scene; he dragged Juliet out of the tomb as if she had been a bundle of old clothes; before falling, he spread an enormous silk pocket-handkerchief upon the stage, put his opera-hat for a pillow, and then very gently laid himself down. "Ah, you may laugh," he said, in answer to the shriek that hailed this new device, "but I do not intend to soil my nice new velvet dress upon these dirty boards." Shouts of "encore" followed his death, and he obeyed the demand with alacrity, swallowed the poison over again, and repeated all the symptoms of a violent *mal de mer* with more gusto than before. The performance was demanded a third time, when Juliet, entering into the absurdity of the situation, rose up, and advancing to the footlights, gave a quotation from the play, very aptly altered :—

> "*Dying* is such sweet sorrow,
> That he will die again until to-morrow."

This, however, was not Mr. Coates's first exhibition; as he had already appeared as Lothario in *The Fair Penitent*, the audience knew what was in store for them, and came armed with apples, oranges, turnips, and carrots, which were showered upon him at the fall of the curtain. He was a well-known character about town, conspicuous from the extraordinary vehicle in which he rode, a carriage modelled in shape and brilliancy of hue upon the fairy car of a pantomime, drawn by two white horses, each of which had a silver cock with outspread wings as large as life attached to its neck. The buckles of his shoes and the buttons of his coat were of diamonds. He was supposed to be immensely rich, but it was afterwards discovered he had only £10,000, which he had devoted to these follies, and an income of £500 a year.

Although the Haymarket was a thriving speculation, George Colman was always in the hands of the Jews. In an evil moment, in 1805, he took his brother-in-law, Morris, into partnership, and made over to him and another man, named Winston, one half of the property; an attorney, one Tabourdin, purchased another eighth, which, contrary to the conditions of sale, he secretly made over to Morris, whose design was to get everything into his own hands. This led to endless disputes and litigation, which, in 1813, landed Colman in the King's Bench, closed the theatre for a whole season, and finally obliged him to resign all share in the management.

It is a curious circumstance that the four responsible managers which the Haymarket had known up to this period were all eminent dramatic authors. Here, as we have seen, were produced many of Fielding's burlesques, and nearly all Foote's excellent farces, to which posterity has never assigned their rightful place among the humorous and witty productions of the eighteenth century. Foote was the English Aristophanes, and like the great Athenian, was nothing if not personal; consequently most of his fun and satire are now incomprehensible without a commentary, and even then can never have the point for us that they had for the contemporaries of the victims. But for the student of manners they are brimful of interest and information. As I have before said, Colman the elder's contributions to the Haymarket *répertoire* were very insignificant, being merely farces, such as *Polly Honeycombe*, *The Manager in Distress*, and one or two alterations of old plays. George the younger gave most of his best work to this house, together with a number of dramas now fallen into oblivion. Here were first performed *The Heir at Law*, and *The Mountaineers*. When Colman was appointed examiner of plays, he made himself the bugbear of actors and managers. All "damns," and even the words "Providence," "Heaven," "hell," "Oh lud!" "paradise," were blotted out of the MSS. submitted to him. And his avarice was equal to his purism; he would not permit a song, or even an address, to be interpolated without exacting his fee. He exercised this tyrannic jurisdiction until his death in 1836.

Morris, now sole lessee, in 1820 demolished the old building, to erect, at a cost of £20,000, on a site a little to the north of it, the theatre with which we are all familiar. It opened on July 4th, 1821, with *The Rivals;* Terry, Oxberry, Jones, and Miss de Camp in the principal parts. In 1822 the company included Vining, Charles Kemble, Jones, Elliston, Oxberry, Mrs. West, Mrs. Glover, Miss Kelly, and Madame Vestris. Two years later it was joined by William Farren. 1825 was the *Paul Pry* year; this comedy ran 114 nights to overflowing houses. But what a cast it was! Farren, Mrs. Waylett, Mrs. Glover, Madame Vestris, and Liston, whose only successor in the part was Wright.

Up to this time no comic actor had ever held so high a position upon the London stage or received so large a salary as John Liston; £50, and even £60, a night were paid him in town and country; his genius was farcical, extravagant, but irresistibly comical. Yet he was grave, and even stately in appearance, though abnormally ugly, and to his dying day believed that his forte was tragedy.

The remaining years of Morris's management may be passed over in a few sentences. Season after season the same plays were performed, with now and again a novelty in the shape of comedy, farce, or a musical trifle, usually written for the particular talent of one actor or actress; but audiences seemed to be content year after year to see William Farren in Sir Peter Teazle or Lord Ogleby, and other parts in old comedy, sparingly diversified by an occasional new character. Madame Vestris, Mrs. Waylett, Mrs. Honey, could always draw delighted audiences by their charming singing and acting, while Liston and John Reeve kept them in a roar of laughter. In the stock company were the elder Vining and James Vining, Buckstone, and Mrs. Glover. This lady made a sensation here in 1833 by appearing as Falstaff in *The Merry Wives of Windsor*. The elder Kean starred here during several seasons, and Charles Kemble played a round of his famous parts in 1835. In 1836, Sergeant Talfourd's *Ion* was produced with Ellen Tree in the title-rôle and Vandenhoff as Adrastus, fine performances both.

Turning over the playbills of this period, we are struck by an air of repose in things theatrical such as we experience in wandering through some quiet and little-frequented picture-gallery. Generation after generation the walls are covered by the same masterpieces growing mellower and mellower with time; occasionally a new canvas is added to their number that attracts the visitor for a while, but only to send him back more lovingly to his old favourites, the beauties of which grow upon him with each visit.

Benjamin Webster, who had been a member of the company since 1829,[1] became lessee of the Haymarket in 1837, and under his direction the house more than maintained its old prestige, both from a dramatic and a histrionic point of view. Phelps made his London débût in the August of that year as Shylock. He was then under an engagement to Macready for Covent Garden at £12 a week. So successful was he that Macready confessed that when he read the criticism in the *Morning Herald* he was depressed by it. This jealousy bore fruit at Covent Garden, for after Phelps had performed Othello, Macduff, and Jaffier with marked approbation from the audience, he was dropped out of the bill. Macready,[2] Helen Faucit, Mr. and Mrs. Charles Kean played long and frequent engagements during the next few years, Creswick had a three years' engagement in 1847 at the Haymarket, while comedy was represented by Farren, Charles Mathews, Strickland, Buckstone, Tyrone Power, Mrs. Glover, Madame Vestris, Mrs. Nisbett, Mrs. Stirling. Here Madame Celeste, of whom I shall write more fully when I come to the Adelphi,

[1] His first appearance was in London at the Cobourg in 1818. He was afterwards a member of the West London Company. In 1824 he was at Drury Lane; it was undertaking the part of Pompey in *Measure for Measure*, at a very few hours' notice, in consequence of Harley's illness, that first brought him into notice.

[2] Macready played his last engagement here in 1851, previous to his farewell performance at Drury Lane.

made her first great mark as an actress in such dramas as *The Wept of the Wishton Wish*, *Marie Ducange*, and others of the romantic school.

Among the dramatic productions of this period were Lord Lytton's *Money*, Douglas Jerrold's charming *Time Works Wonders*, several of Westland Marston's finest plays, *Heart of the World*, 1847, *Strathmore;* Sheridan Knowles's *Love Chase*, and Charles Reade's and Tom Taylor's *Masks and Faces;* Mrs. Stirling's Peg Woffington and Anne Carew in *A Sheep in Wolf's Clothing*, brought out at the Lyceum in 1857, were perhaps her finest impersonations.

In February, 1852, Barry Sullivan made his first appearance in London at the Haymarket as Hamlet, with some measure of success; he afterwards acted in other plays. He returned to the little theatre three years later, and played a round of leading parts with Helen Faucit. He was afterwards seen at Drury Lane. Sullivan was a competent actor of the old bow-wow school; but though an enormous favourite in Ireland and the provinces, he never took any firm hold of the metropolitan public.

Webster made many improvements in the Haymarket: he widened the proscenium eleven feet, and introduced gas, this being the last theatre in London in which candles were used.

When Webster went over to the Adelphi in 1853, the Haymarket passed into the hands of John Baldwin Buckstone, who, as the author (in all) of about 150 plays, and as a low comedian of the first rank, was already a great stage favourite. Twenty-five years had elapsed since he made his first bow at the Adelphi as Bobby Trot, in his own drama of *Luke the Labourer;* previous to which he had been a favourite at the Surrey, and during the latter years of Morris's management had been connected, both as author and actor, with the theatre of which he now became the manager.

A charming actress and a beautiful singer, Miss Featherstone, afterwards Mrs. Howard Paul, came over here from the Strand in October, 1854, to play Captain Macheath in *The Beggar's Opera.* A lovely woman, with a fine figure and the dash and fire of a *jeune premier*, she looked and acted the part splendidly, and her singing of the music was little inferior to Sims Reeves', of whom she used to give a wonderful imitation. For many years Miss Featherstone was a great favourite on the London stage in this character, as Apollo in *Midas*, and other parts. In 1869 she performed a *tour de force* at Drury Lane, doubling Hecate with Lady Macbeth.

J. L. Toole made an appearance here in the same year as Simmons in *The Spitalfields Weaver*, one of Wright's best parts, but I think he played only a few nights.

Covent Garden having been converted into an opera house, and Drury Lane being little better than a huge show, Buckstone was enabled to gather about him all the available comedy talent of the day, and although it was not equal to that at the command of his predecessors, we look back upon the performances of the old comedies under his management with a belief that, for *ensemble*, we shall not see the like again. The Shakespearian clown of the stage died with Compton, who joined the new lessee in his first season, and for eighteen years remained true to his chief. He founded his style upon that of Harley, who had received the traditions of King and Woodward. Such a Touchstone, such a clown in the *Twelfth Night*, it is hopeless to look for now; they had the true Shakespearian flavour—dry, quaint, antique. And his creations in modern comedy and farce were equally admirable. Quite as excellent in his way was Buckstone: his Tony Lumpkin, his Bob Acres, his Backbite, his Sir Andrew Aguecheek, still remain unrivalled. Clever actors have played them since, and have made us laugh heartily; but their humour is quite a different thing to the author's humour, it is the humour of the nineteenth century masquerading in the costume of the eighteenth. Indeed, it is that distinction which renders all representations of old comedy at the present day so unsatisfactory; the modern actor is so much the child of his age that he cannot even simulate the form of any other.

A famous actor, William Farren, who had been before the public for many years, and whom we shall meet again at the Olympic and the Strand, took his leave of the stage in 1855, surrounded by his old associates. He survived until 1861.

One of the earlier successes of Buckstone's management was Perea Nena.[1] Amy Sedgwick, in the summer of 1857, made a great success as Hesther Grazebrook in Tom Taylor's *Unequal Match.* In the style of entertainment the new lessee followed closely in the steps of his predecessors; revivals of old comedies were relieved by the production of new ones, of melodrama, domestic drama, a sprinkling of tragedy, while not infrequently the bill of fare would consist of four light pieces—a comedietta, perhaps by Dance, and three farces.

Buckstone's first season extended over five years, and during that period the house was not closed one night when the law permitted it to be open. That the profits were as remarkable as the length is very doubtful.

[1] See p. 205

The Haymarket was at this time a very late house, being usually open until one o'clock in the morning. In the opera season—those were the days of half price[1]—numbers, after leaving Her Majesty's, would go over to the little theatre opposite to see some favourite actor in a popular character. Wright was paid £50 a week for some time to appear in a farce about midnight; the receipts after that hour averaging £100 a week. But the conditions of social life are entirely changed; most people lived in London proper in those days, or at least within a mile or two of the centre, and were not afraid of a little walk; there was no rush for the train or omnibus; men and their wives walked leisurely home, or adjourned to some quiet place for a little supper. They went to the theatre to enjoy the play and the little treat afterwards; and not because it was "the thing" to see some mediocre production that had been running five hundred or eight hundred nights. Very few people go to the theatre nowadays for mere pleasure; you have only to watch the bored expression on the faces of returning playgoers in the trains to be assured that they have derived little enjoyment from their visit. And it is the same with all other exhibitions; the number of people who do bitter penance yearly by gazing upon the walls of the Royal Academy would fill a martyrology. But whatever is "the go" for the hour everybody, from the duchess to the greengrocer's lady, must follow; individuality is dying out; everyone you meet dresses in the same manner, talks in the same manner, does the same things, goes to the same places—and that is why certain playhouses fill.

Edwin Booth made his first appearance in England at the Haymarket as Sir Giles Overreach in 1861, and

[1] Half price was not established at the Haymarket until about 1835.

afterwards appeared as Shylock and Richelieu, but without making any monetary success; though at that time, or near about it, Gustavus Brooke was drawing crowded houses at Drury Lane.

The fortunes of the theatre were at the very lowest ebb, and a crash was imminent when, as a mere *pis aller*, Edward Sothern from Laura Keene's was engaged to appear November 11th, 1861, as Lord Dundreary in Tom Taylor's *American Cousin.*

Sothern's American success in the part was one of those instances in which greatness is thrust upon a man against his will. As the piece was originally written, Asa Trenchard, created by Jefferson, was the principal character; and Sothern, at that time the light comedian at Laura Keene's, was so disgusted with the part of the silly lord, that he was induced to play it only on condition that he would be allowed to gag and do as he pleased in it. So he resolved to turn it into ridicule, and make it perfectly unendurable to the audience. He gagged, he hopped, he lisped, fully expecting to evoke a storm of disapprobation. To his astonishment, the audience laughed and applauded, and professional instinct told him that he had made a hit instead of a fiasco. Night after night he added some new gag, some new absurdity, until the once despised part overshadowed every other and was *the* thing of the comedy.

Edwin Booth ended his engagement on the Saturday night, and on Monday *Our American Cousin* was produced without any previous announcement. On the first night it was such a deadly fiasco that Buckstone put up a notice in the green-room: "Next Thursday, *She Stoops to Conquer.*" Charles Mathews, who was in front, went behind and said, "Buckstone, you push this piece." "But it is an offence to all the swells."

"Don't you believe it," cried Mathews; "you push it, and it will please them more than anybody else." Buckstone was induced to give it further trial. The critics had not been slow in recognising the originality of the conception. John Oxenford, in the *Times*, took the exact measure of the actor and the part when he said that, although generations of fops had been seen upon the London stage, no fop exactly like Lord Dundreary had ever before appeared. "To test him by anything in the actual world would be to ignore his special merit, which consists in giving a conventional notion the most novel and fantastical expression that can be imagined."

Although those who came to the theatre heartily enjoyed this new dramatic sensation, it was not, however, until the Cattle Show week brought the country people to the house that the performance took any real grip upon the public. The piece was withdrawn before Christmas, and Sothern was engaged to appear after the run of the pantomime, for at that time, and much more recently, every London theatre produced its Christmas annual. "But don't come back with that infernal Lord Dundreary," were Buckstone's parting words.

The pantomime was evidently a failure, for it had to be backed up by five-act plays and a lady star—long since extinguished. Sothern returned on January 27th, and as Lord Dundreary had been much talked about in the interim, he reopened in that character to a crowded house. From that night the craze, that most of us have heard about, set in, and the first of "the long runs" was inaugurated by one of the worst plays ever perpetrated by a competent playwright, and one of the most *outré* performances that ever caught the public taste. It ran four hundred nights, and Buckstone realised £30,000 clear profit by it.

Sothern's next original part was David Garrick in Robertson's comedy of that name, which, in the hands of Sir Charles Wyndham, is still a trump card. It was brought out in the April of 1864. The author of *Caste* was then an unknown playwright, a hack translator of French dramas for Lacey, the theatrical bookseller, and he received only £40 for his work, at least that was the sum stipulated, though Sothern behaved very handsomely when success was assured. With provincial starring engagements between each new play, Sothern appeared in *Brother Sam* at the end of 1864, and in Westland Marston's *Favourite of Fortune* and Robertson's *Home*, a version of *L'Aventurière*, 1865. These plays, with *The Hero of Romance* (1868), were, after Dundreary, the most successful of his impersonations.

The first appearance in England of Madame Beatrice in a version of that fine play, *Mademoiselle de Belle-Isle*, October, 1864, should not be passed unnoticed. Miss Madge Robertson made her first appearance in London here, in 1865, as Ophelia to Walter Montgomery's Hamlet. In the meantime, however, Buckstone had become a mere cipher in the management, and, as is so frequently the case, the ally he had called in to his succour now pushed him from his throne.

No man with less pretensions to histrionic excellence than Sothern ever made a great success. As a comedian he was decidedly inferior to Charles Mathews, while in serious parts he was mediocrity personified; in fact, he was Lord Dundreary in everything he attempted, even in Claude Melnotte. He was the fashion, however; he was received in the best society, hunted with dukes, was the guest of millionaires, and, above all, was ever overflowing with high animal spirits and a *bonhomie* that rendered him as great a social as he was a histrionic success.

Sothern's popularity, however, was greatly on the wane at the close of the "sixties," and in 1870 the production of Gilbert's *The Palace of Truth*, which was followed by *Pygmalion and Galatea*, in which Madge Robertson (Mrs. Kendal) first made her reputation, once more raised the sinking fortunes of the Haymarket. But charmingly original as were these fairy comedies, the vein was but a shallow one, it was soon exhausted, and the third of the series, *The Wicked World*, 1873, failed to draw.

Buckstone's next ally was J. S. Clarke, whose wonderfully grotesque performance, Major Wellington de Boots, had already rendered him a great favourite with London audiences. Poor Buckstone was one of the old type of managers, extravagant and unbusinesslike, and for years lived upon the sufferance of Jews, and of Christians scarcely as merciful. Once more the ally became the master, and the name of John Baldwin Buckstone in 1878 disappeared from the Haymarket playbills to give place to that of John S. Clarke. A farewell benefit was arranged for the veteran actor in August, 1879. *Money* was to be the play, and he was to appear as the Old Member in the Club scene; but before the date fixed Buckstone was stricken with paralysis, and the idea had to be abandoned. Later on another benefit was arranged, and Barry Sullivan appeared as Benedick.

In that same year Adelaide Neilson appeared here as Juliet and Rosalind with the most brilliant success. Unhappily it proved to be her last engagement in London. By-and-by came the news of her untimely death in Paris. There is nothing else in Clarke's management that calls for notice here.

In 1880 the Haymarket, reconstructed and rendered

the most luxuriously splendid theatre of the time, came under the Bancroft management. The disturbances on the opening night, February 1st, during the performance of *Money*, augured ill for the new régime. A keen judgment that seldom erred, or when it did, hastened to retire from its false position, a sympathy that usually anticipated public taste and feeling, and had been one of the secrets of the Bancrofts' success at the Prince of Wales's, here seemed to wholly desert them. The abolition of the pit was a false move, and for ever wrecked the popularity of the management. Nor were the performances to be compared with those which had been given in Tottenham Street. The best of the old company, the Kendals, Hare, John Clayton, had become managers on their own account; again, the actors, accustomed to a very small stage, seemed lost in the larger area of their new home, and oscillated between extravagance on one side and inaudibility on the other.

The reception of the new lessee was about the stormiest that had been heard in a theatre for many years. Mr. Bancroft stated his case fairly enough, but he did not satisfy his old supporters, who ever after had a grudge against him. The pit has always been one of the most time-honoured of English theatrical institutions, and it was particularly so at the Haymarket. In no theatre in London, except the Lyceum, would the innovation have raised so formidable an opposition. As an instance, Mrs. John Wood abolished the pit at the St. James's without exciting a murmur; and the Opera Comique had not one worthy of the name; but the Haymarket was always what is styled a "pit-house," that part of the theatre being invariably well attended, and by a good class of persons; it was these who resented being excluded from their favourable resort.

When the Robertson comedies were transferred to the Haymarket, they were like Dutch pictures expanded to a large canvas, and the real flimsiness of the material was fatally apparent; though it must be added, in defence of the works themselves, that the cast was inferior, that Mrs. Bancroft, especially as Mary Netley, in *Ours*, had fallen into exaggerations to make the scenes "go," and that, above all, the school had seen its day, and that a more robust style of play as well as of acting was coming into vogue.

Most of the old Prince of Wales's successes, *Money*, *Ours*, *Caste*, *School*, *Masks and Faces*, *Diplomacy*, *School for Scandal*, and one of Buckstone's famous pieces, *The Overland Route*, were repeated here. Of the new plays produced, *Fedora*, perhaps, in which Mrs. Bernard Beere gave a performance second only to Sarah Bernhardt's, was the most successful. An attempt, May, 1884, to present in the home of traditional old comedy a rendering of *The Rivals*, archæologically correct as a picture, but entirely modern in arrangement and in histrionic treatment, deservedly failed. Pinero's *Lord and Commons*, 1883, was produced here, but it was not one of his successful works.

On the 20th of July, 1885, Mr. and Mrs. Bancroft retired from the management of the Haymarket, and from the stage as well. It was the most important theatrical farewell that had taken place, perhaps, since Macready's, for actors, as a rule, nowadays linger superfluous upon the scenes of their old triumphs, most frequently until their powers are exhausted, and a younger generation is cynical about their traditions, so that their death or disappearance excites little attention. But Mrs. Bancroft retired in her full maturity, though it cannot be denied that during the last few years she had developed a tendency to over-accentuation, the growth of which has marred so many fine actors and actresses of the past.

On that parting night all differences between manager and audience were forgotten; from two o'clock in the afternoon crowds gathered about the doors, anxious to do honour to those who had so admirably catered for their amusement and intellectual gratification during twenty years, and to catch a last glimpse of the charming actress, who, at different theatres, had been the delight of London audiences for nearly thirty. The bill was made up of selections from *Money*, *Masks and Faces*, *London Assurance*, supported by the *bénéficiaires*, Charles Wyndham, Coghlan, Arthur Cecil, Ellen Terry, Mrs. Kendal, John Clayton, Mrs. Stirling, and a host of others. Henry Irving delivered an address, and Toole made one of his droll speeches, in which he referred to his first meeting with Marie Wilton on the stage of the Lyceum at the first rehearsal of *Belphegor*, when she was a trembling débutante unknown to London. Both Mr.—he was not Sir Squire in those days—and Mrs. Bancroft played engagements in after years, the former at the Lyceum, in the *The Dead Heart*, and both in the revival of *Diplomacy* at the Garrick, where the lady also reappeared as Lady Franklin in a revival of *Money* and on one or two other occasions.

The Haymarket was reopened in September by Messrs. Russell and Bashford—the latter had been the Bancrofts' acting manager—with a version of Hugh Conway's *Dark Days*, but it was not successful. Nor was the sporting drama, *Hard Hit*, in which Willard and Marion Terry acted very finely; nor Mrs. Brown-Potter and Kyrle Bellew in a revival of the old Prince of Wales's play, *Man and Wife*.

Another fiasco was *Nadjesda*, a powerful but uneven play, the first act dealing with a risky situation, in which Emily Rigl, an Austrian actress of great ability, was treated with a sample of British ruffianism from pit and gallery that aroused a storm of indignation from all decent people. It was as Prince Zabouroff, in this drama, that Beerbohm Tree first threw off certain crudities of manner which marred his earlier performances, and gave us one of those studies of restrained and consummate art with which he has been identified ever since. A great success was made with Sir Charles Young's powerful drama, *Jim the Penman*, which was performed in the seasons of 1886–7.

But the Russell-Bashford régime was a brief one, and in the autumn of 1887 the historic playhouse passed into the hands of Mr. Beerbohm Tree. Among the most notable of his productions were Haddon Chambers's *Captain Swift*, a striking play that afforded the manager one of his finest impersonations; *A Man's Shadow* (1889), in which Miss Julia Neilson made her first hit as Julie, and the veteran, James Fernandez, thrilled and astonished the house by his great acting as De Noirville, the advocate; *A Village Priest* (1889), in which Rose Leclercq, as the mother, greatly distinguished herself. In *The Dancing Girl* (1891), Julia Neilson attained the high-water mark of her reputation, and it was a prodigious success. The same cannot be said of *The Tempter*, a picturesque, poetical, mediæval play, exquisitely produced, by the same author. But *Trilby* created a furore; *Hypatia* (1893) was staged with a classic beauty beyond all praise. Oscar Wilde's two best comedies, *A Woman of No Importance* and *An Ideal Husband*, the latter under Lewis Waller's tenancy, were brought out in 1893–4. There were revivals of

The Merry Wives of Windsor, of *Henry IV.* (1896), for Tree to play Falstaff, and *Hamlet*, in which Mrs. Beerbohm Tree gave the finest *realistic* rendering of Ophelia's mad scene that I can remember. There were other plays, *John a' Dreams*, *A Bunch of Violets*, etc., each and all produced with an artistic care, a perfection of detail, and a poetic insight that have only been exceeded by his later work.

Mr. Tree having passed over to his new theatre, Messrs. Harrison and Cyril Maude took up the lease of the Haymarket in October, 1896, and started their campaign with a success, a version of Stanley Weyman's *Under the Red Robe; The Little Minister* was another great draw; revivals of *She Stoops to Conquer*, *The Rivals*, the inevitable *School for Scandal*, *Caste*, *The Black Tulip*, a new version of *The Ladies' Battle*, all of which owed so much of their success to the delightful acting of Winifred Emery and the artistic performances of her husband. Longest run of all was *The Second in Command.* One of the latest revivals was *The Clandestine Marriage*, in which Cyril Maude played with his usual artistic care the old beau, Lord Ogleby. *Cousin Kate*, by a new writer, is keeping up the extraordinary run of luck that has followed nearly all the productions of the present management. Mrs. Cyril Maude's unfortunate absence, however, has left a void that there is little prospect of being satisfactorily filled up.

PART III

THE BYGONE THEATRES OF THE WEST

ROBERT WILLIAM ELLISTON.

CHAPTER I

The Olympic, 1805-99—Its History—With some account of the rise of the minor Theatres and the Repeal of the Licensing Act of 1737.

THE rise of the London minor stage and the fall of the great patent houses give us one of the most curious chapters in theatrical history. In a country like France, where the histrionic art is a part of the national life, such a collapse as that of Drury Lane and Covent Garden would have been impossible; but in England, where art of all kinds is an outside matter, only to be thought about when business is done, in a nation in which the great mass of all classes, when they take amusement, require only something to laugh at, or something "to stretch the gaping eyes of idiot wonder," perhaps the most remarkable part of the case is that the patent houses should have held their ground so long; and, indeed, as I have endeavoured to show in the preceding pages, it was only through pandering to the aforesaid vulgar tastes with raree-show and buffoonery that, after Garrick's time, these managers averted the ever-threatening ruin.

During the sixty or seventy years that succeeded the passing of Sir Robert Walpole's Licensing Act the metropolis grew apace, and though two theatres might have sufficed for 1737, it by no means followed that they were adequate to the requirements of the earlier decades of the next century. Why should East London,

South London, North London, which were every day extending farther and farther away from Central London, not enjoy theatrical amusements if the people desired them? Such a plea it was impossible to deny; and one after another new theatres were allowed to open during the summer months, under the permission of the Lord Chamberlain.

But, in order to evade the Licensing Act, the Italian word "Burletta" was introduced to designate the new style of theatrical entertainment. It proved a very elastic term, comprehending opera, serious and comic, farce, pantomime, melodrama, burlesque, in fine, anything except tragedy and comedy; the one hard and fast rule being that a certain number of songs should be introduced, and the notes of a piano occasionally struck throughout the performance. Since the days of Garrick a new theatrical audience had been gradually developing. Until the close of the eighteenth century, or perhaps more correctly speaking the opening years of the nineteenth, the lower orders of our great city cared little for indoor amusements. Pugilism, cock and dog fighting, bear and bull baiting, and such-like sports and pastimes, were alone to their tastes; and even the galleries of Drury Lane and Covent Garden were mostly filled, only excepting the servants of the nobility, by the people who now patronise the dress-circle; the pit was the resort of barristers, doctors, and critics, and only nobility, or the richest gentry, frequented the boxes. Thus, with the exception, perhaps, of pantomime time, the audience in its entirety was an educated one. When Sheridan brought horses and elephants to Drury Lane, and the Covent Garden management had to follow suit, a lower order of spectators was attracted; and as the working classes grew less brutal in their habits, they occasionally varied the delights of the cock-pit and the bull-baiting field with the tamer recreation of the playhouse.

But poetry and wit had no charms for these new patrons of the drama; they required something more highly spiced, something that would produce in a milder form the excitement of seeing a dog gored to death by a bull, or a couple of bantams spurring each other to shreds. What kindred feeling had they with the woes of *Romeo and Juliet*, or with the fine ladies and gentlemen of the *School for Scandal?* Such people were not of their world; they wanted mimic murders and deeds of violence with all the coarse realism of the *Newgate Calendar* to satisfy their old appetite for blood, and if there were woes and love-making and jesting, it must be of the kind with which they were familiar. And it was not long before caterers sprang up ready and eager to supply such viands.

Yet it was not the lower orders alone who were bringing about these changes in theatrical amusements; the tastes of the great bulk of the playgoing public were tending in the same direction. Both in literature and the drama the classic was everywhere receding before the romantic. Fielding and Miss Burney were forsaken for Mrs. Radcliffe and "Monk" Lewis; we were invaded by the German school of horrors; everything seemed flat and insipid that was not flavoured with them, and the great theatres found that such pieces as *A Tale of Mystery*, *Raymond and Agnes*, *The Castle Spectre*, *The Miller and his Men*, were more attractive than Shakespeare or Sheridan.

Here was the door by which the Licensing Act could be evaded; and to supply this new demand, and to cater for these new audiences, small theatres began to be built, first in Central London and afterwards in more remote districts where, as there were neither trains nor omnibuses, nor any other cheap modes of conveyance in those days, they secured a veritable monopoly. It was no wonder the managers of the patent houses, with their enormous rentals and expenses, fought desperately against this innovation, which was decimating their pits and galleries, while fashion had almost deserted the dramatic for the lyric stage. Within twenty or thirty years from their first starting the summer houses were firmly established. Although their liabilities were smaller, the minor managers had as hard a fight for existence and complained as bitterly of the lack of public support as did their aristocratic brethren at Drury Lane and Covent Garden; but they were under the impression that if they could only succeed in abolishing the privileges of those houses, all would be well with them; while the patent holders, on their side, believed that could they fully exact the monopoly given them by law, golden days would return. Thus, while "the minors" were petitioning the Lord Chamberlain to relieve them of all restrictions, the patentees were constantly urging him to abolish these obnoxious rivals altogether.

As I have previously stated, the minor theatres were privileged to be open only during the summer months, when Drury Lane and Covent Garden were closed, but gradually the seasons of the latter were extended beyond their usual time, which brought forth remonstrances from the other side, who, to retaliate, continued to perform after the great houses had commenced their winter campaign. As the patent theatres, however, fell from their high estate and passed into the hands of mere adventurers, who devoted them to opera, wild-beast shows, circuses, and melodrama, rather than to those plays by which they held their privileges, the incongruity of the monopoly became more and more apparent. Most actors were in favour of unrestricted competition, not from any artistic consideration, but because it would give them a wider field for their vanity and profit; even William Macready petitioned Parliament to that effect. As time went on, the Press, the public, and the House of Commons began to take sides in the discussion, and mostly favoured free trade in things theatrical. Sentimentalists urged that the Licensing Act was inimical to the intellectual advancement of the people, and drew charming pictures of Southwark, Whitechapel, and Shoreditch crowding in their thousands to listen to the words of "the immortal bard" and to laugh over the wit of Sheridan; blood and murder, vulgar farce, and inane pantomimes, they prophesied, would no longer be tolerated, and the golden age of the drama would be indeed inaugurated.

During several years influential men, Sir Edward Bulwer Lytton among the rest, had been urging upon the House the necessity of a change in the law; but it was a long time before our legislators could be induced to appoint a Committee to investigate the question; actors and other experts were examined, and at length, in 1843, Sir James Graham introduced and carried a Bill, by which the patent privileges were abolished, and all London theatres placed under the jurisdiction of the Lord Chamberlain. No sooner did this Act become law than the managers of the minor theatres made a rush upon Shakespeare. But a very brief experiment convinced them that they had been reckoning without their audiences, and that although Whitechapel or Shoreditch might occasionally like to see a "well-mouthed actor" in Richard, Macbeth, or Hamlet, it preferred for its staple fare *The Murder of Maria Martin* and *The Bandit of the Blind Mine.* In only one outlying theatre, Sadler's Wells, did the new Act in any way fulfil the expectations of its admirers, and there, indeed, it scored an absolute triumph.

From an artistic point of view the change, though inevitable and unavoidable, was not an unmixed blessing; it scattered the talent that should have been concentrated, it lowered the standard of excellence, and it fostered the vanity and petty ambition of men who, with just ability enough to represent Banquo or Laertes, aspired to Macbeth and Hamlet. Histrionic talent has never been so abounding in any age or country that competent artists for the representation of high tragedy and comedy could be found more than sufficient for two or three theatres.

The first of the West End minor theatres that won a prominent position was the Wych Street house. In the reign of Elizabeth, Drury Lane was known as the Via de Aldwych. Drury House, built towards the end of the sixteenth century, gave a new title to the thoroughfare, running northward, while the southern end came to be known as Wych Street. Close to Drury rose Craven House, erected by the Earl of Craven for the reception of his bride, James the First's daughter, the titular Queen of Bohemia. It was a fine mansion, shut in by iron gates, and with extensive grounds in the rear. Long after its fellows had disappeared, and "the drabs and bloods of Drury Lane" had become a byword, Craven House still stood, shorn of its gardens, and converted into a public-house that bore the name of "The Queen of Bohemia," in memory of its former mistress. To save the building from falling it was pulled down in 1805, and, upon the ground being cleared, a portion of the site was taken on lease by Philip Astley, the founder of the Amphitheatre,[1] so long known by his name, for the purpose of raising a circus thereon.

The Olympic Pavilion was built chiefly out of the materials of an old French warship, the *Ville de Paris*—*Wheel de Parry* Astley called it—which was sold, with some other naval prizes, about this time. No sooner was the lease signed than Astley proceeded to collect workmen out of the neighbouring public-houses and set them to work. Seated in a little one-horse chaise, that he used to drive about in, but which was scarcely capacious enough to contain his very rotund figure, from morning until night, in all weathers, he directed the operations, and saw that there was no idling or shirking. There was very little brickwork in the building; the yards and bowsprits of the ship formed the uprights and supports, the deck was used for the stage and flooring, the sides for the outward walls, while the roof was of tin.

The Pavilion was in the form of a tent. There was one tier of boxes, a pit, which surrounded the circle, and, at the back of the pit, a gallery. There was no orchestra, the musicians being placed in two stage-boxes facing one another. The entire cost was only £800. Obtaining a licence, through the influence of Queen Charlotte, for music, dancing, burlettas, pantomime, and equestrian exhibitions, Astley opened the place in 1806.

But it was a complete failure from the beginning. No attraction could draw the public to "Astley's Middlesex Amphitheatre," not even pugilistic exhibitions by such renowned heroes of the prize-ring as "Dutch Sam," and others of equal celebrity; so, after losing

[1] See "Astley's Amphitheatre."

about ten thousand pounds, Astley tried to let it, and, in 1813, sent circulars round to the various theatrical managers describing its peculiar advantages.

"We'll throw the bone, Johnny," he said to his son, "and let the dogs fight for it; someone will snap at it."

The dog that did snap at it was that eccentric genius Elliston, whom we have already met at Drury Lane. "The very thing for me," he exclaimed, "so near to Drury Lane; it will be quite a family circle." He entered into negotiations with Astley, and arranged to give him £2,800 for the building, and an annuity of £20 during the remainder of his life. Not long was he burdened with the latter payment, as Astley died in the following year. Elliston's opening night was April 19th, 1813, the name of the house being changed from the "Olympic Pavilion" to "Little Drury Lane." The rivalry of an actor so popular as Robert William Elliston was not to be ignored by the patent houses, the managers of which presented a memorial to the Lord Chamberlain, setting forth that the licence granted to the late Philip Astley extended only for the time during which the Amphitheatre in Westminster Road was closed, and was restricted to equestrian exhibitions. The result of this representation was the closing of the theatre in the following month. But Elliston was not a man to be easily beaten; he had good friends at Court, through whose influence he obtained a new licence, under which he reopened the house in the December of the same year; but, as a sacrifice to the susceptibilities of the great managers, he reverted to the old name—the Olympic Pavilion.

This minor stage only just missed the honour of introducing Edmund Kean to London; during the interregnum Elliston had been in correspondence with him. The following letter from the famous actor, who was at the time only a poor unknown stroller, steeped to the lips in poverty, is so full of suggestion that it needs no comment :—

"*Barnstaple, Oct. 2nd,* 1813.

"SIR,—I have this moment received your proposal for the Wych Street Theatre, *id est,* Little Drury Lane, and much deplore your letter not finding me. Neglect does not rank in the catalogue of my follies. The terms Miss Tidswell, by your authority, mentioned to me is the superintending of the stage, the whole of the principal line of business under all denominations of acting, and an equal division of the house on the night of my benefit, with three guineas a week salary. The pecuniary terms, I own, do not justify the renown of your establishment; but I place so firm a reliance on your reputed liberality that, on the proof of my humble abilities and assiduity towards the promotion of your interests, you will not be unmindful of mine. I accept, Sir, your present proposal, simply requesting you will name what time you expect me in London, etc.

"Your obedient servt.,
"EDMUND KEAN."

Until he had obtained the licence it was impossible for Elliston to fix the date of opening, and in the meantime Kean had received an offer for Drury Lane, which he at once accepted. Thereupon Elliston asserted his prior claim, and no entreaties from the poor stroller could turn him from prosecuting it. His conduct, to say the least, was harsh and uncharitable, as the name of Edmund Kean on the playbill at that time was not worth a shilling. The dispute, which very nearly lost Kean his chance at Drury Lane, was ultimately arranged by his finding a substitute, an actor named Bernard; but as Elliston had to pay this man £5 a week, Kean undertook to give the £2 extra out of his own pocket. When Robert William heard of the little man's success he, no doubt, greatly repented of his lenity.

Pantomimes, ballets, farces, melodramas—all bearing the orthodox title of "burlettas"—were, as in other minor theatres, the stock bill of fare, and to these were added such other attractions as tight-rope dancers, performing dogs, and one Baker, a professional pedestrian, who had walked a thousand miles in twenty days, appeared here to sing songs and dance hornpipes in "the identical shoes" in which he had performed his famous walk. In 1818 the manager again roused the active wrath of the great patentees by playing Milman's *Fazio*, a five-act tragedy; but although all the influence of the powerful Drury Lane committee was brought to bear against him, he once more survived the storm, and came out of the struggle stronger than ever. In that year he rebuilt the theatre at a cost of £2,500, and engaged a superior company, in which Wrench, the light comedian, and Mrs. Edwin, one of the finest melodramatic actresses of her day, were included. To add still further to the attractions, he himself acted here for the first time, in a new piece called *Rochester*, which, together with an extravaganza, ran through the entire season, drawing large and fashionable audiences.

Planché, some of whose earliest dramatic efforts were produced at the Olympic, tells a good story of Elliston at this period. He had written for him a sort of speaking pantomime called *Little Red Riding Hood*. On the first night everything went wrong in the mechanical department. When the performance was over, Elliston summoned all the carpenters and scene-shifters on to the stage, in front of a cottage scene, having a practicable door and window; leading Planché forward, and standing in the centre, with his back to the footlights, he harangued them in the most grandiloquent manner, expatiating on the enormity of their offence, their ingratitude to the man whose bread they were eating, the disgrace they had brought upon the theatre, the cruel injury they had inflicted on the young and promising author by his side; then, pointing in the most tragical attitude to his wife and daughters, who were in his box, he bade them look upon the family they had ruined, and, burying his face in his handkerchief to stifle his sobs, passed slowly through the door of the scene, leaving his audience silent, abashed, and somewhat affected, yet rather relieved at being let off with a lecture. The next minute the casement was thrown violently open, and thrusting out his head, his face all scarlet with fury, he roared out, "I discharge you all." "I feel utterly unable," says the writer, "to convey an idea of this ludicrous scene, and I question whether anyone unacquainted with the man, his voice, action, and wonderful facial expression, could thoroughly realise the glorious absurdity of it from verbal description."

In 1819, Elliston became the manager of Drury Lane, and, according to the articles of his lease, he was prohibited from being connected with the management of any other theatre. During the next five years the Olympic conducted four *entrepreneurs* to the bankruptcy court. In 1824, Elliston having lost everything at Drury Lane, the mortgagees sold the Olympic Pavilion, building, scenery, wardrobe, and all, for £4,860. An engraving of the theatre at this time shows a high brick wall, with a verandah-like abutment and tent-like entrance. Mr. John Scott, who had built the Sans Pareil, afterwards the Adelphi, was the next manager, and he inaugurated a reign of red-hot melodrama.

At the latter end of the year 1830, Madame Vestris, being out of an engagement, made up her mind to take a theatre, and the Olympic being the only available one in the market, it was Hobson's choice. She opened it on January 3rd in the following year with a drama on the subject of Mary Queen of Scots, in which Miss Foote, who appears to have been for a short time in partnership with her, played the heroine, and an extravaganza by Planché entitled *Olympic Revels*. It is at this point that the real history of the Wych Street theatre, which now took an acknowledged and a high position among the places of amusement of the metropolis, may be said to commence. Madame Vestris was the first of the manageresses, as was set forth in the address spoken by her on the opening night, which commenced :—

> "Noble and gentle, matrons, patrons, friends,
> Before you here a venturous woman bends ;
> A warrior-woman, that in strife embarks,
> The first of all dramatic Joans of Arc ;
> Cheer on the enterprise thus dared by me,
> The first that ever led a company !
> What though, until this very hour and age,
> A lessee lady never owned a stage !"

During Madame Vestris's second season, Liston was one of the stock company, and James Bland, who, until the appearance of Robson, had no equal as a burlesque actor in the mock-heroic style that depends for its humour upon the exaggeration of passion, instead of buffoonery. Encouraged by the success of her undertaking, each year she made greater efforts to attract public favour, and in 1833 her company included Keeley, Liston, Bland, James Vining, Frank Matthews, Mrs. Orger, Miss Goward (Mrs. Keeley), and her incomparable self. The entertainment was of the lightest and brightest—comedietta, farce, extravaganza. Planché was the dramatic *genius loci*, and no other could have been found so exactly suitable to the requirements of the management. Planché had a delicacy of touch in burlesque that has never been equalled by any other English writer. Classical subjects have been travestied for the stage since the days of Henry Fielding; but Planché, while travestying the ancient myths, did it with a refinement unknown to his predecessors. His chief triumphs, however, were in a field until then unexplored by playwrights—the fairy lore of France, as it exists in the pages of Perrault and the Countess d'Aulnoy. Under his hand those exquisite fairy tales never degenerated into mere nonsense, and though every character was treated from a humorous point of view, no beautiful thought or creation was held up to ridicule; street slang was never called in to eke out shortness of wit, and when puns were introduced—which was not too frequently—they were real puns, appropriate to the situation, and not dragged in for the mere purpose of word-twisting; the fantastic, the grotesque, and the poetic were combined in almost equal degrees. And what an interpreter he had in Madame Vestris! one endowed with histrionic abilities that were brilliant even in the highest range of comedy, with a voice equal to the requirements of the finest music, with a taste the most refined, and a personal beauty that was peerless! To quote Planché's own words: "The extraordinary and continued success of this experiment was due, not only to the admirable singing and *piquante* performance of that gifted lady, but also to the charm of novelty imparted to it by the elegance and accuracy of the costume, it having been previously the practice to dress a burlesque in the most *outré* and ridiculous fashion. My suggestion to try the effect of persons picturesquely attired speaking absurd doggerel fortunately took the fancy of the fair lessee, and the alteration was highly appreciated by the public. But many old actors could never get over their early impressions; Liston thought to the last that Prometheus, instead of the Phrygian cap, tunic, and trousers, should have been dressed like a great lubberly boy, in a red jacket and nankeens, with a pinafore all besmeared with lollipops."

Nor were her reforms confined to the burlesque part of the programme. Writing of the Olympic at this time, in his autobiography, Charles Mathews says: "There was introduced for the first time in England that reform in all theatrical matters which has since been adopted at every theatre in the kingdom. Drawing-rooms were fitted up like drawing-rooms, and fitted with care and taste. Two chairs no longer indicated that two persons were to be seated. A claret-coloured coat, salmon-coloured trousers, with a broad black stripe, a sky-blue neckcloth with a large paste brooch, and a cut-steel eyeglass with a pink ribbon, no longer marked the light-comedy gentleman, and the public at once recognised and appreciated the changes."

Never for a moment did the fair manageress relax her vigilance; when not acting, she was always in her box watching the performance and detecting the slightest faults or shortcomings.

It was on December 7th, 1835, at the age of thirty-one, that "young" Charles Mathews made his first appearance upon the public stage at the Olympic. The event is thus described in a newspaper of the day: "Olympic.—On Monday this house was crowded in every part; the announcement of the first appearance of Mr. Charles Mathews was sufficient to excite the curiosity of the general playgoer, as well as the actors, who mustered strong upon the occasion. We never recollect on any previous one so many performers congregated in the audience part of the theatre. Liston introduced him to the public, and appeared satisfied with the talent displayed by the new débutant. Two burlettes were produced—the first a translation by Mathews, in which he performed 'the Hunchback'd Lover'; the second a clever and original piece, entitled *Old and Young Stagers*, by Leman Rede. In the latter, Liston enacted the Old Stager, and Mathews the young one. We are not disposed to be too severe on the juvenile aspirant, and will make every allowance for a first appearance. His performance throughout was such as to give promise of future excellence; at present he wants that repose which only time and study can accomplish. He occasionally reminded us of his late father, particularly in a song which he introduced, and which he executed exceedingly well; it called forth an unanimous encore. We shall wait his appearance in some other character before we give a decided opinion of his talents, but at the same time must do him the justice to say it was one of the most successful débuts we have ever witnessed."

Mathews was educated for an architect, he had also been a protégé of the Earl of Blessington's, and accompanied that nobleman and his famous countess to Italy for the purpose of pursuing his studies. From that time he moved in the most fashionable circles of society, and contracted habits and associations very unsuited to a struggling professional man. His father lost all his money by bad speculations, theatrical and otherwise, and at his death young Charles found that he must set to work in earnest to gain a livelihood; so he took an empty room in Furnival's Inn, and had his name painted upon the panels with the addition of the word "Architect." As no one appeared to be desirous of testing the young man's powers of construction, his friends advised him to try for a district surveyorship. There was a vacancy in the district of Bow and Bethnal Green, and Mathews enlisted all the interest he could muster to obtain the post. To continue in his own words: "The emoluments arising from the appointment were not startling, and about £40 per annum compensated me for my agreeable labours—that is, would have done, had I received it; but there was the difficulty. It consisted of fees, fees to be collected by myself in person, and a pretty time I had of it. At one house I knocked humbly, after considerable hesitation; the door was opened cautiously with the chain up, and a stout, suspicious-looking dame, in a pair of nankeen stays, asked me if I 'came arter the taxes or summat?' 'No, madam,' I answered deferentially, 'I am the district surveyor from Cutthroat Lane, and——' 'Oh, bother!' said the lady, 'summons me if you like; I'm not going to be humbugged by you.' Another defaulter kept an oilcloth warehouse in Whitechapel. I was some time before I could summon up courage to enter, as there were several customers assembled. However, I ventured, and was met by an appeal that was irresistible. 'What?' he said, 'you, a gentleman, come to a poor man like me for such a paltry sum as that! You ought to be ashamed of yourself.' Then turning to the customers, 'What do you think of this? Here's a gentleman who——' I did not wait to hear the rest, but made my exit at once, thinking I was lucky to escape being tossed in a blanket."

This was not the kind of experience to suit the associate of D'Orsay, the pet of earls and countesses, and although averse to the stage as a profession, he now turned his thoughts in that direction. He had been a writer of light pieces, and an amateur actor in the private theatres of his friends from boyhood; and, born as it were within the shadow of the green baize, it was no raw novice who made his first bow to a London audience on that December night.

The Olympic, however, was the only theatre at that period upon which he could have achieved a success, for his style was new, was entirely opposed to the stage traditions that still ruled the dramatic world, and were to rule it for many years to come. His light comedy was quite a different thing from that of the *outré*-dressed, swaggering, back-slapping, restless, loud-talking gentleman who then possessed the stage; it was the most perfect blending of art and nature, or rather it was the most perfect example of natural art, the English stage has ever known. Mathews did not, as superficial observers used to say, do and talk precisely as a man would in the privacy of his own drawing-room; no landscape can be transferred to canvas exactly as it exists, but only as it appears through the medium of the painter's eye; no character can be drawn, no story, however realistic, can be told until it has been sublimated in the novelist's imagination; and no actor can tread the stage without imparting a certain artificial colouring and polish to his creations, unless he would have his efforts condemned as crude and *un*natural. However closely art and nature may approach each other, the moment they are confounded together each loses its distinctive charm. It was the very perfection of Charles Mathews's art that made it look so much like nature; founded upon the best French school, his acting was quite equal to his models. No English rival approached that combination of consummate ease, nonchalance, polished manner, and brilliant vivacity that marked his performances until he was nearly seventy years of age. Whatever he did was apparently without effort; even in such extravagances as *Patter versus Clatter* and *He would be an Actor*, in which he assumed several different characters, we had the same delightful repose; when he suddenly changed from the young officer to the chattering barber, or the man with a cold in his head, or from the Welsh gardener to the French lady, he never resorted to caricature to emphasise the change; he was never haunted by the memory of the previous character, and a fear that he might be falling back upon it. He had full confidence in his skill and fine judgment. How admirably was the latter displayed in the second act of *Used Up!* Sir Charles Coldstream approached only as near to a ploughman as a gentleman could. I have seen other actors approach very much nearer, because in their coarse art they thought a violent contrast should be made between the first and the second act.

But to return to our chronicle. When Liston retired from the stage, in the season of 1836–7, William Farren joined the company. Farren, who is the father and grandfather of the living actors of that name, and was son of the original Careless in *The School for Scandal*, was one of the finest actors of his time. As early as 1818 he made a great success at Covent Garden as Sir Peter Teazle, with Young, Charles Kemble, Blanchard, and Liston in the cast, and from that time until his retirement in 1855 retained his prestige as Sir Peter, Lord Ogleby, Marrall, Dr. Primrose, Grandfather Whitehead, Sir Anthony Absolute, etc.

Imagine a *lever de rideau* acted by Charles Mathews, Keeley, James Vining, Mrs. Orger, Mrs. Keeley,

Madame Vestris, and Farren! They all appeared together in *You Cannot Marry Your Grandmother.* It will be somewhat startling to present-day playgoers to be told that with such a magnificent array of talent the highest price of admission was four shillings; indeed, there were but two prices, as in 1837 Madame Vestris abolished the gallery, converting it into boxes; the pit was two shillings. Though general salaries were small, both Liston and Farren took very large ones, and the manageress and Charles Mathews must have put themselves down for a pretty considerable sum weekly. The wonder is, how the theatre could possibly have been kept on at such a tariff.

In the July of 1838, Charles Mathews and Madame Vestris were married in Kensington Church, and directly afterwards started for America. Mathews's account of their trip goes very far to prove that there was not much exaggeration in Dickens's pictures of the Americans of that generation. Arriving at an hotel in New York, fatigued by their voyage, in the midst of some public ball, they naturally desired privacy, and because they objected to show themselves like prize oxen, it was voted that they had insulted the American citizens; a clique was formed against them, the prospects of their tour were ruined, and by Christmas they were once more in London. And not a day too soon, for the Olympic company had been playing to a heavy loss during the whole time they had been absent.

It may be supposed that the little theatre no longer satisfied the Mathews' ambition, as, in 1839, they quitted the Olympic for Covent Garden. During the next ten years the fortunes of the Wych Street house were extremely chequered. George Wilde, a penniless adventurer, George Bolton, another, Kate Howard,

Davidson, etc., etc., came like shadows and so departed, leaving no record behind, except in the books of their creditors. Those were followed by Miss Davenport, and, in 1848, by Walter Watts, a clerk in the Globe Insurance Office, who lavished a lot of money, not his own, upon the theatre.

It was under Watts, January, 1848, that Gustavus Brooke made his first appearance in London as Othello. There was a great similarity between the careers of Edmund Kean and the Irish tragedian; both were reckless and dissipated, and both passed their early years in strolling companies. While at Manchester, where he played second parts, Brooke attracted the attention of Macready, who engaged him for Drury Lane in 1845. Finding himself cast for the unimportant part of Salanio in the *Merchant of Venice*, however, he broke his engagement and went back to strolling. Only a few months before he opened at the Olympic he was playing in a theatre built under a railway arch at Kilmarnock, and was driven to such extremities that he had to take up his abode there night and day.

Brooke had a good stage-face and presence, a voice deep and musical as a full-toned organ, and great power. Though he was guilty at times of "tearing a passion to rags, to very tatters," there was a soul in his rant, and a reality in his bursts of passion, that hurried the spectator on and blinded one to his exaggerations. No such sensational début had been made since the night Edmund Kean played Shylock for the first time at Drury Lane; "the pit rose" at him as it had at "the little man in the capes," and applause culminated in an enthusiastic demonstration. Yet never were the critics more divergent in their opinions, for while the *Times* pronounced him to be purely original, exquisite in his pathos, and overwhelming in his rage, the *Examiner* considered him utterly conventional and a mere mouther.

Whatever might have been Brooke's faults, there was no Othello between his and Salvini's. His Sir Giles Overreach was a remarkable piece of acting. I have never seen anything more startling upon the stage than his last act, especially that point where, in the full tempest of his fury, he was rushing sword in hand upon his creature, Marrall—the sudden stop, as one struck by palsy, the horror of the face, the gripping of the wrist that refused to perform his will, and the muttered cry: "Some undone widow sits upon my arm!" Even the actors engaged in the scene were appalled by the terrible realism, and almost forgot their parts. Brooke was also an admirable comedian in certain Irish characters, such as O'Callaghan in the once favourite farce of *His Last Legs*. He was afterwards as great a success at Drury Lane as he had been at the Olympic.

The public took prodigiously to the new star, and Brooke might have held a permanent position upon the London stage but for that sin which has proved the destruction of so many actors; it was the story of George Frederick Cooke over again: a disappointed or an outraged public in town and country that soon grew disgusted with their favourite. There was a touch of heroism in his death: he went down in the wreck of the *London*, January, 1866, while on his way to Australia, and he was last seen working manfully at the pumps. Perhaps "there was nothing in his life became him like his leaving it."

On March 29th, 1849, at five o'clock in the evening, the Olympic was discovered to be on fire, and in a little while all that remained of Philip Astley's "*Wheel de Parry*" was a mass of smouldering ruins. There was a strong suspicion of incendiarism.

The house was rebuilt and reopened by Walter Watts at the end of the same year, but was abruptly closed in March, 1850, in consequence of the manager's arrest for enormous defalcations and forgery, which made his name rather famous in Old Bailey records.

After another fiasco by George Bolton, William Farren came here from the Strand with a fine company —Mrs. Glover, Mrs. Stirling, Compton, Leigh Murray; he afterwards engaged Helen Faucit for a series of legitimate performances.

Yet with all his efforts and all the talent at his command, Farren could not draw the public to any profitable extent. There is one factor, however, to be taken into consideration; Farren, though not then seventy years old, was a mere wreck; his speech was so indistinct that he might have been acting in a foreign tongue for all that could be understood of his utterances, and as he persisted in playing principal parts, this circumstance might have had something to do with the bad business.

On Easter Monday, 1853, Frederick Robson made his first appearance on this stage in an old farce entitled, *Catching an Heiress.* Robson had for some years been low comedian at the Grecian Saloon. He then went to Dublin for two or three seasons, where Farren saw him act and engaged him for the Olympic. Robson, however, attracted no particular attention until Talfourd's burlesque on *Macbeth* was brought out a few weeks later; then his tragi-comic style burst upon the town with all the force of a new creation. Three months afterwards he appeared as Shylock in another burlesque by the same author, and the next morning the *Times* pronounced him to be the greatest actor that had been seen upon the stage since Edmund Kean. This was followed by a wonderful impersonation, and a wonderful comic song in one of the trashiest of farces, *The Wandering Minstrel*,—"Villikins and his Dinah," that he had sung hundreds of times at the Grecian; it now drew all fashionable London for a twelvemonth. It was more than a success, it was a furore. Everybody was singing "Too roo ral, too roo ral, too ral li da." It was introduced upon the most extraordinary occasions, even by a counsel in his address to the jury; "Villikins and his Dinah" was the ballad *par excellence* from the Belgravia drawing-room to the St. Giles's beershop.

Farren took leave of the Olympic in September, 1853, as Lord Ogleby, and on the 17th of October Alfred Wigan inaugurated his reign with *The Camp* at the Olympic, and Tom Taylor's *Plot and Passion*, in which Mrs. Stirling, Wigan, and Emery played superbly, and Robson made another enormous hit as the spy Desmaret. I may note that the stalls were now raised to five shillings.

A first appearance has to be noted, that of Miss Herbert, who had come over from the Strand, in a powerful play called *Retribution*; we shall meet her again at the St. James's. But Robson was the unique attraction. The ghoul-like *Yellow Dwarf* was followed by the still more wonderful impersonation of *Medea*, with its wild, savage intensity, and grotesque commonplace. *Masaniello* was little inferior with the song "I'm a Shrimp," in which he reduced his body to boneless limpness, and the weird, mad scene, with his imitations of Charles Kean. And his success was equally great in domestic drama. What a wonderful performance was his Daddy Hardacre; it was the very ferocity of avarice. Hardly less successful was his Sampson Burr, in *The Porter's Knot*, but the sentimentality was somewhat strained and mawkish. Robson was a great genius; who that saw him when in the full possession of his powers can ever forget the strange-looking little man with the small body and the big head, who played upon his audience as though they had been the keys of a piano, now convulsing them with laughter as he perpetrated some outrageous drollery, now hushing them into awe-struck silence by an electrical burst of passion or pathos, or holding them midway between terror and laughter as he performed some weirdly grotesque dance? The impression he conveyed in those moments of extreme tension was that of a man overwrought by excitement to the verge of madness; the wild, gleaming eyes, the nervous twitchings of the marvellously plastic features, the utter *abandon* to the feeling of the moment, whether it were tragic or grotesque, the instantaneous transition from the tragedian to the clown, were no stage-tricks, but an inspiration, an irrepressible impulse. He was morbidly timid and nervous; he could never realise the great position he had attained, and was ever haunted by a fear that his fall would be as sudden as had been his rise; success had a delirious effect upon him, and to deaden the stage-fright, which he could never overcome, he resorted to stimulants—with the usual result.

When in August, 1857, Alfred Wigan retired from the management of the Olympic, it was undertaken by Robson in partnership with the acting manager, Emden. Poor Robson, his career was brief as it was brilliant, and its brilliancy was dulled long before the end. He had been famous scarcely seven years when his powers began to fail, and his terror of facing the audience became so great that while waiting for his cue he would gnaw his arms until they bled, and cry out piteously, "I dare not go on, I dare not!" until the prompter had at times absolutely to thrust him before the footlights.

Robson's last original part was Dogbriar, in Watts Philips's drama, *Camilla's Husband*, produced at the end of 1862; but by this time he was only the shadow of his former self. Melter Moss, in *The Ticket-of-Leave Man*, was written for him, but after a few rehearsals another actor, George Vincent, had to be engaged for the part, and on February 12th, 1864, before the run of that notable play came to an end, Frederick Robson had breathed his last.

The Ticket-of-Leave Man achieved the longest run recorded up to that time. It was one of a species of plays that had been delighting East End audiences for many years; but the style and the acting were toned down, the extravagances pruned, and the West End found a new sensation in scenes of low London life, which had not been so realistically rendered upon the stage since the days of *Tom and Jerry*.

Emden relinquished the management of the Olympic shortly after his partner's death, and was succeeded in the autumn of 1864 by Horace Wigan, the original Hawkshaw of the play last named. The new manager produced during his tenure a series of romantic plays which came to be known as "The Olympic Drama"—as in the days that were passed Buckstone's pieces were called "The Adelphi Drama"—of which Henry Neville, who had made himself famous as Bob Brierley, and Kate Terry were the principal exponents. Neville's impassioned, impulsive style excellently adapted him for the heroes of such plays as *The Serf*, *Henry Dunbar*, while as the heroine of domestic and romantic drama Miss Terry was the true successor of Mrs. Stirling. She was less successful in the legitimate, as she lacked poetry and distinction, although it was as Juliet at the Adelphi, in August, 1867, that she elected to take leave of the London stage. At the end of four years Wigan retired, and Benjamin Webster conducted the house for one season. He was followed in 1869 by Mr. Liston, who made some marked successes with adaptations of Dickens's and Wilkie Collins's novels, chief of which were *Little Em'ly* and *The Woman in White*.

Ada Cavendish spent a large sum of money in 1872 to make the Olympic one of the most charming theatres in London. *The New Magdalen* was her principal production. Miss Cavendish was an excellent actress, endowed with power, passion, and pathos, and but for chronic ill-health might have risen to a high position. Her Mercy Merrick, by which she is chiefly remembered, was a remarkably fine performance of a part that taxed all the beauty and all the art of the actress to enlist the sympathies of the audience and achieve a success. A notable impersonation of this lady's was Miss Gwilt, another of Wilkie Collins's shady heroines.

Miss Cavendish's management was brief as it was profitless, and in 1873 Henry Neville succeeded her, and was lessee for some six years. Tom Taylor's *Clancarty*, with Ada Cavendish as the heroine—the original and the best of all—*The Two Orphans*, *Clytie*, *Buckingham*, *The Scuttled Ship;* revivals of *The Ticket-of-Leave Man*, *Henry Dunbar*, *The Wife's Secret*, were among his productions. W. S. Gilbert's *Gretchen* was staged here soon after Mr. Neville's secession in 1879. John Hollingshead, Edgar Bruce, Geneviève Ward, Agnes Hewitt, John Coleman, etc., tried their fortunes at the Olympic between the last-named year and the closing of the old house in May, 1890, but nothing was done that calls for comment.

Entirely rebuilt and greatly enlarged, with a seating accommodation for three thousand people, and a stage inferior in size only to Drury Lane, the New Olympic was opened by Mr. Wilson Barrett in January, 1891, with a play bearing the suggestive title of *The People's Idol.* But if Mr. Barrett was the people's idol, the worshippers withheld their sacrifices, and although he revived *The Lights o' London*, *Hamlet*, *The Silver King*, and appeared in a new version of *Belphegor*, called *The Acrobat*, which unfortunately called up damaging recollections of Charles Dillon in the part, the ill luck of the old house seemed to have passed on to the new.

Signor Lago started an opera season here in September, 1892, and produced Tschaikowsky's *Eugène Onégin.* The great Russian composer's music was almost unknown eleven years ago, and the work was indifferently received. The season terminated abruptly. A curious dramatic experiment was made in 1895 by the Anglo-American Theatrical Syndicate, when an elaborately got up version of *The Pilgrim's Progress* was staged with a voluptuous ballet—shade of the Bedford tinker!—while Miss Grace Hawthorne represented the pious Christian very much in the guise of a pantomime prince. It was an extraordinary production.

There would be no interest and no purpose in recounting the names of the red-hot melodramas, the plunges into the legitimate—all more or less failures—that succeeded one another in rapid succession until the final closing of the unfortunate house in the autumn of 1899. A troupe of midgets at very low prices were the last who appeared upon its boards. A little while and even its site, traversed by a great thoroughfare, will be forgotten.

CHAPTER II

The English Opera House and Theatre Royal Lyceum—Its Records under the Keeleys, Madame Vestris, Charles Fechter, Sir Henry Irving, etc., 1809-1902

IN 1765, Mr. James Payne, an architect, erected, upon a piece of ground that formerly belonged to Exeter House, a building, constructed for the exhibitions of "The Society of Artists," which he christened the Lyceum. Three years later, divisions taking place among the members, certain of them went off to Somerset House, and there founded the Royal Academy, while the original body soon afterwards sank into oblivion. The premises were then purchased by Mr. Lingham, a breeches-maker in the Strand, who let them for exhibitions, or balls, or meetings, or any other purpose for which he could find a tenant. About 1794, Dr. Arnold, the musical composer, rebuilt the interior as a theatre, but being unable to obtain a licence through the strenuous opposition of the patentees of Drury Lane and Covent Garden, he had at last to give Lingham back his lease and forfeit the improvements with it. By including a large saloon and some smaller rooms, as well as the theatre, in the building, it could accommodate several exhibitions at one time. When the Amphitheatre in Westminster Road was burnt down, it was here that Astley brought his circus. The Musical Glasses (without Shakespeare), phantasmagoria, panoramas, made their home at the Lyceum. It was, by turns, a school of eloquence, a concert-room, a Roman Catholic chapel, the show-place of a white negro girl, and of a porcupine man; here actors out of engagements gave entertainments; and here it was that in 1802, Madame Tussaud, upon her arrival in England, first exhibited her collection of waxwork figures.

Not until 1809 did the Lyceum become a regular theatre. In that year the burnt-out company of Drury Lane obtained a special licence from the Lord Chamberlain to give dramatic performances at the Lyceum, where they performed during each winter, until the new Drury Lane was ready, in 1812. Samuel James Arnold, the son of the composer, and the manager for the Drury Lane Committee, obtained a licence for the performance of English opera during the summer months, on the plea that it would become the nursery of English singers for the patent theatres, and in 1810 the name of the building was changed to the English Opera House. Ballad operas old and new, musical farces, melodramas, such as *Love in a Village*, *One o'Clock; or, the Knight and the Wood Demon*, *No Song no Supper*, *The Devil's Bridge*, were interpreted in different seasons by Braham, Liston, Fawcett, Oxberry, Mrs. Mountain, Mrs. Bland, Fanny Kelly. Here about 1811 was produced Tom Moore's single dramatic essay, *M.P.; or, the Blue Stocking*.

In 1815, having, at the death of Whitbread, retired from the management of Drury Lane, Arnold was granted a ninety-nine years' lease of the Strand property from the Marquis of Exeter, at a ground rent of £700 per annum, and purchased the whole block of buildings that now form a square between Wellington Street and Exeter Street, rebuilding the houses, shops, and theatre, at a cost of £80,000. The northern end of Wellington

Street was not formed until 1829; Exeter Change, the Zoological Gardens and monsters' show-place of that day, occupied the site and projected over the pavement of the Strand; consequently the principal entrance to the theatre was beneath a small stone portico, supported by six Ionic columns, leading into a long, vaulted passage, upon which a door of the adjoining tavern opened, as it still does, into what was the pit passage. The entrances to pit and gallery were in Exeter Court. At prices ranging from one to five shillings, the house was computed to hold £350. The interior was handsomely decorated, but the great feature of the building was a saloon seventy-two feet long and forty wide, fitted up as a winter garden, with flowers and shrubs, and diversified in character each season: sometimes it represented an Italian terrace, then a Chinese pavilion, at another it was adorned with pictures of ancient Egypt. This house was one of the earlier places of public amusement that adopted the use of gas, as the Haymarket was the last, and in 1817 the announcement that gas-lights were introduced over the whole stage was made the great feature in the bills. It had been used at the Olympic, however, two years previously. Later on in the same season this innovation was extended to the auditorium.

The new house was opened June 15th, 1816, with two musical pieces, *Up All Night; or, The Smuggler's Cave*, and *The Boarding House*, and an Address by Miss Kelly. Between 1816 and 1818, Harley, Miss Love, a charming singer, and T. P. Cooke, were in the company. Fanny Kelly, however, was the bright particular star of the theatre. Charles Lamb was in love with her, and a letter dated 1819, in which he proposed to the delightful actress—who declined—has recently come to light.

Fanny Kelly, when she was nine years of age, played the Duke of York to George Frederick Cooke's Richard, on his first appearance in London in 1810; and Prince Arthur to Mrs. Siddons's Constance. She achieved no distinction in her profession, however, until 1814, when her clever acting at this theatre made the success of a pantomime called *Harlequin Hoax.* In the first season of the new house, *The Maid and the Magpie*, an adaptation of a French drama, *La Pie Voleuse*, was produced. It was just after the *cause célèbre* of Eliza Fenning, and a certain similarity between the two stories, together with the exquisite pathos of Miss Kelly as the falsely accused servant, Annette, created a great sensation. Memories of this old drama still survive in Rossini's *La Gazza Ladra*, and in H. J. Byron's burlesque. From that time Miss Kelly became identified with the heroines of domestic drama, and in such parts as Phœbe in *The Miller's Maid*, Lisette in *The Sergeant's Wife*, and many others written expressly to suit her particular style, she had no rival in her own day, nor has she had a successor. She was equally excellent in certain *soubrette* parts in farces, and while never lacking dramatic intensity or broad humour, her style was perfectly natural, no slight commendation in an age when stage art was generally stilted and artificial. Although very plain, she was twice in danger of her life from rejected lovers: one man fired at her from Drury Lane pit, and the bullet passed over her head; at Dublin another love-sick swain was so violent and threatening in his behaviour that she had to give him into custody. The ludicrous side of the story is that both were proved to be insane. "What can it mean?" she said very naively to the Dublin magistrate before whom the latter case was brought. "It can't be my beauty that drives these poor people mad!" We shall meet Miss Kelly again at the Strand and the Royalty.

Another striking success was that of Planché's once famous melodrama, *The Vampire*, for which that greatest exponent of diablerie, T. P. Cooke, was engaged. It was for this piece that the star, or vampire trap was invented. It was a very ingenious contrivance; so perfect were the springs, that when the actor vanished it seemed that he had gone through the solid boards, as no opening was discernible.

The licence granted to the English Opera House extended from July 1st to October; but, except by special permission for some particular occasion, no play belonging to the *répertoire* of the winter theatres was allowed to be performed. The old fare had to be adhered to—ballad opera and dramas, strong melodrama, bearing such titles as *The Death Fetch;* pantomimes and versions of German and Italian opera, cut down to a commonplace serious or comic drama, with songs and duets, most of the concerted pieces being omitted—in the first place, because the company could not sing them, and in the second, because the public would not have cared about them.[1] But the theatre did not pay; and in 1817 the management resorted to the curious experiment of giving two performances a night, the one commencing at six, the other at half-past nine, at reduced prices, a practice that was very speedily abandoned.

[1] The musical taste of the period was barbarous in the extreme. When *Oberon* was first produced at Covent Garden, in 1823, all the concerted pieces were cut out, and it was thought the audience would not stand even the exquisite "Mermaid's Song." At the very house I am writing of, when *Il Barbière* was brought out as a sort of musical comedy, Rossini's score was varied by excerpts from Dibdin, Philips, and three or four other composers.

It was on this stage, in 1818, that Mathews the elder first appeared in his famous entertainment *Mathews at Home*. His extraordinary powers of mimicry had for some time overshadowed his great abilities as an actor, so that, as he complained in his opening address, both managers and the Press had fallen into the habit of regarding him as a mere mimic, and on the opening of the great theatres he occasionally found himself left out in the cold. Years before, Charles Dibdin had appeared at the old house in a musical and mimetic entertainment, and it was this that suggested the idea of the *At Home* to Mathews. Arnold, the manager, offered to engage him for seven years at a thousand a year, terms with which, never anticipating the enormous success that the entertainment would achieve, he at once closed. The *At Home* was to be given each year in April and May at the English Opera House, and in the provinces during the remaining months. When the success was assured, more favourable terms for the artist, however, were arranged. The following copy of the first bill of Mathews's entertainment may prove interesting to the curious reader :—

THEATRE ROYAL, ENGLISH OPERA HOUSE, STRAND.

The public are respectfully informed that they will find Mr. Mathews "At Home" this evening, Thursday, April 2nd, 1818; Saturday the 4th, and on the Monday, Tuesday, Thursday, and Saturday following, when he will have the honour of presenting his visitors with an entertainment called

MAIL COACH ADVENTURES;

Affording an introduction for various comic songs, imitations, &c. Previous to which he will address the company on the subject of his present attempt.

PART FIRST.

Recitation—Introductory address—General improvement in the conveyance of live lumber, as exemplified in the progress of heavy coach, light coach, caterpillar and mail—Whimsical description of an expedition to Brentford.

SONG—*Mail Coach.*

Recitation—Description of the passengers—Lisping Lady and Critic in Black.

SONG—*Royal Visitors.*

Recitation—Breaking of a spring—Passengers at Highgate—Literary Butcher—Socrates in the Shambles—Definition of Belles-Lettres—French Poets—Rhyming Defended.

SONG—*Cobbler à la Française.*

Recitation—Theatrical Conversation—Dimensions of Drury Lane and Covent Garden stages—Matter-of-fact Conversation—Satire on Truisms.

SONG—*Incontrovertible Facts in various Branches of Knowledge.*

PART SECOND.

Mr. Mathews will deliver an experimental lecture on Ventriloquy.

PART THIRD.

Recitation—Digression on the Study of the Law; Whimsical Trial, Goody Grim *versus* Lapstone—Scramble at Supper—Drunken Farmer—Extract from Hippisly's Drunken Man.

SONG—*London Newspapers.*

Recitation—Imitation of Fond Barney of York—Arrival of a Scotch Lady—Long Story about Nothing.

SONG—*Bartholomew Fair.*

Recitation—A Quack Doctor—Mountebank's harangue—Anecdote of a Yorkshire man.

SONG—*Nightingale Club.*

The entertainment to conclude with novel specimens of Imitation, in which several tragic and comic performers will give their different ideas how "Hamlet's Advice to the Players" should be spoken.

Mathews has had many imitators in this kind of entertainment, his own son among the number, but never an equal. To judge by the stories related by

Mrs. Mathews, his powers of mimicry, or rather of transformation, must have been nothing less than marvellous, for without make-up, change of dress, or any stage trickery, he could so transform his personality as to deceive his most intimate friends. He was once expelled from behind the scenes of the Liverpool Theatre, where he was actually playing at the time, as an intrusive stranger; and the next moment, after simply allowing his features and figure to assume their normal appearance, passed through the stage-door again and was recognised as Mr. Mathews. In those days the *habitués* of the boxes had the *entrée* of the green-room of Drury Lane; among those who availed themselves of the privilege was a curious old gentleman, whose name, it was understood, was Pennyman, and whose behaviour was so eccentric that he soon became a notorious character. "No one," to use Mrs. Mathews's words, "could tell how the gentleman got admittance, and therefore there was no mode of excluding him. Every night he attracted inconvenient numbers to the green-room; and on the nights when my husband performed it was a matter of much regret to the performers that Mathews always came to the theatre too early or too late to see a subject whom he, of all others, ought to see. It was really surprising that no suspicion of the truth arose. One night, in the midst of a greater excitement than was usually created by him, he suddenly revealed himself to the assembled crowd as Mr. Mathews." When Godwin was writing *Cloudesley*, he asked Mathews to furnish him with some hints upon the possibilities of disguise. Mathews invited him to dinner, and while his guest was conversing with Mrs. Mathews, slipped out of the room; almost immediately afterwards a servant entered to announce a Mr. Jenkins. Mrs.

Mathews looked vexed, and had scarcely time to explain that it was a troublesome and eccentric neighbour, when the new visitor entered. He was introduced to Mr. Godwin, and began to talk so incessantly about that gentleman's works, and made such impertinent inquiries concerning the forthcoming one, that the illustrious author, bored and annoyed, rose from his seat and went to the window, that opened on to the lawn; but Mr. Jenkins was not to be so easily evaded; he pushed before him and officiously offered to unfasten the window; after fumbling a little, he threw it open and turned round; then, to his astonishment, Godwin saw another man—not Mr. Jenkins, but Charles Mathews. After this Mathews became a terror to judges and barristers whenever he was seen in court. One day, while on a provincial tour, he strolled into the sessions-house at Shrewsbury during a trial. Presently an usher came to him with the judge's compliments to inquire if he would like a seat upon the bench. Rather astonished, as he had no acquaintance with his lordship, Mathews followed his conductor and was most effusively received. Relating the incident some years afterwards to a legal friend, he was commenting upon the politeness shown him, when the listener burst out laughing. "I've heard the judge tell the story," he said, "and I remember him saying, 'I was so frightened when I caught sight of that d——d Mathews in the court with his eyes upon me that I couldn't fix my thoughts upon the case, for I believed he had come there for the purpose of taking me off on the stage that night, so I thought it was best to be as civil to him as possible.'"

Small as were the privileges accorded to the minor theatres, the managers of the patent houses endeavoured to curtail them by prolonging their own seasons further into the summer, and there were appeals to the public from one side and to the Lord Chamberlain from the other. There is a good story illustrative of this feud told in an unpublished letter of Peake's. Dr. Kitchener, who was a general friend of the theatrical people of the day, hit upon what he considered the splendid idea of inviting the four belligerent managers of the Haymarket, English Opera House, Covent Garden, and Drury Lane to a dinner, at which there should be no other guests. The arrangement was kept a close secret, and each arrived profoundly ignorant of the others' presence. Their combined astonishment may be imagined. But, after a little awkwardness, they could not withstand the ludicrousness of the situation, and, bursting out into a hearty laugh, shook hands and put a good face upon the matter. The doctor now tried hard to introduce the subject of their differences, but for a time they parried all his efforts, until at last Elliston, then lessee of Drury Lane, rose, and with an air of overwhelming hauteur laid his hand upon Arnold's head and exclaimed, "Minor manager, I will crush you!"

Masquerades and costume recitals were given at the English Opera House to fill up the winter months, and occasionally special permission was obtained for some distinguished actor to appear in a round of legitimate characters. It was in 1821 that Mrs. Glover played Hamlet for her benefit, and a year or two later Mathews was allowed to appear in some of his famous characters of legitimate comedy. Here, in 1821, was produced the operatic version of *Guy Mannering*, Miss Kelly being Meg Merrilies. Liston and Madame Vestris in 1823 were playing in *Sweethearts and Wives*.

In the same season was given a dramatic version of Mrs. Shelly's weird romance *Frankenstein*. T. P.

Cooke's Monster was a wonderful performance, which he afterwards repeated at the Porte St. Martin, and for eighty nights thrilled the Parisians as he had thrilled the Londoners. No less hair-stirring was his Zamiel, in an English version of *Der Freischütz*. Though the score was very much condensed, the great opera was an enormous success. The minor house could still boast of the finest talent of the day; in addition to the actors already named may be added Miss Stephens, Henry Phillips, Miss Romer; two celebrated juvenile prodigies of the time—Clara Fisher and Master Burke; James Bland, Keeley; and, on July 2nd, 1825, the bills announced that Miss Goward, from the Theatres Royal, Norwich and York, would make her first appearance in London as Rosina in the ballad opera of that name, and Little Pickle in *The Spoiled Child*. That lady was destined to become one of the greatest favourites, scarcely excepting Fanny Kelly, that ever trod those boards, but she was better known thereafter as Mrs. Keeley.

During 1828, an explosion of gas having compelled the closing of Covent Garden, the company appeared here, and Kean played some of his finest parts—Shylock, Sir Giles Overreach, Sir Edward Mortimer. A famous melodramatic sensation, *The Bottle Imp*, in which O'Smith, who was to be Cooke's successor in diablerie, played the Imp, and Frank Matthews made his first appearance, was produced in the same year, and ran forty-four nights.

On February 10th, 1830, while in the occupancy of a French company, the English Opera House died the natural death of all theatres—by fire. It was a terrible conflagration, sweeping away one side of Exeter Street, and involving a loss to Mr. Arnold of £8,000. During the next three years the company played now at the Adelphi, now at the Olympic; and it was not until July, 1834, that the present building was finished and opened under the name of the "New Theatre Royal, Lyceum, and English Opera House." Beazeley, the architect, made a curious omission in the plan—the gallery stairs were forgotten; this extraordinary oversight was not discovered until the building was finished, and a temporary wooden staircase, which, however, remained for several years, had to be hastily put up for the ascent of the gods to their Olympus. By this time the entire neighbourhood had been transmogrified. Old Exeter Change had disappeared several years previously, Wellington Street had been opened, and the principal entrance to the theatre was transferred from the Strand to the new thoroughfare, an alteration that can scarcely be said to have been for the better.

The first success at the New Lyceum was made with John Barnett's charming opera, *The Mountain Sylph*, Miss Romer and Henry Phillips in the principal parts; it was played a hundred nights to crowded houses, and the season was extended, for the first time, through November. Frederick Lemaître played Robert Macaire and other of his famous characters here in 1835, and, by royal authority, the house was allowed to open in April, and to continue open until the following January,[1] but with such ill results that, after trying the experiment of reduced prices, the management became bankrupt, and was ultimately resolved into a commonwealth among the company. Arnold lost during the two seasons £4,000. Then came Italian Opera Buffa and French plays, an English version of *La Sonnambula*,

[1] This was the first advantage gained by the minor houses over the patentees. See the preceding chapter.

with Miss Romer as Amina, *The Dice of Death*, *Les Huguenots* as a musical drama, Mrs. Keeley playing Valentine—all more or less failures.

It was at this house, in the winter of 1838–9, promenade concerts, called *Concerts à la Musard*, from the name of the conductor, announced as a novelty from Paris, were first introduced into this country. The music was entirely instrumental. As they were continued for several seasons, from November to May, it may be presumed that they were tolerably successful. Here, in 1837, Compton made his London début as Robin in *The Waterman*, and two years later Mrs. Stirling joined the company.

A commonwealth, chiefly composed of actors from Covent Garden, opened here in 1840, and next year Balfe undertook the management with a great flourish of trumpets, and with what appeared to be an excellent chance of success—a real national opera, after the continental form; no mere string of ballads, but works worthy to stand beside the productions of Italy and Germany, were to be produced. The Queen headed the list of subscribers. Orchestra-stalls were formed for the first time, and the prices of admission raised to seven shillings. A spectacular opera upon an Egyptian subject, called *Keolanthe*, composed by the manager, was produced on the opening night, and Macfarren was to set to work upon something to follow. But these were all castles in the air; very soon there was a defection of the principal artistes; everything went wrong, and after a ten weeks' struggle the doors were suddenly closed. Perhaps the failure is more easily explainable than the disappointed *impresario* cared to admit. The people who could appreciate Mozart and Rossini, and even Bellini and Donizetti, would not care to listen to

Keolanthe, of which probably not a bar survives in anybody's memory; and as in those days every girl had not learned to strum upon the piano—happy days!—the taste for even such music as this had not yet risen among the masses. *Hinc illæ lacrymæ.* After this came German opera, with stalls at ten shillings and sixpence, the first time we hear of such a price in a theatre; but the German went the way of the English; the Italian school had the monopoly of fashionable patronage, and the music of the Teutons was "caviare" to our *dilettanti*.

Jullien and his band performed here early in 1842; then came Vestris's company from Covent Garden, at the break up of her management, and in September the house was converted into an "American Amphitheatre," a wild-beast show, with the famous Carter, the lion king, for star. Later on in the same year, in April, charming Mrs. Waylett undertook the management; the tariff was reduced and half-price taken to all parts of the house; and to heighten the attraction, Signor Nano, the Gnome Fly, was engaged to crawl upon the ceiling, walk up perpendicular walls, and fly about the place like a veritable diptera — a very extraordinary exhibition, but it could not save the management from coming to an abrupt termination.

This house was one of the first to avail itself of the change in the licensing law; and on the 29th of January, 1844, the English Opera House became the Theatre Royal Lyceum. The season opened with Shakespeare's *Henry IV.*, an aspiring amateur, Captain Harvey Tuckett, playing Falstaff; the rest of the company were taken from the rank and file of the patent theatres. A fortnight's trial, to empty benches, cured the Lyceum of its ambition for the legitimate, and on Easter Monday in the same year, the Keeleys, who had long been supreme favourites at this house, took up the sceptre. They gathered about them an admirable company for the class of pieces they performed—farce, extravaganza, and strong domestic drama, which made up an evening's entertainment at once solid and bright, and so various as to suit almost any taste.

Dickens was then in the very zenith of his popularity, and dramatic versions of his novels were sure cards. *Martin Chuzzlewit* scored a great success here, running ninety nights. The cast was admirable. Sam Emery, whom some of us remember, and who made his first appearance in London upon these boards in 1843, was the Jonas; Alfred Wigan, the Montague Tigg; Frank Matthews, the Pecksniff; Keeley, Sairey Gamp; Mrs. Keeley, young Bailey; Miss Woolgar and Mrs. Wigan, the two girls. Then followed *The Chimes*, in which little Keeley was Trotty, and his wife, Margaret Veck; *The Battle of Life*, *The Cricket on the Hearth*—Mrs. Keeley was an incomparable Dot—and numerous extravaganzas by Mark Lemon, Gilbert à Beckett, and others. The *Caudle Lectures* were also dramatised, with Keeley as Mrs. Caudle.

The Keeley management terminated on June 11th, 1847, in consequence of a disagreement with Arnold, the principal landlord, and on October 18th, Madame Vestris succeeded to the vacant throne, with one of the finest comedy companies of modern days—Mrs. Fitzwilliam, Mrs. Leigh Murray, Miss Fairbrother—a charming and beautiful actress, afterwards the morganatic wife of the Duke of Cambridge—and Mrs. Stirling; Charles Mathews, Frank Matthews (no relation beyond the name), whose mellow, unctuous old men were a delight to witness, Leigh Murray, a very fine comedian,

Meadows, Charles Selby, Harley, quaintest of comedians, Buckstone, oiliest and raciest of his kind, and last, but not least, the manageress herself, though then, alas! falling into the sere and yellow leaf.

The opening piece was *The Pride of the Market;* but the successes of the season were *Used Up*, *Box and Cox*, and *A Rough Diamond.* The Lyceum, under the new management, became the most delightful theatrical resort in all London. Extravaganza and burlesque, as written by Planché and as mounted by Vestris, were brought to the highest excellence of which they were capable—*Riquet with the Tuft*, *King Charming*, *The King of the Peacocks*, *The Island of Jewels*, were among the most famous.

It was in *The Island of Jewels* (1849), Planché tells us, that the first approach to a transformation scene was introduced. In the last scene William Beverley, who was the scenic artist, arranged the leaves of a palm tree to fall and discover six fairies, each supporting a coronet of jewels. "It produced such an effect," he adds, "as I scarcely remember having witnessed on any similar occasion up to that period, and every theatre rushed into imitation." Such was the small beginning of those elaborate displays of scenic art. There were revivals of *The Merry Wives of Windsor*—Vestris, Mrs. Ford; Mrs. Yates, Mrs. Page—and of *The School for Scandal*, and the production of Dance's once favourite comedy, *A Wonderful Woman*, in which Madame and Frank Matthews played so superbly.

Madame Vestris had at this time passed the meridian of her powers, but Mathews was in the perfection of his, with a charm of style, an exquisite polish, that had no rival off the Parisian stage. In comedy, farce, or burlesque he was equally at home; he could carry a whole piece upon his shoulders, without ever wearying an audience; and in powers of transformation he was surpassed only by his father. It was on this stage that *Patter versus Clatter*, and *He would be an Actor*, with their marvellous changes, mostly in front of the audience, together with the famous *Game of Speculation* (1851), first saw the footlights. A curious piece called *The Chain of Events*, in eight acts, was brought out in 1852, with wonderful scenery and a built-up ship that was tossed about in a storm, the earliest mechanical stage effect of the kind.

There was no lack of public support; but, as everybody knows, the speculation ended in bankruptcy. Let the manager himself explain the causes of this disaster.

"For seven years we worked day and night, with unvarying success, but the want of capital to fall back upon was for ever the drawback upon our efforts. Every piece used to be got up upon credit, and the outlay had always to be repaid before a profit could be realised; and all the large receipts accruing from the brilliant houses from Christmas to Easter were more than swallowed up by the utter blank that followed from Easter to Michaelmas. . . . During these seven years, buoyed up by hope, I battled with my fate, and made head against my increasing difficulties, till one heavy fall of snow at Christmas spared me the trouble of continuing my existence." The fact was, Mathews entered upon the lesseeship burdened with debts standing over from the Olympic and Covent Garden failures, and was never out of the hands of the Jews. Then he had for wife one of the most extravagant of women, to whom the most costly luxuries had become necessities of life. In such a small item as gloves, for instance, she would sometimes use up a box in a single night; if a pair, or half a dozen pairs in succession, fitted with the slightest crease, they were cast aside, and for every scene a fresh pair was put on. When lace curtains were required upon the stage they were real lace, and everything else was on the same scale; while so minutely particular was she in small matters, that she would pass a white laced handkerchief over the furniture of the green-room, and even the balusters of the staircases leading to the dressing-rooms, and woe to the cleaners if the delicate cambric was soiled. All that this meant can, perhaps, only be appreciated by those who are acquainted with that temple of dust—behind the scenes of a theatre.

Mathews was made bankrupt, but obtained a first-class certificate. Soon afterwards he was arrested by an inveterate creditor and thrown into Lancaster gaol. More than once before he had had a narrow escape of such a fate, *à propos* of which he used to tell some amusing stories. One night, as he was entering the stage-door of the Lyceum, a bailiff tapped him upon the shoulder. "Why have you not renewed the bill?" asked the man. "He" (the creditor) "wouldn't renew it," replied Mathews. "Well, then, just write your name across this," said the man, producing a long slip of blue paper with a stamp in the corner. Mathews did so. "Now I'm your creditor, and shall be happy to renew if you can't pay at the end of the time." And with these words he disappeared. He had paid the debt out of his own pocket to save the actor from a prison. Who shall talk about stony-hearted bailiffs after that?

"How many times," Mathews writes, "have I gone upon the stage with a heavy heart and a merry face, to act the very part in jest that I was playing behind the scenes in earnest, and not a sympathetic smile to pity me. On the contrary, everybody seemed to believe that

I revelled in it, and every allusion I had made to duns and bailiffs was hailed by the audience as the emanation of a light heart and most unctuous enjoyment. Had I been a tragedian and walked on with a melancholy air and serious face, I should have cause for feeling my unfortunate position—'Poor fellow, see how down he is!' But the painfully successful effort of assuming gaiety and joyousness—difficult as it was—robbed me of all sympathy. 'Pooh! pooh! he doesn't care, he likes it; he's in his element.'" After being incarcerated for nearly a month in Lancaster gaol he was released. He had taken his seat in the railway carriage, bound for London, when a man sitting opposite to him pointed to the Castle, as they steamed by, and remarked to a lady sitting beside him, "That's were Charley Mathews is!" "Really," answered the lady sympathetically, "poor fellow!" "Poor fellow! not at all," answered the other; "he revels in it. Lord bless you, he's been in every prison in England!" A few days after his release Madame Vestris died. She had retired from the stage in 1854, in consequence of ill-health. The last piece she played in was a version of *La Joie Fait Peur*, called *Sunshine through the Clouds.*

Professor Anderson with "Magic and Mystery," and a season of Italian opera, consequent on the burning of Covent Garden, with Adelaide Ristori on the off nights, for opera was performed only three times a week in those days, filled up the interregnum between the passing of the Vestris-Mathews management and the coming of Charles Dillon.

Dillon opened the Lyceum in 1856 in his great part Belphegor, and achieved an immediate success; picturesque, glowing with passion, and with a power of pathos that has never been surpassed and seldom equalled, he roused the audience to the highest pitch of enthusiasm. J. L. Toole played Fanfaronade, and Marie Wilton, who had acted the part with Dillon at Bristol, where she had already made a brilliant reputation, was the Henri, a most exquisite bit of acting, which, with her *piquante* and sprightly performance of Perdita in Brough's burlesque on *The Winter's Tale*, that concluded the programme, secured for her an emphatic success.

Dillon's next character was D'Artagnan in *The Three Musketeers*, and not since Elliston had such robust and vividly picturesque acting been witnessed upon the stage. Charles Dillon well deserved to be called the English Frederick Lemaître. Nor was his talent confined to melodrama; there were scenes in his Virginius the like of which had not been seen since Macready, and his King Lear has not been equalled by any succeeding English actor.

Italian opera and Ristori occupied the theatre during the summer months, and the Pyne and Harrison company during the autumn; the latter drew immense houses with *The Rose of Castile*. Dillon resumed the management at Christmas with a splendid spectacle, *Lalla Rookh*, in which Miss Woolgar and J. L. Toole appeared. Miss Helen Faucit supported the manager in *Macbeth*, *The Lady of Lyons*, and *Much Ado about Nothing*. His last production was a revival of *Louis XI*.

Dillon had the ball at his feet, and had he possessed the tact, the culture, and the judgment of Henry Irving, he might have anticipated the latter's success. But Dillon had been trained in a bad school; he had risen out of the mire of the profession, and, with little education beyond such as he had picked up in his professional career, he could not shake off old habits and associations. When he should have been attending to the business of the stage, he was at the bar of a public-house surrounded by unworthy parasites. After a tedious and ineffective rehearsal, to which he paid little attention, he would dine off a rump-steak and a pot of porter in his dressing-room; then, cigar in mouth, stroll round into the Strand to see the people flocking to the pit, dress hurriedly at the last moment, and when the performance was over carouse "potations pottle deep" with some of his satellites. Though he lived in no style beyond keeping a plain brougham, he was always over head and ears in debt, borrowed money at 100 per cent., and often paid 200; so that although the receipts of the theatre were very large, as fast as the money came in it was appropriated by greedy creditors, and at the end of two seasons he had to retire.

It is worth noting that it was under Charles Dillon's management that stalls were permanently established at the Lyceum; the charge was at first only five shillings, but was afterwards raised to six.

Edmund Falconer was the next manager, and made a great hit with *Extremes; or, Men of the Day*, of which he was the author. But the one success being followed by several failures, the theatre again became tenantless, until it was opened by Madame Celeste. Her principal success was a dramatised version of *A Tale of Two Cities*, in which she gave a wonderful rendering of Madame Dufarge. But at the end of the second season she retired a heavy loser by her speculation. More Italian opera with Titiens, Alboni, Giuglini, after which Falconer again took up the management. His first production, August, 1861—*Woman against the World*, with Mrs. Charles Young, afterwards Mrs. Hermann

Vezin—was a go. His second, *The Peep o' Day Boys*, was played considerably over a twelvemonth, and all London flocked to see the great quarry scene and the heroine precipitated from the breaking bridge, which in breathless excitement rivalled the water-cave of *The Colleen Bawn.*

When Falconer went to Drury Lane the famous French actor, Charles Fechter, took over the lease. Fechter inaugurated a new era in English histrionic art that led to the great theatrical revival of the nineteenth century. He began by revolutionising the stage. The ancient grooves, trap-doors, and sticky flats were abolished, the flooring so constructed that it could be taken to pieces like a child's puzzle, scenery could be raised or sunk bodily, and all the shifting was done on the mezzanine stage beneath; ceilings were no longer represented by hanging cloths, or the walls of a room by open wings, but were solidly built,[1] the old glaring "floats," which used to make such hideous lights and shadows upon the faces of the performers, were sunk and subdued, and set scene succeeded set scene with a rapidity that in those days, when seldom more than one set was attempted in each act, was regarded as marvellous.

But it was not alone in the mechanical and artistic departments that Fechter wrought such startling changes: he shook to their foundation the worn-out traditions of the old school of acting, which, however excellent it might have been in its time, had become musty and pedantic.

Fechter was well known to the London public, as he had already played Hamlet at the Princess's, when he

[1] There is nothing new under the sun. Goethe, in his Autobiography, part 3, book xi., says that in the French theatres (even in his youth) they shut in the sides and formed real walls for the interior scenes.

opened the Lyceum on January 10th, 1863, with *The Duke's Motto*. Henri Largardère was one of his most brilliant parts, and he crowded the Lyceum for many months with all the brains and all the fashion of London. Yet its magnificent mounting was surpassed by that of *Beldemonio*, which followed, and was succeeded by *Hamlet*. Of Fechter's interpretation of the part I shall have something to say when I come to the Princess's.

The King's Butterfly (*Fanfan la Tulipe*), *The Roadside Inn* (*Robert Macaire*), *The Mountebank*, a version of *Belphegor*, and *Ruy Blas* made up the principal work of the second season, which ended with a loss. In the third a poor drama, entitled *The Watch Cry*, in which Fechter played a dumb part in wonderful pantomime, was followed by one of his finest efforts, *The Master of Ravenswood;* his delineation of Scott's fated hero was superb; very beautiful was Carlotta Leclercq's Lucy; Emery's Caleb Balderstone was a gem, and the quicksand effect in the last act has never been excelled, either in effect or ingenuity. The play was a great success. A revival of *The Corsican Brothers*, with several important innovations from Kean's method, came next, and such a rendering of the twin brothers has never been seen before or since. Boucicault occupied the stage in the autumn following with his own drama, *The Long Strike*. Fechter returned at Christmas with *Rouge et Noir*, an adaptation of the famous *La Vie d'un Jouer*, previously known in England by a version called *The Hut of the Red Mountains*.

The great French actor was admirably seconded by Kate Terry, Carlotta Leclercq, Hermann Vezin, Emery, George Jordan, Addison, Harry Widdicombe, Mrs. Ternan, Miss Henrade, etc. His last important production was *The Lady of Lyons*. Bulwer's hero is essentially French, and, taken for all in all, perhaps, the author's conception was never before so vividly realised; the high-falutin speeches put into the mouth of Claude were, for the first time, not premeditated declamation, but bursts of natural emotion, and even that most artificial harangue in the cottage scene had such intensity of conviction and *abandon* that the tinsel seemed gold. Fechter's power lay in that glowing passion, that wonderful picturesqueness, which carry away the imagination of the audience, qualities that are no longer to be found upon our stage. The reign which commenced so brilliantly closed but gloomily on May 24th, 1867, with a performance of *The Duke's Motto.*

E. T. Smith carried on the theatre for the next two seasons. He produced Westland Marston's *Life for Life*, in which Adelaide Neilson made her first great hit as a poetical actress; Bulwer Lytton's very much out-of-date play *The Sea Captain*, renamed *The Rightful Heir*, during the same season, was the only other event of note that need be recorded here.

Under the management of the Mansell brothers an experiment in opera-bouffe was made by the production of *Chilpéric,* but proved a dismal failure. And when, in the autumn of 1871, Mr. H. L. Bateman entered upon the speculation, everyone prophesied a like fate for him. And at the start it seemed as though their gloomy vaticinations would certainly be realised. Bateman took the Lyceum especially to bring forward his daughter Isabel, in whom he believed he had a prize equal to her sister Kate, of Leah fame. He commenced his campaign with a dramatic version of George Sand's *La Petite Fadette*, called *Fanchette.* Both play and actress failed. *Pickwick*, with Irving as Jingle, was a *succès d'estime*, but there was no money in it. Matters were growing desperate, and as a *pis aller* a piece by Leopold Lewis, founded upon one of Erckman-Chatrain's celebrated stories, at that time in Henry Irving's possession, was put in the bills.

Bateman had regarded that fine character-actor, George Belmore, as the second string to his bow, for although Irving had made his mark at the St. James's and at the Queen's in Long Acre, and more especially at the Vaudeville, as Digby Grant, no one was prepared for such a revelation of power and originality as burst upon the town on that November night in 1871, when he gave his first performance of the ghost-haunted Burgomaster, Mathias.

We must go back to the night when Robson first played Shylock to find a parallel to the sensation he made. The drama ran 150 nights to overflowing houses. Later on Irving appeared as Jeremy Diddler in *Raising the Wind*, and Kate Bateman as Leah, and Medea, in a new version of the classical tragedy by Wills.

Irving's next hit was in *Charles I.*, September, 1872, which ran 180 nights, a beautiful poetical play, and Irving's acting in it "one entire and perfect chrysolite." The stage has never given us anything finer of the kind in dignity, in pathos, in kingliness. Isabel Bateman played the Queen excellently, but it was not until Ellen Terry took up the character that we could realise all the awful agony of the parting in the last scene, that drowned the house in tears. In the following year we had *Eugene Aram*, a powerful drama, but not very successful. Yet Irving has done few things more striking than the first scene with Houseman; the sudden transition from the calm, poetical scholar to the fierce, determined man revealed the whole psychology of the character by a single flash.

Richelieu was a production of 1873, a fine performance, which in the anathema rose almost to greatness. *Philip*, a charming drama, followed in February, and was admirably acted both by the leading actor and John Clayton.

But it was in the following season, on October 31st, 1874, when Irving appeared as Hamlet, that his popularity rose to its greatest height. Manager Bateman was a king among *entrepreneurs;* he worked the Press for all it was worth, and sent invitations to the editors of all the great provincial papers. They accepted, and next morning their eulogies were scattered all over the kingdom. *Hamlet* ran until June 25th, 1875, outliving poor Bateman, who died in the previous March.

Macbeth was the *pièce de résistance* of the autumn of 1875, and was splendidly staged; from the first scene, where the weird sisters loomed out of the chaotic darkness by flashes of lightning, to the black, ponderous stonework of Glamis Castle and the towers of Dunsinane, bathed in blood-red sunset, we were never out of the fateful atmosphere of the mighty tragedy. When he reproduced the play in 1888, Irving had greatly improved upon his first rendering, notably of the murder scene; there were some very fine points in the fourth act—the sense of doom in the gloomy utterance and haggard face—but the craven conception of "the noble Thane" can never be acceptable, and the last act was weak. Miss Bateman was the Lady Macbeth.

It is best to pass over *Othello*, February, 1876, in silence. It soon gave place to Tennyson's *Queen Mary*, in which Miss Bateman played the title-rôle and Irving Philip of Spain; another failure. It was followed by *The Belle's Stratagem.* The Carl Rosa Company had possession of the house during the autumn, and Miss

Bateman opened the dramatic season with *Fazio*. The next great revival was *Richard III.* from the text, in January, 1877. I have always considered this to be one of Sir Henry's best Shakespearian parts. The last act was deficient in physical power, but the conception was full of intensity and subtlety, while some of the scenes were remarkably striking.

The Lyons Mail followed *Richard*. Then, at the beginning of the new year, *Louis XI.*, the finest thing he had yet done; a wonderful study. *Vanderdecken* was the next production. This was Mrs. Bateman's last season, and on December 30th, 1878, Henry Irving became sole lessee of the Lyceum. He began with an elaborate revival of *Hamlet*, and Ellen Terry made her first appearance here as Ophelia. *The Lady of Lyons* ended the season. The next opened with *The Iron Chest*, but it was not a success, and soon gave place to one of Irving's most notable revivals, *The Merchant of Venice*. It was a dream of ancient Venice, bathed in an atmosphere of enchanting poetry. And what a piece of acting was Ellen Terry's Portia! How tender, how womanly, and altogether delightful. Irving's Jew was very fine, but a little too mild. The revival was a prodigious success, achieving the longest run on record, to celebrate which the manager gave a sumptuous supper on the stage after the performance, on the hundredth night, at which Lord Houghton presided.

A very elaborate get-up of *The Corsican Brothers* commenced the next season. Irving followed Kean's conception of the dual rôle, but after Fechter, who threw all the fierce Corsican nature into the last act, the deadly *northern* calm of Irving, where he confronted Château Renaud, was not convincing.

I could never understand why *The Cup* (1881) was

never revived after its first production. No grander scene was ever set upon the Lyceum stage than the Temple of Artemis, and Miss Terry's Camma was a beautiful performance. In May, Irving and Booth alternated Othello and Iago. Both the Othellos were bad, but Irving's Iago was consummately fine. A revival of *The Two Roses* must be mentioned, since it introduced George Alexander to the London stage in the part of Caleb Deecie.

The event of 1882 was the production of *Romeo and Juliet.* Irving made three huge mistakes when he played Othello, Claude Melnotte, and Romeo, and it was only in certain scenes, notably that with the Nurse, that Miss Terry rose to the occasion. Terriss was utterly conventional as Mercutio; the only well-played parts were the Nurse of Mrs. Stirling and the Apothecary of Tom Mead. And yet with such exquisite art was the tragedy evolved, that never was I so impressed by its marvellous beauty as on the three occasions that I witnessed it at the Lyceum. I was living in the halls and streets of mediæval Italy; I felt the glow of the sunshine, the chill of the vault of all the Capulets, and I was overwhelmed by the fatalism of the immortal love story. The genius of a great artist pervaded the whole, and communicated its sense of harmony to the spectator.

If Ellen Terry fell short of our desires as Juliet, she infinitely exceeded all expectations as Beatrice, when *Much Ado about Nothing* was produced in October, 1882. She played Leonato's daughter as it had never been played before; she broke through every tradition of the part, she was a law unto herself in it; yet even the most orthodox of old actors grew enthusiastic over her, and some even declared her to be the most delightful Beatrice they had ever seen.

Miss Mary Anderson made her London début here in 1883, while Irving was on his first American tour, and by her beautiful face and figure and graceful pose captivated the town as Galatea and in other parts. Another American, Lawrence Barrett, a good actor, failed to make much impression in a play called *Yorick.* Later in the year 1884, Irving, on his return from America, revived *Twelfth Night.* Not one of his happiest efforts, but Ellen Terry was an exquisite Viola.

During the summer extensive alterations were made in the theatre, the roof of the gallery was raised, the dress-circle enlarged, and the principal entrance reconstructed. In the autumn Miss Anderson attempted Juliet in a costly get-up of Shakespeare's tragedy.

Calling up, as I write, memories of famous Lyceum first nights, not one is more delightful than the *première* of *Olivia*, May, 1885. As *Romeo and Juliet* was fired with the passion and turbulence of mediævalism, so was *Olivia* steeped in the pastoral quietude of the eighteenth century, when there were no unrest and "burning questions," and life passed drowsily and evenly. Irving's Vicar was charming; it revealed a depth of pathos never suspected by his admirers. Olivia was one of Miss Terry's most adorable performances. When she struck Thornhill with the cry "Devil!" what a thrill went through the house, then a hurricane of applause. But how risky it was; only the intense conviction of the actress saved it from a laugh. The scene between father and daughter, and the return of the wanderers were never surpassed in pathos; there was not a dry eye in the house; even the hardened critics blew their noses and furtively wiped their cheeks.

But it must be conceded that the 19th of December, 1885, the first night of *Faust*, was, after all, the greatest of Lyceum *premières.* The applications for reserved seats would have taxed the capacity of a dozen theatres —*thousands* came from Germany alone. People gathered about the pit and gallery doors at nine in the morning; by six o'clock the crowd was half-way across the road of the Strand. Scores of despairing women gathered in the vestibule in the forlorn hope of returned seats, casting beseeching eyes upon Joe Hurst, whose visage was stern and inexorable; some were so desperate that they seemed more than half inclined to make a rush up the stairs. It was a wonderful production. The old German streets, Margaret's garden, the Brocken with the wild, grey, misty revel, and eldritch screams of the witches whirling round the crimson, electric figure of the fiend. And after all the terrors, the dawn-lit ancient city of Nuremberg. I think Irving was at his best on the first night; he was more reposeful, yet more terribly intense than afterwards. What a fiasco poor Conway made as Faust, as great as Alexander's success in Valentine. The latter soon afterwards succeeded to the title-rôle. But vivid above all other impressions of the play is the Margaret of Ellen Terry; from the few words of her first entrance, through the joyousness of the jewels scene, the simple pathos and exquisite tenderness of the love duologues, the overwhelming agony at the fountain, the frantic despair in the church, and the madness and death of the end. What a performance it was!

The 138th night of *Faust,* which closed the season, was notable as marking the last appearance of Mrs. Stirling upon the stage, after a service to her art of fifty-seven years. In her early days she was an incomparable heroine of domestic drama, and a good all-round actress; in her later years a supreme exponent of the old woman of classical comedy. Mrs. Malaprop died with her. Martha was her last character.

The continuity of the Irving management was now constantly broken by the American tours. Sarah Bernhardt was here with *Theodora* in 1887; Richard Mansfield, the American actor, appeared in a version of Stevenson's *Dr. Jekyll and Mr. Hyde*, with little success; and Miss Anderson gave an elaborate revival of *The Winter's Tale* in 1888. In the June of the same year Miss Terry appeared in one of the most exquisite of her creations, Ellaline in *The Amber Heart*, and Irving played Robert Macaire. In the summer of 1889, Verdi's *Otello* was first sung in England with Tamagno and Maurel; and Sarah Bernhardt played another season, in which she acted *La Tosca* for the first time in London.

The autumn production was *The Dead Heart*, of which nothing good can be said; then followed *Macbeth*, with Miss Terry as the Lady, a character she should never have attempted. *Ravenswood* could not compare with Fechter's version, especially in the acting.

1891, another trip to America, during which great improvements were again effected in the theatre. Splendidly redecorated, it was opened by the Daly company. 1892, *Henry VIII.* Not even on this stage was the revel at York Place, with the masque, "the white satin dance," to Edward German's quaint music, which is now known to everyone, surpassed. Irving's Wolsey was a well-considered performance; Miss Terry's Queen Katherine—another mistake. *King Lear* belongs to the same year. Lear was quite outside the limits of Irving's art, and in avoiding the traditions of his predecessors, he stripped the character of all grandeur, while in the mad scenes he not only failed to indicate a powerful intellect shattered, but he degraded the once great monarch to the level of a doddering lunatic. A creation so stupendous as King Lear cannot be dragged down from the sublime heights, where it stands beside Œdipus and Prometheus, to the gutters of realism, without the incongruity being apparent to the least artistic intelligence. The grand *mise en scène* and Ellen Terry's Cordelia—and never had Shakespeare's heroine a more exquisite interpretation—were the only redeeming features of a very inadequate production.

But this fiasco was atoned by the glorious triumph of Tennyson's *Becket* (1893). Many, like myself, consider that Irving attained to the zenith of his art in this tragedy, and that the martyr of Canterbury is the greatest piece of acting he has given us. Never before did he equal the grandeur of his defiance of the nobles in the Hall of Northampton Castle, the stern asceticism, the devotional fervour of the later scenes, or the solemn impressiveness of the death. Rosamond, perhaps, was the last of those beautiful creations by which Miss Terry will be chiefly remembered in the years to come, for her Imogen was a disappointment.

Ellen Terry was the one poetical actress of her generation—her own sister, Marian, was nearest to her; all her most celebrated contemporaries were realists. Charles Reade said of her: "She is an enigma; her eyes are pale, her nose rather long, her mouth nothing particular. Her complexion a delicate brick-dust, her hair rather like tow. Yet, somehow, she is beautiful. Her expression kills any pretty face you see beside her. She is a pattern of fawn-like grace. Whether in movement or repose, grace pervades the hussy." As in private life, this rare fascination was one of the secrets of her public success; a fascination so absolute that it carried you away without the power to criticise. Her Ophelia, Desdemona, Cordelia, Portia, Beatrice could never have been surpassed by the actresses of past days, and leave all of her own generation far behind. Sarah Bernhardt has said that her greatest treat was to see Ellen Terry act, and Wendell Holmes, when she was in America, after her mad scene of Ophelia, paid homage to her by kissing the hem of her dress. Yet in her early days she showed no promise of future excellence. The Bancrofts were the first to draw forth the latent fire in Portia. But it was only under Henry Irving that her genius was fully developed. One regret of all playgoers is that they have never seen her in the part of parts, of which she would have been an ideal representative—Rosalind; another, that she should ever have attempted characters so utterly outside her limits as Lady Macbeth, Queen Katherine, and *The Viking* heroine. But such mistakes have been made by all great artistes in all ages.

Irving was never famous for the companies he gathered about him; his confrères were efficient, and that was all. William Terriss was, perhaps, the most conspicuous; his best parts were Squire Thornhill, Henry VIII., and Henry II.

And now briefly to resume the chronicle of the Lyceum. *King Arthur* was the not very commendable production of 1894; *Don Quixote* and *A Story of Waterloo* of 1895. As Corporal Brewster, Irving scored another triumph; he has done nothing more perfect; perhaps in no other part has he so completely sunk Henry Irving in the character he represents.

Another of the manager's American trips left the Lyceum in possession of Forbes Robertson and Mrs. Patrick Campbell. *Michael and His Lost Angel,* a fine piece of work, was, from causes which I have not space to discuss, strangled in its birth. *For the Crown*, a noble play, though well acted, was beyond the genius of its exponents. Irving's autumn production, *Cymbeline*, 1876, was not remarkable from any point of view. It was followed by a reproduction of *Richard III.*, and in 1897, Miss Terry played Réjane's great part, Madame St. Gêne, not unsuccessfully. *Peter the Great* and *The Medicine Man*, 1898, need not be dwelt upon.

The splendid fortune which had shone upon the Lyceum since the first night of *The Bells*, thanks to plays that did not catch on with the public *and* Irving's repeated and long absences in the States, was waning fast. Irving relinquished the management, which was taken up by a syndicate, with Mr. Comyns Carr as managing director. Much abuse has been heaped upon the head of the actor-manager; yet he has, at least, a love for his art, and, whatever mistakes he may commit through egotism, he has some knowledge of it; but a syndicate of business men would sacrifice the genius of the world, from Homer to Tennyson, to add one per per cent. to a dividend, and the voice of one man of culture is certain to be overpowered by the clamour of the Philistine board.

Coquelin appeared as Cyrano de Bergerac in the summer of 1898, and during the autumn and winter Forbes Robertson and Mrs. Campbell again occupied the boards. *Robespierre*, 1899, was the next Irving production. Wilson Barrett followed with revivals of *The Silver King* and other plays, and the Benson company played a season before Sir Henry returned to stage *Coriolanus*. No character could have been more unsuited to his subtle, purely intellectual style than Caius Marcius, which requires the greatest breadth and physical power. By, as in Lear, pedantically ignoring the traditions of his predecessors, he rendered the part colourless; the Coriolanus of Plutarch did not sneer at his enemies, he bullied them, and the flying legions of Rome would certainly not have rushed back to victory had they been objurgated in the style adopted by Sir Henry Irving. Lewis Waller followed on with *The Three Musketeers* in the autumn, and *Henry V.* began the new century. In 1901, *Sherlock Holmes* took the stage. In the following year there was a revival of *Faust.* Oh what a falling off was there! And on July 19th, 1902, the curtain fell, for the last time, on a performance of *The Merchant of Venice* and *Waterloo*—and the story of the Lyceum was ended.

I have dwelt at some length upon the history of this house, as for many years it was the premier theatre, the Comédie Française of England, and the Irving management its supreme factor. It would be scarcely possible to over-estimate the benignant influence which Sir Henry has exercised over the English stage. The soul of generosity, with a personality that has won for him the friendship of all sorts and conditions of men, he attracted to the theatre people of all shades of thought, from the bishop to the scientist; and, completing the work initiated by Fechter and the Bancrofts, he has been chiefly instrumental in raising the drama and the actor from the pitiful slough of the middle Victorian period to the position they held under James I.

Poor old theatre, to which for so many thousands of nights all the intellect, all the beauty, all the fashion from all parts of the world flocked eagerly, whose doings were discussed from India to Land's End, scene of such brilliant assemblies, of such delightful memories, of the triumphs of so many great artistes, living and dead, thou art now but the *salle des pas perdus;* the applause is hushed, the lights are extinguished for ever, the rats are thy only tenants, the dust of death is over all, and thou art only awaiting the coming of the housebreaker to be among the things that have been and are not.

Any account of the Lyceum would be incomplete without some reference to a famous institution which, during fifty years, had its home within those walls. I refer to the Sublime Society of Beef Steaks, founded by John Rich in 1735.

During seventy years the meetings were held in a room in Covent Garden. When the theatre was burned down in 1808, the society took up its quarters for one year at the Bedford Coffee House. Thence in 1809 it removed to the Lyceum. Upon the rebuilding of the house after the fire, a couple of rooms were added for their especial accommodation, and there all meetings were held until the dissolution of the club in 1867. Sir Henry Irving used them as reception-rooms. The "Steakers" were very aristocratic and very exclusive. It was rigidly laid down that their number should never exceed twenty-four, and they would not make an exception even for the Prince Regent, who had to wait his turn. The members met every Saturday night to eat beef-steaks and drink port wine. At the end of the dining-room was an enormous grating in the form of a gridiron, through which the fire was seen, and the steaks were handed from the kitchen. Over this was the quotation :—

> "If it were done, when 'tis done, then 'twere well
> It were done quickly."

There was perfect equality, and the last-made member,

even were he of royal blood, was made the fag of the rest.

There is a capital story told of this peculiarity of the society. On a certain occasion, when a large and distinguished party had met, a wealthy and pretentious Liverpool merchant was among the guests. Something occurred to rouse his suspicion that the royal and titled persons were myths, and he communicated this conviction to his host, remarking that it was a very good joke, but he saw through it. The idea was instantly seized, and the Beefsteaks, to keep up the delusion, resolved themselves into a society of tradesmen. The Duke of Sussex reproached Alderman Wood for the tough steaks he had sent last Saturday. The Alderman retorted upon his royal brother by complaining of the ill-fitting stays he had sent his wife. Sir Francis Burdett told Whitbread his last cask of beer was sour, and the latter accounted for it by saying that it had been left too long in the Tower. A leaf had to be withdrawn to shorten the table, and in closing it the chair of the Duke of Leinster, who was president, was overbalanced, and both the duke and the chair fell into the grate. No one moved, everybody roared, and His Grace had to scramble to his feet as best he could. This confirmed the merchant's scepticism. "Why," he said, "if he had been a real duke, would they not all have run to pick him up?"

CHAPTER III

The Tottenham Street Theatre, better known as The Prince of Wales's, 1809-82—A Curious Chapter in Theatrical History.

SOMEWHERE in the latter decades of the eighteenth century a Signior Paschali built a concert-room in Tottenham Street, Tottenham Court Road, which was afterwards purchased and enlarged by the directors of the "Concerts of Ancient Music," whose entertainments were "patronised by royalty." In 1802 the building came into the hands of a society of amateur actors called the Pic Nics, who frequently provoked the satiric pencil of Gilray, and their success was great enough to bring down upon them the hostility of the legitimate theatres.

Six years later the concert-room was converted into a circus, which, however, enjoyed a very brief existence. After being closed for a time, Mr. Paul, a gunsmith and silversmith in the Strand, whose wife fancied she had a call for the stage, and would speedily become a second Vestris, bought the place and fitted it up as a theatre. The lady opened as Rosetta in *Love in a Village*. At the end of a few months the unfortunate husband was in the bankruptcy court, after which the assignees and some tradesmen attempted to carry on the theatre; but the loss was so heavy that they soon gave up their undertaking.

In the December of 1814 the property, which had cost

£4,000, was sold to Mr. Harry Beverley for £315, and the scenery and other accessories were thrown in for another £300 ; while the rent was only £177 per annum and the taxes £35. After some considerable alterations it was opened early in the following year under the name of the Regency Theatre of Varieties. It was essentially a minor, with a very mediocre company, though the manager—the father, by-the-by, of William Beverley, the famous scenic artist—and his brother, Roxby Beverley, were both exceedingly clever actors who, had they chosen to remain in London, would have been in the foremost rank of comedians ; but preferring to reign in the provinces rather than to serve in a principal London theatre, they became the proprietors of a circuit in the north.

The Regency, thanks to the restrictive laws, did not provide a very elevated style of entertainment for its patrons, melodrama and farce being the staple fare. After six years' struggle the Beverleys retired in favour of Brunton, but they returned for a season or two in 1826. Brunton, on assuming the management, re-christened the house the West London Theatre, and introduced a superior style of entertainment, while his daughter, afterwards Mrs. Yates, of whom some account will be found in the chapter on the Adelphi, became the bright particular star. Talk about driving a coach and four through an Act of Parliament, that feat was certainly accomplished by Brunton when, in spite of the patent theatres, he played *She Stoops to Conquer*, *The School for Scandal*, *The Wonder*, and called them "bur-lettas," introducing a song or a few chords of music here and there to keep up the farce.

A little later on Planché describes the place as "about as dark and dingy a den as ever sheltered the children of Thespis." The stage was only twenty-one feet wide at the proscenium and thirty-six feet deep; the prices ranged from four shillings to one; the auditorium would hold about £130. A picture now before me representing the exterior of the theatre in 1826 shows that no alteration was ever made in the street frontage; there is the ugly squat portico and the blank wall beyond, just as they appeared to the last.

In 1826 the West London became the home of the French companies who visited London. There was a subscription season of forty nights; the plays, however, were given only once or twice a week during winter and spring. It is suggestive to mention that when Mdlle. Georges was engaged, the prices were raised to two shillings and five; but the aristocracy, who at that time alone supported foreign companies, would not pay the price, and the great Parisian actress appeared to empty benches.

During. 1829, three different managers tried their fortunes at the West London—Tom Dibdin, Watkins Burroughs, and Mrs. Waylett. The latter, who made her London début at the Adelphi, was now in the first rank of English cantatrices, rivalling Mrs. Honey, and even the great Vestris herself.

It is curious to mark how certain forms of art flourish and then disappear. During the early years of the nineteenth century there was a positive glut of English songstresses, Miss Stephens, Miss Love, Mrs. Honey, Mrs. Waylett, Madame Vestris, all of whom for beauty of voice, exquisite method and expression, especially in what, for lack of a better word, I must call the serio-comic style—an expression horribly vulgarised by the music-hall "artistes"—have no successors in the present day. These ladies, with the exception of the last, who frequently soared into a much higher region of art, were essentially ballad singers, and their favourite songs were brought into every piece they appeared in, with an utter disregard of the fitness of things which seems quite amazing to an age that prides itself upon its rigid correctness in theatrical details ; as an instance, in a dramatic version of Beaumarchais's *Mariage de Figaro*, in which she played Susanna, Mrs. Waylett sang "The Soldier's Tear," "I'd be a Butterfly," "The Light Guitar," "My Own Bluebell," while in a version of Boieldieu's *Jeanne de Paris* she introduced, as the Princess of Navarre, "I've Been Roaming," "The Merry Swiss Boy," "Oh, No, We Never Mention Her," and "The Dashing White Sergeant."[1]

The fair manageress surrounded herself with a capital company, including Miss Jarman, afterwards Mrs. Ternan, a charming actress; Vining, Alexander Lee, etc.; but, although she added melodrama to these more elegant pieces, the public did not support her, and she soon gave place to other ambitious spirits.

Mrs. Fitzwilliam seems to have been one of these,[2] but was very soon succeeded by Melrose and Chapman, who so greatly embroiled themselves with the patentees that the owners of the theatre expelled them.

In January, 1831, after being closed some little time for alterations and decorations, the theatre in Tottenham Street, as it had been called during the past two years, was once more rechristened the Queen's, and reopened under the management of Mrs. Nisbett, who brought with her Mrs. Glover, Mrs. Humby, and a good stock company. If it had been possible to make this unlucky

[1] See also p. 278.

[2] It is very difficult to ascertain the actual managers from the playbills as very frequently their names do not appear at all.

theatre pay, that feat should have been accomplished by one of the most beautiful women and exquisite *comédiennes* of the time.[1] Old playgoers still speak rapturously of that silvery laugh, to hear which alone was worth a visit to the theatre; of that wonderful *verve* and "go" which, in the fullest sense of the word, created such parts as Constance in *The Love Chase* and Lady Gay Spanker in *London Assurance;* but although she and Mrs. Glover played nightly in light pieces, Mrs. Nisbett, in April, had to engage an extra attraction in the person of a French pantomime actress, Madame Celeste, who here made her first appearance in London, at the age of fifteen,[1] as a dumb Arab boy, in a piece called *The French Spy*, a part which, as she could not speak one word of English, was played throughout in dumbshow; yet by the beauty and grace of her dancing and action she made a decided hit.

In 1833 the name of the house was changed to the Fitzroy; but not for long, as two years later it once more became the Queen's, with Mrs. Nisbett's name again at the head of the bill. The person who found the money, however, was the notorious Ephraim Bond, the money-lender, who kept a gambling-house in St. James's Street, second only in importance to Crockford's (the

[1] Mrs. Nisbett, then Miss Mordaunt, had made her first appearance in London, as the *Widow Cheerly*, at Drury Lane, October 16th, 1829; but she had been on the stage from childhood, having played Juliet at ten as a juvenile prodigy.

[2] Young as she was, Celeste had already played an engagement in America, where she married an officer named Elliot, who died shortly afterwards; she had also appeared in Liverpool as Fenella in *Masaniello*. She returned to America in 1834, where she created so much enthusiasm that at Washington the people yoked themselves to her carriage and proclaimed her a citizen of the United States, while General Jackson himself presented her to the Council of Ministers. Leaving America with a considerable fortune, she reappeared at Drury Lane in 1837, and afterwards performed at the Haymarket and the Adelphi.

Ephraim Sharpe of Disraeli's *Henrietta Temple*); he seems to have taken it for beautiful Mrs. Honey. There was an admirable company—Wrench, Elton, Tilbury, Morris Barnett, Tom Green, John Reeve, Mrs. Orger, Miss Murray, Mrs. Honey, and Mrs. Nisbett. The lightest of light pieces were performed, sometimes as many as six one-act trifles making up the bill.

During the Lent of 1837 and 1838—by which time Mrs. Nisbett's name no longer figured as manageress, she being at that time at Covent Garden with Macready—Madame Vestris and Charles Mathews, in consequence of some absurd regulations, being unable to play at their own theatre, the Olympic, brought their company to Tottenham Street, when the theatre was again known as the Fitzroy.

In the October of 1839 the house, rechristened the Queen's, came into the hands of Mr. C. J. James, a scenic artist, who, from that time until the final close of the theatre, was never dissociated from the management. For years the Queen's, or the Dust Hole, as it was irreverently called among actors, was one of the curiosities of London. Mr. James began by reducing the prices to two shillings, one shilling, and sixpence, and this tariff was afterwards lowered to one shilling and sixpence, eightpence, and fourpence, with half-prices to boxes and pit. Melodramas of the most terrific description, bearing the most tremendous titles, were performed. Only fancy going to see *Footpad Joe, the Terror of Charing Cross; or, the Dog of the Abbey; The Death Wedding; or, the Witch of the Heath; The Inn of Death; or, the Dog Witness.* The great star of the latter was Jack Matthews, who used to boast that he was the only "Dog Hamlet." At booths and fairs this gentleman played the Prince of Denmark with a large black dog at his heels, who used to "bay the moon" at the sight of the ghost and throttle the king in the last scene, which would be arrived at in about half an hour after the commencement. *The Skeleton of the Wave; or, the Ocean Spirit*, was another favourite play at the Queen's; but what a feast of horrors for one night was *The Demon Lord; The Poison Tree; or, the Law of Java*, which in future bills became *The Poison Tree of Java; or, the Spectre Bride and the Demon Nun;* and to wind up on this particular night, *The Death Plank*; *or, the Dumb Sailor Boy.* These highly seasoned dramas were, however, occasionally diversified by the engagement of Mrs. Nisbett, Mrs. Honey, and by Shakespearian productions. The style in which the plays were rendered may be imagined; no burlesque was ever half so extravagant; in one piece the villain was thrown into the corner fifteen times by the hero, and invariably consoled himself by the remark that he "must dissemble," or that a "time would come." The acting, as may be imagined, was in unison with the drama. Anything so utterly stilted and unnatural it would be impossible to conceive at the present day; burlesque could not exaggerate it, as it was beyond the reach of exaggeration, even in the utterance of the simplest words. If a character asked for a piece of bread and cheese he would raise and lower his eyebrows three times, pause between each word, which was dragged up from the very pit of his stomach, and intoned as tragically as though he had requested a cup of poison.

The Queen's shared with the Bower Saloon in Stangate the reputation of being the lowest theatre in London; and then the neighbourhood! always impregnated with "an ancient and fish-like smell" from the fried fish, which was the staple commerce of the street. Such was the house that Miss Marie Wilton, in 1865, being at that time in search of a theatre, fixed upon as a home for elegant comedy. Truly it had been under the direction of Mrs. Nisbett, Mrs. Fitzwilliam, Mrs. Waylett, Madame Vestris, but that was a generation ago, and the experiment cannot be characterised as anything less than daring in the extreme.

What she saw one night upon visiting the theatre might have daunted the boldest resolution. I will give it in her own words: "Some of the occupants of the stalls (the price of admission was, I think, a shilling) were engaged between the acts in devouring oranges (their faces being buried in them) and drinking ginger-beer. Babies were being rocked or smacked to be quiet, which proceeding in many cases had an opposite effect. A woman looked up to our box, and seeing us staring aghast with, I suppose, an expression of horror upon my face, first of all 'took a sight' at us, and then shouted, 'Now then, you stuck-up ones, come out of that, or I'll send this 'ere orange at your 'eads.' Mr. Byron went to the back of the box and laughed until we thought he would be ill. He said my face was a study. 'Oh, Byron!' I said, 'do you think the people from the West End will ever come into those seats?' 'No,' he replied, 'not those seats.' Of course he made jokes the whole evening. One woman in the stalls called out, 'I say, Mrs. Groves, 'ere's one for you,' at the same moment throwing a big orange; upon which Mr. Byron remarked, 'Nice woman, Mrs. Grove—*orange grove.*' I think, if I could, I would at that moment have retired from my bargain; but the deed was done, and there was no going back from it."

The money required to start the speculation, £1,000, Mrs. Bancroft informs us, was borrowed of her brother-in-law, Mr. Francis Drake, and with this the decorators and upholsterers were set to work to cleanse and furbish up the Dust Hole. When this task was done a balance of only £150 was left in the treasury, but from that time, again to quote her own words, "Not one shilling further was ever borrowed by me from, or given to me by anyone, living or dead, in connection with this enterprise." H. J. Byron was in partnership with Miss Wilton, but risked only his work. The Prince of Wales having given permission for the use of his name, the theatre was opened under its new management in September, 1865, with a comedietta by J. P. Wooler, entitled *A Winning Hazard*, Byron's burlesque of *La Sonnambula*, in which Marie Wilton played Elvino, and the farce of *Vandyke Brown;* the company included "little Johnny" Clarke, Fred Dewar, Bancroft, Miss Fanny Josephs, Miss Goodall, Miss Lavine, and three Miss Wiltons. The speculation was a success from the first, and even on the opening night hansoms, for the first time for twenty-five years, drove up to the doors of the Tottenham Street Theatre. Yet on that first night the Prince of Wales's had the narrowest escape of being burned to the ground through a bundle of shavings having taken fire beneath the pit.

The next programme was Byron's *War to the Knife*, and a second burlesque from the same pen, *Lucia de Lammermoor*. But although the house paid from the beginning, the first really great success was Tom Robertson's *Society*, produced on November 11th, 1865; this soon became the talk of the town. Robertson had previously made a hit with *David Garrick* at the Haymarket; but *Society* had gone the round of the managers, and had been rejected almost with contempt; indeed, one wrote "bosh" across it. So much more depends, however, upon the circumstances under which a play is put before the public than on the play itself. Many a fine work has failed simply from the fact that it was produced under inauspicious influences, while mediocre productions have attained a success far greater than their merits warranted, because they have happened just to fit an occasion and have been favoured by surroundings. *Society* was clever, but not great, and the managers who rejected it were not so short-sighted as they may now appear to have been; played under the conditions of dramatic art that then obtained, it would certainly have fallen flat; as a new departure in the drama it required a new departure in histrionic art for a successful interpretation; that it secured at the Prince of Wales's, and at once hit the public taste.

At the Christmas of 1865, Miss Wilton appeared as Little Don Giovanni; her last burlesque part. Another comedy by H. J. Byron, *A Hundred Thousand Pounds;* and then, on September 15th, 1866, Robertson's second comedy, *Ours*, suggested by Millais's picture "The Black Brunswicker." In *Society* the Robertsonian method was only in embryo, in *Ours* its form was fully developed, but it was reserved for *Caste,* produced April 6th, 1869, just after the dissolution of the Wilton-Byron partnership, to display its highest capabilities. The story was so human that it appealed to every kindly feeling of our nature, and was as sympathetic to the stalls as it was to the gallery. It was the Alpha and the Omega of the Robertsonian method; it contained all that had gone before, anticipated all that was to come.

The author, although a very bad actor, was a genius as a stage manager. After reading his comedies, people wonder what there was in dialogue, at times so bald, to fascinate an audience and draw them night after night to hang delightedly on every word. It was not exactly the play, it was the novelty of the representation and the skill with which it was rendered that constituted the charm. The style of acting was a surprise; nothing so perfectly realistic, so devoid of staginess, had ever yet been seen in an English theatre. But Robertson dominated all. "I don't want actors," he said; "I want people that will do just what I tell them"; and he certainly contrived to infuse the very souls of his creations into those who personated them. Looking back now, after a lapse of many years, when the school has passed away and a new order obtains in things theatrical, the glow of remembrance is almost as fervid as when those performances were the talk of every drawing-room. What a charming piece of acting was Younge's George D'Alroy; his many successors never hit the simple-hearted, noble-minded gentleman, as Robertson conceived him, so perfectly as he did. Some tried the lisp, but it never had the same effect; it was an excrescence with them, while with him it was full of suggestion; again, all succeeding George D'Alroys were a little too clever to fall in love with the poor ballet-girl; but when Younge played the part, you never for a moment were in doubt as to the probability, for it was exactly what *that* George D'Alroy would have done. Bancroft's drawling but fine-hearted swell was admirable in its freshness and departure from old types. Another memorable performance was the Sam Gerridge of John Hare, his first appearance in London. And George Honey! was there ever such an Eccles? Some thought it extravagant, and perhaps it was; yet who, with a soul for humour, would have lost one touch of its vivid colours, who would have had its inimitable drollery less emphasised? It was the exaggeration of a Dickens, of a man thoroughly possessed by the relish of his own drollery, and communicating by its very intensity the relish to the spectators. But even above all this excellence was the delicious Polly Eccles of Mrs. Bancroft, so saucy, so *piquante*, such a blending of laughter and tears, in fine, so thoroughly human. Pages might be written in analysis of this matchless performance, but those who have seen it will be able to recall its every detail, and those who have not, well, words cannot paint it for them. Yet she tells us that she preferred Naomi Tighe. We do not think many will agree with her. Delightful as was Naomi Tighe, it was artificial, whereas Polly Eccles was the quintessence of nature. It was probably a surprise to old playgoers to hear that in length of run *Caste* stood as low as fifth, when compared to other plays produced at this theatre. Of Robertson's comedies, *School* ran the greatest number of nights, and *Ours* came second. *Diplomacy* and *Masks and Faces* both exceeded *Caste* in longevity.

A long run was made by Wilkie Collins's *Man and Wife*, founded upon his novel of that name, which excited almost as much indignation in athletes, from the attack it made upon their order, as did Kipling's "flannelled fools" and "muddied oafs" not long ago. A gruesome piece. Coghlan was very fine in it.

It was in 1874 that Mr. Gilbert's delightful little comedietta, *Sweethearts*, was produced; and it was as Jenny Northcote that Mrs. Bancroft's art was at its finest. It was the marvellous flow of animal spirits, the intense enjoyment of the actress in her own conception, which made the laughter as spontaneous as the tears that carried the audience away with Polly Eccles; but a much higher art was revealed in the performance of Mr. Gilbert's heroine. Yet the *ars celare artem*, to use a horribly hackneyed phrase, was so perfect that every aspiring amateur thought she had only to ape the forward schoolgirl in the first act, and powder her hair and look lacrymose in the last to emulate Mrs. Bancroft; in her stupid self-conceit she never thought of the flashes, the subtle touches revealing the love and tenderness that palpitated beneath the *espièglerie* of the wayward Jenny, the exquisite bits of business, that required such delicacy in handling. Even finer was the last act; the deep pathos that was veiled by that calm, placid face, the story of the blighted life that you read, not through any conventional stage emotion, but by the mere drooping of an eyelid, the least quiver of the lip, the faltering on a syllable were as perfect as anything the French stage could show.

Poor Robertson's share in the triumphs of the Bancroft management was as brief as it was brilliant. Artistically, however, his vein was exhausted; he had done his work, he had swept away old conventionalities; but had he written many more pieces he would have established affectations even more objectionable than those he had displaced. All the characters of the plays lived in the best of all possible worlds, in which the troubles of early years were for the happiness of later, tears were always dried up by the sunshine of smiles, and the curtain fell upon love and kisses. The teacup-and-saucer-trousers-pocket-school was very good in its way in the hands of its original exponents, but was carried to an absurd extent by their imitators, and to be quite inaudible and utterly inanimate were beginning to be considered the acme of good acting. A rude shock to the school was experienced when *The Merchant of Venice* was subjected to its cult, though we should all look leniently upon that error, since it first revealed to us the powers of Ellen Terry in the part of Portia.

It is worthy of note that a more robust style of drama, such as *Diplomacy*, one of the most perfect performances given at the Prince of Wales's, *Peril*, etc., followed the Robertson comedies. *Money* was the best acted of the Bancroft old comedy revivals ; Mrs. Bancroft's Lady Franklin was admirable, and Coghlan rendered that stilted sentimentalist Evelyn for the first time endurable. *The School for Scandal* and *Masks and Faces* were admirably staged ; but the tone of the Prince of Wales's was essentially modern, there was no conviction about the powdered wigs and velvet coats; if the dresses were of the eighteenth century, the men and women were essentially of the nineteenth ; but, again, the highest praise must be accorded to Coghlan's Charles Surface ; no actor within my memory has equalled him in Sheridan's gay hero. He was the full - blooded, port-wine drinking, boisterous young gentleman of the eighteenth century.

The secret of the success of the Bancroft management was its practical, business-like conduct ; the Bancrofts gathered about them the finest talent, compatible with their style of entertainment, and frequently contented themselves with subordinate parts in the interests of the piece. When they made a mistake they never failed not only frankly to acknowledge, but to retrieve it as quickly as possible, no matter at what cost. Everything they attempted in scenery, in costume, in acting was finished to the minutest detail. An evening at the Prince of Wales's was an artistic pleasure undisturbed by any jarring chord.

The Bancroft management came to an end in 1879, and the theatre passed into the hands of Edgar Bruce. His first success was Geneviève Ward in *Forget Me Not*, a most powerful performance. This was followed by

Burnand's *Colonel*, 1881, which was destined to exceed the longest of the Bancroft runs. Curious to relate, this piece was accepted and even put into rehearsal by the previous manager and then declined. The judgment, however, that so determined can scarcely be questioned, considering that *The Colonel* was but a new rendering of an old piece from a French original, *The Serious Family*, which had been a stock comedy at the Haymarket in Buckstone's days; and who could have had sufficient forethought to foresee that the transference of the satire from sham piety to sham æsthetics would have so seized upon the public taste? Beerbohm Tree made his début as Lambert Streyke in this play.

Although other pieces were produced by Mr. Bruce, with *The Colonel* all that is interesting in the history of the theatre terminates. A dispute between the lessees, Bancroft and James, and the tenant as to which of the three should be responsible for the alterations insisted upon by the Board of Works ended in closing the doors of the Prince of Wales's for ever as a theatre in 1882. And the old house, associated with so many delightful memories, became a Salvation Army barracks—to what base uses may we not return! The last remains of the building have only just disappeared, and I understand that Mr. Frank Curzon intends to erect a new theatre upon the site.

CHAPTER IV

The Holborn Theatre (known also as the Mirror and the Duke's)—The Holborn Amphitheatre (*alias* the Connaught, the Alcazar, the Theatre Royal, Holborn)—The Queen's, Long Acre—The Globe—The Opera Comique—Toole's (The Charing Cross, The Folly).

THE utter stagnation into which theatrical speculation had fallen by the middle of the last century is testified by the circumstance that from 1841, when the Princess's was opened, until 1866 no new theatre was added to central London, and that several could not find tenants.

The first person who ventured upon what had long been regarded as the forlornest of hopes—an addition to the number of our dramatic temples—was Mr. Sefton Parry, who, in 1866, erected a theatre upon the site of an old coach-yard and stables, and called it after the thoroughfare in which it was situated, THE HOLBORN. It was opened in the October of that year with *Flying Scud*, a sporting drama, which, with a real horse and that fine actor George Belmore as the old jockey Nat Gosling, proved a hit. But it was a solitary one. When Mr. Parry retired from the management in 1868, it was undertaken by Miss Fanny Josephs; and in the following season she gave place to Mr. Barry Sullivan, an actor of the old school, who, with Mrs. Hermann Vezin as his leading lady, played a round of the old-fashioned legitimate drama, such as *The Gamester;* but the abrupt closing of the theatre in the January of 1871 told its own story.

When, in 1875, Mr. Horace Wigan became lessee, the Holborn was renamed the Mirror. His brief tenancy was marked by one important production, *All For Her*, the first of the dramas founded upon the Sydney Carton episode (which Dickens had borrowed from Dumas). When John Clayton, who had hitherto been esteemed only an indifferently good actor, appeared in this play, a great future, as an exponent of the romantic drama, was predicted for him. It was the most picturesque and poetic performance that had been seen since Fechter's *Ruy Blas*. But *All For Her*, though moved from theatre to theatre, was never more than *un succès d'estime*, and curious to say, Clayton never made another hit in the romantic drama, unless it was as Osip in *Les Danischeffs*. Truly his ever-increasing obesity afterwards unfitted him for the heroic, yet it does not quite explain the why and the wherefore of the circumstance.

After Horace Wigan the house was again re-christened, this time the Duke's Theatre. Many were its managers and as many were their disappointments. Messrs. Holt and Wilmot broke the spell of ill luck with Paul Merritt's *New Babylon* in 1879. On June 4th in the following year the Duke's was burned to the ground. A portion of the First Avenue Hotel now covers the site.

An almost forgotten place of dramatic entertainment, which was first called the Amphitheatre, Holborn, and opened as a circus in 1868, and then converted into the Connaught Theatre, afterwards the Alcazar, and finally THE THEATRE ROYAL, Holborn, may be dismissed in a few sentences. It was John Hollingshead who started it as a dramatic speculation in 1874, at cheap prices. Beginning with pantomime he leaped to Beaumont and Fletcher's *Maid's Tragedy* and other old-world plays, which were interpreted by one or two serious actors, and the rest from the Gaiety. Perhaps he intended it for a huge joke and did not mind paying for the fun. George Rignold played a short season here in a version of *Adam Bede* and other pieces. But it was a hopeless affair from the first, and about 1888 was converted into a building called the Central Hall.

On October 24th, 1867, St. Martin's Hall, Long Acre, having been reconstructed, was opened as THE QUEEN'S THEATRE. Although Alfred Wigan's name appeared at the head of the bill, it was an open secret that the lessee was Mr. Labouchere. During its brief existence the Queen's took a very important position among London houses. The first piece produced upon its boards was an adaptation of Charles Reade's *White Lies*. Mr. Liston, who afterwards took the Olympic, succeeded Wigan; then came Ernest Clifton, under whom most of the most notable successes of the house were achieved. It was here that Mrs. Rousby made her London début in 1869 as Fiordelisa in the *Fool's Revenge;* and drew very large audiences in '*Twixt Axe and Crown*, and *Joan of Arc*. A beautiful face and the enthusiastic patronage of Tom Taylor, made for this actress one of those meretricious and transitory reputations which are common enough in stage annals; though she might have held the public longer had not her own follies robbed her of its respect.

The Queen's could always boast of one of the finest companies in London. J. L. Toole and Lionel Brough were the stock comedians; and it was here, after his engagement at the St. James's, that Henry Irving, in such plays as *Dearer Than Life*, *The Lancashire Lass*, firmly established himself as an actor of exceptional powers. Miss Nelly Moore and Miss Henrietta Hodson, two *ingénues* that even the French stage might have been proud of, were chiefly identified with this theatre; John Ryder, Sam Emery, Mr. and Mrs. Frank Matthews, Hermann Vezin, Charles Wyndham were also at different times members of the company. Phelps played Bottom in a very fine revival of *A Midsummer Night's Dream* in 1870, and also appeared in one or two new plays. *Cymbeline* was produced in the following year; there was also a revival of *The Tempest*, both for Henrietta Hodson. Some may remember the fiasco of *The Last Days of Pompeii*, which was so mercilessly burlesqued. And in 1872 George Rignold, a robust, picturesque actor of the Dillon school, who had he not gone away to Australia might have raised himself to a fine position on the London stage, made his mark in Watts Philips' *Amos Clark*, in which Miss Wallis first appeared. In the same year Colonel Richards's *Cromwell*, brought out as a counterblast to *Charles I.*, offered Rignold another chance of distinguishing himself, as the Lord Protector. This was followed by *Old London*, a new version of *Jack Sheppard*, in which Miss Hodson played Jack. Here ended the Labouchere management, and for a time the tenants were various.

The Queen's scored but few successes, *The Turn of the Tide*, a version of the old Victorian drama *The Black Doctor*, produced early in its life, and Mrs. Rousby's engagements being the chief. Under Mrs. Seymour's direction, in 1873, Charles Reade's *Wandering Heir* was given, with Mrs. John Wood, and afterwards Ellen Terry, as the heroine. In 1875 Salvini, who came from Drury Lane, appeared here as Othello.

One of the greatest pieces of tragic acting the world has ever seen, not only in overwhelming power, but in subtle art: it created a profound impression. Salvini also appeared as Macbeth, Hamlet, and while at Covent Garden, in 1884, King Lear; all were fine performances, but none equalled Othello. By the perfection of its mechanical plant the house was admirably adapted for spectacular drama. After Drury Lane it was the largest theatre in the West End. It was converted into the Clerical Co-operative Stores in 1878, and was no more fortunate in business than it had been in art.

THE GLOBE was erected by Sefton Parry upon a portion of the site of Lyon's Inn, an old Inn of Courts that dated back to the time of Henry VIII. But for many years previous to its demolition it had been the resort of shady characters.[1] The Globe was opened in December, 1868, with one of H. J. Byron's best comedies, *Cyril's Success*, in which W. H. Vernon made his first bow to a London audience. Cyril's was the only success scored by Parry, and in 1871 the Globe passed into the hands of Harry Montague, who, having disagreed with his partners at the Vaudeville about the importance given to burlesque, in which he did *not* play, seceded from the triumvirate. Montague was the women's darling, and the most fascinating actor of his time. He began at the St. James's under Webster. London managers did not care about engaging novices in the days of "Old Ben," but Montague was so persevering that Webster said afterwards, "D——n the fellow, I was obliged to give him an engagement to get rid of him!"

[1] It acquired a notoriety at the beginning of the nineteenth century as having been the abode of William Weare, a turfite, who was murdered by his associates, Thurtell and Probert.

His principal productions at the Globe were H. J. Byron's *Partners for Life;* Albery's *Forgiven; Oriana;* Frank Marshall's *False Shame;* a revival of Douglas Jerrold's *Time Works Wonders;* a dramatic version of *Dombey and Son*, with Sam Emery as Cap'n Cuttle, and Helen Barry as Mrs. Dombey. Montague had an excellent company, which included Haymarket Compton and Miss Carlotta Addison, then a charming juvenile lady; but the theatre never paid, and he went away to America, never to return.

Edgar Bruce rented the Globe for a time, and brought from the Aquarium Theatre the adaptation of "Bleak House" called *Jo*, in which Miss Jennie Lee gave that powerful, wonderfully pathetic, and haunting performance of the street arab, that must ever linger in the memory of those who saw it. Edward Righton succeeded Bruce, and was fairly successful with revivals of *Money*, *She Stoops to Conquer*, with Merritt's *Stolen Kisses*, the burlesque of *My Poll and My Partner Joe*, interpreted by Henry Neville, Righton, William Farren, John Ryder, Mrs. Chippendale, Mrs. John Wood.

Comyns Carr's version of *Far From the Madding Crowd*, April, 1882, with Mrs. Bernard Beere as Bathsheba, will be remembered on account of the dispute between Mrs. Kendal, Mr. Pinero, and Mr. C. C., as to the originality of *The Squire*, which bore such a remarkable resemblance to Mr. Hardy's famous novel. But whatever might have been the rights of the case, the St. James's play was an overwhelming success, and the Globe's was a failure. After the production of Sydney Grundy's comic opera, *The Vicar of Bray*, Mrs. Bernard Beere became manageress, and made a fiasco with Tennyson's *The Promise of May*, November, 1882. The second night was rendered remarkable by the late Marquis of Queensberry, of prize-ring celebrity, rising up in the stalls to proclaim himself an agnostic and denounce the poet's type of that cult, as embodied in the character of Edgar. A dramatic version of *Jane Eyre*, by G. W. Wills, with Charles Kelly as Rochester and Mrs. Beere as the heroine, was scarcely more fortunate. In 1884 we find the names of John Hollingshead and J. L. Shine at the top of the bill; but a year later Charles Hawtrey took their place with *The Private Secretary*, brought from the Prince's with its third and most successful Rev. Robert Spalding, Mr. Penley. A failure at its birthplace, it here became one of the greatest successes of the century.

Very few theatres so frequently changed hands and styles of entertainment as the Globe. Richard Mansfield, the American actor, whom we have met at the Lyceum, produced *Richard III.* on a magnificent scale in 1889, and was very wroth with the British Press and public because he shared the same fate with so many of his predecessors. In the following year Mr. F. R. Benson commenced his first London season with a beautiful revival of *The Midsummer Night's Dream*, in which the now famous dramatic poet, Mr. Stephen Phillips, played the small part of Flute, the bellows-mender.

Norman Forbes was the lessee in 1891, but quickly retired, a poorer if not a wiser man. One of the most charming of comic operas, *Ma Mie Rosette*, with that delightful singer, Eugene Oudin, as Henry IV., was brought out here in 1892. And early in the next year *Charley's Aunt*, transferred from the Royalty, commenced its record-breaking run of four years. Translated into French, it was played five hundred nights at the Theâtre de Cluny. In the English provinces the success of this mediocre farce was and is equally phenomenal. Yet another man-in-petticoats piece, *Miss Frances of Yale,* with Grossmith, in 1897, failed to attract the laughter-loving public.

Lewis Waller brought out his version of *The Three Musketeers* here in 1898 ; and John Hare, in the same year, gave us E. V. Esmond's *A Bachelor's Romance,* revivals of several of Tom Robertson's comedies, and best of all, Pinero's *The Gay Lord Quex,* 1899. I do not know of a finer piece of dramatic work in the whole range of comedy than the second act of this play. No scene ever more gripped an audience in breathless suspense, or evoked a wilder burst of applause at the end, than the duel between Sophie—so splendidly played by Miss Irene Vanbrugh—and my lord. The way in which the natural vulgarity of the ex-lady's-maid broke through the genteel veneer of the manicurist, the alternations of bully, triumph, entreaty, the tenacity of her fidelity to the woman for whose cause she was fighting, and her final burst of admiration for the magnanimous foe who yielded at discretion, was most perfect acting.

Wilson Barrett made some successes here, and a very remarkable one was achieved by Miss Julia Neilson in *Sweet Nell of Old Drury,* 1901, originally played at the Haymarket, an extraordinary perversion of history, in which the saucy orange-girl, whose coarseness of speech and manner is historical, is transformed into a sentimental philanthropist, who might at the present day be the pet of an evangelical parson. But the multitude flocked to see the whitewashing of Nell, so *n'importe.* And with a revival of this drama on the 22nd March, 1902, the doors of the Globe Theatre finally closed. It was a jerry-built house, run up with a view to the long-deferred Strand improvement. If a fire had broken out it would have burned like a match-box. It is curious that those guardians of the public safety, the County Council, who are so severely conscientious where other managers are in question, should have been unaware of this fact and have continued to let it without alterations. It held about 1,000 people at a money value of £210.

THE OPERA COMIQUE, like the Globe, was erected upon the Lyon's Inn site, and was opened in October, 1870. It was at that time one of the most artistically decorated theatres in London. But its scattered entrances in three thoroughfares, interminable passages, and draughty stalls, that threatened every visitor with neuralgia and catarrh, and the "outlandish" name, heavily handicapped it from the first.

The opening season was an utter fiasco. But in the next it was fortunate enough to secure the company of the Comédie Française, which, driven from its home by the German invasion, performed for the first time in its history out of Paris. Madame Ristori, after a long absence from this country, played an engagement here in 1873, appearing as Marie Antoinette, Lucrezia Borgia, and in the sleep-walking scene of Lady Macbeth—a wonderful piece of acting that realised all the Siddons traditions.

It was at this house that the Gilbert and Sullivan combination practically commenced—though the *Trial by Jury* first saw the footlights at the Royalty in 1875—in November, 1878, with *The Sorcerer*, one of the best of the long series of comic operas that delighted the English public for a score of years. I can see little Grossmith now hopping round the fire like a frog in the creepy-droll incantation scene. Lady Sangazure was played by Mrs. Howard Paul, her last appearance upon the stage. *H.M.S. Pinafore* came next with its breezy humour and catching melodies; *The Pirates of Penzance*, and everybody was singing the policemen's chorus; then *Patience*, a delightful piece of work. And what artistically finished performances they were; every performer was so perfectly fitted and trained—Grossmith, Temple, Jessie Bond, Leonora Braham, Miss Everard, Rutland Barrington, Alice Barnett!

When, in 1881, D'Oyley Carte removed the company to his new theatre, he certainly carried away with him the luck and prestige of the Opera Comique. Musical pieces in imitation of the Gilbert and Sullivan school, French comic operas were tried with indifferent success. Lotta, one of the most famous of American *comédiennes*, who is said to be a millionaire, appeared here in the double rôle of Little Nell and the Marchioness, and other parts, but failed to attract.

Mrs. Bernard Beere conducted the season of 1887–8, and created a great impression as Lena Despard in *As in a Looking-Glass*, breaking a lance, many thought, with the divine Sarah herself in the terrible death scene. Arthur Roberts made a success here with a burlesque on *Joan of Arc* in 1891. In the next year there was a season of French plays. David James was "sole lessee" for a time; Compton tried legitimate comedy; Willie Edouin was manager for a while. Just before their departure for Australia (1893), the Dacres opened the theatre for a few weeks. Nellie Farren took the house to bring out a burlesque upon *Trilby*, but Arthur Roberts had anticipated her elsewhere, and the venture failed, as had most of the others. *Alice in Wonderland*, 1898, and a drama by Simms, *A Good Time*, April, 1899, were the last productions before the house was finally closed for demolition.

TOOLE'S THEATRE, now covered by the new buildings of

the Charing Cross Hospital, was developed out of the Polygraphic Hall, which was chiefly remarkable for the monologue entertainment "My Carpet Bag," given by Woodin, one of the numerous imitators of the elder Mathews. The Hall was converted into a tiny playhouse in 1869, and christened the Charing Cross Theatre. But it held no position until it came into the hands of J. S. Clarke, of Major Wellington de Boots fame, in 1872. His most notable production was *The Rivals*, in which Mrs. Stirling gave her splendid performance of Mrs. Malaprop for the first time, and Clarke appeared as Bob Acres, a very humorous and clever piece of acting, but *not* "fighting Bob."

When Mr. Alexander Henderson took the house in 1876, he rechristened it the Folly, and his wife, charming Lydia Thompson, was the great attraction in burlesque. In 1878 a phenomenal success was achieved with *Les Cloches de Corneville*, in which Miss Violet Cameron made her first hit as Germaine, and Shiel Barry gave a performance of Gaspar, the Miser, such as had not been seen since Robson's Daddy Hardacre.

J. L. Toole undertook the management in November, 1879. Pinero's first comedy *Imprudence* was brought out here in 1881, and a second, *Boys and Girls*, in the next year; both were failures. The author was too unconventional for the audiences of that time, and his originality, it must be added, was crude and ill-digested, being in the process of crystallisation. H. J. Byron's *The Upper Crust*, and others by the same author, and burlesques on popular plays, such as *Stage-Dora* and *Paw Claudian*, or *The Roman Awry*, in which that bright clever actress Marie Linden gave her delightful imitations, were much more successful.

In 1882 Mr. Toole initiated the objectionable

American practice of calling the theatre after his own name, and so it was thenceforth known as "Toole's." The Daly Company made their first appearance here in 1884. The theatre was let to various companies and managers during the frequent absence of the lessee, but during the rest of its existence there is little that calls for notice.

J. M. Barrie's first play, *Walker, London*, was produced in 1892, and enjoyed a long run. The house was considerably enlarged, though after the alterations it could not seat more than 900, and improved by the genial comedian, who has unfortunately been lost to the laughter-loving public for so long a time through a prostrating illness. His last production was *Thoroughbred* in February, 1895, and the theatre, which was not very prosperous in its last years, having been acquired for the extension of Charing Cross Hospital, was closed in the spring of that year.

CHAPTER V

The old Gaiety—The Alhambra—The Empire—The (New) English Opera House—The Sans Souci, etc.

THE old GAIETY was constructed out of the Strand Music Hall, which had proved a failure in the days when the music-hall was not so much in favour as it is at present, by the late Mr. Lionel Lawson of *The Daily Telegraph.* It was opened on December 21st, 1868, with an adaptation from the French, *On the Cards*, Alfred Wigan playing the leading part, and a burlesque on *Robert the Devil*, with the Daubans, Nelly Farren, who came from the Olympic, and Fanny Josephs, as the chief attractions. Thirty years ago and much more recently, a burlesque was considered by most theatres in town and country to be an indispensable wind-up to the evening's entertainment. The Gaiety from the first produced burlesque upon a more lavish scale than any of its rivals.

But in its earlier days "the sacred lamp" was not always alight. A romantic play entitled *Dreams*, by Tom Robertson, was brought out in 1869. Mr. and Mrs. Charles Mathews appeared in 1873 in *Married for Money*, and at the end of the same year Phelps, Toole, Charles Mathews, Hermann Vezin, acted together in *John Bull*, a combination that drew all theatrical London. Phelps also appeared in several of his celebrated comedy rôles.

Toole began a career of some years in H. J. Byron's *Uncle Dick's Darling.* Irving played Chevenix, and very much impressed Charles Dickens by his acting. "That young man will be a great actor," was his prophecy. Another hit of Irving's at this theatre was Bob Gasset in *Dearer than Life.* Adelaide Neilson was in both pieces.

Madame Angot represented opera-bouffe here, and *Zampa,* with Santley in the title-rôle, serious opera. French companies played here every season from 1874, and it was on this stage that Sarah Bernhardt made her first appearance before the English public with the company of the Comédie Française on their second visit to England in 1879. There was an immense rush to see the actress, whose fame had preceded her; every seat was taken, and crowds nightly and daily besieged the doors of pit and gallery.

The greatest house was on the night she played Donna Sol in *Hernani*—£571. She also created a profound impression in *Phèdre.*

I have always thought that from a purely artistic point of view, she has never acted so finely as in combination with artistes who could claim something like equality with the diva in their own line of art. She was then the central figure of a great picture, in harmony with all the subordinate parts; since then she has too frequently made the mistake of surrounding herself with mediocrities, which destroys the sense of proportion; she has studied only her own effects, without relation to the whole, and has developed strong mannerisms, the constant repetition of which often fatigues the ear. For several years she appeared in London only at this theatre.

When the Gaiety opened for the season, in December,

1878, the manager informed his patrons that during the ten years of its existence the theatre had been closed only ten weeks, and as a balance against that interval there had been morning performances equal to one year and three months. It was Mr. Hollingshead who first abolished the infamous system of fees, which, however, has come into force again under managers who ought to blush for countenancing such extortion. What would a man say to be charged sixpence at an hotel for the menu of the dinner he sat down to eat? Not but what some of the blame is due to the public, who would persist in tipping the attendants in spite of all notices against the usage. Another institution initiated by John Hollingshead, the matinée, for the production of untried plays, proved a plague to dramatic critics, who had to sit stewing on hot summer afternoons to witness inanities that were never heard of again. This is a thing of the past, and afternoon performances, as at present understood, are a great boon to the dwellers in suburbia.

Between whiles old comedies and dramas were given—Congreve's *Love for Love*, Sheridan's *A Trip to Scarborough*, *The Critic*, *George Barnwell*, *The Castle Spectre*—to exemplify Hollingshead's theory that the old drama was very inferior to the modern; and played as it was by actors in up-to-date style, with their tongues in their cheeks, he had no difficulty in communicating his faith to a Gaiety audience. Charles Mathews played most of his later engagements at the Gaiety, and there created his last famous character, Mr. Councillor Punch, in *My Awful Dad*, 1875. H. J. Byron was also closely identified with the house both as actor and author. As the years passed on, burlesque became more and more absolute on those boards. But the

Gaiety school never equalled that of the Strand; it was coarser, less artistic, too much to please "the boys." Yet its record bears a good array of names—Toole, Edward Terry, Tom Thorne, Kate Vaughan, Edward Royce, Lonnen, and, greatest of all, Nelly Farren and Fred Leslie.

Miss Farren, who had been principal burlesque actress at the Olympic, was on the staff of the Gaiety from the opening night; for a time, however, she played seconds to Patty Josephs, but not for long. I remember her and Toole in *The Princess of Trebizonde*, in the early days; how *piquante* and droll they were. She played a number of comedy parts in the seventies and early eighties—Miss Prue in *Love for Love*, Miss Hoyden in *The Man of Quality*, Clemency Newcombe in *The Battle of Life*, Nan in *Good for Nothing*. How delightful she was in *The Grasshopper*, *Carmen Up to Data*, *Little Faust*, *Little Don Cæsar*, *Babes in the Wood*, and how many more! Nellie Farren was much more than a mere burlesque actress; there were flashes of passion and intensity, especially in her street arabs, that thrilled with true tragic power. But what she is chiefly remembered by are her wild spirits, her audacity, her *verve*, her "go." In Fred Leslie, who joined the company in 1885, she had an *alter ego*. Never was buffoonery carried to such an excess upon the dramatic stage as by those two in *Monte Cristo*, *Ruy Blas*, and especially between Little Jack Sheppard and Blueskin. But the fun was so real, so apparently spontaneous, so thoroughly enjoyed by the buffoons themselves, that it was irresistible. It was during the run of *Cinder-Ellen*, in 1892, that poor "Nellie" was struck down by rheumatism, brought on, it is said, by damp tights; in order to make the silk fit close to her limbs, she was in the habit of first dipping them in water. And Leslie did not long survive his co-mate. The Gaiety never replaced them as artistes. There was always that note of intensity in Leslie's acting, without which burlesque is tomfoolery; witness his "looking-glass" song in *Cinder-Ellen*, what a touch of quite tearful pathos there was in the old man lamenting the loss of his youth.

It was about 1881, with Burnand's *Whittington and His Cat*, I think, that Hollingshead instituted that dreary thing, the three-act "burlesque drama." But it extended on into Mr. George Edwardes's management, until early in the nineties, when was introduced the American variety show, called musical comedy.

Nat Goodwin appeared in the off season of 1900, but gradually the new departure has monopolised the stage, each specimen usually for a couple of years. An endless line of "Girls" has been varied by one "Boy," all so much alike that it would puzzle most of the audience to differentiate them. Costly dresses, beautiful scenery, and lively song and dance, however, made the Gaiety the best paying house in London.

It is a very significant commentary upon English dramatic art, that while the classic Lyceum, with its splendid intellectual memories, closed its doors almost unnoticed, the great Temple of Nonsense ended its career in July with an éclat unparalleled in the history of the stage. Enormous prices, perhaps the highest ever given, were paid for all the reserved seats, and a very distinguished audience came to do honour to the occasion. That every old Gaiety actor available should appear upon the stage that night to awaken memories of the past was a matter of course, and Sir Henry Irving gave a dignity to the occasion by delivering a farewell address. *The Toreador*, which had had a very long run, was the last piece played upon the old Gaiety boards.

There is something melancholy in the disappearance of so many of our old haunts wherein many of us have spent such delightful hours of our lives, haunts which have echoed to the voices of men and women whose names were once household words, most of whom have passed away into "that undiscovered country from whose bourne no traveller returns." Even the very site of the buildings will very soon be obliterated, and a future generation will be as indefinite about the situation of the Olympic, or Lyceum, or the Globe or the old Gaiety, as we are concerning the spots upon which the Shakespearian theatres stood.

It was in 1871 that THE ALHAMBRA was converted from a music-hall into a theatre. This building had undergone several transformations. When erected in 1854 it was called the Panopticon of Science and Art, and was opened as a joint-stock undertaking by certain enthusiasts who were desirous of imparting scientific truths in a popular and amusing form, after the old Polytechnic mode. After about three years it was closed, and in 1858 the ubiquitous E. T. Smith took it on lease, and renaming it the Alhambra from its Moorish style of architecture, opened it as a place of general entertainment for horse-riding, panoramas, athletics, etc. Both the exterior and interior of the building remained unaltered. In December, 1860, it underwent another change, a stage was erected, and it was converted into a regular music-hall. After a while it became noted for its ballets; but it did not excite very much attention, except as a favourite resort of very fast young men, until the period of the Franco-German War, when the singing of the "Marseillaise" and the "Wacht um Rhein" on the same night roused the national rivalries, not only of the French and Germans, but of their English partisans as well, to fever heat. The Alhambra was crowded nightly by people who came to hiss and applaud and by those who rushed to enjoy the fun. While the excitement lasted the house was a gold mine. In 1871 Mr. John Baum, the then lessee, obtained a theatrical licence With a good opera-bouffe company, ballets superbly mounted, and the best ballet dancers in London, which could always be procured by paying larger salaries than the theatres and giving permanent employment, with an excellent band far exceeding in number that of any one of the more legitimate houses, it might have been thought that the Alhambra would certainly pay; so it did for a time, but the *habitués* missed the lounge, the smoking and drinking, and its previous reputation caused the more prim portion of the public to look askance upon it. Several well-known opera-bouffes were produced here and very elaborately mounted, notably *Le Roi Carotte* and the *Black Crook.* Burned to the ground at the end of the year 1882, it was rebuilt and reopened as a theatre with a revival of Burnand's burlesque of *Black-Eyed Susan*, in December, 1883. So direful, however, was the failure of the dramatic entertainment this time that the proprietors closed the house, and in the next year, under the old licence for music and dancing, reopened it as a music-hall.

The Empire, originally called the Alcazar, built upon the site of Saville House, notorious in the forties for the exhibition of Madame Warton's Poses Plastiques, was opened at the end of 1883 with a very superbly staged version of *Chilpéric*, and with what was then a novel employment of electricity, incandescent lights breaking out upon the breastplates and helmets of the ballet. It was the first time such an effect, which has since become quite common, was attempted. In July, 1884, John Hollingshead brought the Gaiety company here with the burlesque of *The Forty Thieves.* In the next year Hayden Coffin and J. L. Shine appeared in a comic opera, *The Lady of the Locket.* In 1886 a version of Jules Verne's and D'Ennery's *Round the World in Eighty Days* was splendidly mounted here under the direction of Marius, with Charles Cartwright, Collette, Kate Vaughan; and another elaborate spectacle, *The Palace of Pearl*, was produced. Not long afterwards, 1887, the dramatic was abandoned for the variety show.

Expectation was on tiptoe when, in the first week of February, 1891, D'Oyly Carte opened his magnificent new theatre, with its marble vestibule and staircase and splendid decorations, in Cambridge Circus as THE ENGLISH OPERA HOUSE, with Arthur Sullivan's grand opera *Ivanhoe.* The supposition, however, that an opera could be forced into a long run like a drama was one of those absurd calculations which experts so often make. Soon came the fiasco. There was not another English opera ready, and the house that was built for the purpose of exploiting national music had to fall back for its second work on *La Basoche!*

Sarah Bernhardt appeared as Cleopatra here in 1892. D'Oyly Carte turned the theatre into a company, who converted it into a variety show, but for a long time it was a terrible muddle.

Even when the company was placed under the management of Augustus Harris, the muddle was quite as bad. I shall never forget the first night of the new entertainment, the mixture of variety turns and melodrama; poor William Rignold as a brave British officer killing his wife to save her from the sepoys. The entertainment struggled on long after midnight, amid the jeers and hostile demonstrations of the audience. Nothing prospered at the house until Mr. Morton, who I verily believe would make a theatre pay on the top of a Dartmoor tor, undertook the management. From that time the Palace Theatre has been one of the best paying of the variety shows.

* * * * * *

There still remain a few more extinct West End theatres, now quite forgotten, to be mentioned, to render my list complete.

At the end of the eighteenth century, Charles Dibdin fitted up a little theatre at the corner of Leicester Place—the post office now occupies the site—for his entertainment of songs and sketches, which he called THE SANS SOUCI. Edmund Kean, when a boy, appeared here in some acrobatic performances. After Dibdin's time it was used more by amateurs than professionals, except for benefits. "Baron" Nicholson, in his memoirs, 1820, calls it "an elegant little theatre," but it was too small for any effective representations. In 1832 it was opened by subscription for vaudevilles. Two years afterwards a French company occupied it. After that it was closed.

From 1819 to 1823 THE ARGYLL ROOMS, Regent Street, was fitted up for French plays, under the patronage of the aristocracy. These were given by subscription every Friday from March to September. The performance commenced at nine and terminated at twelve; after which the company adjourned to the ballroom to finish up the night's amusement with dancing. This, however, was a private theatre, as only subscribers were admitted.

In 1832 a theatre was opened in Windmill Street, Haymarket, and called THE ALBION, a name which, three years afterwards, was changed to the New Queen's. Its entire existence extended over only four years. The famous tragedy actress, Sally Booth, performed here, though its ordinary programme was very pronounced melodrama.

In the same year (1832) an undertaker named Gale, of York Street, Westminster, erected upon a plot of ground he owned (for which it may be presumed he could find no other purpose) THE WESTMINSTER THEATRE. It stood just about the spot on which is now the stage entrance of the Imperial. Its first manager was T. D. Davenport, who is generally believed to have been the original of Dickens's Crummles. Dibdin Pitt and John Douglass were his successors, and several actors who afterwards won a name for themselves, William Davidge, Joseph Rayner, and Munyard, appeared here. The Westminster Theatre never obtained a licence, and was in existence only about four years.

Between 1834 and 1840 there was a theatre in High Street, Kensington, called THE ROYAL KENT; but it was a mere box, and would hold only about two hundred and fifty persons. Nevertheless, it had "a royal entrance" down a back court. Brown, a well-known light comedian, Wynne, an actor of some repute, the brother of Augustus Sala, frequently mentioned in the memoirs of the latter, and Denvil, the original representative of Manfred, were, at one time, among the company. Indeed, it was from here that Bunn engaged Denvil for Drury Lane, to play the part of Byron's melancholy hero.

For a few months, during 1841, there was a theatre opened at the back of the Colisseum, Regent's Park, and called the Colisseum Theatre, Albany Street. Tully' the well-known composer and conductor, figured there as a comedian.

PART IV

THE NORTHERN, SOUTHERN, AND EASTERN THEATRES PAST AND PRESENT

CHAPTER I

THE NORTHERN THEATRES

Sadler's Wells (the oldest theatre in London); a curious history—The Grecian—The Albert Saloon—The Britannia—The Variety, Hoxton—Highbury Barn—The Park Theatre—The King's Cross—The New Theatres.

ALTHOUGH most of the old Northern, Southern, and East End theatres are extinct, or have fallen too low for consideration, it is not so long ago since they were important factors of theatrical London. But affairs theatrical have been utterly revolutionised during the last fifteen or twenty years. Formerly each of these district theatres had its own particular audience, that seldom attended any other; now, thanks to cheap conveyances, such audiences are ubiquitous. Again, the local music-halls have drawn away the old gallery frequenters and many of the pittites, while genteel respectability either go to the West End or to the handsome new suburban houses, where they can see all the West End pieces, and sometimes with the original castes.

Until 1843 all theatres, except Drury Lane, Covent Garden, and the Haymarket, were alike called minor theatres, and little or no distinction, except from the accident of situation, was made between those of Whitechapel and those of the Strand. The same authors wrote the same kind of piece for the Adelphi, the English Opera House and Olympic, as for the Victoria, the

Surrey, and the City of London. Edward Stirling, Leman Rede, Fitzball, Mark Lemon, John Oxenford, and Douglas Jerrold wrote for all.

But there was another class of writers which was especially attached to these houses, and, after the new Licensing Act, became responsible for the entire repertory —Egerton Wilks, Edwin Travers, George Almar, Dibdin Pitt, Charles Hazelwood, and many others. The plays of these men, though destitute of literary merit, were usually cleverly constructed, with an exciting plot, and plenty of strong situations. The writers were invariably actors, and for a salary of two pounds ten, or three pounds, played parts, and wrote a play a week. *The London Journal*, and such-like publications, were largely laid under contribution; originality could scarcely be expected at the price.

Although, on the broad lines, all East End dramas of this latter period were pretty much alike in their violent and exaggerated contrasts between vice and virtue—for the playgoers of Whitechapel, Shoreditch, and Hoxton did not care for fine-drawn distinctions or "paltering in a double sense" between the angels of light and darkness—each house had a style of its own. As an instance, Norton Folgate liked a strong flavour of romance, and did not object to the supernatural—indeed some of the best work of this kind was given to the City of London. The Britannia had a preference for the purely domestic; the village maiden pursued by the libidinous Squire, in sticking-plaster boots, but always preserved by the serious countryman who spouted sermons by the yard, or by the comic chambermaid—as the manageress, Mrs. Lane always chose those parts—who with an umbrella could put as many ruffians *hors de combat* as a Surrey sailor could with a quid of tobacco.

The hatred of aristocrats was even more pronounced, perhaps, at the Pavilion and the Effingham, where every actor who appeared in a black coat, a silk hat, and white Berlin gloves was at once recognised to be a villain, while rags always covered an honest heart, even though it might be associated with a damaged reputation. The last-named theatres, being largely supported by the Jews, usually contrived to introduce a Hebrew into the pieces; he was always a model of every Christian virtue, who held forth eloquently upon the wrongs of his race, and was usually the good genius of the play. Not that any house restricted itself within hard-and-fast lines; romance and ghosts were no more eschewed by the Britannia than were the lovely work-girls persecuted by libertine lords, and afterwards married to dukes, by the City or the Pavilion. The plots of all were very much alike; there were not more than a dozen chords to the whole gamut. As these dramas were written for the uneducated, it followed as a matter of course that the language was of the most superfine description; in many, however, dialogue was a matter altogether of secondary importance, every half-dozen sentences being followed by action or situation, which succeeded one another with an ingenuity of invention that is really surprising.

At the southern theatres was preached the gospel of rags and 'orny-'anded virtue, especially at the "Vic," but from the days of *Black-Eyed Susan* until within the last twenty years nautical dramas were first favourites with the Surreyites.[1] The virtuous sailor fought terrific combats with half a dozen "lubbers," the agnomen he bestowed upon all landsmen, with a short basket-hilted

[1] Sadler's Wells was the first of the nautical drama theatres, for reasons which will appear further on.

sword, two or three times in the course of the performance; while at Astley's it was "the fiery, untamed steed," usually a mild quadruped that would not have trampled upon a worm, and fierce Tartar khans and Indian moguls, with an insatiable appetite for slaughter, that were the great attraction.

The actors who interpreted these dramas were of course equally in accordance with the tastes of the audience. These suburban minor theatres arose at a time when the histrionic art was a mere bundle of traditions and conventionalities. Edmund Kean was the model usually affected by the tragedians, and they imitated him by ranting and roaring without intermission. Yet many of them possessed considerable real dramatic power, such as N. T. Hicks, Charles Freer, Bengough, Cobham. And there was not such a great difference between their style and that which obtained in the Strand; the colours were laid on more heavily, but the actors were scarcely distorted reflections of their West End types. Three actresses, mostly associated with the East End—Mrs. Honner, Mrs. Yarnold, and Miss Vincent—though a little more emphatic, might have stood beside Mrs. Yates or Mrs. Stirling; while Mrs. Lane, at the Britannia, could have held her own in broad comedy against Mrs. Fitzwilliam. As the West End minor houses, however, took a higher position, the acting became more and more refined and natural, while that of the outsiders descended to mediocrity, and the manner grew more and more stilted and inflated.

No burlesque actor could possibly exaggerate the peculiarities of the old "transpontine" or "East Ender"; his walk, every motion of his arms, and every syllable he enunciated were the quintessence of burlesque, so absurdly grandiose, so utterly unlike anything human that it would be very difficult to persuade the present generation that anything so innately ludicrous could ever have been taken seriously or witnessed without roars of laughter. It is only within the last thirty or forty years that this style began to die out, and it has now quite disappeared.

The prices of admission to these theatres usually ranged from 3*d.* or 4*d.* to the gallery, 6*d.* to pit, and 1*s.* 6*d.* to boxes; the highest price did not exceed 2*s.* 6*d.* But the houses were very much larger, especially in the cheap parts, than those of the West, and could be more tightly packed.

The oldest and most interesting of all the outlying theatres of London is SADLER'S WELLS. In the year 1684, while some workmen were digging gravel in the grounds of Mr. Sadler, a surveyor of highways, at Clerkenwell, they struck, at some distance below the surface, upon a flagstone, which, upon being raised, disclosed a well. This was very soon identified as one that had belonged to the Priory of Clerkenwell, and in the Middle Ages had been accredited with miraculous powers. It was just about the time that inland springs were coming into vogue, and chalybeate waters were acquiring the reputation of being a golden specific for all complaints. In a very little time hypochondriacs and valetudinarians were flocking to Mr. Sadler's gardens, until the average number of daily drinkers at this new fountain of life amounted to five or six hundred. The proprietor enclosed the gardens, planted them with shrubs, had a marble basin formed for the spring to rise into, engaged a lady to discourse sweet sounds on the dulcimer in an artificial glen, from five to eight on summer evenings; while, in a shell-work grotto, a man played the pipe and tabor for those who loved to dance.

During the last years of the Commonwealth, the stage being still under the ban of Puritanism, places of amusement, called "Musick Houses," were opened in different parts of the metropolis, and gave a miscellaneous entertainment of singing, dancing, tumbling, much after the style of the modern music-hall. To add to the other attractions of the Wells, Sadler, in partnership with a dancing-master named Forcer, erected a wooden "Musick House" in his grounds; a platform at one end served as a stage, and a bench on each side accommodated the musicians; there was no separate charge for admission, which was the privilege of those who took refreshments at the bar. Ned Ward, the author of *The London Spy*, in his *Walk to Islington*, gives us such a vivid picture of the humours of the "Musick House" in 1699, and of the company that frequented it, that I cannot do better than quote as much of his description as the modern reader would find palatable. He and a female companion, being out for a stroll in the Clerkenwell fields, make their way to Sadler's Wells.

> "We enter'd the house, were conducted upstairs,
> There lovers o'er cheesecakes were seated by pairs.
> The organs and fiddles were scraping and humming,
> The guests for more ale on the tables were drumming;
> Whilst others, ill-bred, lolling over their mugs,
> Were laughing and toying with their fans and their jugs,
> Disdain'd to be slaves to perfections, or graces,
> Sat puffing tobacco in their mistresses' faces.
> Some 'prentices, too, who made a bold venture,
> And trespass'd a little beyond their indenture,
> Were each of them treating his mistress's maid,
> For letting him in when his master's abed."

Having refreshed, they

> "Look'd over the gallery like the rest of the folk,
> Without side of which, the spectators to please,
> Were nymphs painted roving in clouds and in seas.

Our eyes being glutted with this pretty sight,
We began to look down and examine the pit,
Where butchers and bailiffs and such sort of fellows
Were mix'd with a vermin train'd up to the gallows,
As buttocks and files, housebreakers and padders,
With prizefighters, sweet'ners, and such sort of traders,
Informers, thief-takers, deer stealers, and bullies;
Some dancing, some skipping, some ranting and tearing,
Some drinking and smoking, some lying and swearing,
And some with the tapsters were got in a fray,
Who without paying reck'ning were stealing away."

"Lady Squab," now by the side of the organ, favours the company with a song, at which

"The guests were all hush, and attention was given,
The listening mob thought themselves in a Heaven."

After she retires amidst vociferous applause from the butchers,

"Then up starts a fiddler in scarlet, so fierce,
So unlike an Orpheus, he looks like a Mars,
He runs up in Alt with a hey-diddle-diddle,
To show what a fool he could make of a fiddle."

When this is over, a girl of eleven comes on and executes a sword-dance.

"Arm'd Amazon-like, with abundance of rapiers,
Which she puts to her throat as she dances and capers,
And further, the mob's admiration to kindle,
She turns on her heel like a wheel on a spindle."

Next appears

"A young babe of grace,
With Merc'ry's limbs, and a gallows in his face,
In dancing a jig lies the chief of his graces,
And making strange Musick House monkey-like faces."

He again is followed by Thomas, the waiter, who, dressed as a clown, performs a dance, etc., etc.

The whole neighbourhood of Clerkenwell, though at

this period nearly surrounded by open country, was a nest of ruffianism and the centre of the cruel sports which were the delight of all classes. At no great distance from Sadler's Wells, on the site of what is now called Ray Street, formerly Rag Street, stood the notorious grounds of Hockley-in-the-Hole, so frequently referred to in the literature of the early decades of the eighteenth century, notably in *The Beggar's Opera*, and in one or two of Steele's papers in the *Spectator*. Here were carried on the brutal pastimes of bull and bear baiting, and cock-fighting; here, in the days before pugilism became a science, backsword players displayed the nicety of their fence, fighting with sharp weapons that inflicted grievous wounds, for sport had no zest for our ancestors unaccompanied by bloodshed. Sadler's Wells occasionally rivalled its near neighbour by providing similar fare as an additional attraction for its patrons, though rope-dancing, pantomime, and tumbling were always its staple amusements.

When George II. came to the throne, Sadler and dancing-master Forcer both had passed away, and the son of the latter, a barrister, had succeeded to "the Wells." The new lessee seems to have given a more theatrical turn to the entertainment by adding musical interludes, and under his *régime* the Spa was more flourishing than ever, being patronised by royalty; for in 1735 the Princesses Amelia and Caroline went thither to drink the waters, in consequence of which the nobility flocked in such numbers that the proprietor would take nearly £30 during a morning.

Forcer junior died in 1743. Under the next manager, one Warren, the "Musick House" was most villainously disreputable. In Kirkman's *Memoirs of Macklin* we find the following description of the place as one of the reminiscences of the old actor: "I remember when the price of admission here was but threepence, except a few places scuttled off at the sides of the stage at sixpence, and which were usually reserved for people of fashion, who occasionally came to see the fun. Here we smoked and drank porter, or rum and water, as much as we could pay for; and every man had his doxy that liked it, and so forth; and though we had a mixture of very odd company, for I believe it was the baiting place of thieves and highwaymen, there was little or no rioting. Some hornpipes and ballad-singing, with a kind of pantomimic ballet, and some lofty tumbling, and all was done by daylight, and there were four or five exhibitions every day. The length of each depended upon circumstances. The proprietor had always a fellow on the outside of the booth to calculate how many people were collected for a second exhibition, and when he thought there were enough, he came to the back of the upper seats and shouted, 'Is Hiram Fisteman here?' This was the cant word agreed upon with the performers. Upon which they concluded the entertainments with a song, dismissed the audience, and prepared for a second representation."

In 1744 Sadler's Wells was presented by the Grand Jury of Middlesex as a place injurious to public morals. Two years later we find that there was no charge for admission beyond a pint of wine, which cost one shilling, and as a specimen of the kind of amusements provided, it may be mentioned that Hogarth's *Harlot's Progress* was dramatised with all its repulsive details. Harlequins, mountebanks, tumblers, singers, and dancers still, however, formed the principal part of the company. A wonderful equilibrist named Maddox, who seems to have anticipated what we regard as the new tricks of the present professors of the art, appeared here in the middle of the eighteenth century. Balancing himself upon the slack wire, he could toss balls and kick straws into a glass he held in his mouth, balance a cart-wheel upon his shoulder or his chin, and finish up by poising two wheels with a boy standing on one of them. That these amusements were patronised by the upper classes is proved by an advertisement in the *Public Advertiser* to the effect that on certain nights a horse patrol would be stationed on the new road between the Sadler's Wells and Grosvenor Square for the protection of the nobility and gentry.

Rosoman, a builder, whose name still survives in Rosoman Street, Clerkenwell, pulled down the old wooden Musick House in 1765, and raised a stone theatre—the present building—in its place, at a cost of £4,225, the demolition and re-erection occupying, it is said, only seven weeks. Rosoman greatly improved the status of Sadler's Wells; the prices of admission were raised to two-and-sixpence to the boxes, one shilling to the pit, and sixpence to the gallery, while for an extra sixpence a pint of good wine, "that had been four years in the wood," was supplied to all who liked to avail themselves of the privilege.

Until 1796 the auditorium was fitted up exactly like a modern music-hall, with high-backed seats and little ledges behind each for bottles and glasses, and the audience drank and smoked throughout the performance. When Rosoman retired in 1772 Tom King, whom we have met at Drury Lane, took the house and brought fashionable audiences there to patronise him. After a while the interior was entirely remodelled, but the style of entertainment remained much the same as before.

The playbills of the time announced that a Miss Richer will appear on two slack wires, and pass through a hoop with a pyramid of glasses on her head, and Master Richer will perform on a tight-rope with a skipping-rope; that one Joseph Dorton will drink a glass of wine, placed upon the stage, backwards, and beat a drum at the same time; a man named Lawrence will throw a somersault over twelve men's heads; and one Paul Redige will throw a somersault over two men on horseback, each of the men having a lighted candle on his head. Here we have our present music-hall attractions anticipated, and we thought they were novelties!

The great Sadler's Wells sensation of 1783 was a company of performing dogs, and such a rage did they become that the managers in that one season cleared £10,000. Frederick Reynolds, in his *Recollections*, gives the following description of what must really have been a very remarkable performance: "An enterprising actor, of the name of Costello, collected at the fairs of Frankfort and Leipzig a complete company of canine performers, and arriving with them in England, Wroughton, the then manager of Sadler's Wells, engaged him. There were fourteen in all, and unlike those straggling, dancing dogs still seen in the streets, they all acted respondently and conjointly with a truth that appeared almost the effect of reason. The star of the company was named Moustache, and the piece produced for their first appearance was *The Deserter*. The house, crowded nightly, resembled in point of fashion the opera on a Saturday night. I will pass over the performance till the last scene, merely remarking that the actors of Simpkin, Skirmish, and Louisa were so well dressed and so much in earnest that in a slight degree they actually preserved the interest of the story and the illusion of the scene. But Moustache as the Deserter! I see him now, in his little uniform, military boots, with small musket and helmet, cheering and inspiring his fellow-soldiers to follow him up scaling ladders and storm the fort. The roars, barking, and confusion which resulted from this attack may be better imagined than described. At the moment when the gallant assailant seemed sure of victory, a retreat was sounded, and Moustache and his adherents were seen receding from the repulse, rushing down the ladders and then staggering towards the lamps in a state of panic and dismay."

Reynolds then proceeds to explain how the excitement of the scene was worked up: the dogs had been given no food since breakfast, a hot supper with a most appetising aroma was set at the top of the fort—no wonder they stormed it so fiercely—and when the retreat was sounded, Costello drove them back with a whip. Still, whatever tricks might have been resorted to, for an entire play to be performed by dogs was a very remarkable undertaking.

Among the medley of four-legged and two-legged mountebanks and acrobats that occupied the stage of Sadler's Wells at this time, occasionally crop up names that were thereafter to become famous in theatrical annals. In 1786 Miss Romanzini, afterwards better known as Mrs. Bland, one of the most delightful of English ballad singers, made her first appearance here; two years later, "Master Abrahams," who had been seen a twelvemonth previously at the Royalty in Wellclose Square, then a mere boy, sang at the Islington house, before he had disguised his Hebrew patronymic, by cutting off its first and last letters, to Braham. As the nursery of pantomimists "the Wells" was always celebrated; here Boyce, the most finished harlequin of his own day and far surpassing anything that has been seen since, unless an exception be made in favour of Byrne, was first introduced to the public.

But most famous of all names connected with the old theatre is that of Grimaldi. Giuseppe, the father of Joey, came to England in 1760 as dentist to Queen Charlotte. But having been a dancer in his own country he abandoned tooth-extracting to become ballet-master at Drury Lane and Sadler's Wells. Young Joe made his début upon the stage of the latter house as a sprite at the age of one year and eleven months, and soon afterwards appeared as "little clown" to his father at a salary of fifteen shillings a week. At three years old he performed the part of a monkey, and made such a hit that he was put on the staff of the theatre. His father died when he was a mere child, leaving his wife and family totally unprovided for. Joey was then engaged at Drury Lane as well as at "the Wells." Sheridan raised his salary to a pound; the other manager reduced it to three shillings, at which pittance he remained for three years, making himself generally useful both on and off the stage. Nothing could exceed the drudgery of this mere child: every morning he had to walk from Great Wild Street, Drury Lane, where he and his mother lodged, to Sadler's Wells for rehearsal; back to dinner at two; then again off to the theatre, where he worked from six to eleven; after that he had to walk home. At times he performed both at Sadler's Wells and Drury Lane on the same night; on one occasion he was so pressed for time that he ran from "the Wells" to the Haymarket Opera House, where the Drury Lane company were performing during the rebuilding of their own theatre in 1794, in fourteen minutes, and after walking on in a procession, which was all he had to do, ran back to Sadler's Wells, to play clown in the pantomime, accomplishing the return journey in thirteen minutes. But by this time he was receiving £3 a week from the Drury Lane treasury and £4 from Sadler's Wells, and was rapidly rising in fortune and reputation.

In the meanwhile, however, many changes had taken place in the management of Sadler's Wells. At the end of ten years, that is to say in 1782, King gave it up in consequence of being appointed Sheridan's manager at Drury Lane, and sold his interest to Arnold, his partner, and Wroughton, a Drury Lane actor, for £12,000. After Wroughton's time, at the close of the eighteenth century, Mrs. Siddons' husband took up the lesseeship. During his term a boy named Master Carey, the great-grandson of that Henry Carey who wrote "Sally in our Alley," and composed many of the most successful ballad operas for this theatre, made his début here under the title of "The Pupil of Nature," and recited Rollo's speech from *Pizarro*. Little thought Mr. Siddons that this boy, under the name of Edmund Kean, was destined, "at one fell swoop," to destroy the great Kemble school that then reigned supreme.

It was not until 1804, when the house was under the management of Charles Dibdin, a Mr. Hughes being the chief proprietor, that Sadler's Wells began that series of nautical dramas, with sensational effects and real water, that obtained for it the name of the "Aquatic Theatre," and formed its principal attraction during the next forty years. For these effects a gigantic tank, fed from the New River, was constructed beneath the stage, and a drama entitled *The Siege of Gibraltar* was produced; in this piece real vessels floated on real water for the bombardment of the fortress; the heroine fell from the rocks into the sea, and her lover plunged after her; there were a naval battle and a ship on fire, from which the sailors sprang into the waves to escape the flames, and in another scene a child was cast into the water and rescued by a Newfoundland dog. The tank was ninety feet long, five feet deep, and in some places twenty-four feet wide; there was a second over the stage, fifteen feet square and five feet deep, for waterfall effects. In a play called *The Island*, founded upon the story of the Mutiny of the Bounty, the stage was raised bodily to the roof for one act which was performed upon the tank.

That the writer of the finest of nautical songs, "Tom Bowling," should have been the creator of the nautical drama was highly appropriate, and that at the period when the English Navy was at the height of its glory it should prove an immense success was a matter of course. The sailors who fought under Nelson were to the public all Tom Bowlings, careless, generous, tender-hearted, brave as lions, yielding up their lives at the call of duty, unconquered and unconquerable; this was the type that remained a chief favourite with East End and transpontine audiences for considerably over half a century, or until burlesque and cynicism, and the inevitable decay which in time destroys every species of dramatic composition not based upon the eternal truths of human nature, cast it into the limbo of thousands of other fashions of the hour. But for the genius of T. P. Cooke, who roused the emulation of a host of imitators, however, it might not have enjoyed so long a term of life. An appalling calamity overshadowed the fortunes of Sadler's Wells in October, 1807, in consequence of a false alarm of fire raised during the performance.

Twenty-three persons lost their lives, suffocated, trampled to death, or dashed to pieces by leaping from the gallery into the pit. The theatre was opened two nights for the benefit of the relations of the deceased, and of the large number who lay dangerously injured in the hospital, and then closed until Christmas.

In 1817, in consequence of a disagreement with the management, for the first time for many years Grimaldi was missing from the bills. The next season, however, unfortunately for himself, he returned as manager, being at the same time a large shareholder. This speculation resulted in a heavy loss for our poor clown.

The bills of Sadler's Wells are very monotonous. Year after year we find terrific melodramas with astounding titles, and ballets and pantomimes succeed each other with persistent regularity. The subjoined, taken from *Hone's Every Day Book*, is a curious and representative specimen of the programmes of the time. The date is 1825.

SERIOUS NOTICE.

IN PERFECT CONFIDENCE,

The following extraordinary comic performances at

SADLER'S WELLS

Can only be given during the present week. The proprietors, therefore, most respectfully inform that fascinating sex, so properly distinguished by the appropriate appellation of

THE FAIR!

And all those well inclined gentlemen who are happy enough to protect them, that the amusements will consist of a romantic tale of mysterious horror and broad grin, never acted, called the

ENCHANTED GIRDLES,

or

WINKI THE WITCH,

AND THE LADIES OF SAMARCAND.

A most whimsical burletta, which sends people home perfectly exhausted from uninterrupted risibility called

THE LAWYER, THE JEW,

and

THE YORKSHIREMAN,

With, by request of 75 distinguished families, and a party of 5, that never to be sufficiently praised pantomime, called

MAGIC IN TWO COLOURS;

or

FAIRY BLUE AND FAIRY RED,

or

HARLEQUIN AND THE MARBLE ROCK.

It would be perfectly superfluous for any man in his senses to attempt anything more than the mere announcement in recommendation of the above unparaleled representations, so attractive in themselves as to threaten a complete monopoly of the qualities of the magnet; and though the proprietors were to talk nonsense for an hour, they could not assert a more *important truth* than that they possess

The only Wells from which you may draw

WINE,

THREE SHILLINGS AND SIXPENCE

A full Quart.

Those whose important avocations prevent their coming at the commencement will be admitted for

HALF PRICE AT HALF-PAST EIGHT.

Ladies and gentlemen who are not judges of the superior entertainments announced are respectfully requested to bring as many as possible with them who are.

N.B.—A full moon during the week.

The reference to the full moon is intended for those living westward, who had to cross the lonely regions of Battle Bridge and the New Road which were still infested by footpads.

But to return to Grimaldi. His pecuniary losses were not his worst; his long life of arduous toil had brought on premature decay. At length he was compelled to relinquish his engagement at Covent Garden, which brought him in £1,500 a year, including a benefit. And on Monday, March 17th, 1828, the Sadler's Wells playbill announced that on that night Mr. Grimaldi would make his last appearance at that theatre, and bid his patrons and friends "Farewell."

The house for that event was crowded to the ceiling—Londoners are always faithful to their old favourites; the low, faltering accents in which the old actor bade adieu to those present, many of whom had followed his career from boyhood, were listened to in tearful silence, to be followed by burst upon burst of applause. A little over three months afterwards he took his final leave of the stage at Drury Lane, of which an account has been already given.[1] He survived his retirement nearly nine years, dying in the May of 1837.

Grimaldi was the Garrick of pantomime; he was the creator of the modern clown, which scarcely existed before his time, and of the harlequinade of our boyish days. Yet, wonderful as was his grotesque humour, creating inextinguishable laughter, Grimaldi was much more than a mere buffoon. On one benefit night he gave the dagger scene of *Macbeth* in his clown's dress. R. H. Horne, who was present, says: "Notwithstanding this, and that he only made audible a few elocutionary sounds of the words, a dead silence pervaded the whole house, and I was not the only boy who trembled: young and old seemed to vibrate with the effect upon the imagination." When he sang "An Oyster Crossed in Love," such touches of real pathos trembled through its grotesqueness as he sat in front of the footlights, between a cod's head and a huge oyster that opened

[1] See p. 94.

and shut its shell in time to the music, that all the children were in tears; while everyone roared over "Tippitewichet," "Hot Codlins," "Me and my Neddy."

During the next ten or fifteen years the history of the "Aquatic Theatre" presents few points of interest. During the twenties Mrs. Egerton—the house was under the management of her husband—a very fine actress in such parts as Madge Wildfire and Meg Merrilies, well known in the West End, was the bright particular star of this northern hemisphere. In 1832 Sadler's Wells was presided over by the celebrated Mrs. Fitzwilliam; Buckstone was a member of the stock company, and wrote pieces for it. For several years Honner—the husband of a famous melodramatic heroine of the olden time, better known in the East than the West, however—ruled the destines of the old Islington house.

The style of entertainment given at "the Wells" had gradually improved; dramatic versions of Sir Walter Scott's novels, and, when a star came, occasional incursions into the realm of the legitimate drama, varied the highly-spiced fare which had formerly been invariably presented to the patrons of this theatre, and it was on these lines that the later lessees conducted the house until 1844, when, most important of all events in its history, it was let to Samuel Phelps and Mrs. Warner—the latter one of the finest *tragédiennes* of the day.

We have already met Phelps at the Haymarket, Covent Garden, and Drury Lane.

While the legitimate drama could be performed only in the three principal theatres of the metropolis, a tragedian had little option. But when free trade was established in the dramatic kingdom, the aspect of things theatrical underwent an entire change. Nevertheless, it was as daring a project as that conceived by Marie Wilton more than twenty years afterwards, to convert such a theatre as Sadler's Wells, which for nearly two centuries had been the resort of the roughest audiences of London, from the home of the lowest form of dramatic entertainment to the most legitimate temple of the drama that had been known since the days of the Blackfriars. Even more remarkable than the idea were the energy and tenacity of purpose that enabled Samuel Phelps to carry it out with supreme success. The first thing he did was to establish order in the unruly gallery. Few men would have had the courage to discard one set of patrons on the mere chance of securing a better ; and that was exactly what the new lessee did ; upon the slightest disturbance the offenders were instantly expelled, and he would even put on a cloak over his stage dress and go up into the gallery himself to enforce order.

Phelps opened Sadler's Wells on May 27th, 1844, with *Macbeth*, Mrs. Warner being Lady Macbeth, and Marston Macduff. Within two years his fair partner retired, and in the July of 1846 the theatre, after some very considerable alterations had been effected, was announced to be under the management of Messrs. Greenwood and Phelps. They started with a production of *The First Part of Henry IV.*, in which Phelps played Falstaff for the first time, and Creswick was the Hotspur. The highest price of admission for years had been only two shillings, but this season a first circle was added, for which three shillings was charged —the highest throughout this management.

Henry IV. was the first of that noble series of Shakespearian revivals which included all the great dramatist's plays, except *Titus Andronicus*, *Troilus and Cressida*, and the three parts of *Henry VI.* Although not equal in cost or splendour to similar productions of Macready's at Drury Lane or Charles Kean's at the Princess's, all these works were admirably mounted, and with a correctness and attention to details and a reverence for the text that have seldom been equalled.

He also revived plays by Beaumont and Fletcher, *A King and No King*, *Rule a Wife and Have a Wife*, *The Honest Man's Fortune*, and an alteration of *The Maid's Tragedy* renamed *The Bridal;* Massinger's *The City Madam*, *The Fatal Dowry*, *A New Way to Pay Old Debts;* also Webster's *The Duchess of Malfi*, Rowley's *A Woman Never Vext*, Otway's *Venice Preserved*, Macklin's *Man of the World*, Cibber's *The Fop's Fortune*, Vanbrugh's and Cibber's *The Provoked Husband*, Rowe's *Arden of Feversham*, Goldsmith's *The Good-Natured Man*, Cumberland's *The Wheel of Fortune;* as well as other plays by Leigh Hunt, Byron, Knowles, Bulwer Lytton, Colman, Mrs. Centlivre, Sheridan, Selous, the Rev. James White, and Tom Taylor's *The Fool's Revenge*, a version of Hugo's *Le Roi S'Amuse.*

Among the actors who were at different times enlisted under his banner were Henry Marston, George Bennett (the last of the Kemble school), Creswick, Hoskins (afterwards a favourite tragedian in Australia), Frederick Robinson, William Belford, Hermann Vezin, Miss Glyn, Mrs. Hermann Vezin, Miss Cooper, Fanny Vining, Margaret Eburne, Mrs. Marston (a very fine "old woman"), Fanny Huddart, and many others well known in their day but now only names. Here was an array of talent that the patent houses could not equal.

Under the rule of Samuel Phelps the drama fulfilled

its highest purpose—that of interpreting and bringing home, both to the cultured and the uncultured, the noblest truths of poetry, the grandest conceptions of genius. While the once great patent theatres were handed over to wild-beast shows, and were sunk in the deepest slough of degradation, while the fashionable world deserted the drama for the opera, the little remote suburban house—for it was remote in those days from the great centres of London—was nightly filled with an eager and a rapt audience, most of them fresh from the workshop or the counter, drinking in immortal ideas, of which but for the stage they would have lived and died in ignorance. To the refining and educating influences of the actor's art under such conditions there is no limit.

Those who did not see Phelps in the great parts of tragedy until his last seasons at Drury Lane were scarcely fair judges of his capacities, for his powers were then on the wane. He was the last of the old school of tragedy; with him the traditions that, through Betterton, Booth, Garrick, Kemble, Macready, had been handed down more or less faithfully from Shakespeare himself, died from utter senility and decrepitude, for what had once been the spontaneous outcome of genius had now shrunk by constant repetition into the merest conventionalism. Phelps was always thoughtful, artistic, and imbued with a thorough knowledge and appreciation of his author; his delivery of "To be or not to be" was among the most impressive I have heard; in the mad scenes of Lear he was very fine; there were points even in his Othello that for subtlety of interpretation it would be difficult to surpass; his address to the soldiers in *Henry V.* would rouse his audience to enthusiasm; but he lacked poetry and distinction; nor did he ever electrify by any flash of genius, he never passed the invisible line that separates the *good* actor from the *great*. To see him in one of Shakespeare's tragic parts was an intellectual pleasure, satisfying the judgment, though seldom appealing to the imagination.

But as a character actor, in certain rôles, he stood supreme. The stage has never given us anything more perfect than his Sir Pertinax Macsycophant—and oh, ye gods, his Bottom the weaver! who that had the privilege of seeing it can ever forget that marvellous performance? Before his time actors had made the part a mere buffoon; but the manner in which Phelps elaborated and drew subtle meanings out of every line, his delivery of the soliloquy after the awakening—a few broken sentences, conveying to the ordinary reader nothing—but, as he pronounced it, a whole psychological history; the manner in which the conceited clown after his transformation became densely asinine, ever surreptitiously feeling for the long ears that had gone; this was indeed great acting. Justice Shallow, Job Thornberry, King James, Trapbois, were in their way equally fine; nor must we forget his powerful performance of Manfred and Werner.

The last-named play recalls a memorable night at Sadler's Wells—it was somewhere in 1861—when the lessee's son, Edmund, made his first appearance upon the London stage in the character of Ulric to his father's Werner. Perhaps the old actor never performed the part so finely as he did on that night. The identity between the real and the ideal relations of the characters was as vivid to him as to the audience, and gave a deeper intensity, on both sides, to the scenes between father and son. More than once the self-control so necessary to the artist in the very tempest of passion, nearly forsook him; but such falterings struck home to every heart, rousing the spectators to yet stronger sympathetic demonstrations, that mounted higher and higher to the end of the tragedy, and culminated in a rising *en masse* and bursts of cheering as both actors were summoned again and again before the curtain. The mantle of the father, however, did not descend upon the son, for Edmund Phelps never rose above mediocrity. His career was a sadly brief one, and his early and sudden death was a blow from which the father never recovered.

Samuel Phelps's latest biographers deny that he was an imitator of Macready; but those who have seen the two famous actors in Werner aver that the one rendering was a facsimile of the other; indeed, Phelps was not only Macreadyish on the stage, but off it as well, and was too much given to reproduce the moroseness and overbearing airs of his former chief, accompanied by those grunts and mutterings which made the elder tragedian a constant butt for imitators. There was little or nothing of the professional type about Samuel Phelps, and an actor was about the last thing that a stranger would have taken him to be. He was an ardent disciple of Izaak Walton; for several years during the summer vacation he went down to Farningham, and put up at the hotel there to enjoy a little fishing; everybody about, it would seem, took him for a quiet country gentleman. But during the run of *The Doge of Venice*, a farmer of the neighbourhood happened to go to Drury Lane; there was no mistaking those nasal tones, and, after listening to the Doge for some little time, he whispered to a companion, "Why, dang me if that ain't our old fisherman!"

The retirement of Greenwood in 1860 was the beginning of the end of the Phelps management, for it would seem that the actor had no capacity for the commercial side of the speculation. Two seasons afterwards, in 1862, he grew weary of absolute government, and bade adieu to his old home, though he afterwards visited it on several occasions as a star.

Captain Morton Price and Miss Lucette, with a light style of entertainment, occupied Sadler's Wells for a season; and in the autumn of 1863 it came into the hands of Robert Edgar, who, chiefly through the talents of his wife, Miss Marriott, a noted lady Hamlet, was lessee for the next six years. A mixture of the legitimate and strong domestic drama, such as Boucicault's *Jeannie Deans*, were the usual entertainments during that period. For the next few years the house sank to very low depths, it was turned into a skating rink, it was the scene of a prize-fight, it was closed as dangerous.

In 1879 Mrs. Bateman, upon leaving the Lyceum, became the manageress, reconstructed the interior, and made an attempt to revive something of the old prestige. A round of legitimate drama, with Kate Bateman as the leading lady and a fairly good company, failed to draw. When Mrs. Bateman died in 1881, her daughter Isabel carried on the theatre for a while. But since the days of Greenwood and Phelps that revolution in things theatrical, which I have descanted upon at the beginning of this chapter, was changing the old order, and the generation of playgoers that had hung delightedly on the lips of *their* oracle had passed away, tastes had changed, and audiences persistently turned their faces westward. After the Bateman management the old house went from bad to worse, and its later history is not worthy of record. It has for a long time given two performances a night at very cheap prices.

Although the interior is for the most part new, the

outward walls are the same that Rosoman raised a hundred and forty years ago, when the New River flowed in front of them, so that Sadler's Wells is certainly the oldest theatre in England, and probably in Europe.

Half a century ago, and much later, the gardens of the Eagle Saloon, afterwards better known as The Grecian, in Shepherdess Walk—a name reminiscent of rurality—was a favourite cockney resort in summer time, where *al fresco* singing and dancing by the light of variegated lamps could be indulged in. In 1832, Thomas Rouse, or "Brayvo Rouse," as he was usually hailed by his patrons, opened a theatre in the grounds. As a caterer for the public taste, Rouse was before his time; his ambition was to provide a superior class of entertainment to that which obtained at the other cheap theatres. He engaged a good band and chorus, and capable singers and actors to interpret some of the lighter operas of Auber, Boieldieu, and Adolphe Adams, which were heard for the first time in England in the humble precincts of the City Road.

Augustus Sala writes in his little book on Robson: "Drinking and smoking went on during the performance, but the pieces put on the stage were all of a high class, and the scenery and appointments would not have disgraced the Olympic during the brilliant reign of Vestris and Planché. The admission fees were low, the place was comfortably and luxuriously fitted up, the entertainments were on the most liberal scale, and the proprietor sat every night in a box in full view of the audience, keeping order with as much dignity as the Speaker of the House of Commons."

Rouse lost about £2,000 a year by attempting to improve the musical taste of his patrons; but as the tavern brought in about £5,000, the debit and credit accounts were very well balanced. The Eagle was likewise celebrated for its buffo singing. Chief among these singers were Henry Howell and Robert Glindon. The latter wrote his own songs, and "Biddy the Basket Woman," "The Literary Dustman," and several others were very celebrated in their day. In the gardens, during the summer months, dancing and singing still went on as in the old time.

Robson's first London engagement was at the Grecian, 1844, where he remained about five years, and played, without exciting any particular attention, in *The Wandering Minstrel*, *Boots at the Swan*, that afterwards drew all London to the Olympic. After the play was over a miscellaneous concert was given in one of the large saloons attached to the grounds, and he often sang "Vilikins and his Dinah" and "The Country Fair," between eleven and midnight, little dreaming of the rage these ditties would create in the years to come. Sims Reeves was first heard here as a member of the chorus.

It was in 1851 that Conquest succeeded Rouse as the manager of the Grecian Saloon. The theatre had a huge area, within a few feet of that of Drury Lane; the ground floor formed an enormous pit, and at the back was a circle. The new management began with a revival of *The Midsummer Night's Dream*, and legitimate tragedy and comedy kept the stage for two or three years, to the great loss of the speculator. By-and-by the house was rebuilt, the ground lowered some eighteen feet, and two tiers of boxes and a gallery formed. After the alterations the Grecian would hold 3,400 people. Ballets, under the direction of Mrs. Conquest, who was a very fine dancer, supported by her pupils, became the great feature of the theatre. There were still a dancing-room, and *al fresco* entertainments in the grounds as well, to add to the attractions of the place, and the gardens were opened on Sundays for sacred music.

From the time George Conquest took an active share in the management, which was about 1857, pantomime and strong melodrama reigned paramount. As a daring gymnast, Mr. Conquest has never had a superior, and the Grecian pantomime became one of the things of the Christmas season. The name Saloon was long since changed to Theatre, and in 1876 it was again rebuilt at a cost of between £8,000 and £9,000. Only three years afterwards Mr. Conquest disposed of the property to a man named Clark, at one time lessee of the Adelphi. Clark had made a large fortune in the marine store trade, and lost it all at the Adelphi and the Grecian; the £9,000 for which he sold the City Road property to the Salvation Army in 1881 being all that he saved out of the £21,000 he had given for it.

Miss Kate Vaughan and Miss Lingard were pupils of Mrs. Conquest. Messrs. Harry Nicholls, Herbert Campbell, Arthur Williams, Miss Victor were for years members of the stock company. It was here also that Paul Merritt and Henry Pettit produced their first dramatic essays.

In Shepherdess Walk, close by, there was formerly another saloon theatre called THE ALBERT; but when it was first opened or closed I have been unable to discover.

In High Street, Hoxton, was a theatre that was once perhaps the best paying in London, but one unknown, unless by name, to all except the residents in the immediate neighbourhood. THE BRITANNIA SALOON, as it was originally called, was opened by Sam Lane in 1841; his widow, Sarah Lane, an excellent actress of *soubrettes*, who continued to act to within the last years of her life, succeeded him in 1849, and was the manageress until her death, which occurred in 1899. No theatre was ever before so long under one management, and in every other respect it was unique; actors joined the company in their youth and remained, some of them, until they were incapacitated by age, or had strutted and fretted their last hour upon the stage of life. Authors wrote exclusively for the house, and the Britannia was the last to give up its peculiar style of drama—which mostly preached the gospel of rags and 'orny-'anded virtue and the wickedness that was engendered by wearing a decent suit of clothes—and adopt second-hand West End pieces. Formerly the pantomimes at this house ran up to Easter and were well staged. The Britannia, as I have said, was entirely supported by the inhabitants of North London, especially those of Hoxton and Kingsland.

The site now partly covered by the Britannia was once occupied, in the time of Elizabeth, by a noted hostelry and gardens called "the Pimlico," and, like Totten Court and White Conduit Gardens, was a favourite resort of London citizens for many generations. On Easter Monday, 1841, the house and gardens were opened by Mr. Lane with the following advertisement:—

"ROYAL BRITANNIA SALOON.—Britannia Tavern, Hoxton. Licensed pursuant to Act of Parliament. Proprietor, Mr. S. Lane. Open every evening, with splendid decorations *à la Watteau* (by Mr. Fenhoult, of the Theatres Royal). Variety Entertainment—Talented Company—Grand Concert—Opera and Vaudeville—Rope and other Dancing—Ballet—Laughable Farce. Neither talent nor expense is spared. Prices, Reserved seats 6d., and Upper Stalls 1s., for which a refreshment ticket is given. Doors open at 6 o'clock, commence at half-past. Chorus master, Mr. Rudford; Ballet master, Mr. Smithers; Leader of the Band, Mr. Jackman; Machinist, Mr. Rowe."

After the passing of the new Licensing Act, melodramas were produced with a strong company, and in 1850 the premises were greatly enlarged and improved, though the house was not closed a single night. In 1851, James Anderson was engaged here at a salary of £120 a week, to play a round of Shakespearian parts, and frequently returned on similar terms. Once a year there was always a week or two devoted to Shakespeare, the parts being played by the stock company. On June 29th, 1858, the old Saloon was closed for ever; some adjoining houses were bought, and a new and colossal theatre, that would hold three thousand people, opened in the November of the same year, was erected on the ground. Every variety of entertainment has been given at the Britannia, from Pepper's Ghost to Tom King the pugilist, from champion swimmers, giants, acrobats, to Arthur Orton.

In an interview which Mrs. Lane granted not very long before her death, she remarked upon the change that had come over the audience. *The Middleman* had just been performed there with great success. "I can remember the time, many years ago," she said, "when *The Middleman* wouldn't have drawn at all after the first night. In those days we used to put on such awful rigmaroles as *Sweeny Todd, the Barber of Fleet Street*, who used to murder the people that came to be shaved, cut them up, and sell them to Mrs. Lovat, a pastry-cook, to make pies of them. But," she added, "the play must have a good moral, whatever it is; our people wouldn't care for anything that hadn't a moral."

Not far from the Britannia is THE VARIETY THEATRE, Hoxton, formerly a music-hall; it obtained a theatrical licence in 1871, but has always blended the two styles, playing short pieces, with singing and other entertainments between.

A theatre called THE ALEXANDRA was erected in the grounds of Highbury Barn, by Giovanelli, in 1865, for the performance of farces and light pieces, in which Danvers, J. G. Taylor, Rachel Sanger acted. It disappeared with the gardens in 1871.

Camden Town had its theatre thirty years ago. Built in 1871, it was first called THE PARK, and it was fondly imagined by the proprietor that it might be made a second Prince of Wales's; West End actors were engaged, a West End author wrote a burlesque especially for it, but a lady, with not the least pretensions to talent, by choosing to assume the principal parts in every production, defeated all such possibilities. In 1873 the name of the theatre was changed to the Alexandra, and in 1881 its miserable existence was put an end to by fire.

In Liverpool Street, King's Cross, was a squeezed-up building, with a small portico, that had a curious history attached to it. Built originally by Lanza, a teacher of singing, for the exercise of his pupils, also for musical entertainments, and called the Panharmonium, it was, in 1832, opened by Mrs. Fitzwilliam and Buckstone as THE CLARENCE THEATRE. The speculation proved so unremunerative that these celebrated players quickly abandoned it. The interior was very fantastic, being constructed after the pattern of a Chinese pavilion. In 1838 it was rechristened the "New Lyceum." Manager succeeded manager, and under each speculator it sank lower, until tickets were issued to admit four persons to the boxes upon the payment of threepence. So utterly disreputable did the audiences become, that the house was at length closed by order of the magistrates. It was then converted into an amateur theatre, and called the Cabinet, and ultimately the King's Cross. In 1870 some witless person once more attempted to convert it into a regular theatre; it soon afterwards sank into oblivion, and was heard of no more in connection with the regular drama.

At the end of 1870 the Philharmonic Music Hall, in the High Street, Islington, became THE PHILHARMONIC THEATRE, under the management of Messrs. Head and Morton. A great success was achieved in the following year by one of the most popular of operas-bouffes, *Geneviève de Brabant*, with Miss Emily Soldene, who had opened the house in *Chilpéric*, as Drogan; so admirably was the house appointed, and so excellently was the opera staged and cast, that this suburban theatre soon came to be patronised by West End audiences; *Madame Angot*, a revival of the *Grande Duchesse*, etc., followed *Geneviève de Brabant*, and other operas-bouffes, and occasionally dramas, with more or less success, until the Philharmonic fell a prey to the flames in September, 1882. A new and handsome theatre, THE GRAND, rose upon its ashes, and was opened in the autumn of 1883. Its existence was a brief one, as it was burned down at the end of December, 1887. Rebuilt upon a yet more elaborate scale, it was reopened in the December of the following year, and again perished by fire in February, 1900. It was re-erected and reopened at the end of the same year. With the exception of the Christmas pantomime, the Grand, like all other suburban theatres, is chiefly kept open by West End stars and travelling companies.

Handsome theatres have been erected at Dalston, Stoke Newington, Muswell Hill, and Camden Town, but they have no separate existence; their entertainments are chiefly drawn from the West End stages. Each member of these travelling companies is drilled into a slavish imitation of the original, from which he or she must not depart; the actors are thus converted into automata. No training could be worse, since it does away with all individuality. Now and again some melodrama or farcical comedy that has not received the *cachet* of the west, written and exploited by some performer of provincial fame, varies the monotony, but seldom or ever runs more than a week. But in the care bestowed upon the productions, the beauty and the comfort of the auditorum, these suburban houses are equal to all, except the highest-class theatres of the more fashionable districts, and very much cheaper.

CHAPTER II

THE SOUTHERN AND THE EAST END THEATRES

Astley's Amphitheatre—The Surrey—The Victoria—The Old Peckham Theatre—The Bower Saloon—The Rotunda—The Deptford and Greenwich Theatres—The Elephant and Castle—The New Southern Theatres—The Royalty, Wellclose Square—The City Theatre, Grub Street—The Pavilion—The Garrick—The City of London—The Standard—The East London—The Oriental—The New Theatres.

IN the year 1770, one Philip Astley, formerly a trooper, who had greatly distinguished himself in action, and who had always a great fancy for breaking in and training horses, took upon a lease a piece of waste ground near the foot of Westminster Bridge, and opened what he called a riding-school, though it was really a circus; there was a ring in the centre open to the sky, and seats all round ranged under a canvas roof; the prices of admission were threepence and sixpence. At first he performed without a licence, and proceedings were instituted against him by the Surrey magistrates. One day, however, the King happened to be passing over Westminster Bridge upon a horse that proved unmanageable; Astley, who was looking on, came forward to His Majesty's assistance, and soon rendered the beast docile, for which service he was a few days afterwards rewarded with a licence in due form.

In 1780 he erected a wooden building, with gallery, pit, and boxes, out of the old Covent Garden hustings, which had just been used for an election ; this débris was the perquisite of anybody who chose to remove it, and was usually made into a bonfire by the mob to celebrate the return of the successful candidate. Astley offered gin and beer to those who would bring him the wood instead of burning it, and therewith built his new Amphitheatre. The interior being decorated so as to resemble an avenue of trees, it was called the "Royal Grove." The prices ranged from two shillings to sixpence. The entertainments consisted of performing dogs, tumbling, and feats of horsemanship. In 1787 he added burlettas and pantomime. Seven years later the building was burned to the ground. In less than seven months a new one rose in its place. In 1803 this was also destroyed by fire. Without losing a day the sturdy old trooper set about raising a successor. Morning, noon, and night, in snow and rain, drilling his workmen as though they were a troop of soldiers, he personally superintended the work, as he did later on in Wych Street, until all was completed. The new house opened on Easter Monday, 1804, with, for the first time, an equestrian spectacle, though, as will be presently shown, he was not the originator of the kind of dramatic exhibition, for which the house was thereafter to be famous.

After having erected in France, Great Britain, and Ireland no fewer than nineteen amphitheatres, Astley died in 1814. He was succeeded by his son, who had been for some years the actual manager. Young Astley was a famous rider, and created such an impression in Paris that Marie Antoinette presented him with a gold medal encrusted with diamonds, and gave him the name of the English Rose, a very high honour, as it placed him beside the greatest of male dancers, Vestris, who was called the French Rose. In 1817 he relinquished his government in favour of Davis, who had been in partnership with him some years, and the theatre was rechristened "Davis's Amphitheatre." Under Davis the equestrian spectacles were produced on a more extensive scale. One, *The Blood-Red Knight*, brought in £18,000 to the treasury; *The Battle of Waterloo*, and *The Burning of Moscow*, in which an actor named Gomersal —the one whom Colonel Newcome was so struck with—made an immense hit by his portraiture of Napoleon, which drew all London over Westminster Bridge.

To Davis succeeded the famous Andrew Ducrow, perhaps the greatest rider that was ever seen upon the equestrian stage, as well as the most perfect of pantomimists. How glowingly has "Christopher North," in the *Noctes Ambrosianæ*, dilated in the following passage upon the exceptional powers of this remarkable and very eccentric actor.

"*Tickler*. The glory of Ducrow lies in his poetical impersonations. Why the horse is but the air, as it were, on which he flies. What god-like grace in that volant movement, fresh from Olympus! What seems the feathered Mercury to care for the horse whose side his toe but touches, as if it were but a cloud in the ether? As the flight accelerates, the animal absolutely disappears, if not from the sight of our bodily eye, certainly from that of our imagination, and we behold but the messenger of Jove. . . .

"*Shepherd*. Since as Ducrow takes his attitude as steadfast on the steed as on a stane, there ye behold stanin' before you, wi' helmet, sword and buckler, the image of a warrior king. . . . These impersonations by Ducrow prove that he is a man of genius. . . . Thus, to convert his frame into such forms, shapes, attitudes, postures, as the Greek imagination moulded into perfect expression of the highest state of the soul, *that* shows that Ducrow has a spirit kindred to those who in marble made their mythology immortal."

Ducrow, however, was noted for a profound contempt for the literary part of the drama. "Cut the dialect (dialogue) and come to the 'osses," was his favourite direction. During the rehearsal of an equestrian piece one morning, after listening with growing impatience to a long dialogue between the two leading actors, he at last broke in with :

"Hold hard, gentlemen; here's a deal o' cackle without any good in it. I'll show you how to cut it. You say 'Yield thee, Englishman!' Then you (indicating the other) answer 'Never!' Then you say 'Obstinate Englishman, you die.' Then you both fights. There, that settles the matter; the audience will understand you a deal better, and the poor 'osses won't catch cold while you're jawing."

Bunn, in *The Stage*, relates the following anecdote of this eccentric genius. Ducrow, *loquitur:* "I don't know how you find it, but as soon as I put up the last nights of the season, the beggars begin to give themselves airs. I went to the theatre the other night, and seeing a prime little roasting pig on a nice white napkin in the hall, I told someone to take it upstairs to Mrs. Ducrow. The fellow said it wasn't for me, but for Mr. Roberts. He's the chap, you know, as orders the corn for the 'osses; I'm only the chap as pays for it. Then them confounded carpenters sneak in of a morning with their hands in their pockets, doubled up as though they'd got the cramp, and at night they march out as upright as a dart. 'Cos why? Every one of 'em's got a deal plank up his back. Then the supers, every one on 'em, takes out a lump o' coal in his hat, and they all club their priggings together and sell the lot for drink. As to the riders, they come into rehearsal gallows grand, 'cos they've had all the season a precious deal better salary than they're worth; and at night they come in gallows drunk and, forgetting they may want an engagement next year, are as cheeky as a bit of Billin'sgate."

Although so illiterate that he seldom ventured upon a speaking part, however small, Ducrow's taste and talent as a stage manager in contrasting colours and arranging groups was unrivalled. Nor was his reputation confined to the Westminster Amphitheatre, it was world-famous. In Paris, while performing at Franconi's, the Duchesse d'Angoulême presented him with a gold medal; after the run of one of his pageants at Drury Lane, *St. George and the Dragon*, Queen Adelaide presented him with a hundred pounds, and Count D'Orsay with a pair of gilt pistols and a dirk mounted in ivory and gold.

Astley's has been immortalised by Dickens in *The Old Curiosity Shop*, and the name always calls up memories of the visit of Kit Nubbles, Mrs. Nubbles, Barbara and little Jacob. And Thackeray associates it with Colonel Newcome.

In 1841 the Amphitheatre was again destroyed by fire, and his losses, amounting to £20,000, so preyed upon Ducrow's mind as to cause his death a few months afterwards. The house was rebuilt by Batty, who changed the name to Batty's Amphitheatre.

After Batty came the well-known circus manager, William Cooke. Cooke turned *Macbeth* and *Richard III.* into equestrian dramas, and made White Surrey a leading part.

In 1863, Dion Boucicault, with a loud flourish of trumpets, supposed to be a warning note of coming destruction to all West End managers, converted the famous old Amphitheatre into the Theatre Royal, Westminster, but the result was a miserable failure. His most notable production was a version of *The Heart of Midlothian*, which Miss Marriott played for years afterwards at Sadler's Wells and throughout the country. In the following year, under the management of the ubiquitous E. T. Smith, the old house returned to its former ways. It was in the October of 1864, the famous Ada Isaac Menken made her first appearance here as Mazeppa. For a number of nights she actually accomplished what Mr. Boucicault had threatened to do—brought fashionable London across Westminster Bridge. For many years afterwards the house was under George Sanger's management. It was closed in 1895, and a row of shops now covers the site.

The drama of Astley's Amphitheatre was peculiar to itself; its most salient features were noise, blood, thunder, and gunpowder; tyrant kings and savage chiefs of the most ferocious types of theatrical humanity, and heroes of the most impossible bravery and virtue. Every great battle from Waterloo to Kassassin, probably, was depicted upon that stage.

Next in order of the transpontine theatres comes the SURREY, which commenced its career as an amphitheatre. In 1771 a famous equestrian performer and "strong man" named Charles Hughes opened a riding-school and exhibition, in opposition to Astley's, in Stangate. Twelve years later he and Charles Dibdin, the song writer, entered into a partnership and raised a building which cost £15,000, near the Obelisk in Blackfriars Road. It was opened in 1782, under the name of the Royal Circus.

"Horsemanship," says Dibdin, in his *Professional Life*, "was at that time very much admired, and I conceived that if I could divest it of its blackguardism it might be made an object of public consequence; I proposed, therefore, that it should embrace all the dexterity and reputation of ancient chivalry; that tournaments, running at the ring, and other feats of equestrian celebrity, should be performed. I proposed to have a stage, on which might be represented spectacles, each to terminate with a joust or tilting match, or some other grand object, so managed as to form a novel and striking *coup de théâtre*, and that the business of the stage and ring might be united."

From this we gather that the equestrian drama did not originate at Astley's, but was borrowed by that house from the Surrey.

At first children were the only performers, the idea being to make the Royal Circus a school for actors; these were sixty in number, and among them were several destined thereafter to make some figure in the theatrical world, notably the future Mrs. Charles Kemble, Mrs. Bland, Mrs. Mountain, etc. Grimaldi, the father of famous Joey, was engaged as ballet-master, and the speculation promised every success. But the Surrey magistrates, who seem to have been greatly opposed to theatrical amusements, closed the place as an unlicensed building; such resistance, however, was offered by the audience that the Riot Act had to be read, and the military called out. The following year, a licence being obtained, the house was reopened. The ground landlord, Colonel West, who was the principal proprietor, dying soon afterwards, the other partners fell by the ears. Dibdin was put into the King's Bench by his creditors and renounced by his treacherous associates.

The management of the Royal Circus was a crown of thorns. Breaches of the law were continually involving the managers in prosecutions; one Justice Hyde was their determined enemy, and at the head of a posse of constables would make raids upon the theatre and seize the offending parties. On one occasion, after arresting a man named Barret, he carried him off to a neighbouring public-house, and there opened a commission, the result of which was that the unfortunate actor was committed to Bridewell. Yet at this very time at a low public-house, called the "Dog and Duck," in St. George's Fields close by, the resort of the vilest characters, the cruel sport of duck-hunting, amidst scenes indescribable, was permitted to be carried on every Sunday.

The Royal Circus had not only the honour of introducing equine performers to the London stage, but was also the first place at which canine actors appeared. The Thespis and Susarion of the bow-wow stage were called Geler and Victor, and such was their popularity that they held daily receptions, and people flocked in hundreds to gaze upon and fondle these canine phenomena. Dog pieces became quite the rage; they even invaded the classic stage of Drury Lane, as we have seen. The actors who owned the animals were called "dog stars." They always travelled in pairs; one played the villain, the other the virtuous individual; the latter was always attended by his faithful "dawg," who protected him from all the machinations of his enemy. At the wind up the latter took "the seize," as it was called, that is to say, at a given signal the dog sprang at his throat, which was guarded by a thick pad—invisible, of course, to the audience—covered with red cloth, and never let go until the malefactor had expired in great agony.

In 1803 the Royal Circus was burned down. Rebuilt, it was opened in the following year with the usual style of entertainment. Not until 1809, when it came under the management of William Robert Elliston, was it converted into a theatre. Elliston paid a rental of £2,200 per annum ; he transformed the arena into a pit, and the stables into saloons. The opening bill was unique ; the performance commenced with a drama entitled *Albert and Adela; or, the Invisible Avengers*, and to evade that stumbling-block of all minor managers, the Patent Act, *Macbeth* was converted into a *ballet d'action*, in which the lessee took the leading part. The *Beaux' Stratagem*, *Hamlet*, and many other legitimate plays were similarly treated.

Upon Elliston's retirement, in 1814, the house was again turned into a circus. But in 1816, Tom Dibdin, after making considerable alterations, reopened the Royal Circus as the "Surrey." Under his directorship versions of Scott's novels were given, and Milman's *Fazio*. After seven years Dibdin came to grief, and so did the theatre. Pieces of the most degraded description were produced, notably one upon the murder of William Weare, in which the identical gig used by the murderers was brought upon the stage.

When Elliston quitted Drury Lane, the Surrey being vacant, he again, in 1827, undertook the management. At this time Douglas Jerrold, then a young man, was writing dramas for Davidge of the Cobourg for five pounds a week. One day he and Davidge quarrelled, and instead of delivering over the MS. he had in his pocket he carried it to Elliston, who immediately accepted it. The drama was *Black-Eyed Susan*. T. P. Cooke was engaged for William at the then enormous salary of £60 a week, and a half clear benefit every sixth week.

The first performance was on January 26th, 1829. The success of the piece was not marked on the first night until it came to the catastrophe, but the curtain fell upon a whirlwind of applause, and with each succeeding performance the attraction increased.

"All London," wrote Hepworth Dixon in the *Athenæum*, at the time of Jerrold's death, "went over the water, and Cooke became a personage in society, as Garrick had been in the days of Goodman Fields. Covent Garden borrowed the play, and engaged the actor for an after-piece. A hackney cab carried the triumphant William in his blue jacket and white trousers from the Obelisk to Bow Street, and Mayfair maidens wept over the stirring situations and laughed over the searching dialogue, which had moved, an hour before, the laughter and tears of the Borough. On the three hundredth night of representation the walls of the theatre were illuminated, and vast multitudes filled the thoroughfare. When subsequently produced at Drury Lane, it kept off ruin for a time even from magnificent misfortune. Actors and managers for a time reaped a golden harvest. Testimonials were got up for Elliston and Cooke on the glory of its success, but Jerrold's share of the gain was slight—about £70 of the many thousands it realised for the management. With unapproachable meanness, Elliston abstained from presenting the youthful writer with the value of a toothpick. When the drama had run three hundred nights he said to Jerrold with amusing coolness, 'My dear boy, why don't you get your friends to present you with a bit of plate?' For the four hundred nights *Black-Eyed Susan* was played at different theatres during the first year, Jerrold received about the sum that Cooke was paid for six nights at Covent Garden."

Jerrold wrote several more pieces for this house; among others a five-act blank-verse tragedy called *Thomas à Beckét*. Elliston died manager of the Surrey Theatre. His last appearance was in June, 1831, only twelve days before his death, in the character of Sheva in Cumberland's *Jew*, upon which occasion *Black-Eyed Susan* was played as an after-piece for the two hundred and twentieth time.

At the end of the performance he made a speech—he was nothing if not a speech-maker—in which he humorously supposed himself to be the descendant of an old actor, one Mr. Elliston, who had for many years enjoyed the public favour, but who a few weeks before had judiciously

> "Walk'd sober off, before a sprightlier age
> Came tittering on, to thrust him from the stage."[1]

A noted actor, named Osbaldiston, was the next Surrey manager, and he also was so fortunate as to secure a highly successful piece in Fitzball's *Jonathan Bradford*, which even exceeded the run of Jerrold's

[1] Elliston never missed an opportunity of addressing an audience, and his speeches, wild and inconsequent to a degree, were not the least amusing part of the entertainment. Here is one delivered to a noisy gallery, which, in its grandiloquent commencement and intensely commonplace termination, is exquisitely comic:—"Ladies and gentlemen, I venture as a most unobtrusive individual to take the great liberty of addressing you. It is of rare occurrence that I deem it necessary to place myself in juxtaposition with you. (*Noise in the gallery.*) When I said juxtaposition I meant *vis-à-vis*. (*Increased noise.*) When I uttered the word *vis-à-vis* I meant contactability. Now let me tell you that *vis-à-vis*, which is a French term, and contactability, which is a truly English term, very nearly assimilate to each other. (*Disturbance redoubled.*) Gentlemen, gentlemen, I am really ashamed of your conduct. It is unlike a Surrey audience. Are you aware that I have in this establishment most efficient peace officers at my immediate disposal? Peace officers, gentlemen, mean persons necessary in time of war. A word to the wise. One more word—if that gentleman in the carpenter's cap will sit down (*pointing to pit*) the little girl in red ribbons behind him—you, my love, I mean—will be able to see the entertainment."

drama, and brought to the fortunate *entrepreneur* the sum of £8,000. And yet no poorer specimen of dramatic work was ever given even to the stage of a transpontine theatre. It was the story of a celebrated murder, but the chief attraction lay in a scenic effect, since common enough, but then a startling novelty. The stage was divided into four compartments, and four actions were carried on simultaneously. It was this that, for two hundred and sixty nights, crowded the Surrey to the ceiling.

Davidge followed Osbaldiston. A miserly, grinding curmudgeon, he was Douglas Jerrold's abhorrence; the famous satirist never forgave the ill-paid drudgery he had imposed upon him in his youth. "May he keep a carriage and not be able to ride in it," was Jerrold's bitter invocation. And the wish came to pass; Davidge made a respectable fortune, but ill-health destroyed all his enjoyment of it. His death taking place early in the evening, Jerrold remarked, "Well, I didn't think he'd go before half-price came in!"

Next came Drury Lane Bunn, Miss Romer, and opera. Then, in 1848, "Dick" Shepherd, a name that was for many years to be associated with the house, entered into a partnership with Osbaldiston; it was a very brief one, and Shepherd was afterwards joined by Creswick, the tragedian. A more ill-assorted pair never coalesced; Creswick was nothing if not legitimate; he had all the pompous grandiloquence of the old actor; while his partner, a famous representative of the Surrey sailor, swore by rough-and-tumble melodrama, was vulgar and slangy, and always spoke of Creswick as "Mr. Bill Shakespeare." Yet their partnership endured, with one interruption in 1863, from 1848 to 1869, when both retired.

On the night of January 30th, 1865, just as the audience were leaving the theatre, fire broke out, and soon the whole building was in flames. It was a terrible conflagration; fortunately no lives were lost, though it was with great difficulty that the poor ballet-girls were dragged out. The house was immediately rebuilt on a larger and superior scale.

After the termination of the Shepherd and Creswick régime, there is nothing worth chronicling until George Conquest, a clever actor, playwright, and incomparable pantomimist, took up the management in 1880. With sensational dramas, many written by the lessee, well staged and acted, and exactly suited to the tastes of the audience, and a good Christmas pantomime, the Surrey was a flourishing house for many years. Since Conquest's death, in May, 1901, the Surrey has not kept up its old prestige, and no more need be said of it.

When the foundation-stone of THE COBOURG THEATRE was laid, it was on the western side of one of the great ditches that drained Lambeth Marsh, a large portion of which was at the time still open fields, the New Cut was not yet formed; the foundations were the stones of the old Savoy Palace, then just being pulled down for the opening of Lancaster Place. The theatre was built by subscription, the Princess Charlotte and her husband, Prince Leopold, heading the list, and the house was named after him. But in spite of royal patronage, the Cobourg might never have been finished had not a wealthy tallow-chandler, named Glossop, with a passion for the drama, advanced a considerable sum, with the aid of which it was completed at a cost of £12,000, and opened in the May of 1818. The play was *Trial by Battle; or, Heaven Defend the Right.* It was founded on a *cause célèbre*—the murder of Mary Ashford; in which the accused, one Abraham Thornton, appealing to an old, forgotten statute, claimed "the wager by battle" against his accuser, the brother of the deceased, declared himself ready to defend his plea of not guilty with his body, and threw down a gauntlet, after the manner of a knight-errant. The challenge was not taken up, the prisoner was discharged, and the crime has remained an undiscovered mystery to this day. This extraordinary case had been decided only a week or two before the opening of the theatre.

In addition to the drama there was "a grand Asiatic ballet," and a harlequinade arranged from the *Masque of Comus*. The newspapers informed the public that "a large and fashionable audience" was present on the first night; and the playbills stated that it was the intention of the proprietor "to have all the avenues to the theatre well lighted, while the appointment of additional patrols on the Bridge Road, and keeping them in our own pay, will afford ample security to the patrons of the theatre." But fashionable audiences did not long continue to visit the Cobourg, which very soon became the resort only of the aborigines. "It is the very haunt and refuge of the melodramatic muse," writes a critic, during its earlier years; "there 'murder bares her red arm' with most appalling vividness; there the genius of robbery reigns triumphant on his festive throne; there the sheeted ghosts do squeak and gibber across the frighted stage, and all the sublimities of horror are to be found there, in their most high and palmy state."

The Cobourg was considered a very handsome theatre, and the looking-glass curtain, which was invented in 1822, and used for several years as an act-drop, was one of the sights of London. It was thirty-six feet high, thirty-two wide, composed of sixty-three divisions, enclosed in a gilt frame, and was raised bodily. It was ultimately done away with, as its enormous weight endangered the roof. Pieces were excellently mounted—for those days—the scenery was well painted, indeed, Clarkson Stanfield was at one time among the scenic artists, and the acting of its kind was good. Miss Vincent, thirty or forty years ago, was as famous a heroine of domestic drama on the south side of the Thames as Mrs. Stirling on the north, and allowing for difference of style, their abilities were probably equal. Old Surrey-side playgoers used to talk of her acting in *Susan Hopley*, a version of Mrs. Crowe's once-famous novel, that for hundreds of nights drew crowded houses. N. T. Hicks, "Brayvo Hicks," as he was called, Bengough, Watkins Burroughs, Osbaldiston, Henry Wallack, Henry Kemble, "Jack" Bradshaw, called the Paul Bedford of the "Vic," and many others, all of whom figured in those famous pictures known as penny plain and twopence coloured, in their favourite parts, with legs wide apart and sword or pistol in hand, and a large reserve in their belts, were members of the Cobourg company.

West End stars occasionally crossed the river; Edmund Kean acted here two nights and received a hundred pounds for his services. The Lambethites preferred Tom Cobham, a famous melodramatic actor, in Richard to Kean, and did not conceal their preference, much to the disgust of the great little man. Paganini played here one night. Buckstone made his first London appearance upon these boards, and many other distinguished actors at different times trod them. But none were so successful as local favourites. In 1833 the Cobourg was rechristened the Victoria, in consequence of the late Queen having once, when Princess, paid the theatre a visit.

For many years the old "Vic," as it was familiarly called, held a unique position among London theatres; both its plays and its actors were regarded as representatives of the most extravagant phases of melodrama, and furnished the burlesque-writer with endless fun. The audience was the lowest and vilest in London, the very scum of Lambeth. "The lower orders rush there in mobs," wrote Charles Mathews, "and, in shirt sleeves, applaud frantically, drink ginger-beer, munch apples, crack nuts, call the actors by their Christian names, and throw them orange-peel and apples by way of bouquets." The "Vic" was notorious for accidents, and a very terrible one occurred there in 1858, when sixteen persons were crushed to death through a false alarm of fire.

On the 9th of September, 1871, the Victoria, then under the management of Mr. Cave, ceased to exist as a theatre. In order solemnly to commemorate the occasion, the drama upon which its curtain had first risen, more than half a century before, *The Trial by Battle*, was the piece chosen. It was converted into the Victoria Coffee House Palace, where concerts and operatic selections are given at low prices.

There was formerly an old theatre in the High Street, Peckham, at which a very hazy tradition asserts that Nell Gwynne once played. It was used for dramatic performances, and was for several years under the management of Penley, a Drury Lane actor, as late as 1822, when the premises were converted into a Lancastrian school for boys.

A theatre that, during its latter years, gained a notoriety as unenviable as that of the Victoria was THE BOWER SALOON, Stangate; it was built and opened, in 1838, by a scene-painter named Philips. Many

East End theatrical notabilities made their first appearance upon that stage, and some who have since pleased West End audiences, while many good actors out of engagements would accept a temporary situation there until they could procure something better. Mr. George Hodson, the father of Miss Henrietta Hodson, was one of the early managers; then Biddles, the father of Mrs. Calvert, who as Miss Adelaide Biddles made her first appearance there. James Fernandez was at that time a member of the company. Between thirty and forty years ago it was nothing better than a "gaff," to use a slang theatrical word for which there is no equivalent, and the audience was principally composed of the *gamins* of the New Cut and all the back slums of the Surrey side; every kind of entertainment was given, from *Maria Martin* to *Macbeth.* The managements were usually extremely brief, the actors seldom paid, and the theatre more frequently closed than open. The Bower Saloon finally disappeared in 1879, but long previous to that it had been a thing of the past.

The Rotunda, in Blackfriars Road, which had once been occupied by the Museum of Sir Aston Lever, by the Surrey Institution, and subsequently used as a concert-room, was opened in the September, 1833, as THE GLOBE THEATRE. Five years afterwards it was again a concert-room, and ultimately descended to a "gaff."

In the years gone by there had been a wretched tumble-down old building at Deptford known as THE THEATRE ROYAL. In 1866 Sefton Parry built a neat little theatre at Greenwich to take its place. A few years ago a fine theatre was erected in the Broadway, Deptford.

In 1872 a new theatre was built at the northern end of the New Kent Road and named THE ELEPHANT AND

Castle. It has been mostly devoted, when open, to lurid melodrama and a pantomime at Christmas. After being closed for some time it has been entirely reconstructed, and was reopened in August, 1902. Since then the style of entertainment has been much improved.

Kennington, Balham, Brixton, Camberwell, have now handsome theatres that need not fear comparison with those of the west, but, as I have said of the northern, they have no history, being used only by travelling companies.

From the disappearance of Odell's theatre in Ayliffe Street, and Giffard's in Goodman's Fields, of which some account has been already given, until 1787, the east end of London was deprived of all theatrical amusement. In the year just named a new theatre was erected in Wells Street, Wellclose Square—so called from an ancient well that formerly existed in Goodman's Fields. The chief promoter of this speculation was the celebrated John Palmer, whom we have met at Drury Lane, and his partner was Lee Lewes,[1] another well-known member of the patent theatres companies; while Quick, Bannister, Ryder, Johnstone, Mrs. Gibbs, and other performers of good standing were engaged. Palmer, it would appear, was under the impression that the Lieutenant of the Tower and the magistrates of the Tower Hamlets had the power to license the house, and it was not until the building was announced to open that he was made aware of his unfortunate error.

The managers of Drury Lane and Covent Garden took alarm at an opposition so powerful, and put forth an advertisement in the public prints reciting the various penalties entailed by such a breach of the law, together

[1] He was the grandfather of George Henry Lewes, the critic.

with their determination to put them in force and to prosecute everyone concerned in any breach of the Patent Act. This had the effect of detaching several actors and actresses from Palmer's company. But he himself, not to be daunted, opened his new theatre on June 20th, under the name of THE ROYALTY, WELLCLOSE SQUARE, with *As You Like It.* In order to evade the law he announced the performance to be for the benefit of the London Hospital. The house was crowded; but there was some disturbance, organised, no doubt, by the West End managers, and cries were raised for Palmer to produce his patent.

The Royalty was not again opened until the 3rd of July. But the patentees were determined to enforce their rights, and show no mercy; and one morning Palmer was summoned by the local authorities to appear before them at a certain tavern in the neighbourhood—magisterial business being not infrequently transacted at public-houses in those days—to show under what authority or licence he was acting. Palmer, who was known in his profession as "Plausible Jack," as a constable was waiting, had no alternative but to obey the summons; he presented himself before the magistrates with an air of excessive humility, and in answer to their queries said he had a document which he hoped would fully justify his conduct in their worshipful eyes; it was at home, he had come away so hastily, fearful of keeping them waiting, that he had forgotten to bring it; but if they would so far indulge him as to delay a few minutes he would fetch it—he lived close by—he would not be two minutes. His request was granted, and, laying his hand upon his heart and invoking the blessings of Heaven upon their heads, he left the room. After some time, as he did not return, the magistrates rang for the waiter, who, upon trying to open the door, found it locked and the key gone.

Fearing that he might be summarily committed to prison, Palmer had made prisoners of the quorum to gain time to get away, and the highly incensed gentlemen could not be released until a locksmith was sent for to force the lock. Both he and Bannister, however, were arrested, but released on bail, and a timely submission to the autocrats of Drury Lane and Covent Garden settled the difficulty.

The first time Palmer met Sheridan after his escapade it was with the air of Joseph Surface, a white pocket-handkerchief in his hand, his eyes turned up, his hand upon his heart. "Mr. Sheridan," he began, "if you could but know at this moment what I feel *here*." "Stop, Jack," broke in the manager, "you forget *I wrote Joseph Surface*." Palmer was ruined by his mad speculation, and although he was reinstated in his old position at Drury Lane, and with a considerable rise of salary, he was never again free from difficulties. He died upon the stage at Liverpool in 1796, while playing *The Stranger*.

In 1788 Macready, the father of the great actor, permission having been obtained from the Lord Chamberlain for the performance of burlettas and pantomimes, undertook the managment of the house for a time, but soon grew tired of it. After the fire at Astley's in 1794 the burnt-out company performed at the Royalty. For many years it held on the usual precarious existence of such places; but as, from its remote situation and style of entertainment, it could not possibly clash with the West End houses, the patentees instituted no further proceedings.

In 1810 it was known as the East London, and

sixteen years afterwards was burned to the ground. Having been rebuilt, it was reopened under the name of the Brunswick, and only a few days afterwards was destroyed by a most appalling accident. The walls, though only two and a half bricks in thickness, were 118 feet in height, and 117 in length; upon this superstructure, with the idea of rendering the building fireproof, an iron roof was set. Again and again the proprietors had been warned that the supports were not adequate to sustain this ponderous mass; but iron roofs were little understood sixty years ago, and, in their haste to get the house open, the builders totally disregarded such warnings, and continued to attach further burdens to the already overweighted girders. On the third morning after the opening, February 28th, while the company were rehearsing *Guy Mannering*, the theatre fell in, killing fifteen people and injuring twenty more; among the former, by a strange fatality, as he had succeeded in escaping from the building into the street, was Mr. Maurice, the man whose obstinacy had caused the catastrophe.

No attempt was made to rebuild the unfortunate house, but theatres soon began to spring up rapidly at the east end of London. In 1830 a disused chapel in Grub Street, now Milton Street, immortalised in the chronicles of the eighteenth century as the abode of the literary hack, was converted into a theatre. It was named THE CITY THEATRE, and afterwards the City Pantheon. John Bedford, a well-known comedian, was the first manager; he was succeeded by Chapman, the husband of Miss Ann Tree, Mrs. Charles Kean's sister, thereafter manager of the Tottenham Street Theatre. The Grub Street Theatre had the honour to introduce Miss Fanny Clifton, afterwards Mrs. Stirling, to the theatrical profession. It was here she made her first appearance upon the stage in the humblest walk of the drama, delivering messages and speaking a few lines. Edmund Kean played Shylock here in May, 1831, and in the July of the same year Ellen Tree and James Vining performed in a French translation entitled *One Fault*. The first stage version of Gerald Griffin's *Collegians*, upon which *The Colleen Bawn* was founded, entitled *Eily O'Connor*, was brought out the same year. An admirable company was engaged at this time, and *Love in a Village* was performed with a cast equal to any that the West End could show: Miss Forde, Rosetta; Mrs. Chapman, Lucinda; Chapman, Hawthorn; Blanchard, Justice Woodcock; Buckstone, Hodge. *Black-Eyed Susan* was given with Mrs. Chapman as Susan, and James Vining as William. Mr. and Mrs. Davidge from the Surrey, Miss Apjohn, afterwards Mrs. Frank Matthews, and John Reeve, were at different times members of the company. Chapman had been fined £350 for playing the legitimate drama at the Tottenham Street Theatre, and the persecution of the patent managers still pursuing him for defying their privileges, he retired from Grub Street in 1831 in favour of Davidge. The City Theatre was now worked in conjunction with the Cobourg, the same performers appearing at the two places nightly, being conveyed backwards and forwards in hackney coaches. Miss Smithson, the *tragédienne*, who afterwards became the wife of Hector Berlioz, was the principal attraction in 1832. A great hit was made in the same year with Leman Rede's "moral drama" *The Rake's Progress*. Webster was manager for a while, with Mrs. Waylett as "the star." Moncrieff the dramatist had the house for a time, and as dramatic performances were forbidden tickets were sold at a pastrycook's opposite. In April, 1833, the fifteen years' lease, at a ground rent of £210 per annum, was sold by auction for 310 guineas. 1836 was the last year in which the theatre was opened, and warehouses were erected on the site.

The year 1829 saw yet another theatre added to the East End list—THE PAVILION in Whitechapel, which opened under the direction of Wyatt and Farrell. The latter engaged Fanny Clifton from Grub Street. Perceiving she had great promise he put her forward, and it was at this house that she made the first step towards the brilliant career that awaited her at a more fashionable end of the town. The first Pavilion was burned down in 1856 and immediately rebuilt. Within the last few years the proprietor, Mr. Morris Abrahams, has had the house reconstructed, and it is now a spacious and handsomely appointed theatre, upon the stage of which dramas are produced in a most effective manner, and are interpreted by thoroughly competent companies. Its principal patrons are the English Jews of the neighbourhood.

In 1830 a new theatre was opened in Leman Street, Whitechapel, and from its proximity to the scene of "little Davy's" début was called THE GARRICK. Wyman and Conquest—the father of George—were the managers. It was burned down in 1845, and rebuilt. It always held a very low position even among East End theatres, and could seldom attract a responsible manager. At times it fell to the level of a penny show, with performances twice a night. In 1873 or 1874, J. B. Howe, a great favourite in Whitechapel, took the house, renamed it the Royal Albert, furbished it up, and, with a fair company and a better style of entertainment, endeavoured to resuscitate its fortunes; but all his efforts were in vain, and he quitted the speculation bankrupt. The Garrick has long since ceased to be numbered among metropolitan theatres.

The next in order of the East End houses was a second City of London, built in Norton Folgate, by Beazeley, the architect of the Lyceum. It was opened on the 30th of March, 1835, under the management of Cockerton. For a brief season, in 1837, it was under the direction of the famous Mrs. Honey, after which it again came into the hands of Cockerton, who was presently joined by Richard Shepherd, afterwards so well known as the manager of the Surrey. Mr. and Mrs. Honner opened the house in the summer of 1846, and in addition to a series of original dramas produced several of Shakespeare's plays, in which Mrs. Honner, a very fine actress, George Bennett, Saville, etc., appeared. There was also an excellent dramatic version of Dickens's *The Battle of Life* given, in which the lady just named played Clemency in a style that could only have been surpassed by Mrs. Keeley. But the most prosperous days of the City were under the directorship of Johnson and Nelson Lee who came here from the Standard. Johnson and Lee were the successors to Richardson in his famous booth, which they conducted until it was finally broken up. They were the first, at the City of London, permanently to reduce the prices of admission; previous to their time there was no lower price than sixpence to the gallery at any of the East End theatres, they made it threepence, and sixpence to the pit; the experiment proved highly successful. The "old City" was the best of the East End theatres. After the repeal of the Patent Laws nearly all the leading tragedians from the West End houses starred here in the legitimate drama, and the companies, though of the melodramatic school, were excellent. When Nelson Lee ceased to direct its destines, about 1865, the house fell to a very low level, and the stage being required for the extension of the North London line, between Shoreditch and Broad Street, it finally closed in 1868. The frontage in Norton Folgate is still standing.

THE STANDARD, Shoreditch, was opened about six months after the City. From 1837 it was, for several years, under the directorship of Johnson and Lee. It was put up for sale in 1849, and fell into the hands of John Douglass, who, like Lee, had been a showman. After his death it passed to his sons. The "Royal Standard" was burnt down in 1867. Rebuilt on a much more extensive scale, it was reopened as the "New Standard" in the following year. This theatre, although it usually kept a good stock company, was the first of the East End houses that attracted the stars from the west and West End plays. Twenty, thirty, forty years ago all the best actors of the day appeared at different times upon its stage, a circumstance which, at that time, rendered it unique among theatres of its class, and drew to it a very much superior audience, chiefly from the northern suburbs. It has an enormous capacity. It was asserted to be the largest theatre in London, and was handsomely decorated. In the days of Richard Douglass, who was a very fine scenic artist, a pupil of Beverley's, its pantomimes ran those of Drury Lane very close.

The Melvilles—father, widow, and sons—have been the lessees for many years. Walter Melville is the author of several lurid dramas, written especially for the Standard, two of which have recently been seen at the Adelphi. A particular feature of the Standard, ever since I can remember, has been an annual season of opera, usually by J. W. Turner's troupe. The Grand, the Dalston, the Stoke Newington have taken away most of the old patrons of the house, which is now, I think, chiefly dependent upon the locality for its supporters, and for them necessarily the management has to cater.

The Effingham Saloon, Whitechapel, was first opened somewhere about sixty years ago. Rebuilt in 1867, it was renamed THE EAST LONDON. It was the favourite resort of the sailors and inhabitants of Wapping and the dock neighbourhood, and the pieces represented were adapted to their primitive tastes. It was one of the lowest audiences in London. The East London was burned down in 1879. As the theatre had not paid for some time, it was not rebuilt. But of late years a house for the performance of Yedisha plays for the Polish Jews, now called "Wonderland," has been opened upon the old site.

A music-hall in High Street, Poplar, was, in 1867, converted into a theatre called THE ORIENTAL, but after a few years it reverted to its original form of entertainment. It was once considered a very remote house, but Stratford can now boast of two well-conducted, well-paying theatres, where West End plays and West End stars are frequently seen. Sir Henry Irving has appeared there.

SADLER'S WELLS THEATRE.

PART V

THE WEST END THEATRES OF TO-DAY

CHAPTER I

The Adelphi, 1866–1903, and Famous Adelphi Dramas and Actors—The West London Theatre.

THE first founder of THE ADELPHI THEATRE was a colour maker and sort of Jack-of-all-trades in the Strand, named John Scott. He had accumulated a very large fortune by the invention of a washing blue, called the "Old True Blue," manufactured from the sooty deposit of some peculiar wood; a discovery he had made by accident while travelling in the Black Forest. Being fond of the society of actors, whom he was in the habit of entertaining, his daughter conceived a passion for the stage, and persuaded him to buy some ruinous old property in the rear and at the side of his dwelling-house and build a theatre.

The colour merchant was rash enough to invest £10,000 in purchasing leases and building a small theatre, which he christened the Sans Pareil. It was opened on November 27th, 1806, with an entertainment consisting of songs, recitations, imitations *à la* the elder Mathews, the whole being written and delivered by Miss Scott; the performance winding up with a display of fireworks.

Such speculations on the part of outsiders almost invariably prove a disastrous failure; this, however, was a brilliant exception. John Scott was one of those persons who succeed in everything they undertake; he was indefatigable in his management, and of an evening would take off his coat, go into the cheap parts of the house, and pack the people close together; he used to boast that he thus often increased the takings by five pounds a night. Miss Scott also seems to have been a clever girl, who most ably seconded her father off the stage by her talents on.

It was not long before the monologue and pyrotechnic entertainment developed into the dramatic, and the Sans Pareil became another thorn in the sides of the lessees of the patent theatres. The usual prices were charged: boxes, 4*s.*; pit, 2*s.*; gallery, 1*s.*; the doors were opened at 5.30, and the play began at 6.30,[1] with half-price to boxes at 8.30. The company was evidently of the most mediocre description, everything depending upon that tremendously energetic and industrious lady, Miss Scott, who not only performed in all the pieces except the pantomimes, but, according to the playbills, wrote them nearly all; at the bottom of three-fourths of the programmes there is a line in italics, which informs the reader that "the whole of this evening's entertainment is written by Miss Scott." Sometimes this statement is modified—Miss Scott has only rearranged the scenes and situations—but she has always had something to do with the entertainment; her name has invariably a line to itself, is preceded by an "and," and is printed in very large caps., which strongly contrast with the very small type that was deemed sufficient for everybody else; unless it be some stray star from Drury Lane or Covent Garden—a star at the

[1] This was the usual time of commencement even seventy years ago; in the middle of the 18th century it was six; the lack of a complete set of playbills at the British Museum renders it impossible to trace the intermediate times back to the three o'clock of Pepys's days.

Sans Pareil, though a very small satellite in its own dramatic horizon. Upon one occasion, Miss Scott indignantly disclaims any connection with any other Scott who may be playing elsewhere, and emphatically declares that she has never yet appeared in any other theatre. Melodramas, styled burlettas in the bills, bearing such titles as *The Red Robber*, *The Old Oak Chest*, *The Amazon Queen*, are the *pièces de résistance*, and musical farces—also called burlettas; these again are frequently supplemented by monkeys from Paris, slack-rope dancers from Vienna, wonderful dwarfs, and, at holiday seasons, by pantomimes.

John Scott was as lucky with his theatre as he had been with his "Old True Blue," and made, it is said, thereby another large fortune. In the year 1819 he sold the Sans Pareil to Messrs. Jones and Rodwell for £25,000. His daughter retired with him, at least I do not again come across her name in the playbills. The name of the house was changed with the management from the Sans Pareil to the Adelphi, and opened under that title on October 18th, 1819. The announcement informed the public that it had undergone considerable improvements, and, after the first week, it was further added that "the brilliant effect of the gas chandelier suspended from the dome is the subject of universal admiration." In this year John Reeve made his first appearance here upon the London stage, and his remarkable talent in broad comedy quickly rendered him a rival to the great Liston himself.

The style of entertainment under Messrs. Jones and Rodwell was a decided improvement on that favoured by the proprietor of the "Old True Blue"; melodramas of the red-hot school were still performed, but they were varied by dramatic adaptations of Walter Scott's novels.

The management having, it would seem, prospered, the Adelphi in 1821 underwent further alterations, and the opening bills descant glowingly upon the splendid decorations, the enlarged passages, that rendered the house, in aspect, entirely new. This season was remarkable for the first appearance in London of that inimitable droll, "little Keeley." No less important was the début of Mrs. Waylett, one of the most charming singers and *piquante* actresses of the century, whom we have met in Tottenham Street.

The Adelphi hitherto had excited scant notice from the Press, which in those days seldom deigned to note the doings of a minor theatre, while its audiences were chiefly drawn from the humblest classes. But during the season of 1821 it became the most popular house in London.

It was during this year that a journalist of a very low type named Pierce Egan, who afterwards founded *Bell's Life*, a writer whose pen was principally devoted to the reports of the prize-ring, in a sporting vernacular that was long peculiarly associated with pugilism, brought out a periodical work, with coloured plates by the two Cruikshanks, entitled *Tom and Jerry; or, Life in London.* Before the second number was published, Mr. Egan, whose style was the apotheosis of slang and vulgarity, found himself famous. It was one of those curious crazes which at times seize upon the public for some book, some play, or actor, whose merits are not infrequently in the inverse ratio of its or his popularity. The publisher of this *recherché* work was suddenly overwhelmed with orders, his shop was besieged by eager purchasers; the press could not turn out copies fast enough, and a small army of women and children were employed day and night in colouring the engravings.

With each number the madness increased; pictures of Bob Logic, Corinthian Tom, and Jerry Hawthorn adorned every print and bookseller's window, everybody became Corinthian; tailors advertised the Corinthian coat, the Corinthian pantaloons; shoemakers made only the Corinthian shoe, and hatters filled their windows with the Corinthian hat.

A dramatic version of the famous book was produced at the Adelphi; but, as it has happened to so many great stage successes, the piece was received on the first night with such hostility that Rodwell declared it should not be played again, and it was with great difficulty his partner induced him to alter his determination. How much reason he had to thank him for his advice is a matter of history. The cast was exceptionally good, his part fitting each actor like a glove. That excellent comedian, Wrench, was the Tom; Reeve was Jerry; Wilkinson, Bob Logic. Referring to this piece in his *Experiences*, Serjeant Ballantine says: "A little unknown man who had been given some three lines to say contrived in doing so to create roars of laughter. His part was written up, and from that time to his death he was recognised as one of the most comic actors that ever delighted an audience. This was Robert Keeley." He played the small part of Jemmy Green. Even Walbourn, who went on for Dusty Bob, and who had scarcely a line to speak, became a celebrity; he took a tavern at Battle Bridge, and George Cruikshank painted the sign, representing him in his famous character. The author recorded his opinion that it was "one of, if not the greatest triumph of histrionic art ever exhibited upon the stage!" Kean declared that during the whole course of his theatrical career he had never seen any performance equal to it. This, of course, was an exaggeration. Far more significant was the unconscious testimony of an actor of the day, who, while witnessing the performance from the front, exclaimed, "Good heavens! is it possible? It certainly *is* a real dustman they've got upon the stage. I am very sorry that our profession has sunk so low as to be compelled to go into the streets to get a person of that description to support the character!" And he left the house in disgust. Nor was the actor the only one so deceived; so life-like were the presentments of Tattersall's and its frequenters in the scene representing the famous repository at Hyde Park Corner, of Tom Cribb, the noted pugilist, and other sporting characters in *Tom Cribb's Parlour*, that bets were made that it was these notabilities themselves who nightly appeared upon the scene.

The piece ran through the remainder of the season, which was considerably more than a hundred nights, opened the next, and was revived again and again with unabated success; nothing like it had ever been previously known in theatrical annals, seats were taken weeks in advance, people made journeys from the remotest parts of the country to witness it—and in the old stage-coach days that meant more than it does now—and five guineas were at times paid for one seat. The Puritans were up in arms; they stood at the theatre doors laden with tracts, which they tried to thrust into the hands of everyone who entered; the serious Press inveighed against it, ministers denounced it from the pulpit, the Lord Chamberlain was petitioned to suppress it; he went to the Adelphi to sit in judgment, saw, and enjoyed the piece so hugely, that he went again and took my lady with him. All opposition only swelled the success and made everyone more eager to see it. In 1822 there were ten theatres in and about London, to say nothing of the provinces, playing *Tom and Jerry*, and everywhere with the same success.

For a time the high-falutin of tragedy, the artificial humours of comedy, the nightmares of melodrama were set aside, and *Life in London* was presented as it was, from Almack's in the West to All Max—the beggar's home—in the East; from the ball of the opera to the dancing crib in Ratcliff Highway. No wonder it was successful. The man about town was curious to see how nearly the presentment of such scenes approached to the reality, while respectability—always eager to get a peep behind the curtain that conceals the forbidden—flocked to catch a glimpse of that naughty world it dared not visit in any other way. At the bottom of the bill was the following curious announcement: "A facsimile of the treadmill, by a French artist in ivory work, drawn from his actual experience on the spot for the last three months!"

Life in London was followed by *Green in France; or, Tom and Jerry's Tour*, in which the two heroes were transported to Paris, and made to pass through a series of adventures illustrative of fast life in the French capital. But though it was produced in a far more elaborate and costly manner than its predecessor, like all sequels, *Green in France* proved a failure, and after being forced for thirty-five nights, was shelved, and *Life in London* revived. Another piece by Pierce Egan, *The Life of an Actor*, produced September 4th, 1824, was more successful. It was a coarse burlesque upon the theatrical profession, its shifts, its poverty, its seamy and ridiculous side; the thing chiefly owed its success to the farcical humour of John Reeve, in the part of Abraham Delawhang, in which he gave his imitations of contemporary actors.

But the time was not ripe for the realistic, except as a change, and by-and-by a tremendous melodramatic spectacle, entitled *Valmondi; or, the Unhallowed Sepulchre*, with a hero who had drunk of the elixir of life, an attendant demon, an *auto-da-fé*, and a catastrophe in the infernal regions, occupied the boards upon which Black Sal and Dusty Bob had recently performed their wonderful breakdown. This terrible drama had fatal consequences for one of the managers of the Adelphi; a theatrical magazine for March, 1825, which announces the decease of Mr. Rodwell, informs us that "the anxiety and fatigue he endured in arranging for the representation of the melodrama of *Valmondi* brought on the complaint which ended in his death."

Jones immediately retired from the management, and on October 10th the Adelphi opened under the direction of Terry and Yates. Both had been members of Drury Lane and Covent Garden companies, and Yates had made some mark at the former. Wrench, John Reeve, T. P. Cooke, Tyrone Power, who had joined in the previous year, Mrs. Fitzwilliam, and Miss Brunton, afterwards Mrs. Yates, were among the company engaged. Under the new management the Adelphi advanced rapidly in public favour and reputation. Its first great hit was the dramatic version of Fenimore Cooper's famous novel, *The Pilot*. Fitzball, the adapter, shifted the odious and ridiculous parts assigned by the author to the British to the Yankees themselves; and Scott tells us in his *Diary* (October 21st, 1826) that "the Americans were so much displeased that they attempted a row, which rendered the piece doubly attractive to the seamen of Wapping, who came up and crowded the house night after night to support the honour of the British flag." This will go a great way to account for the extraordinary run—extraordinary for those days—of two hundred nights, which *The Pilot* enjoyed.

The great feature of the performance was T. P. Cooke's Long Tom Coffin. Cooke had served in the Royal Navy, and distinguished himself at the battle of St. Vincent. In 1804 he quitted the main-deck of a man-o'-war for the stage, and made his first appearance at the Royalty Theatre in Wellclose Square. He was afterwards a member of most of the metropolitan companies, including that of Drury Lane and the English Opera House, where we have met him. When, in 1825, he appeared at the Adelphi he was an actor of considerable reputation, and in Cooper's nautical hero presented upon the stage, probably for the first time, a real seaman. How Cooke acted the sailor is graphically described in the following passage from the delightful *Noctes Ambrosianæ*.

"*Shepherd.* But tell me, Sir, did you gang to see Mr. Tay Pay Cook in *The Pilot?*

"*North.* The best sailor that ever trod the stage.

"*Shepherd.* Do you ca' yon treddin' the stage? Yon's no treddin'. When he first loupit out o' the boat on dry laun', tryin' to steady himself on his harpoon, he garred me find the verra furm aneath me in the pit shovin' up and down as if the earth were lousen'd from her moorin's, I grew amaist sea-sick.

"*North.* Nothing overdone; no bad bye play, blabbing of the land-lubber; not too much pulling up of the trousers; no ostentatious display of pigtail; one chunk of tobacco into his cheek without any perceptible chew, sufficient to show that next to grog quid is dear; no puling, no whining, when on some strong occasion he pipes his eye, but merely a slight choking of that full, deep, rich, mellow voice, symphonious, James, in all its keys with the ocean's, whether piping in the shrouds, or blowing great guns, running up, James, by way of pastime, the whole gamut; and then so much heart and soul, James, in minute particulars, justifying the most passionate exhibition when comes crisis or catastrophe.

"*Shepherd.* What for do you no mention the hornpipe? I wad gie fifty pounds to be able to dance yon way. Faith I wad astonish them at Kirns. The way he twists the knees of him, and rins on his heels, and down to the floor wi' a wide spread-eagle amaist to his verra doup, up again like mad, and awa' off intil some ither nawtical movements: the hornpipe, bafflin' a' comprehension as to its meanin', and then all the while siccan' a face!"

Cooke's next great hit was Vanderdecken in the melodrama of *The Flying Dutchman.* His fine figure and expressive features, his skill in make-up and picturesqueness, imparted to his melodramatic pantomime a wonderful power and vividness.

In 1827 the Adelphi was again enlarged both before and behind the curtain. But at the latter end of 1828, wrecked in health and fortune, having lost all his own savings, £500 lent him by Ballantyne, and £1,250 for which his friend, Walter Scott, had pledged his credit, Terry retired from the partnership. He died in the following June. In the next season Charles Mathews joined Yates, paying £17,000 for a half-share.

Some seasons previously Yates had appeared in a monologue entitled *Sketches of Life and Character;* the two partners now united in a duologue entertainment of a similar kind. Yates possessed great powers of mimicry as well as histrionic talent of a very high order; he was equally at home as Alexander, the roué in *Victorine*, as Mantalini in *Nicholas Nickleby*, as the bold Miles Bertram in *The Wreck Ashore*, and as Quilp in *The Old Curiosity Shop*. During the next few years this house could boast of companies which made the name of the little minor theatre famous throughout the dramatic world. And yet, somehow, it could not be made to pay; whether it was badly managed, or managers lived beyond their means, or the public were not sufficiently liberal in their support, it would be difficult to determine. Yates, however, had a great friend in the Duchess of St. Albans (formerly Miss Mellon), who frequently came to his assistance.

Mathews dying in 1835 a poor man, his son, Charles the younger, took his place, but retired at the end of the first season. Then Yates found another partner, a man named Gladstone, who ultimately became sole lessee, and succeeded in effecting what his far cleverer predecessors had failed in, making the house pay. Poor Yates died broken-hearted in 1842, in the very zenith of his powers, at the age of forty-seven. Edward Stirling tells a good story about him in *Old Drury Lane*, which is worth repeating. During one of the Westminster elections he was seen by the mob entering the Tory polling booth. A cry was raised of "Yates voting against us, oh, oh!" The actor laid his hand upon his bosom, and vowed his heart was with them.

"Ladies and gentlemen," he said, as soon as he could be heard, "on this joyous occasion pray be merciful—on this my first appearance on a political stage, and I promise you *the last*. You may return Old Nick if you like; my wish is ever to please my best supporters, the people."

"Hurrah, bravo! give us 'Jim Crow'!" shouted the

mob. In an instant Yates, with the utmost *sang-froid*, whistled the tune, danced a breakdown round the hustings, and wound up with singing—

> "Wheel about,
> Jump about,
> Vote just so;
> Let your bobs
> Be spent
> On my 'Jim Crow.'"[1]

His wife, *née* Brunton, the sister of the beautiful Louisa Brunton, afterwards Countess of Craven, was an incomparable heroine of melodrama, and an excellent actress of high-class comedy as well. She had made her London début at Covent Garden, in 1817, as Letitia Hardy with brilliant success; as Violante (*The Wonder*), Beatrice, Rosalind, Olivia, and Miss Hardcastle she was admirable, reminding the old playgoers of her time of Mrs. Abington and Miss Farren. Mrs. Yates survived her husband nearly twenty years.

Madame Celeste made her first appearance at the Adelphi in 1833, in *St. Mary's Eve*. In the same year the house sustained a great loss by the early death of John Reeve. Fortunately, an excellent successor was at hand in Edward Wright, who had just made a great success at the St. James's.[2] Wright worthily took the position that had been occupied by Liston and Reeve. His Paul Pry was little, if at all, inferior to the original representative's. As a farce actor he was inimitable, especially in *The Spitalsfields Weaver* and *Domestic Economy*. The

[1] Rice, an American actor, in the thirties, was the first to introduce the nigger upon the English stage at this theatre, in the character of Jim Crow, and his then novel song and dance was for a time the rage in town and country.

[2] His first appearance in London was at the Tottenham Street Theatre, 1830

actor who afterwards made the nearest approach to his drollery was George Honey. Edmund Yates, in his autobiography, relates how, in the helpless exhaustion of inextinguishable laughter, he has fallen a limp mass across the ledge of the boxes at the Adelphi at the irresistible fooling of this comedian, and the writer of these pages can recall similar experiences. Whenever Wright came upon the stage he brought with him an atmosphere of laughter, that alike infected audience and actors, for actors could no more resist the infection than could the spectators; I have seen the action of a scene brought to a standstill while those on the stage were endeavouring to swallow the risibility that choked them. Yet his humour was totally devoid of effort; if you ever thought of asking yourself why you held your aching sides and wiped your streaming eyes, you found the question rather difficult to answer. His costume was seldom what could be called *outré*, when we remember that the fine gentlemen of comedy then attired themselves in light blue coats, salmon-coloured trousers, and pink waistcoats; his make-up was more that of a light than a low comedian; he was not much given to grimace, yet he had but to twiddle his eyeglass and assume that intense look of utter surprise which accompanied his "Bless my soul, you don't say so?" and your "face crumpled up like a damp towel."

But it must be confessed that he was coarse, terribly coarse. When Charles Kean engaged him for the Princess's, the more fastidious audience of Oxford Street would not tolerate his freedom of speech, and for two or three years he received fifty pounds a week without appearing on the stage.. Buckstone paid him that salary to play a farce after midnight at the Haymarket. But he was a fountain of spontaneous humour, a source of inexhaustible laughter. He was never, however, really at home except at the Adelphi.

Wright had an excellent coadjutor in Paul Bedford; but Paul was only a foil, a pantaloon to Wright's clown; a remarkably fine voice rendered him invaluable in burlesque, while his enormous bulk was a natural source of fun. Authors wrote only skeleton parts for these two inveterate "gaggers," who, after a while, usually abandoned the text altogether and trusted to their own resources. Paul Bedford's two greatest hits were Jack Gong in *The Green Bushes,* in which his "I believe you, my boy," became the cant phrase of the day, and Blueskin in *Jack Sheppard.*

And that brings me to another famous Adelphi success, the dramatic version of Ainsworth's noted novel, in 1840, which created scarcely less sensation than *Tom and Jerry.* Paul Bedford's singing of "Jolly Nose" was one of the great attractions of the drama. Mrs. Keeley must have made the most delightful of housebreakers. She was an actress of wonderful variety, since she could equally delight audiences in prison-breaking Jack, poor Smike, Little Nell, Dot, and the slaveys of broad farce. *Jack Sheppard* became the popular craze. It crowded the Adelphi; versions of it were brought out at half a dozen theatres, and everybody was chaunting—

"Nix, my dolly pals, fake away!"

The Chadbands were again up in arms, advertising by their invectives the thing they condemned; the Press took up a severely moral tone, and so much pressure was brought to bear upon the Lord Chamberlain that by-and-by the piece was interdicted.

In 1844, Madame Celeste, in partnership with Benjamin Webster, became lessee of the Adelphi, and those fine artistes divided their services between the Haymarket, of which Webster was then lessee, and the Strand. Celeste, though the range of her characters was very wide, is now chiefly remembered by her association with a school of plays which were known by the phrase of "The Adelphi Drama," though several were produced at the Haymarket. Nearly all of them were written by Buckstone, who, when he migrated from the Surrey, for which he had written several pieces, to the Adelphi in 1829 or 1830, became the stock playwright of the Strand house. The first of the series of dramas was *The Wreck Ashore*, in which Yates and Mrs. Yates, O'Smith, and Mrs. Fitzwilliam acted. *Victorine*, an adaptation from the French, gave the Yateses two powerful parts. Mrs. Stirling made her first appearance at the West End in *The Dream at Sea*, in the part of Biddy Nutts, 1836. These dramas followed on the lines of the ordinary fiction of the period; the language was stilted, the plots were ultra-sentimental, the heroes and heroines immaculate, the villains of the deepest dye, but they were very effective lay figures in their day.[1] The best known are *Green Bushes*, 1845, and *The Flowers of the Forest*, 1849, in which, as Miami and Cynthia, Madame Celeste had her finest opportunities. Those who saw her only in her latter days play Miami could form no conception of what she had been in her prime, of the grace, the picturesqueness of her pantomime, the intensity of love, hate, revenge that she threw into her delineation of the Indian girl. It was in the portrayal of wild, passionate, half-savage natures that she chiefly excelled.

[1] It is curious to note the enormous difference in the remuneration received by dramatic authors in those days and in these. Buckstone was the author of 150 dramas, comedies, and farces; he was paid only £60 for a three-act drama, though he afterwards raised the price to £70 and £10 for provincial rights during a twelvemonth; while a certain living writer of melodramas has received in fees as much as £10,000 for a single piece.

An attempt was made to revive *The Flowers of the Forest* some years ago, but the audience laughed at what they called the old-fashioned twaddle. And as it was *then* interpreted they were not far wrong. But when Mrs. Fitzwilliam[1] was Starlight Bess, Miss Woolgar,[2] Lemuel, O'Smith, Ishmael the Wolf, and Buckstone and Paul Bedford, Cheap Jack and the Kinchin, it was quite a different thing, and, with such a caste, and the text modernised, would tell almost as powerfully upon an Adelphi audience now as it did half a century ago.

Again, modern melodrama with all its striking effects has given us nothing more picturesque than the last scene of that same drama, in which Cynthia, cast out from her tribe, is made by her father to expiate the death of Lemuel by her own self-immolation ; the wild scene, the picturesque groups of gipsies lit up by the smoky glare of the torches, and now and again illumined by flashes of lightning, the powerful acting of the terrible O'Smith, the awful intensity yet the exquisite beauty of Celeste's every utterance and movement, so admirably contrasted with the silent agony of Starlight Bess, formed quite a Salvator Rosa picture. Alfred Mellon, the conductor of the theatre, who afterwards married Miss Woolgar, composed some delightfully appropriate music for the action, which added greatly to the effect.

As a delineator of the terrors of melodrama, O'Smith was scarcely inferior to T. P. Cooke. No doubt we should think him shockingly conventional and unreal nowadays, but he had real power and intensity, together

[1] Mrs. Fitzwilliam, who was identified with Buckstone's management, was one of the most delightful comic actresses of her day. But it was the touch of true pathos, which is the gift of all real humorists, that rendered her Nelly O'Neill, in *Green Bushes*, and Starlight Bess so striking. She died about 1856.

[2] Miss Woolgar made her first appearance at the Adelphi in 1843.

with an intuitive sense of the picturesque. In one of the old dramas, I believe it was *Peter Bell*, he played the part of a drunkard, and in one scene he had to upset a cup of liquor; with a cry of horror he cast himself upon the stage and ravenously licked up the spilled drink. It was one of those daring bits of business that only a strong actor, confident in his own power, would have dared attempt; had it been weakly done it would have raised a laugh; as he did it, it sent a shudder through the house. His death-scene of the pirate, Grampus, in *The Wreck Ashore* was a wonderful piece of melodramatic acting; the ghastly face peering in at the window of the room where the two girls are alone, the moving of the latch by the invisible hand, the firing of the gun by the heroine, and that terrible figure, ragged and emaciated, falling in through the doorway death-stricken. It was grim, horrible if you will, but it was picturesque, intense and imaginative, and therefore could not be revolting.

And this high-priest of terror was in private life a very mild, middle-aged gentleman, with a hobby for collecting butterflies. Was it not a curious contradiction?

In 1853, Webster retired from the Haymarket and devoted himself entirely to the Adelphi, with which he was thereafter to be solely identified. The Buckstone vein of melodrama was by this time pretty well exhausted, and a new series of a higher order followed, with which the names of Charles Reade, Tom Taylor, Watts Philips, and Dion Boucicault are associated; among the most notable of these plays may be named *Masks and Faces*,[1] *Two Loves and a Life*, *The Poor*

[1] *Masks and Faces* was first played at the Haymarket, 1852; it was revived here and became a stock play.

Strollers, *The Dead Heart*, in all of which Webster, and in most Celeste, greatly distinguished themselves.

Webster was an actor of consummate ability, and would have been an acquisition even to the Comédie Française in its best days. He had greater variety than perhaps any other actor of his generation. What a seemingly impassable interval there was between the broad humour of the Somersetshire ploughman, Giles, in *The Queensberry Fête*, and the slimy, snake-like hypocrite Tartuffe—a splendid performance; or the callous drunkard Richard Pride and that most charming of his creations, Triplet. Richard Pride is only a very ordinary melodramatic part, but as played by Webster it was an elaborate psychological study; Richard Pride is drunk almost throughout the play, but there was no monotony in Webster's performance, for in each scene he gave a different phase of the vice. Yet, with fine artistic skill, though he could not help rendering the picture repulsive, he always avoided making it brutal. Janet was another of Celeste's most powerful performances. I can remember nothing more thrilling than her agony after she had left her child at the Foundling, her frantic cries as she tore at the walls to try and get it back again.

No other actor has played Triplet with the subtlety of Webster; the poor dramatist is only a strolling player after all, though with the soul of a gentleman beneath his vanity and bombast, and this Webster showed distinctly. Bancroft, undoubtedly the best exponent of the part after the original, failed to convey this impression; he was too much the broken-down gentleman throughout, while Beerbohm Tree was too lacrymose, missing the hopeful Bohemian spirit, to whom the gift of a guinea would open heavens of delight.

Robert Landry in *The Dead Heart* was another of

Webster's masterpieces; the scene in which he was brought out of the Bastille with brain and body paralysed, the gradual awakening of consciousness and memory, acted only by facial expression, would keep the house riveted in dead silence for minutes. Irving's Robert Landry would not bear comparison with the original. There is only one reading of the part, and that was Webster's; it would not bear modernising nor attempts at *originality*.

It was by the acting, and the acting only, that the old Adelphi won its fame; little care or expense was bestowed upon mounting its pieces; its dresses were usually shabby, and its scenes and sets were little elaborated, while its supers passed into a byword, "Adelphi guests." Ill-health having compelled Wright to retire in 1858, J. L. Toole, at the recommendation of Charles Dickens, was installed in his place, and made his first appearance here in *Good for Nothing*. A year or two afterwards he played Spriggins in *Ici on parle Français*, perhaps the most famous of all his parts.

In the early summer of the same year the old house, that had become a veritable dust-hole, was pulled down, and a new and more spacious building rose in its place, which was opened on Boxing Night in the same year. Most of the famous actors who had made its fame had passed away, or did not long survive the change. Mrs. Fitzwilliam, O'Smith, Tyrone Power, the great Irish actor, were dead; Mrs. Yates had retired many years previously, Wright was seen no more, Madame Celeste remained only a short time, in consequence of disagreement with the management, and of the famous company soon Webster himself, Mrs. Mellon (Miss Woolgar), and Paul Bedford were the only representatives.

The new Adelphi made a promising beginning with

The Colleen Bawn, the first of the sensational dramas, that is to say, the first drama in which a striking mechanical effect was the principal attraction, and the first serious drama in which the actor became of secondary importance to the mechanist and scene-painter. There had been shaking waters and rolling billows and other watery effects before the cavern scene of *The Colleen Bawn*, chief among which was the famous rolling wave in *Acis and Galatea* at Drury Lane in Macready's time; but transparent stage-water had never before been seen, and a few yards of blue gauze did more than all the finest acting in the world could have accomplished, it filled the Adelphi for hundreds of nights, it filled the treasuries of provincial managers, it sent people to the theatre that had never been before, and it made the fortune of the author. Yet it is said that he was not actually the inventor of the wonderful thing, but that the idea first occurred to an old stage carpenter while he was constructing the scene.

Nevertheless the piece was well acted. Myles-na-Coppeleen was, with Shaun the Post, Boucicault's best part; Mrs. Boucicault was a charming Colleen Bawn; Falconer was the Danny Mann; and it could not have been better played; indeed, every part was almost perfect in its way, and the drama was very cleverly constructed. But there is no denying that, but for the blue gauze, *The Colleen Bawn* might not have run twenty nights.

Boucicault had treated the Adelphi audiences to water in his first essay in the sensational school; in his next, *The Octoroon*, produced in November, 1861, he gave them fire.

At this time there were only two kinds of theatrical entertainment the public would patronise—the sensational and the burlesque—and the metropolitan theatres, with one or two exceptions, were divided between the pair. As the person who brought the grist to the mill, Boucicault soon became the paramount power at the Adelphi; an excellent stage manager and a stern reformer, he certainly did considerable service in sweeping away the cobwebs of antiquated tradition which had nowhere gathered thicker than here; and he must be coupled with Fechter and the Bancrofts as among the pioneers in the reform of the English stage.

The Octoroon, however, did not rival its predecessor in attraction, and the audience was sent through fire *and* water after a time, that is to say, the two sensations were given nightly. A wretched piece called *Grimaldi; or, the Life of an Actress*, and a new version of the old drama of *The Vampire* called *The Phantom*, in which the author enacted an Irish ghost, who could only be brought back to a corporeal state by being laid in "the moonbames," afterwards supplemented *The Octoroon*, but with only doubtful success. A quarrel between the two partners sent Boucicault to Drury Lane.

The Dead Heart, however, more than compensated by its popularity for the withdrawal of the great Dion. Miss Avonia Jones, Gustavus Brooke's widow, now varied the reign of melodrama by classical tragedy, and made some impression as Medea. In the autumn of 1863 the Adelphi scored a most emphatic success by the appearance of Miss Bateman in an adaptation of a German play called *Deborah*, rechristened *Leah*. It was a gloomy and monotonous work, but the actress gave so powerful and original a rendering of the central figure that it took with the public at once; gauze waters, burning ships, railway accidents, stone quarries, were all forgotten, and for 210 nights everybody rushed to shudder and weep over the wrongs and to thrill at the awful curse of the vengeful and broken-hearted Jewess. Miss Bateman came to us from America, though she had appeared with her sister in London as a sort of juvenile phenomenon as early as 1850.

After a tour in the provinces, Miss Bateman returned to the Adelphi in 1865, and opened as Julia in *The Hunchback;* but she was essentially a one-part actress, and failed to convince the playgoers as Knowles's disagreeable heroine. Married in 1866, she took a formal leave of the stage at Her Majesty's Theatre, and, as a matter of course, returned to it two years afterwards.

The next great attraction at the Adelphi was Joseph Jefferson, who opened there as Rip Van Winkle, September 4th, 1865. No truer, more pathetic, or purely artistic piece of acting, within its limits, has ever been seen upon the English stage than Jefferson's rendering of Washington Irving's vagabond hero, and it is satisfactory to reflect that without any meretricious effects, without a suspicion of the least pandering to degraded tastes, it crowded the house for 172 nights.

Fechter was here in 1868, when *No Thoroughfare* was produced, furnishing the great French actor with one of the most remarkable of his impersonations, and Webster with his last original character, Joey Ladle. Previous to this, in the same year, a version of *Monte Cristo* was brought out, with a cast exceptionally fine, including George Belmore, Mrs. Leigh Murray, Fechter, Webster, Carlotta Leclercq, Miss Woolgar, Arthur Stirling, Henry Ashley, Tom Stuart; but it was a failure. In the autumn of 1870, Webster, having fallen into difficulties, took Chatterton into partnership, and the theatre was announced to be under their joint management.

Two years later, after a reign of twenty-eight years,

Webster finally retired, upon a rental paid him by Chatterton, whose name now appeared alone at the head of the bills. Fechter played his last engagement in England here in the same year; and Madame Celeste, alas, reappeared upon the scene of her former triumphs, only to sadden old playgoers by comparisons between the past and present, and to excite the incredulity of younger ones. And this was not her last appearance; again at the end of 1874 she exhibited the wreck of her fine powers to an unsympathising audience.

During these years there is little worth recording in the annals of the Adelphi; revivals of old successes, with a sprinkling of new plays, Irish and otherwise, and a short season of English opera under Carl Rosa in 1873, when *The Merry Wives of Windsor* was produced, chiefly distinguished the Chatterton management; a remarkable run was achieved in the last-named year with Burnand's *Proof*, admirably cast. After Chatterton's downfall the theatre fell into the hands of a marine-store dealer named Clark, and the glory of the old house seemed to have indeed departed. I must not omit to mention the very great success achieved by Boucicault's Irish drama, *The Shaughraun*, which had a very long run.

The Gatti régime, however, that started in 1879, was destined to resuscitate its fortunes, though its inauguration was very ominous. Handsomely redecorated and reconstructed, it opened with a melodrama called *The Crimson Cross*, for which Hermann Vezin, Henry Neville, Adelaide Neilson were engaged. But the first night was one of the cruellest fiascoes I have ever witnessed. There was a dead set against the play, which was literally hooted, though I have heard worse well applauded. Revivals and new plays followed, supported by the same "star" company, but with no great results. Charles Warner, whose energy and breadth of style were excellently suited to the house, was leading man for some time, appearing as Michael Strogoff, Richard Pride, and Tom Robinson.

But, perhaps, the first assured success was Henry Pettit's *Taken from Life*, December, 1881. Pettit was an ideal *playwright* in the exact sense of the word; he was destitute of literary form, his dialogue was utterly commonplace, his characters mere lay figures, but he had a knack of constructing plots out of ancient conventions, of dressing up telling situations, and an unerring eye for stage effect that appealed more strongly to the general public than would any work of genius. It mattered nothing that he used the same stories, situations, and puppets, with slight variations, over and over again; people flocked to see his dramas, and were as delighted with the *réchauffé*, nay, far more so, than if it had been the most startling novelty; for the ordinary playgoer loves to anticipate the end of the story, and is dissatisfied if the author prove too cunning for him.

Edwin Booth was here in 1882, and made some impression in *The Fool's Revenge*, his Bertuccio being a very powerful performance. In the next year G. R. Sims first co-operated with Pettit, and *In The Ranks* was their joint production. The partnership proved a phenomenal success, and was carried on until death dissolved it. Dramas by Wilkie Collins, Robert Buchanan, Charles Reade, Comyns Carr, Haddon Chambers, well acted, perfectly mounted, were produced, but none pleased like the Pettit and Sims mixture. William Terriss succeeded Warner as leading man, and in such dramas as *The Union Jack*, *The Silver Falls*, rendered himself a supreme favourite; his handsome person, bold, breezy, aggressive style exactly fitting him for the heroes of Adelphi melodrama. In 1889 he made a trip to America, and on his return went to Drury Lane with *Paul Kauvar*, afterwards rejoining the Lyceum company. His place at the Adelphi was filled in the interim by George Alexander, Kyrle Bellew, Charles Warner, Henry Neville. When, after an absence of three or four years, he returned to the Gattis, his vogue in *The Swordsman's Daughter*, *Boys Together*, *In the Days of the Duke*, and other dramas, was greater than ever. Pettit's death and Terris's cruel assassination, December, 1897, inflicted a fatal blow upon Adelphi drama. Mrs. Brown-Potter and Kyrle Bellew were here in 1898 with *Charlotte Corday*. Gillette made a great success in *Secret Service*, and a less in *The Heart of Maryland*. Sarah Bernhardt played Hamlet here in 1899.

The old house was pulled down, and rebuilt with an extended frontage and handsome auditorium, and re-opened by Mr. Tom Davis as the Century Theatre, on September 7th, 1901, with an American variety show, *The Whirl of the Town*. But the town would have none of it, and the outcry against the barbarous new name brought back, in the following year, the time-honoured "Adelphi." The latest productions have been *The Arizona; Sapho*, 1902, in which Olga Nethersole made a great hit by her powerful performance of Daudet's heroine. *The Christian King*, 1902, with Wilson Barrett, was *not* a successor to *The Sign of the Cross*, and a stage version of *Captain Kettle* did not rival the popularity of the novel. Pending the appearance of Mme. Sarah Bernhardt, last summer, the management called in the most lurid of East End dramas. Yet *The Worst Woman in London* and *Her Second Time on Earth*, which might have been predicted would be ghastly failures, proved what might be called *un succès de curiosité.*

The old and the new Adelphi drama is seemingly played out, and the future of this theatre is problematical.

THE WEST LONDON, 1831–1903.

In 1831 a theatre was opened in Church Street, Marylebone, and called the New Royal Sussex. A few years afterwards it was renamed the Royal Pavilion Theatre, West, and in 1837, the Royal Marylebone. It was for several years under the management of John Douglass, and for some part of his time was little better than a show. An attempt was made in 1847 to regenerate the house when, under the name of the Theatre Royal, Marylebone, it was for a short time directed by Mrs. Warner, the Drury Lane actress; but her efforts were unsuccessful. E. T. Smith was manager in 1852, and J. W. Wallack in the next year. It was in 1858 that Mr. J. W. Cave commenced an association with the house which, on and off, lasted for many years. In 1864 it was rebuilt and enlarged so as to hold 2,000 persons, and became the western home of East End melodrama. The name of the house was once more changed, to the Royal Alfred, in 1866, and a better style of entertainment was attempted. Charles Harcourt was the manager for a while, and he brought the company from the Queen's, under Miss Henrietta Hodson, to play a short engagement here. But four years later the Royal Alfred was again known as the Marylebone, and the natives of Paddington were once more treated to their old bill of fare. Within the last few years the house has been handsomely rebuilt, and is now known as the West London, but it still adheres to its old line—sensational drama.

CHAPTER II

The Strand and the Royalty—A Chapter on Burlesque—
The Strand, 1832–1903.

"THE little theatre" in the Strand stands upon the site of a building that, from 1820 to 1828, was occupied, first by Reinagle and Barker's, and afterwards by Burford's Panorama. When Burford removed his exhibition to Leicester Square, the premises were converted into a temporary chapel by some wandering sectarians, who, after two or three years, departed elsewhere. It was towards the close of 1831 that Benjamin Lionel Rayner, a celebrated impersonator of Yorkshire characters, upon whom it was said John Emery's mantle had fallen, and supposed to have been afterwards the celebrated "Joe Muggins' Dog" of the *Era*, assisted by one Captain Bell, a turfite, and a Mr. Galbraith, who exhibited as a conjurer under the name of Henry, set about transforming the place into a small theatre. The alterations being completed in seven weeks, it was opened on January 25th, 1832, as "Rayner's New Subscription Theatre in the Strand," but was soon afterwards christened the "New Strand Theatre." The house was not licensed, and money was taken by the sale of tickets at an office outside the door.

It was just at the time that the disputes between the patent and the minor theatres were at their acutest stage, the latter daily growing bolder and more defiant, and the opening piece was a skit upon the theatrical situation, entitled *Professionals Puzzled; or, Struggles at Starting;* this was followed by *Mystification*, a trifle written for Mrs. Waylett, and *The Miller's Maid*, in which Rayner appeared in his famous part of Giles, concluded the programme. The interior of the theatre was tastefully fitted up; the decorations were white and gold, with silver pillars. The prices were four shillings, three shillings, two shillings, there being no gallery.

A few weeks after it opened the house was announced as being under the sole management of Mrs. Waylett, who, no doubt, found the money to keep the concern going. Here she introduced her usual light style of entertainment, musical farce and extravaganza, in which her delightful singing and *piquante* acting were the chief attraction. But it was the old story that I have told again and again, there was no public support, and on the second Saturday in November the new theatre was abruptly closed.

In the February of 1833 the doors were reopened, and Fanny Kelly gave her monologue entertainment, "Dramatic Recollections, with Studies of Character," another imitation of Mathews's "At Home"; but it was an utter failure. In October, Wrench and Russell attempted a dramatic season; at the end of the first week the Lord Chamberlain, stirred up by the patentees, closed the house. In 1834, Mrs. Waylett's name again appeared at the head of the bill as sole lessee, and beneath was printed "Admission gratis." Every kind of expedient was resorted to in order to evade the law; at an adjoining confectioner's, people paid four shillings for an ounce of lozenges, and were presented with a box ticket; while with half an ounce of peppermint drops, for which two shillings were given, was handed a ticket for the pit. An arrangement was then made with Glossop, of the Victoria, and the public were informed at the bottom of the playbill that by purchasing a ticket for the Victoria they would obtain a free admission for the Strand. An Indian chief and his squaw were engaged. Mrs. Nisbett "starred" here. New dramas, new musical pieces, new travesties were produced and acted by a good stock company, among which we find the names of Miss P. Horton and Oxberry. A great hit was made by a burlesque upon *Manfred* by Gilbert à Beckett, entitled *Man Fred*, in which Byron's hero was turned into a mysterious and melancholy chimney-sweep, and Astarte, played by Priscilla Horton, was rechristened Annie Starkie. But in March, 1835, the Lord Chamberlain swooped down upon the defiers of his authority, shut the theatre, and fined the actors.

In the next year, however, the New Strand was placed on the same footing as the Olympic and Adelphi, and then (May 1st) passed into the hands of Douglas Jerrold and his brother-in-law, James Hammond, a burlesque actor of considerable talent. The partnership lasted only a few months. Though a dramatic author, theatres, at least behind the scenes, were distasteful to Jerrold; perhaps he had seen too much of them in his young days, when his father was the manager of what was known as the "Kent circuit," which included Deal, Sheerness, and other small towns. Nor was the Strand speculation fortunate enough to overcome such prejudices, though probably his share in it did not extend beyond the productions of his pen.

At the dissolution of the partnership, Hammond spoke an address, evidently written by Jerrold, which throws considerable light upon the affairs of the theatre at this time. "We began with a tragic drama, *The Painter of*

Ghent," he says; "but as the aspect of the boxes and pit was much more tragic than we could wish, we, in sailors' phrase, 'let go the painter.' We tried something like a ballet, which after a few nights (but purely out of mercy to the reputations of Taglioni and Perrot) we withdrew. We found that our legs were not very good, and so we resolved to produce comedy of words and character; in other phrase, mistrusting our legs, we resolved henceforth only to stand upon our heads." Jerrold, under the *nom de plume* of Henry Brownrigg, wrote many short pieces for the little stage within a few months—*The Bill Sticker; Hercules, King of Clubs; The Perils of Pippins; or, an Old House in the City;* and lastly, the one-act tragedy, *The Painter of Ghent.* His Drury Lane success, *The Rent Day,* was also played here. In *The Painter* he himself acted the hero, but his success was not marked, and after a fortnight he quitted the stage, never again to appear upon it until those famous days of "splendid strolling" with Dickens, Forster, Mark Lemon.

Hammond was manager of the New Strand up to 1839, when, unfortunately for himself, he was tempted by the offer of a low rental to venture upon Drury Lane. His greatest hit was a travesty, called *Othello, according to Act of Parliament,* in which was reflected the struggles of the management to meet the requisitions of the law. Hammond's Othello, "an independent nigger from the Republic of Hayti," was a very striking performance, and Harry Hall's Iago was equally happy. A gallery, capable of holding 800 people, was now added to the auditorium, and the prices were lowered to three shillings, one shilling and sixpence, and one shilling, with half-price to all parts. In regard to the entertainment provided, Dickens's novels, then in all the freshness of their first issue, were freely laid under contribution. A dramatic version of the *Pickwick Papers* was brought out under the title of *Sam Weller* in the year of publication, and *Nicholas Nickleby* followed in 1839; drama, however, was almost invariably supplemented by extravaganza.

We next find the conjurer Jacobs in possession of the house. In 1841 the name of Harry Hall heads the bills, and the Keeleys are starring here, and Mrs. Stirling is playing *Aline*, a version of *Linda di Chamouni*. As soon as the novel of *Martin Chuzzlewit* appears, the paste-and-scissors dramatist of the theatre lays his claws upon it. Then there is an attempt at tragedy, which upon that stage must have been very ludicrous. But from Shakespeare the management has quickly to descend to Bos-Jesmen and General Tom Thumb! Fox Cooper is the lessee in 1847, and reduces the prices, to stalls, three shillings; boxes, one-and-sixpence; pit, one shilling; and gallery, fourpence. Oxberry is manager in the following year, and Edward Hooper's name succeeds his with significant rapidity.

After performing at the Strand as a star for a few weeks, William Farren took the house (1848). This is the first notable event in the history of the theatre. *The Clandestine Marriage*, *The Road to Ruin*, *The Love Chase*, and other comedies were given here with Farren, Mrs. Glover, Mrs. Stirling, Leigh Murray and his wife, Mrs. Alfred Philips, Compton, Henry Farren, and Diddear in the principal parts; comedies were varied by the inevitable extravaganzas, and one or two pretty domestic dramas by Mark Lemon. Mrs. Stirling made a success as Adrienne Lecouvreur in *The Reigning Favourite*, a translation of the French play, even after Rachel had recently appeared in the character. *The*

Vicar of Wakefield, with Farren as Dr. Primrose, Mrs. Stirling as Olivia, and Mrs. Glover as Mrs. Primrose, was a very fine performance. It was just at the end of Mrs. Glover's career, it was her last engagement. Farren left the Strand for the Olympic in 1850.

William Copeland, a Liverpool manager, tried his fortune here in the next year, and rechristened the theatre "Punch's Playhouse." Many familiar names appear in the playbills at this time—Walter Lacy, Charles Selby, Tom Robertson, Charlotte Saunders, Mrs. Selby, Edward Stirling; drama and burlesque were the staple fare. But a couple of seasons were sufficient for Mr. Copeland.

He was followed by Allcroft, the box-keeper of Bond Street, and in 1853, Miss Rebecca Isaacs, the well-known vocalist, was directress under that gentleman. Operas were now tried, among others *Der Frieschütz*. Then came Barry Sullivan, who had just been playing at the Haymarket, in Shakespeare. Allcroft, in partnership with Payne, continued to manage the Strand until 1856, when the latter took the whole responsibility upon himself, and brought the theatre to the very lowest ebb. Leicester Buckingham's name headed the bill during the season of 1857.

No theatrical speculation in London seemed more hopeless, when, in February, 1858, the Strand was undertaken by W. H. Swanborough, whose name, however, for pecuniary reasons, almost immediately gave place in the bills to that of his daughter, Miss Swanborough, a very charming actress, and a favourite at the Haymarket. At last, after five-and-twenty years of much cloud and little sunshine, the house was to enter upon a career of prosperity, and for that it was chiefly indebted to the pen of the late H. J. Byron, with whose burlesque, *Fra Diavolo*, the management secured an initial success.

The Strand has been more faithful to its earliest traditions than most other houses. From the first it was a home of burlesque, and with no other theatre, save the Gaiety, is that species of dramatic composition so thoroughly identified.

English burlesque goes back to the days of Beaumont's *Knight of the Burning Pestle* and the famous *Rehearsal.* But it was Fielding who first introduced that medley of song, dance, and absurdity which we now identify with the name; and Fielding took his inspiration from *The Beggar's Opera;* Gay's celebrated Newgate pastoral may be likewise regarded as the originator of the old English comic opera of Bickerstaff and Dibdin, and, indeed, of all the dramatic "musical melanges" that since that day have held a foremost place in the favour of our theatrical audiences. Kane O'Hara's *Midas* was in the late Mrs. Howard Paul's repertory, Apollo, with the beautiful song "Pray Goody," having always been a favourite with English cantatrices. Henry Carey, the author of "Sally in our Alley," wrote several extravaganzas, and *Bombastes* has not long ceased to be a favourite with amateurs. Travesties of Shakespeare were common enough seventy and eighty years ago, but they were of a rough, coarse type, and it was not until the rise of Planché that a more elegant turn was given to these trifles.

The supreme geniuses of the Planché school of extravaganza, Madame Vestris and Mrs. Waylett, however, had passed away, and with them much of the aroma they used to impart to those dainty trifles; as audiences became more mixed, a stronger flavouring was required for the coarser palates. The hour had struck for something new, and the man was there to supply it, a struggling young author just rising into fame, who boldly carved out a path for himself. He took the transpontine drama—of the ludicrous exaggeration of which the north side of the Thames was far from being free—as the butt at which to shoot his shafts of ridicule; the brigand in six-tab tunic and buckled belt stuck all round with daggers and pistols, and basket-hilted swords, with combats to music, the heavy father always invoking his grey hairs, and given alternately to cursing and blessing, the village maiden walking through frost and snow in silk stockings and sandalled shoes, of which playgoers were beginning to tire, here were splendid materials for burlesque. A capital company entered heart and soul into Byron's fun—"little Johnny Clarke," James Rogers, James Bland, who, until the appearance of Robson, was the king of burlesque, Charlotte Saunders, Miss Oliver, and Marie Wilton, who, after leaving the Lyceum, had passed over to the Adelphi, but unable to get "any business there," had, when the old house was pulled down, transferred her services to the Strand.

Nothing more delightfully *piquante* than Marie Wilton in burlesque can be conceived; her style was not that of Vestris or of Waylett, it was her own and nobody else's. As far as it can be described, Dickens admirably hit it off in a letter to Forster:—

"I really wish you would go, between this and next Thursday, to see *The Maid and the Magpie* burlesque," he writes. "There is the strangest thing in it that ever I have seen on the stage—the boy Pippo, by Miss Wilton. While it is astonishingly impudent (must be, or it couldn't be done at all), it is so stupendously like a boy, and unlike a woman, that it is perfectly free from offence. I never have seen such a thing. She does an imitation of the dancing of the Christy Minstrels—wonderfully clever—which, in the audacity of its thorough-going, is surprising. A thing that you cannot imagine a woman doing at all; and yet the manner, the appearance, the levity, impulse, and spirits of it are so exactly like a boy that you cannot think of anything like her sex in association with it. It begins at eight, and is over by a quarter-past nine. I never have seen such a curious thing, and the girl's talent is unchallengeable. I call her the cleverest girl I have ever seen on the stage in my time, and the most singularly original."

Fra Diavolo was the first of the long series of burlesques that drew crowds to the Strand night after night and year after year. It was the operas, varied by such old melodramas as *The Miller and His Men*, that Byron chiefly foisted his fun upon. One of the cleverest of the series was *The Lady of Lyons*, in which Rogers played Widow Melnotte and Charlotte Saunders, Claude. The former was excruciatingly droll, while the latter, who was called the female Robson, gave a very remarkable performance, especially in the last scene where she posed as Napoleon. It was a wonderful picture. He wrote for several successive companies. Bland and poor Jimmy Rogers, both excellent comedians, died before Marie Wilton left the Strand for Tottenham Street, and they were never adequately replaced; but the same facile pen continued to pour forth with equal fluency *The Kenilworths*, *The Ivanhoes*, *The Africaines* for Messrs. James, Thorne, Terry,[1] Miss Raynham, Mrs. Raymond, etc., and their associates, as it had for the original company, and the houses were still crammed to repletion.

[1] Edward Terry made his first appearance in London at the Surrey, in 1867. In the same year he played the Gravedigger in *Hamlet* at the Lyceum, and joined the Strand company in 1869.

And there certainly was a "go," an excitement about burlesque at the Strand in those days that was never approached by any other house. The enjoyment of the performers was really, or apparently, so intense that the wild ecstatic breakdown into which they broke at the end of almost every scene seemed perfectly spontaneous; it was a frantic outburst of irrepressible animal spirits, and they seemed to have no more control over their legs than the audience had over their applause. You might call it rubbish, buffoonery, vulgarity, anything you liked, but your temperament must have been abnormally phlegmatic if you could resist the influence of that riotous mirth and not be carried away by it.

Every vein, however rich, must be exhausted at last, and the same situations and the same word-twistings at length grew monotonous, more especially as the company became more and more mediocre, and the old spirit gradually evaporated. The acme of dreariness perhaps was attained in a burlesque called *The Vampire*, the last, or one of the last, of the long procession of Swanborough burlesques, 1872.

It was in 1868 (November 7th) that J. S. Clarke first appeared here as the immortal Major Wellington de Boots, and from that time was almost an annual visitor, playing *The Toodles* in 1869, while, in 1870, he made his first appearance in England in old comedy, and performed Dr. Ollapad, in *The Poor Gentleman*, for sixty consecutive nights. Byron himself had acted in several of his bright comedies, *The Prompter's Box*, *He's not such a Fool as He Looks* (1872). In the last year Clarke was again the principal attraction, as indeed he continued to be for a certain period during nearly every season. In the meantime the Strand had lost much of its distinctive character; a new species of burlesque, very much inferior to the old in its best days, was initiated with *Nemesis*, which, however, enjoyed as long a run, if not a longer, than any of its predecessors. It was new, piquant French, with Marius in one of the principal parts, and greatly took the public taste.

A new era in the history of the Strand began with the production of Offenbach's tuneful *Madame Favart*, April, 1879. Though she had appeared for a short time as Germaine in *Les Cloches de Corneville* at the Folly, Florence St. John made her veritable London début as Madame, and took the town by storm with her delicious voice, her charming acting, and beautiful face. Miss St. John and Violet Cameron, who played Suzanne, were at that time the two handsomest women on the London stage. *Olivette*, 1881, was as successful.

Condemned by the Board of Works, in consequence of the panic that ensued after the burning of the Ring Theatre at Vienna, the Strand, which had been rebuilt at a cost of £10,000 not many years before, was entirely reconstructed and enlarged, and opened on November 18th, 1882, with a burlesque by Byron and Farnie called *Frolique*. It was a failure, so was the next—*Cymbia*, by Harry Paulton. It is very curious, but the play with which a rebuilt theatre reopens is almost invariably a failure. In January, 1883, J. S. Clarke appeared as Dromio of Syracuse in an elaborate revival of *The Comedy of Errors;* but it failed to attract, and the management returned to comic opera, revivals of *Our Boys* and other once successful plays, and a dramatic version of Anstey's *Vice Versâ*. The latter was a go; but the prestige of the house had waned.

At the death of Mrs. Swanborough, who was in bankruptcy, Clarke announced himself as the lessee—he had been the real lessee some time before. There was a somewhat notable season of old comedies, during which works were resuscitated that had long been lying in oblivion, such as *The Busy Body*, *A Trip to the Jubilee*, in which Sir Harry Wildair figures, *The Suspicious Husband*, *The Wonder*, together with others better known—*The Clandestine Marriage*, *The Road to Ruin*, etc., supported by William Farren, Edward Righton, H. B. Conway, Fanny Coleman, etc.

Early in the nineties the theatre was sublet to Willie Edouin, who conducted it with varying fortunes for several years. *Our Flat* ran 600 nights, for which the authoress was munificently rewarded with £50!

A more legitimate success was scored by that admirable piece of fooling, *Niobe*. Distinctly original, with a subtle, classical flavour; less a burlesque than an irony, almost pathetic in its sharp-edged contrast between antique ideality and sordid modern realism, so artistically represented by Beatrice Lamb as the revivified Niobe, and by Harry Paulton as the Life Insurance Philistine, it had a singular fascination for the public, even for those upon whom the true satire and inner meaning were lost. It ran between 300 and 400 nights.

A curious outcome of the popularity of *Niobe*, which savours more of Paris than of London, was what, at the time, were called "Niobe wedding parties." It was quite the thing for those who had assisted at a wedding to go and see the Strand piece in the evening; one night as many as twenty stalls and two boxes were engaged by a hymeneal party. How this extraordinary function was first started, or by whom, I am unable to say.

During the last few years the Strand has secured very long runs with farcical comedies, notably *Why*

Jones Left Home, *In the Soup*; but *The Chinese Honeymoon*, thanks very much to the irresistible drolleries of Louie Freer and the "go" and the clever imitations of Marie Dainton, promises to reach the record of the house. As I write it is fast approaching its nine hundredth representation and is still going strong.

THE ROYALTY, 1840–1903

It was in 1840 that Fanny Kelly, having conceived the idea of investing the savings of a long theatrical life in establishing a school for acting, took a lease of some property in dingy Dean Street, Soho. The speculation proved so successful that she built a theatre upon a yard and a range of stables attached to the house.

An engineer named Stephenson had patented an invention by which stage and scenery were to be worked by machinery. By means of a series of cog-wheels, placed beneath the stage and moved by leverage power, "the wings" could be shifted, "the borders" changed, the scenery raised or lowered, and even the stage sunk, cleared of whatever might be on it, reset, and wound up again. Miss Kelly received the most encouraging promises of support from high quarters, while the Press, in a series of preliminary puffs, prophesied a complete revolution in stage art.

"Miss Kelly's Theatre," as it was called, first opened its doors on March 25th, 1840, with a drama by Morris Barnet, called *Summer and Winter*, in which the manageress and author sustained the principal parts. But, alas! the wonderful machinery which was to be the making of the house proved its destruction. Stephenson had represented that the whole arrangement could be worked by one man, but when it came to the test a horse had to be employed. The theatre was a mere bandbox, and the trampling of the horse beneath the stage and the working of the cog-wheels shook every plank in the house and gave the audience St. Vitus's dance. At the end of five nights the actors outnumbered the spectators, and the house was closed. But how to get rid of the fatal machine? The iron bars and bolts and stanchions which had been required to secure it were so embedded in the walls that it seemed at first as though the house would have to be pulled down, and, as it was, very expensive alterations had to be made before this white elephant could be removed.

Miss Kelly's Theatre was consequently closed until the autumn, when she reopened it with the monologue entertainment in which she had appeared at the Strand in 1833, but with no better success. It was her last appearance upon the stage. After sinking £7,000 in this unlucky venture, she resumed her school, and amateur performances were given until 1849, when it is said that a conspiracy, into the details of which it is not necessary to enter, was formed to deprive her of her property, which was seized in default of her paying the sum of £130. Miss Kelly survived unto her ninety-third year. At the end of her life a grant of £150 was accorded her from the Civil List; but she did not live to receive even the first instalment.

The persons who had been so anxious to get possession of the theatre opened it in 1850 as the "New English Opera House," with what was called a grand opera in three acts, *The Last Crusade;* but the public would none of it, they would not come to Dean Street.

For the next fifteen or sixteen years there is little worth recording in the history of this theatre, which was let for amateur performances. In 1861 it was chiefly reconstructed, and reopened on the 12th of November under the name of the "New Royalty" and the direction of Mrs. Selby, a well-known London actress; even then the performances were mainly for the benefit of that lady's "pupils," for the house was again "a school for acting." Burlesque was the principal attraction; Ada Cavendish, "a pupil," made her first appearance in public as Venus in the celebrated *Ixion*. In 1865, Adelaide Neilson made her début as Juliet, and even then created considerable sensation among the critics.

In the next year charming Miss Oliver, who had delighted Lyceum audiences under Vestris with her comedy acting, and Strand playgoers under the Swanboroughs in burlesque, ventured upon the New Royalty, and was highly successful for several seasons. *Black-Eyed Susan*, her great hit, was one of the best of the burlesques. Fred Dewar as Captain Crosstree, Edwin Danvers as the Widow, and the manageress as "pretty Se-usan" were as droll and charming as anything the stage has seen in this style of piece. The company was excellent throughout. *The Bohemian Gyurl* was the next production, in which one of the cleverest burlesque actresses even "of the palmy days," Charlotte Saunders, was immense as the Gipsy Queen. And Craven's pretty little domestic dramas, *Meg's Diversion* and *Milky White*, were almost as attractive as the burlesque.

Miss Henrietta Hodson was the mistress of the little house in 1870, but only for a brief period. She revived some old comedies—Tobin's *Honeymoon* and *Wild Oats*, in which she played the leading parts with Charles Wyndham, who had made his first appearance in London upon those boards in 1866 as Sir Arthur Lascelles, in *All that Glitters is not Gold*. As most people know, the famous comedian was on the Medical

Staff of the Federal Army during the American War. There is a story told of his first appearance upon any stage, which, if not correct, is at least *ben trovato.* It was at New York under Mrs. John Wood's husband; the opening lines of his part were, "I am drunk with love and enthusiasm." He got as far as "I am drunk," when, overpowered by stage-fright, the words stuck in his throat, and he could go no farther. It was his first and last appearance upon *that* stage. Actors who rise to eminence usually begin with a fiasco; mediocrity seldom feels nervous. That admirable opera-bouffe actress, Selina Dolares, made a hit here, in 1875, in *La Perichole.* Mr. G. R. Sims's *Crutch and Toothpick* was a great success in 1879. Miss Lydia Thompson, with W. J. Hill and Miss Wadman, played in *Little Orpheus and His Lute* in 1881. Two years later Miss Kate Santley, who is still the lessee, took over the theatre, and had it reconstructed and handsomely decorated. It reopened in May with Sims's and Clay's comic opera, *The Merry Duchess*, a good-natured skit upon the sporting Duchess of Montrose, with Henry Ashley, Kate Munro, Arthur Williams, and Miss Santley in the principal parts. Comic opera was now the go for a time, but there was not much money in it. Mr. Mayer, after he quitted the Gaiety, gave his annual series of French plays in Dean Street during several years. Here Ibsen's *Ghosts* was first played in English, 1891. Mr. Bourchier started as manager here in 1895, and met with some success. Mr. Alexander's name headed the bill at the end of 1896; in the next season Louie Freer was playing in *Oh Susannah!* and Penley in *A Little Ray of Sunshine* in 1899. In the following year Mrs. Patrick Campbell took over the house, had it beautifully decorated and upholstered, and presented *The*

Canary, *The Sacrament of Judas*, a very fine performance of *Magda*, *Fantastics*, Echegary's *Mariana*, *Pellias and Melisande*, and revivals of *The Notorious Mrs. Ebbsmith* and *The Second Mrs. Tanqueray;* Bjornsen's *Beyond Human Power*, etc. When Mrs. Campbell went to America, George Giddens took her place for a season and brought out *A Snug Little Kingdom*, *Sporting Simpson*, *Lyre and Lancet*, but not with satisfactory results. During the present year, Martin Harvey produced a Napoleonic play, *The Exile*, which had a very brief run. A season of German plays, now in progress, ends the chronicles of the Royalty up to the time of writing.

CHAPTER III

The St. James's—Memoirs of the "Unlucky" Theatre, 1835-1903

IF ever a theatre honestly earned for itself the title of unlucky, that theatre was THE ST. JAMES'S, which from the time of its foundation until it came into the hands of Messrs. Hare and Kendal certainly spelt ruin and bankruptcy to all who were rash enough to invest in it.

In the year 1835 the famous tenor, John Braham, then near upon sixty years of age, conceived the ambition to become a theatrical manager, and purchasing a site in King Street, St. James's, upon which stood an old-fashioned hotel, that dated back at least to the reign of the second Charles, called Nerot's, invested a large portion of the savings of a long professional life, £26,000, on its erection. It had taken many years of toil in those times, when hundreds were not paid for a song, to accumulate that amount, reckoning from the days when "Master Braham," at the age of thirteen, made his first appearance upon any stage at the old Royalty, in Wellclose Square. In building the new theatre, Braham, as many another actor has, both before and since, depended upon his personal popularity, and believed that his name at the head of the bill would be quite sufficient to secure a success.

The St. James's opened on December 14th, 1835,

with *Agnes Sorel*, the music by Mrs. G. A. à Beckett; it was styled, in obedience to Act of Parliament, "an operatic burletta," though it was a serious opera. Braham himself sang the tenor part, and was supported, among others, by Stretton and Miss Priscilla Horton, afterwards Mrs. German Reed, then one of the most charming of actresses and vocalists; the heroine being sustained by a pupil of the manager, Miss Glossop, her first appearance upon any stage. The prices were what we should call cheap nowadays: boxes, five shillings; pit, three; gallery, two; with half-price to all. *Agnes Sorel* was not a success, neither were any of the other pieces which were produced during a very short season of little over three months.

People said the theatre was too far west for the general public, and there was a considerable amount of truth in this; for although the St. James's is but a few minutes' walk from the Haymarket and the Opera House, it is only within the last few years that, except to visit the houses last named, theatrical audiences cared to go west of the Strand; and now—so the old order changes—the new theatres are all in that direction. But the main cause of the failure was the common one, the utter indifference of the public to theatrical amusements, and the abstention of the fashionable world, which patronised only Italian opera.

In the following April the St. James's was opened by a Parisian company, under the management of Jenny Vertprée, with Auguste Nourrit as the star; it was the first of that series of French plays with which this theatre was for so many years identified.

On Thursday, September 29th, 1836, Braham re-opened the house, which in the announce-bill he proclaimed to be the most splendid theatre in Europe, with a comic piece by "Boz," called *The Strange Gentleman.* Dickens always had a *penchant* for the stage, and might have applied himself to dramatic authorship had not the success of the *Pickwick Papers* for once and all turned the current of his genius into another channel. *The Strange Gentleman* was founded upon one of the Sketches, *The Great Winglebury Duel*, and is written very much in the style of a modern farcical comedy; it is full of complications, impossible coincidences, and grotesque situations; Harley in the principal part added greatly to the success, and the piece ran about fifty nights. Thereupon Braham pressed for another from the same pen, and Dickens, collaborating with John Hullah, then a young and comparatively unknown man, produced *Village Coquettes*, an English opera, after the style of Bickerstaff's *Love in a Village;* the manager was delighted with it, protested that nothing so good had been done since Sheridan's *Duenna*, and anticipated a great triumph. But all parties concerned were doomed to bitter disappointment. *Village Coquettes* was savagely cut up by the Press, failed to draw, and did not attain its twentieth night. The plot is on very old lines. A village beauty who all but falls into the snares set for her by a villainous squire and his friend, a rustic lover who talks sermons in a strong dialect, and a comic man who comes in for situations; not that its conventionality was any bar to its success, as it was quite in accordance with the tastes of the day. John Parry abandoned his vocal entertainment, to which, however, he afterwards returned, to play in this piece and some others that followed.

This failure, however, did not close Dickens's connection with the St. James's. In the following season, on March 6th, 1837, a farce by the great novelist, entitled *Is She His Wife?* was produced there, but with only moderate success.[1]

Braham in the meantime was appearing in a round of his old parts: as Young Hawthorn in *Love in a Village*—that charming old ballad opera that contains some of the prettiest of old English music; as Henry Bertram in *Guy Mannering*, with Madame Sala as Meg Merrilies; as Tom Tug in *The Waterman*, etc.; in any of which, not many years before, the great tenor could draw large audiences; but whether it was that age had "staled his infinite variety," or the public would not go so far west even to hear an old favourite, it is difficult to say, but the second season closed with another heavy loss. During the third season, Mrs. Stirling, Wright, and Mrs. Honey were added to the company; the first was already a favourite at the Adelphi and the Strand. Nearly three-quarters of a century ago Fanny Stirling was beguiling our grandfathers and grandmothers of their tears in the heroines of domestic drama, in which, after Mrs. Yates had quitted the stage, she held the foremost place, and charming them by her vivacity as a *comédienne*, as she delighted another generation by her inimitable performances of the Nurse and Mrs. Malaprop.

But neither Braham's singing, nor Mrs. Stirling's nor Mrs. Honey's nor Edward Wright's acting, could draw the public to the theatre. "I feel quite proud to-night," said the manager, entering the green-room one evening,

[1] In 1838, Macready desiring to have something from his pen, he wrote a farce for Drury Lane called *The Lamplighter*, but upon being read in the green-room it was so unfavourably received by the company that he withdrew it. Dickens afterwards converted it into a story for *The Pic Nic Papers*, but for some reason it is not to be found in any collected edition of his works. This, if we except such pieces as *No Thoroughfare*, in which he collaborated with Wilkie Collins, and *Mr. Nightingale's Diary*, written for that "splendid strolling" in connection with the Guild of Literature and Art, closes the list of Charles Dickens's writings for the public stage.

"I have just counted the pit, and there are seventeen people in it!" Nevertheless, he bravely held on to the sinking ship, until at the end of 1838 he found all his savings swept away, and himself, at the age of sixty-four, almost penniless.

With an indomitable pluck that few men possess, he arranged a tour through America, where his success, notwithstanding his advanced age, was prodigious. Having replenished his coffers, he once more returned to his native land, and took up his abode with his daughter, the Countess Waldegrave, until his death in 1856, at the ripe age of eighty-three.

But long ere that event took place the unlucky theatre had impoverished several others rash enough to undertake its management. Hooper opened in 1839 with a company that would now nightly cram any house in London: that fine veteran, Dowton; Walter Lacy; Wrench, the Charles Mathews of that time; Mrs. Glover; Mr. and Mrs. Frank Matthews; James Bland, who, until the rise of Robson, had no compeer as a burlesque actor; Alfred Wigan, then in his very early days, and playing small parts; Miss Turpin, a fine singer; charming Mrs. Honey, beautiful as a *houri*, with the throat of a nightingale.

How much the public appreciated such brilliant talent may be gathered from the circumstance that shortly afterwards a "Forest of Wild Animals" was announced in the playbills, and lions, tigers, leopards, panthers, and jaguars were brought to King Street to supplement the two-legged performers. Drury Lane had set the example by converting itself into a menagerie for Van Amburgh, and Bunn had found it to be a splendid speculation, against which Macready, with Shakespeare and a glorious company at Covent Garden, could not contend. "Our youthful Queen" having patronised the wild beast show at Drury Lane twice in one week, everyone was eager to display his or her loyalty by doing likewise, and for once the St. James's—out of the French season—was nightly crowded. When the lords of the forest had sated fashionable curiosity, a troupe of dogs, monkeys, and goats took their place. But ere this the best of the despised human actors had taken flight. Yet even with all his bestial attractions one season was enough for Mr. Hooper; and after the usual French company, which occupied the house during May and June, the "Poet" Bunn opened the theatre on November 5th, 1839, with an opera company. Six weeks of empty benches, and the doors were closed suddenly; and not again opened until the following April.

It was the time of the Queen's marriage, and Bunn thought that a German opera company—then a novelty in London—would, under the circumstances, prove attractive. Accordingly, an arrangement was entered into with Herr Schumann, director of the opera at Mayence, and as a further compliment to royalty the theatre was renamed the Prince's. The Germans proved even more attractive than the wild beasts, not on account of their talent, for, with the exception of one or two of the men, the company, to judge from the strictures of the Press, must have been execrable; but everything German was the rage just then, and the theatre was crowded nightly throughout the season. Unfortunately, Bunn was at the same time the manager of another unlucky theatre, Drury Lane, which brought him to the bankruptcy court. So the St. James's was once more in the market.

Thinking, perhaps, that the spell of ill luck was

broken, Morris and John Barnett, the former a very clever comedian, who had been in Braham's company, and the latter a very popular composer, undertook the management in November, 1840, opening with an opera called *Fridolin*. But these victims of misplaced confidence only just escaped ruin.

It was in 1842 that Mitchell, of Bond Street, became the lessee, and changed the name of the theatre back to St. James's, which it has borne ever since. Under his management, which lasted about twelve years, the house was almost entirely given up to French companies, and each season London had an opportunity of witnessing performances by the finest artistes of the Parisian stage. Mademoiselle Plessy, the delightful Déjazet, the incomparable Frederick Lemaître, Ravel, Levasseur, and, above all, the grand Rachel.

Though it was at Her Majesty's that Rachel Felix made her London début as Hermione in Racine's *Andromaque* in 1841, it is with the St. James's she is chiefly associated in the memories of old playgoers. G. H. Lewes has drawn a curious parallel between the great Jewish *tragédienne* and Edmund Kean, both in their careers, their physical appearance, and their style of acting; but it is with the modern Rachel, Sarah Bernhardt, that the critic of the present day would be most inclined to draw comparisons; both of Jewish extraction, half German, half French, the elder actress being the daughter of a Jew pedlar, born in French territory; in physique and in their careers the similarity is remarkable.

Upon her first appearance in this country at Her Majesty's, Rachel was received with an effusion perhaps even greater than that which has greeted her successor, for it was not only aristocracy, but royalty that was at

Rachel's feet; the Duchess of Kent took a beautiful shawl from her own shoulders and wrapped it about the actress when she complained of cold one night at the wings; the Queen presented her with a splendid bracelet inscribed, "From Victoria to Mademoiselle Rachel." When she fell ill frequent bulletins were issued, and upon her reappearance the Queen and the Queen Dowager were both present at the theatre to congratulate her upon her recovery. Allowing for the absence of royalty, we had a repetition of this furore when "the divine Sarah" used to be led down an alley of aristocracy resting upon the arm of some ducal host.

By the time, however, that Rachel appeared at the St. James's, in 1846, certain details of her private life having oozed out, the drawing-rooms were closed against her, and royalty held aloof, though her transcendent genius still made her the idol of the theatre. The serpent-like grace and the overwhelming passion of Rachel live again in Sarah Bernhardt; but the supreme excellence of the two artistes differs in kind. Rachel was essentially the grand *tragédienne*, the exponent of Corneille and Racine, the lineal descendant of the great tragic actresses of the eighteenth century—of Clairon, Dumesnil, Adrienne Lecouvrer—and though she abandoned the sing-song cadences of her predecessors, she never descended to the level of ordinary humanity; her personations were ideal, heroic, such as their creators conceived them. Amidst the uncompromising realism which universally pervades the spirit of our age, tragedy is impossible; our idea of tragedy is a murder in Whitechapel; Melpomene no longer carries the dagger and the bowl, but the kitchen poker and the carving-knife; tragedy is absorbed in melodrama, for melodrama is essentially realistic.

Sarah Bernhardt is not a *tragédienne*, but a great melodramatic actress; her Phèdre may be as terrible in its intensity as Rachel's, but it is human, while that of the elder actress was a hell-born chimera, a spirit of incarnate evil. Charlotte Brontë has well defined this when she says: "It is scarcely human nature that she shows you; it is something wilder and worse; the feelings and fury of a fiend." In another place she says more strongly: "It was like a glimpse of hell." All agree, however, that Rachel was deficient in the expression of love and tenderness, that she had no pathos; that is to say, where Sarah Bernhardt is strongest she was weakest. Her last appearance at the St. James's was in 1853; her last appearance upon any stage was at Charlestown, December 17th, 1856; after that she returned to France—to die.

Notwithstanding some great successes, Mitchell had his failures; among others the German company, which in 1853 played Goethe's *Faust* and several of Shakespeare's plays in Deutsch. German, however, was a language not greatly cultivated fifty years ago, and the experiment was not a success. At the expiration of his lease, it is said that Mr. Mitchell's balance, like that of all his predecessors, was on the wrong side.

A year later the unlucky theatre was taken by Mrs. Seymour, the lady who was so intimately associated with Charles Reade; an actress of some power, who had formerly held a leading position at the Haymarket and other theatres. The opening piece was by Reade, *The King's Rival*. Among the actors introduced to the London stage under this management may be mentioned the names of Miss Lydia Thompson and J. L. Toole.[1]

[1] Toole had appeared at the Haymarket two years previously, but it was just an appearance and nothing more; this was his first engagement in a London theatre.

Miss Thompson, in *Magic Toys*, made a great hit by her charming dancing, but Toole's metropolitan success was reserved for the Lyceum, under Dillon. An English version of Euripides's *Alcestis*, with Glück's music, the musical arrangements being under the direction of Sir Henry Bishop, proved as great a failure as *Antigone* had been at another house.

Passing over the next few seasons of monotonous failures, we find Augustus Braham, undeterred by his father's fate, taking up the paternal sceptre, and in June, 1859, producing an opera by Edward Loder, called *Raymond and Agnes*, founded upon the ghastly episode in Lewis's *Monk*. Hamilton Braham, George Perren, Susan Pyne, and Madame Rudersdorf were in the cast; but five nights of empty benches ended the speculation.

Each succeeding year brought forth a new manager; and Alfred Wigan's name next headed the bill, and it was during his short tenure that he gave some of those performances by which he is best remembered. I may especially note two plays, *The Isle of St. Tropez* and *The Poor Nobleman*, in which, even after the great French originals who had played them on these boards, he scored a remarkable success.

At the Christmas of 1861 the name of Alfred Wigan gave place to that of George Vining, but before the following year was far advanced, the latter had been deposed in favour of Frank Matthews, a most admirable actor of old men's parts. It was during his season that Miss Herbert, who had been attached to the St. James's since Wigan's management,[1] startled the town by her powerful performance of Lady Audley, at a time when

[1] Miss Herbert, after making her first appearance at the Strand, joined Wigan at the Olympic in 1856, and created some attention by her performance in Tom Taylor's *Retribution*.

Miss Braddon's novel was the sensation of the day. It drew for a while, but Matthews made no lasting success, and after a season Webster stepped into his shoes. He brought a fine company—Charles Mathews and his wife, Mr. and Mrs. Frank Matthews, Miss Herbert, and Mrs. Stirling—who played in a round of charming pieces.

When Webster had grown tired of losing money, Miss Herbert relieved him of his bargain. Herself one of the finest actresses of the day, she gathered about her some excellent associates, including Walter Lacy, Mr. and Mrs. Frank Matthews, etc., and a good repertory of pieces, embracing most of the popular comedies, of Goldsmith, Sheridan, and Shakespeare. Henry Irving made his second appearance in London (1866) as Doricourt, in *The Belle's Stratagem.* He created a favourable impression in the part; but it was not until he played Rawdon Scudamore, the villain of Dion Boucicault's *Hunted Down,* that he made a distinct mark. John Clayton made his début about this time. J. S. Clarke's first appearance in England as Major Wellington de Boots was at this theatre in 1867, and that excessively droll performance caught on at once. Like all her predecessors, Miss Herbert retired from the St. James's poorer in purse.

In 1869, after the brief management of a Mademoiselle de la Ferté, Mrs. John Wood's name became identified with this house, and as her first productions, *She Stoops to Conquer,* and *La Belle Sauvage,* made *the* hit of the season, people began to think that she had solved the problem at last how to make the unlucky theatre pay. If she failed it was not for lack of good acting, when Lionel Brough, William Farren, John Clayton, Henry Marston, Mrs. Hermann Vezin, Miss Lydia Foote, and last, but not least, the clever manageress herself, appeared in the same plays. One of her most important productions was Sardou's *Fernande*, in which Mrs. Hermann Vezin gave a very striking impersonation of Clotilde, and Miss Fanny Brough played the heroine—her début, if I am not mistaken. Fortunately for herself and the public, she soon abandoned sentimental for comic rôles. For a while it was thought Mrs. Wood was making a fortune; but from the season of 1873 she sublet the house to various speculators, and it was not until 1876 that she reappeared in her character of manageress. The next season was notable for an admirable production of *The Danischeffs*, with John Clayton, Charles Warner, Hermann Vezin, Lydia Foote, Mrs. Wood, and Miss Fanny Addison in the principal parts. Produced within a twelvemonth after the French company, with Madame Fargueil and M. Marais in the cast, had played it on these boards, it was a bold experiment though justified by the result.

Miss Ada Cavendish, under the management of Mr. S. Hayes, gave here a series of performances previous to her departure for America in 1878.

Early in the following year it was known in theatrical circles that Mr. and Mrs. Kendal, in partnership with Mr. Hare, were about to leave their snug quarters at the Court, and venture upon the unlucky St. James's. The people who believed in the legend of luck were fully convinced that the new lessees would go the way of the old; how signally their prophecies have failed is known to all. Favourites as great as Mr. Hare and Mrs. Kendal, companies as good, pieces as well mounted, had resulted again and again at this house only in ruin to the speculator; but the new management came upon better days, when the current of fashion, and popular taste as well, was running in favour of dramatic amusements. That it well deserved its success is not to be disputed ; some of the most perfect performances of the London stage were given during their eight years' management at the King Street house. It was Mrs. Kendal, however, who was the backbone of the establishment. She was at that time one of the best all-round actresses upon the English stage, the best grounded in her art, and the best representative of the thorough school. Born, as it were, upon the stage, and bred for her profession in good provincial schools, and under the eyes of parents who were steeped in its best traditions, Mrs. Kendal was proficient from top to toe ; equally at home in the brightest comedy and the deepest pathos of domestic drama, though not in the poetic. Yet this does not quite explain the secret of her popularity ; it is rather that she is the representative of all the proprieties of private life, the wife, the mother, the champion—with a very loud trumpet—of the respectabilities, in fine, it is as the matron of the British drama that the *pater* and *mater familias* of the middle classes especially patronise her, rather than for her talent.

Hare's and Kendal's first season opened on October 4th, 1879, with one of their great successes at the Court, *The Queen's Shilling*—Mrs. Kendal's Kate Greville was one of her most brilliant performances—and a short piece called *M. Le Duc* for John Hare. In January, 1881, Pinero's first successful comedy, *The Money Spinner*, was produced ; a clever, unconventional, but risky piece of work, as everyone in the piece is shady ; but it caught on, and established the author's reputation. A more assured success, however, was that delightful play *The Squire*, brought out at the end of the same year. Never did Mrs. Kendal appear to greater advantage than in Kate Verity. There was a newspaper dispute; Comyns Carr pointed out the extraordinary likeness the piece bore to a version of *Far From the Madding Crowd*, which he had submitted to Mrs. Kendal for approval. Pinero asserted that he had never read the novel, and knew nothing about the play. It was a very pretty quarrel as it stood, in which each party, as usual, protested that he was in the right.

Impulse, 1882, in which Kendal acted so admirably as Captain Crichton, Mrs. Kendal tells us in her reminiscences, was the most moneyful of all the pieces they produced. *The Ironmaster*, 1884, was another success. *William and Susan*, W. G. Wills's version of *Black-Eyed Susan*, afforded the manageress some scenes of heartrending pathos. There were also revivals of *Peril* and *A Scrap of Paper*—Susan Hartley was another of Mrs. Kendal's very best comedy parts—*Clancarty*, and others, to give the lady an opportunity of appearing in her favourite characters. A very excellent production of *As You Like It* brought down upon Mrs. Kendal's Rosalind an almost brutal attack from certain sections of the Press, who had eulogised performances of the part that could not compare with it. John Hare essayed Touchstone. It was the worst I have ever seen, and I have seen some bad ones, but then his style is ultra-modern. Mr. Kendal, who had been a slowly progressive actor from the first, was a very finished artiste in his own line, which is not the romantic or the poetical, but the men of the day, before he left the St. James's.

The expiration of the lease and the secession of Mr. Hare from the partnership ended the management in 1888. It had been in every way a brilliant success, and every production had been perfectly staged and well acted.

Rutland Barrington came next with *Brantingham*

Hall, a drama by W. S. Gilbert. His tenure was brief as it was unfortunate. Mrs. Langtry held the house for a short time, and produced *As You Like It* and *Esther Sandraz*. But the old fatality seemed to have fallen back upon the St. James's until the advent of George Alexander, in February, 1891.

Commencing with a going success, brought from the Avenue, *Sunlight and Shadow*, following it up with Haddon Chambers's clever drama *The Idler* and *Lady Windermere's Fan*—the first of those brilliant comedies by Oscar Wilde, that promised another Sheridan, for such sparkling dialogue had not been heard on the stage since *The School for Scandal*, the new manager made a splendid start. Later on he gave another whimsical piece by the same author, *The Importance of Being Earnest*, which has been recently revived. Both were very much to the public taste. *Liberty Hall*, a pretty bit of Dickensonian domesticity, in which Marion Terry and Edward Righton acted so finely, did not prepare the public for the thunderbolt which was shot upon the Philistines from the stage of St. James's by Mr. Pinero on that May night in 1893, when *The Second Mrs. Tanqueray* first saw the footlights. It was certainly one of the most sensational first nights within living memory; the daring of the play, the extraordinary powers revealed by Mrs. Patrick Campbell, who, until then, had been regarded only as a competent actress, literally electrified audience and critics. "The greatest play of the century," was the artistic verdict. "The most immoral production that has ever disgraced the English stage!" was the whine of the Philistine. Controversy raged between the two parties, clergymen made Mrs. Tanqueray their text; but the work was so great, the acting so striking, curiosity so eager, that the public filled the theatre to overflowing, and Mr. Alexander's courage in accepting a play that even so broad-minded a manager as Mr. Hare feared to undertake was fully justified at the time, and yet more emphatically since. The part has been played by Jane Hading and Duse, studied by Sarah Bernhardt for production, and repeated again and again by Mrs. Campbell.

To the morality that is founded only upon supposed ignorance of vice, which, by putting a white handkerchief over an ulcerous sore, can persuade itself that the sore does not exist, Mrs. Tanqueray is an abomination. But to those who hold that exposure is warning, that it is better for the young to know the pitfalls in the path of life than blindly to stumble into them and be lost in the depths, it is a profoundly moral play. I was standing at the back of the pit one afternoon and heard two young men, evidently of reputable position, discussing the piece. "Well," remarked one, "I tell you this, if I had any connection with a woman like Paula Tanqueray, after seeing this play, I should cut her." So it was a moral to at least one person.

The Masqueraders, by H. A. Jones, which followed, clever as it was, did not enjoy a long run, perhaps because Mrs. Campbell failed as Dulcie Larondie, and Mr. Alexander's next striking success, early in the year 1896, was *The Prisoner of Zenda*, in which Evelyn Millard gave so beautiful an impersonation of the Princess. Plays followed by Pinero, *The Princess and the Butterfly*, 1897, an exquisite bit of work, but too subtle and refined for a general success; *The Conquerors*, 1898, evoked much disapprobation; Haddon Chambers's *The Awakening* was admirably acted by Fay Davis, Gertrude Kingston, and all concerned; Mrs. Craigie's *The Folly of Being Wise*, exceedingly clever, but not convincing; E. V. Esmond's *The Wilderness*, in which Eva Moore was delightful both as a *comédienne* and an emotional actress, and Alexander was at his very best, which is very good indeed. *Rupert of Hentzau* did not rival the success of *The Prisoner of Zenda*, while of the revivals of *As You Like It*, *Much Ado about Nothing*, the glory was to the costumier and the scene-painter rather than to the actors. The Kendals played a season in 1898, and made a great hit with *The Elder Miss Blossom*, in which Mrs. Kendal showed to greater advantage than she had for some time past, in a very fine and pathetic performance.

The notable event of 1902 was the production, on a most magnificent scale, of Stephen Phillips's beautiful poetic play, *Paolo and Francesca*. But it must be admitted the acting left much to be desired. Alexander was out of his element as the hunchbacked Giovanni; Miss Millard lacked freshness as the heroine, in fact, she was a little too staid; the rest of the caste indifferent.

If I were King opened the autumn season. With all its absurdities and perversions of history it was a capital piece of stagecraft, and most admirably acted, from the principal down to the smallest parts; the stage management was perfect, the *mise en scène* beautiful. Never has Alexander acted with more charm and *abandon* than he threw into Villon in the first act; a very striking performance was that of Miss Suzanne Sheldon, as Huguette.

In *Old Heidelberg*, his latest production, Mr. Alexander astonished his admirers by his youthful make-up; he contrived to cast off the years between youth and middle age, and appear as a veritable boy in look and word and action. I do not know when I have been so charmed as by the simple beauty, so fresh, so unstrained, so pathetic, of the love scenes between Ulrich and Katie, the latter so delightfully acted by Miss Eva Moore, who in the early acts reminded me of Marie Wilton in her best days, as no other actress has ever yet recalled the inimitable Polly Eccles. I could not pay her a higher compliment.

Mr. E. S. Willard, after a very long absence in the States, has held the theatre during the lessee's absence with a play by Louis N. Parker, *The Cardinal*, which he brought with him from America, and has proved a success.

The St. James's auditorium was entirely reconstructed in 1900; it is now one of the handsomest houses in town, and shares with His Majesty's the distinction of being the highest-class theatre in London. The only advantage the latter can claim over its rival is that it works upon a larger scale.

CHAPTER IV

The Princess's, 1840–1900—The Great Shakespearian Revivals.

DURING the early years of the nineteenth century there stood upon the north side of Oxford Street, not far from the Circus, a building called the Queen's Bazaar, used for the sale of fancy and miscellaneous goods. Burned down in 1829, it was rebuilt for exhibition purposes. Soon afterwards Hamlet, the noted silversmith, whose shop, at the corner of Sidney's Alley, Leicester Square, was a fashionable lounge for the *jeunesse dorée*, conceived the idea of transforming the place into a theatre, which was opened on October 5th, 1840.

That its construction had occupied some time is evident from a line in the announce-bill stating that permission to call it the Princess's had been obtained from the Queen previous to her accession to the throne; the public was also informed that "this new and elegant theatre was fitted up with a style and splendour never before equalled in this country." The first entertainments given within its walls were Promenade Concerts, the prices being one and two shillings. These were continued for some months with indifferent success; and it was not until December 26th, 1842, after undergoing considerable alterations, that the building was opened for opera, varied by light dramatic pieces. The bill was *La Sonnambula*, sung by Madame Garcia, Weiss, Templeton, and Madame Sala, the mother of the famous journalist; the extravaganza of *The Yellow Dwarf* being the after-piece. English versions of all the most popular Italian operas continued to be performed with such singers as Garcia, Anna Thillon, Miss Paton, while the dramatic company included Henry Wallack, Walter Lacy, Oxberry, and the Keeleys.

Hamlet had at one time been considered a millionaire, but he incurred heavy losses through not being able to recover on certain bonds, for large sums, given him by the Prince Regent and the Duke of York. This and the unremunerative capital he had sunk in the theatre brought him to the bankruptcy court in 1843. The Princess's was mortgaged for £15,000, and the management was now taken over by Maddox, a Jew, one of the principal mortgagees.

Maddox made no change in the style of entertainment. Several of Balfe's forgotten operas were first given here. Various extraneous attractions were added to eke out the operatic: General Tom Thumb was engaged to appear after *Don Pasquale;* Henry Russell sang "I'm Afloat," and other of his popular songs, as a light refreshment after *Much Ado about Nothing;* while an entertainment entitled *Freaks of Fancy*, supported by a Mr. Lands and his "Infant Brothers," mitigated the terrors of *Timour the Tartar;* domestic drama came to the fore in *Gwynneth Vaughan* (1844), with Mrs. Stirling in the title-rôle, and burlesque was represented by Wright, Paul Bedford, and Oxberry, in an extravaganza entitled *The Three Graces.*

The great hit of 1844, however, was *Don Cæsar de Bazan*, which has been so recently revived by Lewis Waller, with James Wallack as the hero. Scribe's piece, suggested by the episode in Victor Hugo's *Ruy*

Blas, took the town immensely, and rival versions cropped up east and west; the Haymarket produced one called *A Match for a King*, in which Charles Mathews played the impecunious Don; but according to those who witnessed the performance, no one ever approached upon the London stage the dash, the romance, and chivalrous bearing of the original. In the next year Wallack further increased his fame by his performance of Massaroni in *The Brigand*, a musical piece founded upon Eastlake's celebrated series of pictures; his spirited and picturesque acting, together with his charming singing of the song "Gentle Zitella," which was presently thrummed and sung by everybody, drew all London to the Princess's. James Wallack afterwards went to America and established in New York the famous theatre that still bears his name.

In the early part of the year 1845, two famous Americans, Charlotte Cushman and Edwin Forrest, made their London début at the Princess's. Miss Cushman commenced her public career as a singer, with a fine contralto voice, that promised to secure for her a high position upon the operatic stage. After making a successful appearance at Boston, her native city, as the Countess in *The Marriage of Figaro*, she took an engagement at the St. Charles's Theatre, New Orleans, as prima donna. Soon after her arrival, probably through injudicious attempts to extend the compass of her voice, her vocal powers entirely failed. This blow was all the more terrible since she had a widowed mother and sisters entirely dependent upon her. Her father had been a merchant of Boston, one of an old Puritan stock, but at his death left little provision behind, and all the hopes of the family were centred in Charlotte's prospects.

An immense distance from home and among strangers, her position became a terrible one. When reduced almost to destitution, a friend suggested that she should try the dramatic stage, and persuaded her to see the leading actor and director of the theatre, Mr. Barton, the father of the writer of these pages, upon the subject. He very soon perceived that she had fine capabilities. "But," he used to say, "I could never draw them out, try as I would, until one day I put her into a towering rage by certain rude remarks I purposely made, and then at last blazed forth the fire and passion I knew were smouldering within." She made her first appearance for his benefit, as Lady Macbeth, in the summer of 1835, and achieved a decided success. So poor was she at the time, that she had not the means of purchasing a dress for the part; pride forbade her making this known until the last moment, and then a costume had to be borrowed from an actress of about double her size, and made to fit as it would.

She now returned to the North, but misfortune still pursued her, for she had no sooner obtained an engagement at the Bowery, New York, than she was prostrated by illness, from which she had scarcely recovered when the theatre was burned to the ground, and all the theatrical wardrobe she had pinched herself to get together went with it. Even without such reverses, it was a terrible uphill fight, since she had to contend against such physical disadvantages as a face plain to ugliness, with a protruding chin, a nose like Macready's, and a raw-boned masculine figure that would have been scarcely acceptable in a male. I can remember her at a much later period, clad in a hideous beaver bonnet, a short, rough jacket, and very narrow skirts, striding up and down the stage during a rehearsal, and discussing the business with a gruff voice suggestive of anything rather than the soft sex. In Romeo she made an immense hit, and a yet greater sensation as Nancy Sikes, considered in America one of her greatest parts, though I do not think she ever performed it in England. In 1844 she was brought from New York to Philadelphia to play the leading parts with Macready, with whose style she from that time became strongly infected.

Having reached the highest pinnacle of fame upon the American stage, it was now her ambition to test her powers upon a London audience, and at the end of the year just named she set sail for England. There was less gush and charlatanism in the theatrical profession in those days; the photographic art was not born; the *quid pro quo* system, "You beat the big drum for me in England, and I'll do the same for you in the States," was unthought of; and when Charlotte Cushman arrived in the old country there was no deputation to receive her, no suppers and no preliminary pars in the papers to rouse the curiosity of the public. She took humble lodgings in a Covent Garden street, made a pound of mutton chops last her three days for dinner, hastened to offer her services to the London managers—and was rebuffed by one and all.

How she ultimately obtained her first engagement in London is related by George Vandenhoff in his *Leaves from an Actor's Note-Book*, as told to him by the manager himself. "On her first introduction, Miss Cushman's personal gifts did not strike Maddox as exactly those which go to make up a stage heroine, and he declined engaging her. Charlotte certainly had no pretensions to beauty, but she had perseverance and energy, and knew there was the right metal in her; so she went to Paris with a view of finding an engagement there with an English company. She failed, too, in that, and returned to England more resolutely bent than ever on finding employment, because it was now more than ever necessary to her. It was a matter of life and death almost. She armed herself, therefore, with letters—so Maddox told me—from persons who were likely to have weight with him, and again presented herself at the Princess's; but the little Hebrew was as obdurate as Shylock, and still declined her proffered services. Repulsed, but not conquered, she rose to depart; but as she reached the door she turned and exclaimed, 'I know I have enemies in this country, but'—and here she cast herself upon her knees and raised her clasped hands aloft—'so help me G— I'll defeat them.' She uttered this with the energy of Lady Macbeth and the prophetic spirit of Meg Merrilies. 'Hullo!' said Maddox to himself, 's'elp me! she's got the shtuff in her,' and he gave her an appearance, and afterwards an engagement in his theatre." Not a day too soon, for her resources were nearly exhausted.

Edwin Forrest was engaged at the same time to appear at the Oxford Street house, and Maddox wished the two débuts to be made together, but Miss Cushman would not consent to this arrangement; she must rise or fall by herself alone. How wise was her determination was soon made evident by the crushing failure of the ranting, roaring Bowery idol.

Miss Cushman's first appearance upon the English stage was on February 14th, 1845; the part she selected was Bianca, in the now almost forgotten tragedy of *Fazio*. As soon as she was fairly in the great scenes of the play, her power and intensity, her pathos and *abandon*, carried away the house. She used to relate in after years how, being so completely overcome by excitement and the nervousness of a first appearance before the most critical audience in the world, she lost for a moment all self-command, and only recovered her presence of mind through the long-continued applause. But when she faced the house, the sight that met her eyes thrilled her in a manner she could never forget. The audience had risen *en masse*, some had mounted on their seats, and were frantically waving hats and handkerchiefs, and wildly cheering. "All my successes put together since I have been upon the stage would not come near my success in London," she wrote to her mother.

Her own success being assured, Miss Cushman made no objection to perform occasionally with Forrest, who, however, soon retired from the scene of his discomfiture. Burning with rage, he accused Macready of having organised a clique and of joining in the hisses against him. There was not a shadow of evidence to support the charge, but it nearly proved fatal to the English tragedian, for when he visited America, Forrest so incited the New Yorkers against him that it led to what were called the Forrest riots, during which some twenty persons were killed; and Macready narrowly escaped with his life.

But to return to Miss Cushman: she played a round of legitimate parts, Lady Macbeth, Julia in *The Hunchback*, Rosalind, and others, with ever-increasing success, but probably produced the most profound impression of all in the character of Meg Merrilies.

Wonderful as it was, the Meg Merrilies of Miss Cushman, however, bore no more resemblance to Scott's old crone than did the witches of Shakespeare to the wretched old hags that Scotch James persecuted. The Meg of Charlotte Cushman was a sibyl, a pythoness, before whose oracular utterances the boldest might have trembled. What a thrill went through the audience as she suddenly darted from the side scene and then stood motionless, with one claw-like finger of a skeleton hand pointed at Henry Bertram; what a face! blanched and tanned and wrinkled and scarred, as it were, by the storms of centuries; blear-eyed, with Medusa-like grey locks straggling from beneath a kind of turban, while the tall, bony figure was clad in a mass of indescribable rags, shreds, patches of all colours. Who that ever heard it can forget her delivery of the prophecy, more especially of the two last lines:—

> "Till Bertram's might and Bertram's right
> Shall meet on Ellangowan's height."

The tall, weird figure on tiptoe, the withered arms thrown up, one holding the staff far above her head, the flashing eyes, the deep, rough voice rising to the shriek of a bird of prey upon the final word—it was not mere acting, it was an inspiration as great as anything Rachel ever achieved. I once heard an old actor, John Rouse, who played Dandie Dinmont with her, say that he had to turn away his head while supporting her in the death scene; and I have seen ladies in the theatre cover their faces with their hands, unable to endure the sight of the dying agonies of that awful face in the last fierce struggle. When all was over, she was borne off the stage. Some little time elapsed between her death and the fall of the curtain, sufficient for her to wash off her hideous mask, and paint and powder her face, though the dress was unchanged, for the call. It was a curious bit of coquetry for so great an artiste, but she invariably did it.

Miss Cushman's engagement at the Princess's extended over eighty-four nights, not consecutive, however; opera and other lighter entertainments alternated with her performances; an arrangement far more favourable to artistic acting than the present grinding and monotonous drudgery of unbroken long runs. Miss Cushman remained in England until 1850, but did not again appear at the Princess's.

Her next engagement was at the Haymarket, where she played Romeo to her sister Susan's Juliet. The great American actress was an ideal Romeo. Perhaps not since the days of Spranger Barry had the Mantuan lover been interpreted with such a glow of passion and such fine fury. Being a woman, she had none of that *mauvaise honte* which has marred all our later Romeos, who, utterly incapable of assimilating the exquisite poetry of the character, have walked the stage in constant fear of a vulgar laugh, and, by that very self-consciousness, have deservedly evoked it. Not even an English hobbledehoy, that quintessence of vulgarity, could have laughed at the rhapsodies of the Balcony Scene poured forth with the fiery eloquence of Charlotte Cushman. Neither was she less effective in the Tybalt and Friar scenes; the vehemence of her rage and despair was as firm and as convincing as the glow of her amorous passion. Again, her appearance eminently adapted her for the part. It was no woman masquerading in male attire, but such a well-built youth as we might imagine young Montague to have been in life, not handsome, but fervid, true, brave, chivalrous, all that would have fascinated the lovely Capulet.

In 1850, Miss Cushman went back to America, but paid a second visit to England in 1852, performing with undiminished success in London, and starring throughout the provinces, until 1857, when, returning to her native country, she finally retired from the stage in New York in 1861. She lived in retirement for fifteen years, dying in 1876.

During the entire period of Maddox's management, opera occupied a prominent position in the Princess's programme; the works of native composers—Balfe, Linley, Loder—alternating with foreign masters. Here was produced, in 1849, Loder's charming *Night Dancers;* in the same year Alfred Wigan delighted London with his fine performance of Achille Dufard, in *The First Night*. In the next year we find Louisa Pyne and Harrison singing in *Gustavus*.

At the close of the season we have arrived at, Maddox grew tired of a speculation which was, to say the least, not remunerative, and on September 28th, 1850, the theatre was reopened under the joint management of Charles Kean and Robert Keeley.[1] The initial performance was *Twelfth Night*, with Mr. and Mrs. Keeley, Harley, Meadows, Addison, Ryder, Vining, etc., in the principal parts. The next revival was *Henry IV.*, with that fine old actor, Bartley, perhaps the last of the Falstaffs, as the fat knight.

The advent of Charles Kean to the management of the Princess's Theatre commenced a most important era in our stage history. In Shakespearian revivals he had been anticipated by Charles Kemble and Macready at Covent Garden and Drury Lane, and the latter had left little or nothing to be improved upon. It was, perhaps, for the acclimatisation of the higher school of French melodrama that his management was chiefly remarkable. *Pauline*, a very powerful drama founded upon one of Dumas's shorter stories, was a new sensation, combining

[1] The partnership was dissolved in the following year, and Kean remained sole lessee until the end.

as it did the incidents of a transpontine play with the refinement of the legitimate. There is a story told of Queen Victoria becoming so excited over one of the scenes that she held the curtains of her box convulsively grasped until the situation was past. This play created a host of imitations, in which a fascinating hero, beneath a polished and gentle exterior, hid the heart of a tiger; while the duel scene, where a loaded and an unloaded pistol are placed beneath the tablecloth, and each combatant draws his weapon by chance, has been copied again and again.

Pauline, and the success of a much more notable production, *The Corsican Brothers*, Gallicised our stage for a generation. The thrilling mysticism of the story of the twin brothers—in those anti-spiritualistic days—that awfully real ghost, without the conventional blue fire of ancient melodrama, that glided upon the scene in so incomprehensible a manner; the weird melody that haunted us night and day after hearing it; that terrible duel, the like of which had never been seen by an English audience accustomed to associate "a terrific combat!!!" with short basket-hilted swords chopped in time to music, the whole thing divested of all the vulgar, noisy elements of the old school, fascinated the playgoer; it was veritably a new dish for his jaded palate, and from that time he was continually craving for more like it.

When the play was revived by Irving, with an elaboration of detail never dreamed of in the days of its first production, the old playgoers flocked to the Lyceum, eager to renew the old impressions; but, alas! the novelty was faded, the ghost music no longer thrilled them; the famous sliding trap was criticised and pronounced clumsy and absurd; and even the duel scene, marvellously as it was done, fell flat. The younger shrugged their shoulders, and thought how much they had advanced in ideas of stage art, while their elders felt disappointed. But the exultation of the one and the humiliation of the other were equally unfounded; the theme of the famous French drama, with endless variations, had been taken up so frequently since its production that it was but an oft-told story to a new generation.

Kean's performance of the twin brothers was a fine and impressive piece of acting, with a peculiar charm in the first act, though not so true to nature as that of Fechter, who was the original at the Porte St. Martin. But no Château Renaud approached the first representatives, Alfred Wigan and Walter Lacy, in ease and polish and quiet intensity.

It was just the period at which the theatre had reached its lowest ebb in popular estimation, and, most fatal of all sins, was unfashionable, that Charles Kean entered upon the management of the Princess's. With one or two exceptions, the West End houses staged their productions in the shabbiest and most slovenly manner: the dresses were barbarously inappropriate and tawdry, the scenery dingy and primitive. Charles Kean reformed this altogether. But in the fifties the time was hardly ripe, audiences were cold and indifferent, and Kean's earnest efforts were not sufficiently successful to tempt another manager to take up the task until Fechter opened the Lyceum.

The performances given by the Princess's company, by royal command, at Windsor Castle seem to have suggested the revivals, which commenced, in the early part of 1852, with *King John; Macbeth* followed in the next year, *Richard III.* in 1854, *Henry VIII.*, *The*

Winter's Tale, and *A Midsummer Night's Dream* in 1856, *Richard II.* and *The Tempest* in 1857, and *King Lear* and *The Merchant of Venice* in 1858. Shakespeare was varied with *Sardanapalus*, one of the most splendid and notable of the Princess's productions (1853), *Faust*, the French version of the story, in which Kean acted very finely as a French Mephistopheles, *The Courier of Lyons*, and *Louis XI.* in 1855. The revivals brought out were played only three times a week, a variety of pieces being performed on the alternate nights. It is remarkable how closely Irving's management at the Lyceum followed upon Kean's lines, in several instances even to the same pieces. Louis XI. was one of Kean's finest impersonations, but Irving surpassed him in intensity and terrible realism; the same may be said of the two Duboscs; of the twin brothers, as I have said before, the conception and execution of the two actors were much alike.

Certain salient points of these revivals seem to have been lost sight of and forgotten. When the Saxe-Meiningen company came over, everybody said that such grouping and such management of crowds had never before been seen upon the London stage; and thereby old playgoers displayed a wonderful shortness of memory, for the public entry of Bolingbroke and the captive king, which Charles Kean introduced as an episode between the fourth and fifth acts of *Richard II.*, was as full of animation, individuality, and colour as the famous Mark Antony scene in *Julius Cæsar*, as represented by the German company.

The writer of these pages has a vivid recollection of this scene—a winding street, filled with a restless crowd, every personage of which was an independent unit, acting apparently upon the impulse of the moment, laughing, jostling, fighting, neck-craning, indulging in horse-play, but never for an instant inert; the doors, windows, and balconies of the antique houses built on each side of the stage were crowded with eager spectators, some watching the vagaries of the crowd, others straining to catch the first sight of the coming pageant. At the distant sound of the trumpets, the street became a chaos, a shouting, scrambling, fighting mob, struggling for each coign of vantage, until the advanced guard, pushing back the people right and left, cleared a path. Then came the realisation of Shakespeare's fine description:—

> "The rude, misgovern'd hands from window tops
> Threw dust and rubbish on King Richard's head."

As Bolingbroke entered upon "his hot and fiery steed,"

> "You would have thought the very windows spake,
> So many greedy looks of young and old
> Through casements darted their desiring eyes." [1]

There were fine things in *The Winter's Tale;* the introduced Saturnalia might have passed unchallenged until the Walpurgis Night was seen at the Lyceum; and a picture more replete with classic beauty, poetic conception, and fine grouping than the Statue Scene it would be difficult to imagine. Notable among the stage effects in Kean's revivals, were the vision of Katharine of Aragon in *Henry VIII.*, in which the limelight was used for the first time, and the burning of the palace of Sardanapalus, a scene unsurpassed in terror until we saw the earthquake in *Claudian.* It is only by such comparisons that we can estimate our progress in scenic illusion, and do justice to the work of the past.

[1] In his present revival of the play at His Majesty's, Beerbohm Tree has followed closely upon the same lines, but with the advantages of a larger stage and the advance in stage arrangements since Kean's days.

In mechanical appliances the Princess's productions were at a disadvantage in comparison with those of to-day; the limelight was only just introduced, the electric was unknown, for stage effects; and the art of building up such scenes as the Temple of Artemis in *The Cup*, or the Garden of Olivia, or the Hall of Ulysses' castle, as seen at His Majesty's, was reserved for a later time. Not less remarkable has been our advance in the cost of stage productions. Kean never spent more than four or five thousand upon a revival, and it was considered marvellous in those days. Irving and Tree more than doubled such sums. Again, salaries were incomparably smaller. For some time John Ryder, who played seconds to Kean, and in such characters as Friar Laurence and Hubert has left no successor, received only £3 10*s*. a week, until discovering that Walter Lacy was in the receipt of eight, he threatened to break his engagement unless his salary was at once doubled; a request which was complied with. Now such an actor would command from £30 to £50 a week. On the other hand, Kean raised the ballet-girls from a shilling a night, their old pay, out of which they had to find shoes and stockings, to a guinea a week, and found them everything. Besides the actors just named, the Princess's company included Alfred Wigan and Harley, who was for some time the Shakespearian clown *par excellence*.

Charles Kean, with all his peculiarities, bad voice, diminutive figure, immobile features, and lack of impulse, was a most intellectual actor; his Richard II. was a very scholarly performance; his delivery of the poetical speeches which Shakespeare has put into the mouth of the unhappy King, his noble and pathetic bearing in the trial and last scene, and the kingly dignity with which he invested his fall, were full of beauty. The same qualities marked his Cardinal Wolsey, while I have never seen his Leontes, more especially in the last scene, approached. Whatever he did—Hamlet, Macbeth, or even Lear or Othello—was distinguished by fine taste, scholarly judgment, profound study of the text, and veneration for his author, and he essentially appealed to the cultured playgoer by his perfect refinement. I have read and heard the highest eulogies passed upon Mrs. Charles Kean, but when I saw her she was very stout and *passée*, with a sharp, high-pitched voice; but that she had been a very fine artiste in the days gone by admits of no dispute. Few actresses, however, retain their powers after a certain age; Helen Faucit was a most remarkable exception.

The runs thirty years ago were not long enough, and the Princess's was too small and the prices were too low—six shillings being the highest—for such costly productions to be remunerative. In the autumn of 1858, Charles Kean announced the farewell season of his management. The last of his Shakespearian revivals was *Henry V.*, produced in the following year, Mrs. Kean performing the part of Chorus. He made his final bow as a manager on August 29th, in the part of Cardinal Wolsey, though he afterwards appeared here in several short starring engagements.

In September of the next year, Augustus Harris, the father of the late lessee of Drury Lane, who had for many years held an important position in the management of the Royal Italian Opera, took the Princess's. Among others whom he engaged was Henry Irving, then a stock-actor at the Theatre Royal, Edinburgh, who appeared first in a piece called *Ivy Hall*, afterwards as Osric in *Hamlet*; but, as many a future great actor has before him, failed to satisfy his manager, and returned to the provinces.

It was in the following year that Harris introduced Fechter to the London public. It was not the French actor's first appearance in England, he had played with a Parisian company at the St. James's as early as 1846, but that was before he had made his reputation in *The Corsican Brothers* at the Porte St. Martin, and as Armand Duval in *La Dame aux Camelias.* He opened as Ruy Blas. We were more insular in those days than we are now, and the French actor had to contend against our prejudices and a strong foreign accent; but the charm of his style, his pathos, his passion, and above all, his beautiful poetical love-making—we have had nothing like it since—were irresistible.

So far he was upon his own ground, a French actor playing a French part, the ideal hero of romantic drama. But when it was announced that he was about to challenge comparison with the great English actors of the past and present, and play Hamlet—with a French accent—British jealousy of the foreigner began to bristle again; nevertheless, the experiment was the sensation of the season. On the night on which Fechter first played the part of the melancholy Dane on the stage of the Princess's Theatre was rung the death-knell of the traditional Prince of Denmark.[1] Whether the classic

[1] There is every probability that an unbroken tradition as to the rendering of certain of Shakespeare's characters, more especially Hamlet, though naturally growing hazier and less defined through each succeeding generation, was handed down from the days of the poet to comparatively recent times. Rhodes, who organised the first theatrical company after General Monk had declared for the King, was prompter at the Blackfriars, and prompters are always storehouses of tradition. Again, many of the actors of the Restoration, notably Mohun and Hart, and the latter was Shakespeare's grand-nephew, had played at the great theatres, and would have associated with people who saw Burbage act, and to whom Joseph Taylor,

grace of Kemble and Young or the new readings of Fechter and Irving be the truer rendering will be answered by each playgoer according to his individual preference. Hamlet, unlike the other great characters of the dramatist, has been a subject of literary controversy for the last hundred years. Hamlet, however, is a creation not of an age, but of all time, and is more *en rapport* with the psychology of to-day than it might have been with the age of his creator.

We have had so many "original" Hamlets during the last forty years, that we can scarcely conceive the effect produced by this daring innovator upon those accustomed to the orthodox rendering; he discarded black velvet and bugles for a flowing costume of plain cloth, and short black hair for flaxen locks; he threw all traditions, all conventionalisms, to the winds; he treated Hamlet as a new part, and played it according to his own conceptions, unbiassed by any that had gone before; he sat where others had stood; he changed all the sides, all the entrances, all the "business"; he ignored all the old "points"; he was free, colloquial, easy; all this was rank heresy to the orthodox, but hailed as a revelation by the majority. Yet it was an unequal performance. Never, perhaps, were the two first acts more beautifully rendered, especially the soliloquy, "Oh that this too, too solid flesh would melt." The scene with Ophelia was exquisite, but his delivery of "To be or not to be"

his successor in all the great rôles of tragedy, was perfectly familiar. Betterton was a pupil of old Rhodes, and must have been well drilled in the ways of his predecessors; and although the influence of the French stage may have considerably modified his manner, he would have religiously adhered to the general "business" of the parts, for which actors used to have such a superstitious reverence that even a change of side for entrance was regarded as little short of heresy. Betterton's traditions descended to Booth and so on to Quin, Macklin, David Garrick, the Kembles, Charles Young, and Macready.

was villainous, the closet scene unsatisfactory, and the last act fantastic and not convincing.

The success that had hitherto attended Fechter's performances received a severe and well-deserved check when he applied his Hamlet method to *Othello*, the English public would not tolerate a nineteenth-century Moor of Venice.

In the October of 1862, Harris was succeeded by a Mr. Lindus, who, like many another man with more money than wit, took a theatre to gratify his wife's craving for publicity; she obtained the publicity she desired, though not in a way gratifying to her vanity, and her husband, in 1863, was glad enough to retire in favour of George Vining. The latter almost inaugurated his management by a first appearance that promised great things. I allude to that of Mademoiselle Stella Colas, whose fine rendering of Juliet evoked the most extraordinary enthusiasm among a large section of the playgoing public. Although a French rather than an Italian Juliet, it was undoubtedly a striking and powerful performance. But she was only a shooting star that quickly disappeared from the theatrical horizon.

Vining gave a number of famous sensational dramas to the stage. *The Huguenot Captain*, in which Adelaide Neilson made one of her earliest successes, with its splendid ballet, French grotesques, and elaborate stage setting. Then came *The Streets of London*, with its then wonderful fire scene, the fame of which, alas! has long since been extinguished by later marvels; *Arrah na Pogue*—the most delightful of all Irish dramas—with its ivy tower effect, that was more attractive to the crowd than even the admirable acting of Mr. and Mrs. Boucicault, or of John Brougham, or of Dominick Murray, immense as was his performance of Michael Feeny, or of charming Patty Oliver.

Never Too Late to Mend was brought out in October, 1865. It was a stormy first night, long remembered. It seems somewhat ludicrous to us who have heard the groans of the man on the rack in *La Tosca*, and the agonising cries of the tortured boy in *The Sign of the Cross*, to read of a dramatic critic—Mr. Tomlins was most probably under the effects of whisky at the time—rising in the stalls to protest against the flogging of the boy Josephs in the model prison scene. There was a great clamour for and against George Vining, who defied the cabal; the critics wrote down the play, but it ran 148 nights, and the profits were £8,000. In that year, 1865, Charles Kean played his farewell engagement here. His death took place in January, 1868.

After Dark was a great hit of the Vining management, though it was only another version of an old East End play, taken from the French by Edward Stirling, called the *The Bohemians of Paris*, with the famous underground railway sensation interpolated. Vining occasionally varied the sensational with more legitimate productions, such as *The Monastery of St. Just*, and *Donna Diana*.

Benjamin Webster succeeded to the management in 1869; Chatterton joined him during the second season, and in 1872 became sole manager. The new director attempted to revive the legitimate glories of the house by the engagement of Phelps, who appeared here in all his most famous parts, alternating with Creswick, Othello and Iago, Macbeth and Macduff, etc. Charles Dillon, a wreck of the man who had made the great success at the Lyceum seventeen years before, played an engagement here in the autumn of 1873, appearing as Manfred in Lord Byron's tragedy, a part utterly unsuited to his style. The management, however, had ultimately to go back to melodrama, to such pieces as *Janet Pride*, *Lost in London*, *The Lancashire Lass*. In November, 1875, Joseph Jefferson reappeared here as Rip Van Winkle, and was as successful as he had been at the Adelphi ten years previously.

And now the days of the old Princess's began to be numbered; the last remarkable production seen upon its boards was Charles Reade's version of *L'Assommoir—Drink* (1879); a gloomy and revolting play that was only redeemed by the extraordinary performance of Charles Warner in the part of Coupeau.

In November, 1880, the new Princess's was opened by Edwin Booth, who utterly failed, and so most inauspicously inaugurated the building.

Wilson Barrett came here from the Court with Madame Modjeska in the spring of 1881. But the Hungarian *tragédienne* failed to draw, and Bronson Howard's play, *The Old Love and the New*, was put on. Fortune, however, frowned upon the management until the production of G. R. Sims's *Lights o' London*, a new departure in domestic melodrama. Upon a purely conventional plot of the old school was grafted a number of clever realistic episodes of street life, which gave a freshness to old faces that at once caught on with the public. The author's next drama, *The Romany Rye*, however, did not quite equal its predecessor in popularity. But Jones and Hermann's *The Silver King*, the next on the list, far surpassed it. That 16th of November, 1882, was a notable first night. From the falling of the curtain on the first act, which gave a novel variety to an old theme, the play was a triumph; and perhaps no better work of the kind has been seen upon the stage. The three dramas were perfectly staged and admirably cast. Mr. Willard, then new to the London public, established his reputation by his original performance of the "Spider," in which he created a new type of the stage villain, and in each succeeding character he more than maintained his position.

After upwards of a year's run *The Silver King* gave place to *Claudian*, a poor play, by W. G. Wills, magnificently mounted, and with that wonderful earthquake effect. I can call up the scene before my mind's eye—the gardens, the porticoed palaces steeped in the soft Italian moonlight, the groups of classic statues, the subdued music, the voluptuous dancing figures, the oppressive hush of the hot summer's night. Then all of a moment blank darkness, a vivid flash of lightning, a crash of thunder, the roll and rumble that shakes the theatre to its foundation; a few moments' death-like silence, and the moonlight steals over the stage again and shows, where late were beautiful gardens and marble palaces, a chaotic ruin of broken walls and pillars. It was really terrifying.

A revival of *Hamlet*, 1884, was notable from a scenic point of view. An artist was sent over to Denmark to take sketches of Elsinore. It was the first time an attempt had been made to impart local colour to the tragedy, and the result, especially in the first act and in the play scene, was very striking. *Junius*, a tragedy by the first Lord Lytton, 1885, was another grand *coup de théâtre*. The ruined temple of Romulus, the streets and palace of the Tarquins, were unsurpassable stage pictures. But *Junius*, like all other classical plays, was a failure, and Mr. Barrett had to fall back upon revivals of his melodramas, until Mr. Jones's *Hoodman Blind*, in which Miss Eastlake gave a remarkable performance in the dual rôle of Nance Yeulitt and Jess, and Willard, another striking study of a villain in Mark Lezzard, was ready. Mr. Barrett was also seen at his very best in Jack Yeulitt.

In Sidney Grundy's *Clito*, Miss Eastlake, who had never yet been seen in heavy tragedy, fairly electrified the house by the daring *abandon*, the fierce power, the wild abject terror of her Helle, the Greek courtesan; the manager was also excellent as Clito, while the staging was quite equal to that of *Claudian* and *Junius*. But the classical drama pretty well absorbed the profits of the realistic. The five years of Wilson Barrett's management are worthy of all praise as a record of strenuous endeavour to advance the higher theatrical art, but, alas! it was only successful with the lower forms of it. Hawtrey succeeded Barrett, and I can remember his production of an effective play of Hamilton's, *Harvest*, in which poor Amy Roselle acted very finely. Then came Grace Hawthorne, who made a success with Pettit's *Hands Across the Sea*. Upon his return from America in 1888, Wilson Barrett appeared here in *Ben ma Chree*. Later on Miss Grace Hawthorne played an English version of *Theodora*, a wonderful get-up—her dresses, it is said, cost £1,500—but they did not draw the ungrateful public. The lady lost some £14,000 before she quitted Oxford Street.

Then came Mrs. Langtry, who revived *Antony and Cleopatra* on a most magnificent scale, and produced several original pieces. But the theatrical current was flowing away from Oxford Street; the gloomy, heavy house, so suggestive of a well, was never popular; and after Wilson Barrett's retirement, public patronage rapidly dwindled. In 1896 an attempt was made to bring it back with East End melodrama, as represented by *In Sight of St. Paul's*, and cheap prices. *Two Little Vagabonds* scored a decided success in the same year, thanks to the sympathetic acting of Miss Kate Tyndal and Miss Sydney Fairbrother. Charles Warner attempted to revive his old triumphs in *Drink* and *Never Too Late to Mend*; old Adelphi dramas were brought back to life with varying, but no permanent success. Versions of *Lorna Doone* and *Dr. Nikola* were brought out in 1901. *The Fatal Wedding*, 1902, was the last piece that had any run. The County Council has since then closed the house until certain costly improvements shall be made.

It is impossible for anyone to glance through these brief chronicles of the older West End theatres without being struck by the deplorable condition of things theatrical during the greater part of the nineteenth century, thanks to the freaks of fashion and the black wave of Puritanism that swept over the country from about 1830 to 1870. The wonder is that the drama did not absolutely die out under the indifference and hostility of the great majority of the people. For dreariness those forty years can only be compared with the reign of "the Saints."

CHAPTER V

The Vaudeville—The Court and the Criterion—Wyndham's Theatre—The New Theatre.

THE VAUDEVILLE, 1870–1903, was built for three of the most popular actors of their time—H. J. Montague, who had been playing the juvenile parts in Robertson's comedies at the Prince of Wales's, David James, one of the great favourites of the later Strand burlesque days, and Thomas Thorne, who had won a reputation at the same house. Such a combination seemed to be a guarantee of success. But it did not come to the opening bill, *Love and Money*, by Halliday, and a burlesque, called *Don Carlos*, April 16th, 1870; and it was not until the production of *The Two Roses* in the autumn that the public really took to the new theatre. Albery's charming comedy was an inspiration of the Robertson school, but the canvas was broader, the colouring brighter and deeper, though the dialogue, by the author's straining after far-fetched analogies, was more artificial even than that of *School*. Henry Irving had already made his mark at the St. James's and the Queen's, but it was as Digby Grant that he first rose to celebrity; it was a wonderful bit of character acting. And then how charming was Harry Montague as Jack Wyatt, and poor Amy Fawsitt as Lottie, and what unction that drollest of comedians, George Honey, threw into the part of Our Mr. Jenkins. It was a delightful entertainment.

The Two Roses had a very long run, and soon afterwards Montague left his partners for the Globe. James and Thorne were joint managers for some years, but ultimately Thorne became sole lessee.

All previous successes in the annals of the stage were left far behind by the record of *Our Boys*, which ran from January 16th, 1875, unto April 18th, 1879, and has been revived again and again, I know not how many times, not only at its first home, but at half a dozen other London theatres, to say nothing of the provinces. Yet there was in it only one piece of acting above the common, David James's Middlewick, but that pat of "dossett" butter did more for the comedy than all the talent of all the actors put together; it came home and appealed to *οἱ πολλοί* as no artistic touch ever could appeal. It was only a mediocre play; when it was first offered to them, the managers might have bought, at least all the metropolitan rights, for a few hundreds, but their faith in it was not equal to such expenditure, for which the author had much to be thankful; he made a fortune by the piece, and James and Thorne cleared between £20,000 and £30,000 each.

The earlier years of the Vaudeville have an excellent record of good plays and good companies; the scene-painter and costumier were always in the background, and the actor to the fore. Old playgoers will recall the excellent revivals of *The School for Scandal*, which ran 400 nights—the record; of *The Rivals*, 1883, in which the Sir Anthony Absolute of Farren, the Mrs. Malaprop of Mrs. Stirling, the Lydia Languish of Miss Winifred Emery, were worthy of the best days of old comedy; of *The Road to Ruin*, with Warner as Young Dornton, Farren as Old Dornton, David James as Goldfinch; of *Money*, with Henry Neville, Farren, Righton,

Thorne, Ada Cavendish, Mrs. John Wood, Miss Alma Murray; of others that I have forgotten. Then came a reign of farcical comedy, such as *Confusion*, which ran a twelvemonth; *Loose Tiles, Doo Brown and Co.*, etc., interspersed with more serious plays—*Under Fire*, by Westland Marston, and best of all, H. A. Jones's *Saints and Sinners*, 1885, a clever play and a keen satire upon the narrow-minded bigotry and hypocrisy of sectarianism, which aroused the bile of the Mawworms and led to a fierce controversy, in which the more enlightened of the clergy took the side of the author, and even recommended their flocks to go and see the comedy. Nothing more charming was ever put upon the Vaudeville stage than Buchanan's *Sophia*, 1886. Kate Rorke was an ideal representative of Fielding's heroine; and never was actor better fitted with a part than was Charles Warner with Tom Jones; he looked it and acted it to perfection. I think Lady Bellaston was Rose Leclercq's first essay in the middle-aged fine lady, and what a fine performance it was; no one has been found to succeed her in that rôle; and Lottie Venne as Mrs. Honor, so full of dainty quaintness and *espièglerie*, while Thorne's Partridge was, perhaps, the best thing he ever did. *Joseph's Sweetheart*, another Fielding dramatisation, though not equal to the first, had a good run. The acting was not as good; Thorne did not realise Parson Adams. Later on it came to Richardson's turn, and Miss Winifred Emery beguiled the town of its tears by her exquisite performance of Clarissa Harlowe, 1889. It was in this play that her future husband, Cyril Maude, I think, made his first appearance.

The later years of Mr. Thorne's management were not so fortunate; perhaps the *actor*-manager was too much *en évidence*. Old successes were revived, but not with the old casts; *Hedda Gabler*, *Rosmersholm*, at matinées, were played for the first time in England (February, April, May, 1891) by Miss Robins, Marion Lea. It was the commencement of the Ibsen craze, and although the British public did not take to the cult it has exercised an enormous influence upon our dramatic authors.

The original Vaudeville had one of those pinched-up frontages which characterised the old London theatres, that always sneaked back from public recognition as though ashamed of their existence. In 1891, the façade was greatly extended and remodelled and the interior redecorated and reupholstered. Little more than a year later, however, Messrs. Gatti took over the house, giving, it is said, £15,000 for the twenty-one years' lease. They inaugurated their season with another revival of *Our Boys*. One of their greatest successes was that uproarious farce *A Night Out*, kept in the bill for hundreds of nights. The engagement of Mr. and Mrs. Seymour Hicks has proved good business, as the long runs of *Sweet and Twenty*, *Alice in Wonderland*, *Quality Street*, and other successes have testified.

The Vaudeville is able to make the same boast as the old Gaiety—it has known only two lessees, and during almost as many years.

The Court, 1870–1903, which was first called the New Chelsea Theatre, was opened on the same night as the Vaudeville—April 16th, 1870—under the management of Messrs. Morgan and Oliver; the prices were cheap, the entertainment a mixture of theatre and music-hall. Rechristened the Belgravia, the theatre dragged on a brief and miserable existence until it came into the hands of the late Miss Marie Litton. The original building was a dissenting chapel, and the builders of the New Chelsea had not made more alterations than were imperatively necessary. The new lessee, however, entirely reconstructed the house, charmingly decorated it, and in January, 1871, it began a new and prosperous career as the Royal Court Theatre. *Randal's Thumb*, by Gilbert, was the opening piece, supported by an excellent company, including Mr. and Mrs. Frank Matthews, Hermann Vezin, and Mrs. Stephens.

An early hit at the Court was Gilbert's adaptation of *Le Chapeau de Paille*, christened *The Wedding March*, one of the most uproariously funny of the Palais Royale musical farces. Many may remember that leviathan, but excruciatingly comic actor, William Hill, as Uncle Bopaddy. After a long run here it was revived at the Folly in 1879.

But the Court never before or since has had such a sensation as the famous burlesque, *The Happy Land*, written by Gilbert himself under another name, upon his own fairy play, *The Wicked World*, 1873, in which the Government of the day was held up to merciless ridicule. Not since Fielding's *Pasquin* had such a pungent satire been put upon the stage. Ayrtoun, most philistine of Ædiles, went to see his "counterfeit presentment" going about with a pot of slate-coloured paint, with which he daubed all public buildings, statues, and monuments. "What is a ship?" asks a competitive examiner. "I don't know," is the reply. "Then you shall be First Lord of the Admiralty," is the dictum. The trio and dance of Gladstone, Lowe, and Ayrtoun with the *ensemble*, "Here a save, there a save, everywhere a save," were frantically encored again and again. But the Prime Minister was wroth, and the Lord Chamberlain ordered the make-up of the actors, which was so marvellously like the originals, to be modified. *The Happy Land* was afterwards revived at the Queen's.

In 1875, John Hare became lessee of the Court, bringing with him the Kendals, Amy Fawsitt, John Clayton, H. Kemble, and for several seasons the Sloane Square Theatre was one of the most enjoyable places of amusement in all London. What delightful performances they gave us of *The Scrap of Paper*, *The Queen's Shilling*, *A Quiet Rubber*, *The Ladies' Battle*, etc., etc. Wilson Barrett came to the Court in 1879, and in the following season the celebrated Hungarian *tragédienne*, Madame Modjeska, played Juliet, and in a new play of Wills's, called *Juana*.

Two years later, John Clayton inaugurated his management with a translation from the French, entitled *Honour*, followed by Boucicault's *Mimi*, founded on *La Vie de Bohême*, a beautiful performance of Marion Terry's as the heroine, but neither of the plays scored. Next a revival of Gilbert's *Engaged*, which was originally played at the Haymarket in 1877, one of the most scathing satires that ever came even from the pen of W. S. G. Henry J. Byron appeared as Cheviot Hill, the part created by George Honey. *The Parvenu*, *Comrades*, a play by Pinero, *The Rector*, a revival of Robertson's *Play*, and other pieces followed too rapidly for any great success. Arthur Cecil joined the management in the second season, and the partners associated themselves with an excellent company—Marion Terry, Mrs. John Wood, Mackintosh, Brandon Thomas, Charles Sugden.

No marked success, however, rewarded the efforts of Messrs. Clayton and Cecil until the production of Pinero's *The Magistrate*, in March, 1885, which literally took the town by storm. Here was a new kind of farcical comedy without a suspicion of French or German origin, without risky situations or a flavour of *double entendre*, and yet as funny as anything we had ever borrowed from Paris; it was a roar from beginning to end. One of the secrets of its success was its *probability*. Such farces as *Pink Dominoes* are utterly extravagant and impossible; but in *The Magistrate* one had only to grant the first premises, to admit the likelihood of an elderly gentleman placing himself in the hands of a boy, as Mr. Posket did in those of Cis Farringdon, for a benevolent purpose, which, as the author put it, was no great strain upon the credulity, and every adventure that flowed therefrom was within the range of possibility. Nor did the piece, like previous three-act farces, rely upon situation alone; the dialogue was witty and even brilliant, and the literary merit of the work incontestable, while the acting, down to the smallest part, both in *The Magistrate* and its successors, *The Schoolmistress* and *Dandy Dick*, all of which had long runs, was as near perfection as we can hope for. Mrs. John Wood, by her inimitable humour, would alone have carried the audience; next to this admirable actress were the infinitely quaint and droll performances of Miss Norreys, especially as Peggy Hesselrigg; next in order came Messrs. Cecil, Clayton, and Eversfield, while the *ensemble* was proportionately excellent.

The old Court Theatre was pulled down to make way for local improvements in 1887.

On the 24th of September, 1888, the new Court opened under the management of Mrs. John Wood and Mr. Arthur Chudleigh, with *Mama*, a version of *Les Surprises du Divorce*, in which the manageress, John Hare, and Arthur Cecil appeared. The new lessees were not as fortunate as their predecessors; Mrs. Wood scored a success in *Aunt Jack* by that nonchalant, daring humour that could say the riskiest things without offending; and a very clever comedy by Pinero, *The Cabinet Minister*, admirably acted by Arthur Cecil, Weedon Grossmith, Brandon Thomas, Mrs. Wood, and a good all-round cast, drew all London, if not to enjoy the satire, to see the ladies' magnificent court dresses, that cost fabulous sums. *The Amazons*, another trenchant satire by Pinero, was given here in 1893.

It is rather curious that at a time when the suburban theatre was becoming an institution that the prosperity of the Chelsea house should so decline. There is little worth recording after Mrs. Wood's secession from the management. *A Pantomime Rehearsal*, brought from Terry's, was played for the 400th time in 1892. The names of Lumley, Charles Hawtrey appear at the head of the bills, then Chudleigh's and Mrs. John Wood's reappear in a piece called *The Old Lady*, 1892; after that Miss Annie Hughes, who revived *Nancy;* Miss Robins followed with a translation of Echegary's *Mariana*.

In 1897, John Hare returned to his old home with much *éclat*, the Prince and Princess of Wales and the Duke of York honouring the event by their presence. The opening play was a revival of Pinero's *The Hobby Horse*, first produced at the St. James's in 1886, but not a marked success. Later on in the autumn, Humperdinck's *The Children of the King* was produced. *His Excellency the Governor* and Pinero's *Trelawney of the Wells* were successes. Mr. Kerr was manager in 1901, and staged a play of Ogilvie's and *The Strange Adventures of Miss Brown*. The first was a deadly failure. During the present summer the old morality play, *Everyman*, a most curious resuscitation, has been the afternoon attraction.

The Criterion, 1874–1903, stands upon the historic site of the old St. James's Market; it was behind the counter of a glover's shop in that market that George III., then Prince of Wales, first met Hannah Lightfoot; and it was at the Mitre Tavern close by, half a century previously, that Farquhar heard the landlady's niece reading *The Scornful Lady*, and struck by her dramatic power, introduced her to the stage, where she was known as Mrs. Oldfield.[1]

The Criterion, which was at first only an adjunct to Messrs. Spiers and Pond's new hotel, was opened in the autumn of 1874. An underground temple of the drama into which it was necessary to pump air to save the audience from being asphyxiated was certainly a novelty. It opened with *An American Lady*, a new comedy by H. J. Byron, Mrs. John Wood playing the principal part. Opera-bouffe, which was then at the height of its popularity, followed, and was initiated by the *Près de St. Germain*. The success of the Criterion however, was far from assured until Mr. Alexander Henderson, in 1877, converted it into an English Palais Royal by the first of a long line of farcical comedies, *The Great Divorce Case* and *On Bail*. The three-act farce was a novelty in England at this period, and, rendered as it was at the Criterion with almost Parisian vivacity and lightness of touch, made a great hit. *On Bail* was succeeded by *Pink Dominoes*, 1877, the first English piece that successfully broke down the icy wall of insular respectability, and induced the Mrs. Grundys to flock to hear naughtiness in their native tongue—in French it was always quite another thing.[2]

See p. 62.

[2] Schneider used to say that her acting was far more *prononcé* in London than in Paris, indeed, that a Parisian audience would not have stood what

Truth, *Betsy*, *Foggerty's Fairy*, *Fourteen Days*, *Little Miss Muffit*, in which Miss Kate Rorke made her first hit, and acted most charmingly in an extremely delicate situation as Mimie. It was also the first occasion on which Mr. Beerbohm Tree came to the fore. These are the best-remembered pieces of the early days of this theatre.

As burlesque has never been played as it was at the Strand in the Swanborough days, so farcical comedy has never been acted in this country, before or since, with the *chic*, the lightness of touch, the refinement, the neatness, the swing of the Criterion company—George Giddens, Alfred Maltby, Herbert Standing, W. Blakeley, Henry Ashley, Harriett Coveney, Lottie Venne, Mary Rorke, W. J. Hill, and others—with Charles Wyndham as the animating and directing spirit of all. Wyndham has always been regarded as the successor of Charles Mathews, but there is much to be differentiated in their individual styles. Mathews had not the *élan* of Wyndham, nor had Wyndham ever quite the easy elegance or the repose that marked the most mercurial flights of the elder Charles. Actors of different generations, each was equally representative of his own. But Sir Charles Wyndham has a power and versatility that Mathews never possessed, he has depth, passion, pathos, whereas his famous predecessor, away from the lighter vein of comedy, was not distinguished.

Wyndham had succeeded Henderson in the management of the theatre. Closed by order of the Board of Works for reconstruction, the house enlarged, superbly

delighted her English patrons. She knew their taste, provided it was done by a French actress and in the French tongue. But ladies who have gone through an elaborate French course at school may always safely be trusted at French plays, as they are not likely to understand a word of them.

upholstered, and lit throughout by electricity—the first London theatre, I think, that trusted wholly to that illuminant—the Criterion reopened its doors in April, 1884, with a revival of *Brighton*. In the following September, J. H. Macarthy's *The Candidate* proved a phenomenal success. At one time the advanced booking amounted to £7,000.

A revival of *David Garrick* was a triumph; Wyndham's prestige was enormously increased by a performance far superior to Sothern's, more especially in the last act, and it has been from that time a never-failing card to play when all else failed. Revivals of old comedies—*Wild Oats*, *London Assurance*, *The School for Scandal*, *She Stoops to Conquer*, etc., with Mrs. Bernard Beere, Mary Moore, most fascinating of *ingénues*, Fanny Coleman, Rose Saker, David James, Arthur Bourchier, in addition to those already named, in the casts, relieved by occasional new plays, such as *The Fringe of Society*, in which Mrs. Langtry appeared, but of no permanent interest, fill up the chronicles of the Criterion until January, 1893, when *The Bauble Shop*, a very clever, if fantastic play, which, though it evoked much unfavourable criticism, won the favour of the public, commenced a new era in the programme of the theatre. The manager's greatest admirers were not prepared for such an exhibition of power and of the highest qualities of the histrionic art as that passionate invective, dignity, tenderness, love which he threw into the character of Clivebrook. From that night Sir Charles Wyndham ranged himself among the most finished actors in Europe.

Another long run was made by that brilliant comedy, *The Case of Rebellious Susan*—this, I think, was Miss Mary Moore's *chef-d'œuvre*. In *Rosemary*, 1896, Wyndham more than confirmed the high opinion he had created in *The Bauble Shop;* here again we had the true ring of passion and pathos, and certainly no other English actor could have sustained a whole act in monologue without killing the play. *The Liars*, one of the very best of Henry Arthur Jones's comedies, and Haddon Chambers's *The Tyranny of Tears* drew large audiences for scores of nights. *The Jest* was a mistake; Sir Charles is essentially a modern actor, he is not happy in doublet and hose. It was most exquisitely staged, but it was a failure. Wyndham took his farewell of the old house, in which he had enjoyed so many triumphs, in the character of Sir Jasper Thorndyke, in July, 1899.

In his parting speech he said: "This house, which ordinarily holds only £220, holds to-night no less than £1,474." The whole of the proceeds was generously given to the Prince of Wales's Hospital Fund.

Sir Charles still remained lessee of the Criterion; for a time after his departure to his new house he was in partnership with Mr. Arthur Bourchier. *Wheels Within Wheels*, *Monsieur de Paris*, and *Lady Huntworth's Experiment*, by Carton, *The Under Current*, *The Girl from Maxim's*, John Hare with a revival of *A Pair of Spectacles*, the transference of *The Marriage of Kitty* from Wyndham's, are the most notable items in the history of the house since the departure of Sir Charles. The latest productions have been *A Clean Slate*, *Just Like Callaghan*, and E. V. Esmond's *Billy's Little Love Affair*, which has decidedly caught on.

As it may be said of Sir Charles that *le théâtre est moi*, I will for once depart from the chronological order I have adopted throughout these pages to jot down some brief notes upon WYNDHAM'S THEATRE, one of the most elegant and charmingly decorated and upholstered houses in London. It was opened in November, 1899, with the evergreen *David Garrick;* the whole proceeds of the first night were given to the Aldershot Fund for the British Soldiers' Wives and Families; a guinea each was paid for seats in the first three rows of the gallery, and the whole amounted to over £4,000.

A revival of *The Liars*, *Dandy Dick*, and then *Cyrano de Bergerac*, which, though beautifully staged (1900), was not a success; as I said before, Sir Charles is not at his best in doublet and hose. *Mrs. Dane's Defence* in the same year, however, made ample amends. Perhaps it is the finest play that Mr. Jones has written, certainly he has done nothing else so subtle and powerful as the scene in which Sir Daniel Carteret draws from the unhappy Mrs. Dane the proofs of her guilt; the perfectly natural manner in which the conviction is evolved is beyond all praise. And the interpreters were worthy of the author; Miss Lena Ashwell established her right to be classed among the greatest emotional actresses of the day, and has since fully maintained it by her wonderful performance in *Resurrection;* while Sir Charles has never surpassed the perfect art, the touches of tenderness, with a *soupçon* of cynicism, that distinguished his impersonation of Justice Carteret. In my whole theatrical experience I cannot remember a scene that held an audience in more breathless suspense than the one referred to, or that evoked a more excited burst of applause, renewed again and again as the curtain fell upon it.

The Mummy and the Humming Bird, *The End of a Story*, two or three revivals, the transference hereto of *The Marriage of Kitty* from the Duke of York's, a brief revival of *Rosemary*, and *Mrs. Gorringe's Necklace*, by a new author, who has suddenly leaped into public favour, *Glittering Gloria*, of which the bulldog, excellently supported by that clever comedian James Welch and others, was the leading attraction, brings us up to the latest success, *Little Mary*. For perhaps the first time an audience did not resent, but actually enjoyed being "sold." The secret of the enormous success of this very peculiar comedy is that it has given London a new catchword; but for that, and Mr. Barrie's extraordinary good luck, it would most probably have been a fiasco.

THE NEW THEATRE, 1903, another outcome of Sir Charles's indefatigable energy, and another very beautiful addition to the metropolitan playhouses, was opened on March 12th in the present year, 1903, with a revival of *Rosemary*. And again the lessee most generously devoted all the takings of the first night to a charitable purpose, connected with our soldiers and sailors. After a brief run of *Rosemary*, Forbes Robertson came hither from the Lyric with *The Light that Failed*, and was followed by Mrs. Patrick Campbell with a translation from Sudermann, *The Joy of Living*, a gloomy and repulsive play, and revival of *The Second Mrs. Tanqueray*. *Mrs. Gorringe's Necklace*, brought from Wyndham's, is still running.

CHAPTER VI

A BUNCH OF THEATRES

The Savoy—The Comedy—The Avenue—The Novelty—The Prince of Wales's—Terry's—The Shaftesbury—The Lyric.

THE SAVOY, 1881–1903, built by D'Oyly Carte, was opened in October, 1881, with *Patience*, which had already enjoyed a good run at the Opera Comique. The Savoy, with its delicate decorations and quilted silk curtain and electric lighting, was one of the prettiest houses in London twenty years ago, when the old theatres had not yet emerged from ugliness, meanness, or tawdriness.

The Gilbert-Sullivan combination was in the height of its popularity, and the glories of the Savoy began, and, up to the present time, has ended, with a partnership that gave delight to a whole generation of playgoers. It was an irony singularly in keeping with that spirit of incongruity and topsy-turveydom which distinguishes Mr. Gilbert's humour, that while its most caustic sallies were levelled against puritan respectability, it was especially from that division of the public that the Savoy audiences were drawn, for the Savoy essentially had an audience of its own, many of whom scarcely attended any other theatre. So Mrs. Grundy sat and saw herself held up to ridicule, and laughed at her own absurd reflection, without any more sense of being in front of a looking-glass than had the original of Foote's

Cadwallader or Molière's George Dandin when subjected to a similar ordeal. Mr. Gilbert had the supreme good fortune of being associated with a musician who was in perfect harmony with his ideas; indeed, the words and the music of the lyrics are so indissolubly mingled that the one loses its significance without the other. Sir Arthur Sullivan wrote to please his public; he was melodious, catchy, and never composed anything that Miss Jones could not strum upon her piano or warble in her drawing-room, or that Mr. Jones could not "get through." In each succeeding opera there were so many comic, so many sentimental songs, a madrigal, the regulation number of duets, trios, sestettes, and concerted pieces, with very much the same phrasing in all. And here was the great secret of the success; people flocked night after night to the Opera Comique and afterwards to the Savoy to catch the airs and imitate the vocalists at home. Yet they were delightful entertainments, when the wit and the music were interpreted by George Grossmith, Richard Temple, Rutland Barrington, Jessie Bond, Miss Brandram, Miss Everard, and others whose names will occur to the reader; and then the *mise en scène* was so beautiful, the stage management so perfect, the whole thing so unique.

What a first night *The Mikado* was! I shall never forget the frantic delight of the audience over "Three Little Maids." It was *the* thing of the night. I do not think *The Yeoman of the Guard* has ever received its due. The Jester's song was an inspiration; Sir Arthur never did anything else in that particular strain half so good. In *Iolanthe* and *The Princess Ida* there was a poetic fantasy that recalled the librettist's fairy comedies. Recent revivals convey little conception of the fascination these operas exercised over the audiences of the seventies and eighties, for the subtle charm, the aroma, so difficult to define, had gone from them.

Even before the rupture between the associates, the inevitable decay that comes at last to all things, whether material or intellectual, marked with inferiority the later productions of those facile pens, such as *The Grand Duke*, 1896, and after they were divorced the glory departed. Yet *Haddon Hall*, of which Sir Arthur composed the music and Mr. Sydney Grundy the libretto, was not without charm, but it had a short run. Clever composers and stage craftsmen have written for the Savoy—Pinero, Comyns Carr, and Sullivan, 1898, Ivan Caryll, 1899, in *The Lucky Star*—but I think the vein was exhausted; even Sir Arthur's last score, which he left unfinished, *The Emerald Isle*, was not exhilarating. And then the old company, that had been educated and steeped in the traditions of Gilbert and Sullivan opera, went one by one, and their successors, clever artistes though they are, lack the mellowness, the peculiar fitness of their predecessors. *The Princess of Kensington* was the last production at the Savoy. The house has been closed some time.

The Comedy, 1881–1903, started on its career on October 15th, 1881, under the management of Alexander Henderson, with Audran's *La Mascotte*, which had already been tried at Brighton; its brightness, tunefulness, humour, the drollery of Lionel Brough, and the *piquante* acting and beautiful singing of Miss Violet Cameron, in Bettina, caught the town at once and filled the new theatre for hundreds of nights. Planquette's *Rip Van Winkle*, in which Fred Leslie gave a performance of the ne'er-do-well Rip that was only surpassed by Jefferson's, was scarcely less popular. *Falka*, with Violet Cameron, Miss Wadman, Ashley, Harry Paulton, Penley, was another well-deserved success.

Miss Violet Melnotte succeeded Henderson in 1884, and comic opera gave place to drama. *The Silver Shield*, a very effective play by Sydney Grundy, 1885, in which the Dacres, Arthur Roberts, Kate Rorke appeared; after *Woman's Victory* and *Bad Boys*, and a comic opera called *Erminie*, came *Sister Mary*, by Wilson Barrett and Clement Scott, with Miss Lingard and Leonard Boyne in the chief parts.

It was at the Comedy that Mr. Beerbohm Tree made his first essay in management, and produced one of his great hits, *The Red Lamp*, 1887. Comyns Carr was the next manager. Two notable plays deserve mention —Sydney Grundy's *The New Woman* and Pinero's *The Benefit of the Doubt*, in both of which Winifred Emery greatly distinguished herself, especially in the latter, in the risky scene where she became half intoxicated, acted by her with most consummate art and restraint. Yet greater was her triumph in that fine play, *Sowing the Wind*, another of Sydney Grundy's. I can remember few things more beautiful than Miss Emery's acting as Rosamond, or than the scenes between the two old men, as played by Cyril Maude and Brandon Thomas.

Ada Rehan made one of her latest appearances in England here in 1896. Charles Hawtrey conducted the theatre for some time, and brought out a number of pieces suited to his particular vein, in which he was admirably supported by that excellent actress, Lottie Venne. Of these, perhaps, *Jane*, *One Summer's Day*, *To-Day* were among the most successful. Arthur Roberts was here in 1898–9 with *Milord Sir Smith*, and a burlesque on *The Three Musketeers*, called *The Tre-Dumas-Skiters*. Mrs. Lewis Waller played *Tess of the D'Urbervilles;* Forbes Robertson appeared as Count Tezma and in the *Sacrament of Judas*, and

Mr. Nat Goodwin and Miss Marion Elliot gave us E. V. Esmond's pretty play, *When We Were Twenty-one*, which had made such a hit in America.

The fortunes of the Comedy, however, were at a very low ebb when Mr. Lewis Waller brought *Monsieur Beaucaire* to their rescue. This is another instance of the impossibility of gauging the caprices of the public taste. The play was regarded as a mere *pis aller*, or at best a stop-gap; it had utterly failed at Liverpool just before, and the enthusiasm with which it was received on its first production in London, and the crowds that from that time flocked nightly—and daily—to the theatre were a surprise astounding as it was agreeable to everyone interested in the result. The run of the play was not exhausted when Lewis Waller closed in the August of the present year, and he has resumed it at the Imperial pending the production of *Ruy Blas*.

THE AVENUE would most probably never have been built but for the supposition that the South Eastern would have to purchase the site for the Charing Cross extension scheme. But the company did without it, and the theatre remains. It opened on the 11th of March, 1882, with *Madame Favart* and a company including Miss St. John, Miss Wadman, Fred Leslie, and Marius. French comic opera was as much the rage twenty years ago as burlesque had been twenty years previously, and *Les Manteaux Noirs*, *Lurette*, *La Vie*, *Nell Gwynne*, and others, new and revived, followed one another under Miss Violet Melnotte's direction.

But the first genuine successes were made by the series of comic operas—*Nadgy*, *The Old Guard*, and others—in which that inimitable droll, Arthur Roberts, kept the house in a roar of laughter by his antics and impromptus. His song and dance, "à la militaire," in *The Old Guard*, tricked out with all the impedimenta of the camp, was one of the funniest things I ever saw. There is a spontaneity, a sparkle in Arthur Roberts's fun, that no other comedian approaches, while his *verve*, his neatness, the quickness of his repartee are rather French than English.

George Alexander made his first appearance in the character of manager at the Avenue in 1890, with *Dr. Bill.* Something of a fluke was the success, but how splendid Fanny Brough was as Mrs. Horton; and the Kangaroo dance with the girl in red, whose name was not in the programme! I believe that dance was the making of the farce. The lurid French drama, *A Struggle for Life*, which was to be the *pièce de résistance* and *Dr. Bill* only a stop-gap, was a failure, and soon gave way to *Sunlight and Shadow*, afterwards transferred to the St. James's. In the next season, Bronson Howard's *The Henrietta* and a version of *Monte Cristo* were the principal features.

In the autumn of 1891, Henry Arthur Jones brought out one of his cleverest comedies, *The Crusaders*, at the Avenue; its caustic political satire, Mr. Palsam, displeased a portion of the Press, and they slated it, while it cut too near the cherished shams of everyday life to be acceptable to Philistia. Miss Olga Brandon's Una Dell and Lewis Waller's Philos Ingarfield, were fine performances. After a revival of *Judah*, Mr. Jones retired.

Mr. and Mrs. Kendal played for a season here, in 1893, *A White Lie*, *The Silver Shell*—a clever Nihilist play, in which Kendal played very finely. During the next few years the records of the Avenue are barren of successes; Miss Annie Hughes revived *Sweet Nancy* and *A Bit of Old China* in 1898, and Forbes Robertson and Mrs. Patrick Campbell were here for a short time in 1899. In the following season, Charles Hawtrey had a trump card in *Lord and Lady Algy.*

The greatest success ever made at the Avenue, however, was *A Message from Mars,* which ran hundreds of nights, though it had been rejected—what an old, old story—by most of the London managers. Yet, without entering upon a controversy, which brought the play into the law courts, I question whether any other actor than Mr. Hawtrey would have made the piece go to anything like the same extent. It was old-fashioned and full of Dickens's conventionalities; in the hands of any other comedian, Horace Parker would have been repulsive; but Hawtrey was so utterly unconscious of his own beastly selfishness, he so fully believed that everybody about him was inconsiderate of his comfort, and he was so genial and good-tempered in his heartlessness, in fine, he was so thoroughly convincing, that he was positively delightful, as very selfish people very often are in real life. There is no actor on the stage so absolutely free from self-consciousness as Charles Hawtrey, even Wyndham could never tell a lie with such an artless tone of undoubtable veracity and such innocent blandness as he does. Hawtrey's art is within very narrow bounds, but it is perfect as far as it goes. In *The Message from Mars,* Arthur Williams did much for the play as the Tramp.

The most fortunate of recent productions at this house have been Weedon Grossmith's *The Night of the Party, The Little French Milliner,* for which Miss Kate Philips was responsible, and *Mrs. Willoughby's Kiss,* in which Miss St. John appeared in a new line of character, the matron. *Dolly Varden,* a comic opera, is now running.

The Novelty, 1882–1903.—The Great Queen Street

Theatre was a ne'er-do-well from the first. A comic opera, *Melita; or, the Parson's Daughter*, opened—and closed the Novelty, as it was first called, in December, 1882. In the next year it was rechristened the Folies Dramatiques, and Miss Nellie Harris's name headed the bill; Miss Ada Cavendish appeared in a revival of *The New Magdalen.* Willie Edouin, Lionel Brough, Buchanan, all tried their luck at the unfortunate house, and with the same result—failure. In 1888 it received its *coup de grâce* by being rechristened the Jodrell!—after a lady who aspired to the honours of theatrical management. In that year the National Russian Opera Company appeared there; an excellent troupe.

During its twelve years of existence the theatre has been closed for longer periods than it has been open. Penley, after having it reconstructed and handsomely appointed, reopened the house as the Great Queen Street Theatre with *A Little Ray of Sunshine*, brought from the Royalty. He afterwards revived *Charley's Aunt*, but the public would not come. During the last two seasons the German company have given some prestige to the theatre, and when in some future age of the world the new street from Holborn to the Strand is finished, Mr. Penley's theatre, if it has not crumbled to dust by that time, may become a popular place of entertainment.

The Prince of Wales's, 1884–1903, originally the Prince's, was considered to be a model of beauty when it was opened by Edgar Bruce on January 18th, 1884, with a revival of W. S. Gilbert's *Palace of Truth;* Kyrle Bellew, Beerbohm Tree, Miss Lingard, Miss Sophie Eyre, were in the cast. A very free adaptation of *The Doll's House*, the first of Ibsen seen in England, called *Breaking a Butterfly*, by Jones and Hermann, was brought out in March; "Flora Goddard" (Norah) was played by Miss Lingard, whose style was quite unsuitable to the character. The play was severely criticised by the Press, and withdrawn within a month.

The Private Secretary, with Beerbohm Tree as the Rev. Robert Spalding, was brought out at the Prince's, but it was so little successful that in less than three months it was replaced by a dramatic version of *Called Back*,[1] which was just then the sensation of the novel-reading world. Macari was one of Mr. Tree's earliest hits; Miss Lingard was Pauline.

Mrs. Langtry was at the Prince's in the season of 1885 and 1886 with a revival of *The School for Scandal*, Coghlan playing Charles Surface to her Lady Teazle, a performance which I have noted elsewhere.[2] But *The Princess George*, another of the lady's productions, was a dire fiasco. Carton's and Cecil Raleigh's first play, *The Great Pink Pearl*, first saw the footlights here in 1885. The house took the name of the Tottenham Street Theatre, which was last under the management of Edgar Bruce, when the latter was taken over by the Salvation Army, in 1886. It has never been identified with any particular form of entertainment. An extraordinary success was made in 1891 by *L'Enfant Prodigue*, that wonderful wordless play, with its fine music, so splendidly acted by Jane May, Zanfretta, Courtis, and their associates. But such is the fickleness of public taste that *A Pierrot's Life*, finely played not long afterwards, failed to attract.

Operatic burlesques—*Paul Jones*, 1896, *Blue-Eyed Susan*, *In Town*, afterwards removed to the Gaiety—enjoyed long runs. In the last named, Arthur Roberts's *café chantant* song, with the *corps de ballet* and the *pas*

[1] See "The Globe," p. 332. [2] See p. 324.

de deux, with Sylvia Grey, were things to remember. Another great hit of Arthur Roberts's, later on, was *Gentleman Joe, the Hansom Cabby*. One of the best of comic operas, *La Poupée*, so admirably sung and acted by Courtice Pounds, Norman Salmond, Willie Edouin, and their *confrères*, was an enormous success.

Mrs. Patrick Campbell and Forbes Robertson were here in 1899, and brought out a curious Japanese play, called *The Moonlight Blossom*. Hawtrey continued the run of *A Message from Mars*, and produced *The Man from Blankney's*, and, on his return from America, *The President*, 1902. *The Country Mouse*, for Annie Hughes; a new version of *Masks and Faces*, for Marie Tempest to play Peg Woffington, also *Becky Sharpe*, for that lady, were productions of Mr. Frank Curzon's management. George Edwardes at present holds the stage with a variety show, *The School Girl*.

Terry's Theatre, 1887–1903, was built upon the site of the notorious "Coal Hole," where the renowned "Baron" Nicholson held the Judge and Jury Club. October, 1887, was the date of its birth. *The Churchwarden* was the first piece, *The Woman Hater* the second, and both were fairly successful. But *Sweet Lavender* brought £20,000 clear profit to the manager, and ran seven hundred nights. It was admirably cast—Brandon Thomas, Kerr, Maude Millett, Carlotta Addison. Terry was at his very best as Dick Phenyl; indeed, he had never done anything so good. Curious to say, however, no one of the several actresses who played the title-rôle quite realised the character; Rose Norreys, so clever in most parts, was quite out of it. Pinero wrote two more pieces for this theatre: *In Chancery*, 1890, *The Times*, 1892. There were some fine things in the latter, but it fell flat. Terry's contributions to theatrical history have been few and little remarkable. *The New Boy*, Jerome's *Old Lamps for New*, *The Pantomime Rehearsal*, were draws—the latter a great one; but it is a long time since the little theatre has enjoyed such a genuine success as *My Lady Molly*, the popularity of which shows no signs of waning.

THE SHAFTESBURY, 1888–1903, under the direction of Miss Wallis, who had been leading lady at the Queen's, Drury Lane, Adelphi, was opened only a year later than Terry's, October, 1888, with *As You Like It*, followed by *The Lady of Lyons*, etc. But the legitimate drama—as pronounced on that occasion in Shaftesbury Avenue—failed to draw the public. Better fortune attended the management of Messrs. Willard and Lart in the following year. *The Middleman* greatly added to Mr. W. S. Willard's reputation—and banking account as well. *Judah*, by the same author, was no less prosperous. But it aroused one of those controversies which have so frequently raged about Mr. Jones's plays, when that dramatist has run counter to the bourgeois conscience, touching the false testimony of a minister of the gospel and the ethics thereof. No doubt this dispute drew larger audiences than the cleverness of the play; people like to say they have been shocked, it testifies to their morality.

Signior Lago did a season of Italian opera at the Shaftesbury in the autumn of 1891, and introduced *Cavalleria Rusticana* to a London public. Then Miss Wallis returned with strong drama—*The Pharisee* and others—not great successes.

Comic opera took the place of drama in 1893 with *La Rosière*, that failed, and was succeeded by *Morocco Bound*, one of, if not the first, of the English variety show pieces, a species that had so long been popular in

America. It owed its success on the first night to Letty Lind's imitation of a society lady's skirt dance—the skirt dance was the drawing-room craze of the hour—which, performed with all the *chic* that actress is famous for, brought down the house.

A version of Marie Corelli's *The Sorrows of Satan* was staged here in 1897, with Lewis Waller in the principal part. The year before, £15,000[1] was lost over a comic opera called *The Little Genius.*

The most successful of all the variety show plays, *The Belle of New York,* was brought here in 1898, and introduced Edna May to the London public, as well as Messrs. Harry Davenport, Sullivan, Lawton, and other clever Americans. The *verve* and "go" of all—principals, chorus, ballet—were irresistible, and those who came to sneer and condemn remained to applaud. Every street boy whistled the tunes, every piano thumped them, and everyone went to hear them.

Since *The Belle of New York* the Shaftesbury has passed into the hands of the Americans, and has become a kind of annexe to the American theatres. *The Fortune Teller, Are You a Mason? All on Account of Eliza, Jedbury Jun'r,* have been among the most recent productions. Fred Terry and Miss Neilson produced a curious mythical-tragical-musical play, called *For Sword or Song,* early in the year, but it had a very brief existence. A nigger troupe, that has certainly caught on, now holds the stage with *In Dahomey.*

THE LYRIC, 1889–1903.—That charming pastoral *Dorothy,* originally produced at the Gaiety in September,

[1] It was computed that within six months just about this time £32,000 was lost over light operas; the largest sum is that named above, then follows *Lord Tom Noddy,* £6,000; *Monte Carlo,* £5,000; *Newmarket,* £3,000; *On the March,* £3,000.

1886, but transferred to Shaftesbury Avenue from the Prince of Wales's, opened the Lyric on December 17th, 1888. It made the reputation of Miss Marie Tempest—and of Hayden Coffin, by the now famous song of "Queen of My Heart," which, I believe, was an interpolation. After a run, at different theatres, of over 800 nights, it was succeeded by another idyll, *Doris*, which, however, had not the vogue of *Dorothy*. Audran's strikingly effective *La Cigale*, with Miss Geraldine Ulmar, caught the public, and was followed by *The Mountebanks*, *Incognita*, *The Golden Web*, *Little Christopher Columbus*, *Dandy Dick Whittington*. Each opera was beautifully mounted and interpreted by a company worthy of the beautiful theatre in which it was framed. Signora Duse made her first appearance in England here in May, 1893.

It was a great change from light and cheerful comic opera to the gloomy melodrama of *The Sign of the Cross*, with its Whitechapel ruffians, Methodist revival meetings, and Gaiety comedy scenes, which would seem to prove that the ancients were quite up to date. But the clergy flocked to see it, and many recommended their flocks to do likewise, so that the home of song and dance became quite a weekday church, and the public rushed in thousands to hear the groans of the martyrs, witness the Neronic saturnalia, and hear Mr. Barrett spout texts and moral platitudes. Everybody considered it as much a duty to go and see the Christian martyrs as afterwards—the Salvation Lass in *The Belle of New York*. British crazes are very varied; they embrace everything—except poetry and art. Mr. Barrett afterwards appeared in his own version of *The Manxman*, *contra* Mr. Hall Caine, and between the two dramatists there arose a very pretty quarrel. Mr. Barrett attempted to repeat the popularity of his Chris-

The Duke of York's, 1892–1903, originally known by the clumsy name of the Trafalgar Square Theatre, was opened on September 10th, 1892, with a comic opera, *The Wedding Eve*, acted by Decima Moore, Kate Chard, Joseph Tapley, George Barrett. As a revival of *Dorothy* followed very quickly, nothing need be said as to the success of the piece. The house was closed in January in consequence of a rupture between the proprietors, Mr. and Mrs. Frank Wyatt, and the manager, Mr. Levenston. It was reopened in the following month with a farcical comedy, *The County Councillor*, in which Mr. Yorke Stephens, Cyril Maude, Fanny Brough appeared; a couple of months afterwards, *Mlle. Nitouche*, with Miss Yohé, was put in the bill. The name of the theatre was changed to the Duke of York's in September, 1895.

Up to the production of *The Gay Parisienne*, in 1896, there is little but failure to record. The great success of the last-named piece was chiefly the work of Miss Louie Freer; it was her London début; her drollery, so original, and her song, "Sister Mary Jane's Top Note," in which she was pictured all over London, made her and the play famous.

Since the Duke of York's has been under the directorship of Mr. Charles Frohman, though he was guilty of such an inane variety show as *The Girl Up There*, several important plays have been brought out: that exquisite little Japanese piece, *Madame Butterfly*, so beautifully acted by Miss Evelyn Millard; Anthony Hope's *Adventures of Lady Ursula;* L. N. Parker's *Twin Sisters* and *The Swashbuckler;* H. A. Jones's *The Lackeys' Carnival* and *The Princess's Nose*, a failure; E. V. Esmond's *The Sentimentalists;* a revival of *The Gay Lord Quex; The Marriage of Kitty*, interpreted by Lewis Waller, H. B. Irving, Miss Millard,

Miss Irene Vanbrugh, Mr. Hare, Miss Marie Tempest. His great trump card, however, has been Barrie's *Admirable Crichton*, which ended with the 330th performance at the end of August, 1903. At first some, at least, of the critics—uncertain whether to praise or to condemn—thought it might prove to be too cleverly fantastic, too utterly unconventional for "the general," though intellectual London took to it at once. Pinero's splendid play, *Letty*, is a huge success. Irene Vanbrugh's Letty is an exquisite performance, and Nancy Price's Hilda the most original and vivid bit of comedy I have seen for some years.

Daly's Theatre, 1893–1903.—During several summer seasons of the eighties and the beginning of the nineties, Daly's American company visited London, playing mostly at the Lyceum. It was a competent troupe of well-trained artistes, who acted together admirably. But a section of the Press gushed over them most fulsomely. We had nothing to compare with certain members, who were the elder Farren and Mrs. Glover *redivivi*—and with something more all their own. While, as to Miss Ada Rehan, to hint that any English actress could come within comparison with her would be an insult to *la belle Américaine.* This was all mere raving; we could show far finer actors in their own particular line than the old man and woman of Daly's company, and although Miss Rehan was an excellent *comédienne* and an admirable artiste in all she did, yet she was not quite the genius that friends proclaimed her to be. I went to see her play Katharine, prepared for raptures. I tried my hardest to think the performance what I had read it was. But I came away with the conviction that that splendid regal-looking woman, so grand and imposing in appearance, with her deep-toned voice and deliberate utterance, was not the quick-tempered, passionate termagant that Shakespeare drew. I suppose the great favour with which his company was received in London by the Press suggested to Mr. Daly the idea of building a theatre in the English metropolis, and on March 12th, 1893, the very handsome house that bears his name was opened with *The Taming of the Shrew.* But the speculation did not commence successfully, and a splendid production of Tennyson's play, *The Foresters*, which the company had previously done in New York, though admirably acted, failed to draw. A revival of *Twelfth Night*, which ought to have been announced on the bills as by Augustin Daly and William Shakespeare, proved no more attractive. Mr. Daly was as much given to mutilating, "improving," and interpolating upon the bard as if he had been inspired by the ghosts of Tate and Cibber; and *The Two Gentlemen of Verona*, brought out in 1895, and *As You Like It*, which had been played many times before at the Lyceum, were elegant extracts from those plays arranged and modified by the facile pen of the American manager.

During the company's absence from England, Mr. George Edwardes occupied the house, and made it pay—a feat which the proprietor never accomplished. At Daly's death he became the lessee, not without some law complications, and produced a series of pieces on the Gaiety model, though of a higher class, especially from the musical point of view. All that beautiful scenery, costly dresses, and the best available talent could do to make a success of *The Gaiety Girl*, *An Artist's Model*, *The Geisha*, *A Greek Slave*—the best of all, and the most refined—was done, and the theatre has been a gold mine.

It may be worth noting that the Carl Rosa company gave the first performance of Humperdinck's *Hansel and Gretel* here in 1898.

The Country Girl is the latest success, and although it has held the bill an abnormal time, no notice is given of its withdrawal.

In 1876 an annexe for theatrical performances was opened in the Westminster Aquarium and called the Aquarium Theatre. Edgar Bruce was the manager, and the first piece presented was *Jo*, with Jennie Lee as the street arab, a performance that afterwards became almost world famous. It was while Phelps was playing an engagement here in 1878 that he broke down, strange to say, in the "Farewell" speech of Cardinal Wolsey, was carried off and never appeared upon a stage again. He died in the same year. In 1879, when the house came under the direction of Marie Litton, it was renamed THE IMPERIAL (1876–85, 1901–3). Miss Litton gave some really excellent revivals of old comedies, first in the afternoon and then in the evening; *The Poor Gentleman*, *The Beaux' Stratagem*, *She Stoops to Conquer*, supported by Farren, Lionel Brough, Kyrle Bellew, Mrs. Stirling, the lady herself, and efficient associates. A version of *The Vicar of Wakefield*, with John Ryder as Dr. Primrose and Miss Litton as Olivia, was another production. Mrs. Langtry appeared as Rosalind in 1882, and in the same year Miss Calhoun made her London début in *An Unequal Match*. By 1885, the building had ceased to be used for legitimate dramatic representations.

At the end of the century, Mrs. Langtry took a lease of the old theatre, rebuilt it on a magnificent scale, all marble and gilt, after the model of a Greek temple, and opened it at the end of April, 1900, with a very bad play, called *The Queen's Necklace*, which some good acting and costly mounting did not save from failure. *Mlle. Mars* followed, but did not redeem the fortunes of the house. Then Herbert Waring took the management to exploit a play called *A Man of His Word*, and met with no better success than his predecessors. In 1902, before she went to America, Mrs. Langtry revived *The Degenerates*, a play that she had produced during her tenure of the Garrick, which had been very hostilely criticised.

In the spring of the present year, Miss Ellen Terry produced an early play of Ibsen's, *The Vikings*, and clad in Amazonian garb, impersonated a sort of Valkyrie woman ; and as if this were not enough, Mr. Gordon Craig used the play as a vehicle for the exploitation of certain extraordinary theories of stage lighting and stage management. Miss Terry abandoned the Viking woman for Beatrice in a revival of *Much Ado about Nothing*. Mr. Craig continued his experiments, concerning which, as I have not seen them, I have nothing to say.

And now Lewis Waller, who played here for a short time, has taken the theatre on lease, and resumed the run of *M. Beaucaire*.

THE APOLLO, 1901–3, was opened in February, 1901, with an American show called *The Belle of Bohemia*, a fiasco ; after which Martin Harvey played *The Cigarette Maker's Romance* and *The Only Way*. But the first success was made by a musical version of *Kitty Grey*, which had been previously played at the Vaudeville as a comedy. It crowded the new theatre for hundreds of nights, and was one of the most enjoyable things of the kind, as sung and acted by Evie Greene, Edna May, Maurice Farkoa, G. P. Huntly, whose up-to-date "Johnnie" was a strikingly original performance, ever given upon the London stage. *What Would a Gentleman Do?* was the next piece. The Apollo is now under the directorship of the ubiquitous

George Edwardes. *The Girl from Kay's* is still in the bill at the time of writing.

There are still the suburban theatres of West London to be briefly noted. Richmond possessed a theatre as early as 1765. Mathews the elder, we are told in Mrs. Mathews' Memoirs of him, paid seven and a half guineas, when he was a very young man, in 1793, for the privilege of playing *Richard III.* on that stage. Edmund Kean performed there in his great days, and died in the house attached to it. There Helen Faucit first appeared upon any stage in 1833. And Amy Sedgwick, twenty years later, fresh from Manchester, made what by a stretch might be called her metropolitan début upon those boards. It was a queer, little, dark, dingy, squat theatre, of a type that no longer exists. It was pulled down, to save it from falling, in 1884. Until 1890 no attempt was made to replace it; then a theatre was fitted up in the Assembly Rooms of an hotel, and opened with some *éclat* by Mrs. Langtry. In 1899 a new and handsome building was erected. THE CORONET THEATRE, Notting Hill, 1898, differs from the rest of the suburban houses in that it has produced several original pieces, and Mme. Réjane has acted there each season since the opening. It was there also the Japanese actors, who were afterwards seen at the Criterion, made their first appearance, 1900. It is a handsome building both within and without, and holds 2,500 people. The same description may be applied to the Grand Theatre, Fulham, which was opened about the same time, though that is devoted to travelling companies. Hammersmith has now two theatres, the King's and the Lyric Opera House, and Ealing has also its temple of the drama.

HIS MAJESTY'S THEATRE.—Of all the new theatres which have been built during the last thirty or forty years, Beerbohm Tree's splendid house in the Haymarket is certainly the most important. It occupies an historic site, it has the most imposing frontage of any theatre in London, 86 feet at the principal entrances, while the measurement of the three isolated sides combined is 332 feet;[1] a spacious auditorium, *à la* Louis Quatorze, decorated in a style as handsome as it is dignified, and a noble stage equal to the production of the most elaborate scenic effects, it certainly ranks as the first theatre in the metropolis, and has taken up the position, though with a difference, which was held by the Lyceum during the Irving régime.

The house was opened at the end of April, 1897, as *Her* Majesty's Theatre—the name being changed to *His* Majesty's by permission of the King at the opening of the season of 1902—with an address written by the Poet Laureate and Sir Gilbert Parker's *The Seats of the Mighty.* A bad choice, as the novel is undramatic. A revival of *Trilby* quickly took its place, while the next play, *The Silver Key*, another version of Dumas's *Mlle. de Belle Isle,* was being prepared. In the following season, after a resuscitation of *A Man's Shadow,* there was a magnificent production of *Julius Cæsar*, which achieved the longest run of the tragedy on record. The principal parts were taken by the lessee, Lewis Waller, McLeay, Mrs. Tree, Evelyn Millard.

From Marc Antony to Ragged Robin was a far leap,

[1] A comparison between the dimensions of the new theatre and the old opera house may prove interesting. The frontage of the old house was 283 feet. The stage was 80 feet between walls; 60 feet from orchestra to back wall; width at curtain, 40 feet; from curtain to back of boxes, 102 feet; width of pit, 65 feet; height, 56 feet. The figures for the new house are: 86 feet front; stage, 70 feet by 50 feet, with recesses for scenery; proscenium opening, 35 feet; width of auditorium, 70 feet; depth, 61 feet; stage floor to gridiron, 60 feet; from floor to cellars, 23 feet; height, 45 feet.

but Mr. Tree has always been given to such violent exhibitions of versatility. *Le Chemineau* of Richepin was converted into a very delightful English idyll by Louis N. Parker, and was admirably acted by the lessee, Charles Warner, Frank McLeay, Lewis Waller, Mrs. Tree, Evelyn Millard. Miss Olga Nethersole appeared here in the early autumn of 1898 in a poetical play, splendidly staged, called *The Termagant*, and the regular season commenced with *The Three Musketeers*, a very brilliant and successful production.

Carnac Sahib, by Jones, and a wonderful revival of *King John*, were the features of 1899. Mr. Tree played the King with much subtlety; the Faulconbridge of Lewis Waller and the Hubert of McLeay were good, while the Constance of Julia Neilson would have scored if it had been distinguished by more nature and less artificiality. But the most important production at the new theatre, up to that time at least, was reserved for the new century. After a revival of *Rip Van Winkle* and a very exquisite staging of *A Midsummer Night's Dream*, in the earlier part of 1900, the manager inaugurated the autumn season with Stephen Phillips's *Herod*. The King of the Jews was and is Beerbohm Tree's finest impersonation in the poetic drama, and even those who had the highest opinion of his histrionic talent were surprised by the power, the picturesqueness, the *abandon* of his acting, more especially in the last act. I do not think that the Press did justice to Maud Jeffries as Mariamne, perhaps the physical labour might have been a little too apparent, but nevertheless it was a fine emotional performance, deserving of all praise. Indeed, the acting throughout the play was of a high order.

Herod revealed to us that England has once more

a poet-dramatist, and it could not have fallen into better hands for a sympathetic interpretation than those of the manager of His Majesty's. From the first scene, in which the Jewish monarch was seated on the throne, looking like an embodiment of one of the stone figures in the Assyrian Room of the British Museum, Sphinx-like of face, clad in all the costly splendour of the East, and surrounded by all its barbaric gorgeousness, Roman, Syrian, Egyptian, Semitic, one's imagination was transported to ancient Asia. Before us, through the marble columns of Herod's palace, lay Jerusalem with its towering hills, now in the glare of noontide, now in the ruddy glow of evening, now in the glittering silvery moonlight, while up from the streets of David's city, through the silence of the night, rose strains of sweet music, until the moon sank and the stars faded in the roseate streamers that heralded the coming of the sun. This noble play opened the twentieth century as a promise of good omen.

Twelfth Night was the *pièce de résistance* of the following year, and within the scope it allowed, was as finely staged as *Herod*. Nothing could exceed in truth and beauty the picture of Olivia's garden, no such garden had ever been seen before upon the stage of a theatre. Here, again, the atmosphere of the serious scenes was steeped in poetry and in music, "the food of love"; the delicious melodies were exquisitely rendered by Courtice Pounds, and the acting was admirable; Lily Brayton's Viola, if not the Viola of Ellen Terry, was full of fervid passion, and created an excellent impression; Maud Jeffries was a charming Olivia. A little more restraint in the comic scenes would have been preferable, but they were carried through with an exuberance of high spirits that it was impossible to resist. It was the finest production of the comedy ever put before an audience.

As a stage manager, Beerbohm Tree is pre-eminent; like Irving, he has the power of impregnating every actor and every subordinate with his own conception, and infusing into them his own energy; thus his every production is a harmony, in which every note is exactly balanced, so as to combine in a perfect *ensemble*. And now and again there bursts out an original touch that flashes upon the observer like an inspiration; such as when, after the hilarious gaiety of the dance at the close of *Twelfth Night*, the clown is left upon the stage footing it to the music of his own pipe, as the curtain falls. The stage manager of the old days would have been horrified at what he would have denounced as an anti-climax. But the new idea was right; it was a return to the keynote of the comedy; it was like the sweet repose that comes to us after a joyous summer's day, and we sit in the waning light and muse over the pleasures past. It was a fine stroke of art. The same trick, if you like to call it so, was repeated with a variation in *The Merry Wives of Windsor*, where, after Anne Page and the uproarious crew had disappeared, Falstaff and a tiny imp were left alone in the moonlight. The absolute success of a play frequently turns upon some little touch that seizes upon the public, and who can tell how much of the success of these two comedies was owing to the unconventional ending, and in the latter to that hilarious dance, brimming over with fun, in which, linked hand in hand, all the characters tripped again and again in and out before the curtain. It raised the delight of the audience to fever heat.

In 1902, another play by Stephen Phillips, *Ulysses*, which gave even more scope for stage effect than *Herod;* Calypso's isle was a dream of paradise, and the scenes in Hades have never been approached in terror, unless by similar scenes in *Dante*, than which it was more convincing; the Hall at Ithaca was a marvellous picture, both from the scenic and the histrionic point of view.

Of the remaining plays produced by Mr. Tree, *The Last of the Dandies*, poor work superbly rendered, and *The Eternal City*, to which the same judgment applies, *The Merry Wives of Windsor*, and *Resurrection* are the most noteworthy. Shakespeare's comedy, thanks to the combination of Mrs. Kendal and Ellen Terry, was the greatest of all the successes. Mrs. Kendal was admirable and in her best form, while her companion was the Ellen Terry of the old days, brimming over with animal spirits, fascinating, beautiful, irresistible. Tolstoi's gloomy and repulsive theme owed much of its success to the great acting of Lena Ashwell.

The six years' chronicle of the productions of His Majesty's Theatre, each one of which would be a record for a season, is quite unique in these days of long runs; the magnitude of the labour they imposed upon the directing mind must have been enormous.

* * * * *

London can boast to-day of more handsomely appointed theatres than can any other capital in the world, not excepting Paris and New York. Though in certain arrangements in the auditorium for the comfort of the audience the latter may be in advance, in the staging of plays we are easily first.

But the playhouse, after all, is only the husk, the play and the actor are the thing! We have many good actors and actresses among us still, but, as in literature and in art, the tendency to a dead level of cleverness, as opposed to greatness, is constantly increasing. We look round in vain for successors to Irving, Wyndham,

Ellen Terry, for that individuality which raises certain artistes out of the crowd. In the drama I cannot see the successors to Pinero, to H. A. Jones, and to three or four others I might name, whose productiveness must wane in time. Yes, there is Barrie, who has great possibilities, and Stephen Phillips; but then Phillips is a poet, consequently his productions are restricted, and would be acceptable only at three or four theatres at the most.

I know that of these remarks it will be said that writers upon the stage have in all generations, as every famous actor was nearing the end of his or her career, been given to shaking their heads and croaking, "The art of acting will die with them." Yet the man has come when the hour has struck, and the stage has gone on much as before. And so I suppose it will be again, at least let us hope so.

It is disquieting, however, to every lover of the drama that each year more and more theatres are given up to variety shows and to mere buffoonery. Even Wyndham's recently went over to farce, and the Criterion is everything by turns and nothing long. The Garrick under its present manager, and the Duke of York's during several seasons have adhered to good-class work, but a change of managers may at any time send these houses over to the majority, so that the St. James's, His Majesty's, and the Haymarket, which, however, has pandered too much to Mrs. Grundy and mawkish sentimentalism of late, are the only firmly established legitimate theatres in the metropolis.

The opening of a number of handsome suburban theatres, that in decorations, stage appointments, and everything appertaining to stage art can hold their own against most of the houses of Central London, and seat the public at less than half their prices, is a startling new departure in things theatrical. It was feared at first that they would have a very damaging effect upon the finances of the West End theatres. I think it was Sir Henry Irving who expressed himself quite cheerfully upon this point by his belief that they would create new audiences, out of people whom the higher tariff and the fatigue and expense of the journey from the suburbs had hitherto kept out of the theatres, that they would prove a sort of school for the theatrical education of the suburbans, which would ultimately lead them to the fountain-head of the art. And I think this view is proving to be a correct one.

As long as the theatre is simply a business speculation, so long must it be conducted upon purely business lines, and its customers must be provided with what they want, and not with what they ought to have. What then about a subsidised theatre? If a theatre be supported by a public grant, that grant must come out of the public purse, and every taxpayer would think that he had a right to have his say about the conduct of the establishment. Now, as we should have all the Puritan element of the country dead against the subsidy, imagine the fate of the subsidised theatre. It would be the deadliest of failures; instead of raising dramatic art it would lower it to the depths of inanity, as it would fall under the dictation of Philistinism. Shakespeare would have to be emasculated even more than he is now; every play produced would have to be written for "the young person," as she is supposed to be, and if there were any derelictions from the seventh commandment, *pater familias* would storm the newspapers with protests against the public money being used to promote immorality. We have only to remember the storm that was raised by certain plays of Pinero's and Jones's to realise what the attitude of a large section of Britishers would be; possibly it would rouse another passive resistance movement, the Nonconformist conscience is so very sensitive—to money. Well, the manager, as a public servant, would have to succumb, and the National Theatre would be converted into an institution for the dramatisation of the works of the Religious Tract Society. No, no national theatre is possible in this country until it is purged of Puritanism, and that desideratum is not likely to be realised until the Greek Kalends.

* * * * *

THE NEW GAIETY was opened on October 26th, 1903, with *The Orchid*, a piece of the usual Gaiety pattern. It is a handsome house, constructed up to the latest improvements, with a stage eighty feet wide and forty feet deep. When on Lyceum first nights people began to gather about the doors at nine a.m., it was considered to be a record. But the earliest first-nighter arrived at the Gaiety at five a.m., and all day long, under the pitiless rain, the crowd was swelling until it reached the church, and hundreds, after hours of patient endurance, could not obtain admission. Another record was the presence of the King and Queen. Royalty scarcely ever honours a *première* by its presence.

NOTES

TIME after time the old error, that has been fostered from the days of Junius, that the actor was by law a rogue and a vagabond, is raked up by some enemy of the stage. During the present year there has been a long controversy in the columns of a daily newspaper upon this subject. Let me endeavour to state the case. I will begin with the much misunderstood statutes of Elizabeth and James, for the interpretation of which I shall once more quote the dialogue between Lovewit and Trueman in Wright's *Historia Histrionica* (1699):—

"LOVE.—After all, I have been told that stage-plays are inconsistent with the laws of this kingdom, and players made rogues by statute. TRUE.—He that told you so strained a point of truth. I never met with any law wholly to suppress them; sometimes, indeed, they have been prohibited for a season, as in times of Lent, general mourning, or public calamities, or upon other occasions when the Government saw fit. Thus, by proclamation, 7th of April, in the first year of Queen Elizabeth, plays and interludes were forbid until All Hallowtide next following. (*Hollinshed*, p. 1184.) Some statutes have been made for their regulation or information, not general suppression. By the stat. 39 Eliz. cap. 4, 2 (which was made for the suppression of rogues, vagabonds, and sturdy beggars), it is enacted: '*That all persons that be, or utter themselves to be, proctors, procurers, patent gatherers, or collectors for gaols, prisons, or hospitals, or fencers, bearwards, common players of interludes and minstrels wandering abroad (other than players of interludes belonging to any baron of this realm, or any other honorable personage of greater degree, to be authorised to play under the hand and seal of arms of such baron or personage), all juglers, tinkers, pedlars, and petty chapmen wandering abroad, all wandering persons, &c., able in body, using loytering, and refusing to work for such reasonable wages as is commonly given, &c. These shall be adjudged and deemed rogues, vagabonds, and sturdy beggars, and punished as such.'*

"LOVE.—But this privilege of authorizing or licensing is taken away by the stat. Jas. I. ch. 7, s. 1, and, therefore, all of them, as Mr. Collier[1] says, p. 242, are expressly brought under the aforesaid penalty without distinction." "TRUE.—If he means all players, without distinction, 'tis a great mistake. For the force of the Queen's statute extends only to wandering players, and not to such as are the King's or Queen's servants, and established in settled houses by royal authority. On such the ill character of vagrant players (or, as they are now called, strollers) can cast no more aspersion than the wandering proctors in the same statute mentioned on those of Doctor's Commons. By a stat. made 3 Jac. s. 1, ch. 21, it was enacted: '*That if any person shall, in any stage-play, interlude, shew, may-game or pageant, jestingly or prophanely speak or use the holy name of God, Christ Jesus, or of the Trinity, he shall forfeit for every such offence £10.*' The stat. 1 Charles I. ch. 1, s. 2, enacts: '*That no meetings, assemblies, or concourse of people shall be out of their own parishes on the Lord's Day, for any sport or pastime whatsoever, nor any bear-baiting, bull-baiting, interludes, common plays, or other unlawful exercises and pastimes used by any person or persons within their own parishes.*' These are all the statutes that I can think of relating to the stage and players; but nothing to suppress them totally till the two ordinances of the Long Parliament, one of the 22nd October, 1647, the other of the 11th (9th) of February, 1647, by which all stage-plays and interludes are absolutely forbid, the stages, seats, galleries, etc., to be pulled down; all players, though calling themselves the King's or Queen's servants, if convicted of acting two months before such conviction, to be punished as rogues according to the law; the money received by them to go to the poor of the parish; and every spectator to pay five shillings to the use of the poor. Also cock-fighting was prohibited by one of Oliver's Acts of 31st March, 1654. But I suppose nobody pretends these things to be laws."

From this we gather that it was only the Puritans who denounced the theatrical profession as unlawful; but as their views

[1] *Short View of the Immorality and Profaneness of the English Stage.* See p. 54.

were precisely the same in regard to the fine arts and recreation of any kind, they certainly cannot be quoted against the actor any more than they can against painters and poets, all of whom were equally obnoxious in the eyes of these miserable fanatics. There was no further legislation affecting the actor's legal position until the passing of the Licensing Act in 1741. But here, again, the *licensed* actor was still recognised as an honourable member of society, the players of the patent theatres were still His Majesty's servants, and the players of Drury Lane were still a portion of the Royal Household, being yearly allowed so much scarlet cloth for vestment as gentlemen of the King's chamber, a custom that had begun under Charles II.,[1] and did not fall into desuetude until after Garrick's time. Baddeley, the original Moses in *The School for Scandal*, was, I believe, the last actor who wore the royal livery. The new Licensing Act of 1843 made no radical alteration in the social standing of the theatrical profession; it simply legalised as many theatres as the Lord Chamberlain chose to license; but any company playing without such authority or a magistrate's licence, in the eyes of the law, are rogues and vagabonds.[2]

The following contrast between the actors and audiences of the early and late years of the eighteenth century, is from the reminiscences of Charles Macklin (Kirkman's life of):—

"The players in the earlier decades all lived in the neighbourhood of the two theatres; Quin, Booth, and Wilks lived almost constantly in Bow Street; Colley Cibber in Charles Street; Mrs. Pritchard and Billy Havard in Henrietta Street; Garrick a greater part of his life in Southampton Street; and the inferior players lodged in Little Russell Street, Vinegar Yard, and the little courts and streets about the Garden. So that all could be mustered to rehearsal by beat of drum, as might be said, and the expense of coach-hire be saved. But now," said the veteran, speaking at the close of the century, "we are strangely altered, we are all looking forward to squares and great streets, high ground and genteel neighbourhoods, no matter how far distant from the theatre, which should be always the great scene of

[1] See p. 48.

[2] The first royal patent was granted by Elizabeth to Leicester—James Burbage was one of his players—and it was under this licence that the first theatre was built.

business. The audience then had also their different situations; a vulgar person was scarcely ever seen in the pit, and very few females frequented that part of the house. It was filled by young merchants of rising eminence; barristers and students of the Inns of Court, who were generally well read in plays, and whose judgment was worth attending to. There were very few disturbances in the house; the gravity and good sense of the pit not only kept the audience in order, but the players also. None but people of independent fortune and avowed rank ever presumed to go into the boxes; all the lower part of the house was sacred to virtue and decorum; no man sat covered in a box, nor stood up during the performance. The *women of the town* who frequented the theatre were then few in number, except in the galleries, and those few occupied two or three upper boxes on each side of the house."

ADDENDUM TO COVENT GARDEN (p. 208)

The new Opera House was opened in the midst of *La Traviata* rage, and Bosio at Covent Garden was no despicable rival to Piccolomini at Her Majesty's. During several years the Pyne and Harrison company occupied the theatre in the off seasons. Grisi took her farewell in 1861; *Faust* was produced in 1863. Covent Garden was turned into a company in 1865, but was under the direction of Mapleson in the following year. The two *impresarii* were partners in 1869. 1872 witnessed the production of the famous spectacle, *Babil and Bijou*, under Boucicault. After Gye's death, in 1878, the fortunes of the house were desperate—"The Royal English Opera," Salvini, then a circus! Lower still, William Holland, of Woolwich Gardens!! Mapleson came to the rescue in 1885; Halud in 1889. During the nineties there were pantomimes, and dramas were on one or two occasions transferred from Drury Lane at Christmas.

INDEX

T

Many other actors are mentioned *en passant*. Theatres omitted will be found in the "List of Theatres Past and Present."

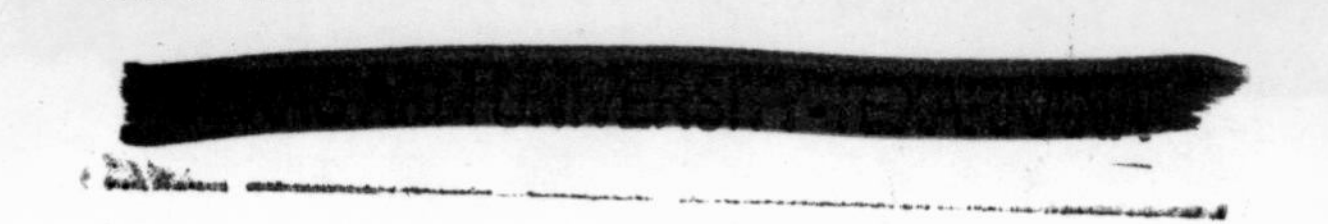